Cuban Socialism in a New Century

Contemporary Cuba

Florida A&M University, Tallahassee
Florida Atlantic University, Boca Raton
Florida Gulf Coast University, Ft. Myers
Florida International University, Miami
Florida State University, Tallahassee
University of Central Florida, Orlando
University of Florida, Gainesville
University of North Florida, Jacksonville
University of South Florida, Tampa
University of West Florida, Pensacola

Contemporary Cuba
Edited by John M. Kirk

Afro-Cuban Voices: On Race and Identity in Contemporary Cuba, by Pedro Pérez-Sarduy and Jean Stubbs (2000)

Cuba, the United States, and the Helms-Burton Doctrine: International Reactions, by Joaquín Roy (2000)

Cuba Today and Tomorrow: Reinventing Socialism, by Max Azicri (2000); first paperback edition, 2001

Cuba's Foreign Relations in a Post-Soviet World, by H. Michael Erisman (2000); first paperback edition, 2002

Cuba's Sugar Industry, by José Alvarez and Lázaro Peña Castellanos (2001)

Culture and the Cuban Revolution: Conversations in Havana, by John M. Kirk and Leonardo Padura Fuentes (2001)

Looking at Cuba: Essays on Culture and Civil Society, by Rafael Hernández, translated by Dick Cluster (2003)

Santería Healing: A Journey into the Afro-Cuban World of Divinities, Spirits, and Sorcery, by Johan Wedel (2004)

Cuba's Agricultural Sector, by José Alvarez (2004)

Cuban Socialism in a New Century: Adversity, Survival, and Renewal, edited by Max Azicri and Elsie Deal (2004)

Cuban Socialism in a New Century
Adversity, Survival, and Renewal

edited by Max Azicri and Elsie Deal

University Press of Florida
Gainesville/Tallahassee/Tampa/Boca Raton
Pensacola/Orlando/Miami/Jacksonville/Ft. Myers

José Luis Rodríguez García, "Cuba: El camino de la recuperación económica: 1995–1999," 1999, reprinted by permission.
Esteban Morales Domínguez, "Variables fundamentales del conflicto Cuba–Estados Unidos en los umbrales del siglo XXI," 1999, (updated original version) reprinted by permission.

09 08 07 06 05 04   6 5 4 3 2 1

Library of Congress Cataloging-in-Publication Data
Cuban socialism in a new century: adversity, survival, and renewal / edited by Max Azicri and Elsie Deal.
p. cm.—(Contemporary Cuba)
Includes bibliographical references and index.
ISBN 0-8130-2763-2 (cloth: alk. paper)
1. Socialism—Cuba. 2. Cuba—Social conditions—1959. 3. Cuba—Economic conditions —1959. 4. Cuba—Economic policy. 5. Cuba—Politics and government—1959. 6. Cuba—Relations—United States. 7. United States—Relations—Cuba. I. Azicri, Max. II. Deal, Elsie. III. Series.
HX158.5.C85 2004
335.43'47—dc22   2004055474

The University Press of Florida is the scholarly publishing agency for the State University System of Florida, comprising Florida A&M University, Florida Atlantic University, Florida Gulf Coast University, Florida International University, Florida State University, University of Central Florida, University of Florida, University of North Florida, University of South Florida, and University of West Florida.

University Press of Florida
15 Northwest 15th Street
Gainesville, FL 32611-2079
http://www.upf.com

For my wife Nickie,
my children, Fanny Rachel, David Leon, and Danielle Sophia,
and my grandchildren, Jared, Ashley, Sarah, and Jake
M.A.

For my sister Pat, who has always done more than her share
E.D.

Contents

List of Figures ix
List of Tables xi
Foreword xiii
Preface xvii
List of Abbreviations xix

I. Introduction

1. Cuban Socialism in the Twenty-first Century 3
   Max Azicri

II. Society

2. From Capitalist to Socialist Culture, and Back to Capitalist Values? 51
   José A. Moreno
3. The Continuing Revolution 65
   Jean Weisman
4. Women's Daily Lives in a New Century 84
   Norma Vasallo Barrueta
5. Demographic Transition and Population Policy 100
   Sonia I. Catasús Cervera

III. Religion

6. The Church of the Past and the Church of the Future 123
   Margaret E. Crahan

IV. The Economy

7. The Road to Economic Recovery 149
   José Luis Rodríguez García
8. Measuring Economic Performance: Strong and Weak Prospects 163
   Andrew Zimbalist

V. Politics

9. The "Single Party of the Cuban Nation" Faces the Future 183
   William M. LeoGrande
10. The National Assembly and Political Representation 206
    Peter Roman
11. Socialism and Elections 223
    Arnold August

12. Presidential Succession: Legal and Political Contexts and Domestic
    Players 242
    Nelson P. Valdes

VI. The Military

13. The Armed Forces Today and Tomorrow 259
    Hal Klepak

VII. Migration to the United States

14. Migrating to the United States: Evolution, Change, and
    Continuity 283
    Félix Masud-Piloto

VIII. International Relations

15. Policy Changes and New Objectives in World Relations 303
    H. Michael Erisman
16. The Cuba-U.S. Conflict in a New Century 320
    Esteban Morales Domínguez

Appendix A 339
Appendix B 342
Appendix C 344

Contributors 345

Index 349

Figures

15.1. Cuban Export Profile   309
15.2. Cuban Import Profile   310
15.3. Cuban Exports to MERCOSUR   317
15.4. Cuban Imports from MERCOSUR   317

Tables

5.1. Main indicators of Cuban demographic dynamics, 1988–2000   105
5.2. A comparison of selected demographic indicators between some world regions and Cuba, 2000   107
5.3. Cuban mortality indicators, 1963–65 to 1998–2000, and life expectancy at birth, 1960–65 to 1994–95   108
5.4. Cuban global fertility rate (GFR) and gross reproduction rate (GRR), 1970–2000   111
5.5. Current and projected Cuban population, 2000–2025   115
8.1. Cuban tourism indicators, 1990–2000   173
11.1. Electoral districts in Plaza de la Revolución municipality   231
11.2. Spoiled, blank ballots cast in national elections, 1993/1998   232
11.3. Spoiled ballots cast in Ciudad de La Habana province, 1993/1998   233
13.1. Evolution of Cuban armed forces, from 1981–82 to 1997–99   273
14.1. Number of rafters by years, 1985–94   288
14.2. U.S. Coast Guard Cuban rescue statistics, 1981–94   293
14.3. U.S. Coast Guard's Cuban interdictions at sea, 1991–2002   297
15.1. Destination of Cuban exports, 1992–98   311
15.2. Sources of Cuban imports, 1992–98   312
15.3. Evolution of intra-MERCOSUR trade   315
15.4. Cuban trade with MERCOSUR   316

Foreword

Against all odds, revolutionary Cuba has survived and, indeed, in some areas has actually flourished. The process has not been easy, however, and Fidel Castro's "pact with the devil" following the implosion of the Soviet Union has come at a high price for Cubans. Social problems virtually nonexistent barely a decade ago have arisen, and the legalization of hard currency has resulted in socioeconomic differences that, prior to 1993, would have been unthinkable in revolutionary Cuba.

Mainstream media in the first world have concentrated (not surprisingly) on what they see as some of the more newsworthy developments in Cuba, usually without any attempt to provide sufficient background material to help understand these developments. The end result is a disappointing record of superficial coverage and mediocre analysis. This book, a collection of essays from Cuba watchers from a variety of ideological positions, backgrounds, and countries, provides a context and valuable insights into the post-1993 developments.

In essence the authors address three fundamental questions: what has Cuba done to keep the revolution alive and at what cost, and what is the current state of Cuban society in the wake of these compromises.

The essays gathered here by Azicri and Deal cover a variety of pertinent topics. The four essays in the section dealing with Cuban society examine significant changes that have had a major impact on daily lives on the island. The issue of religion on the island is discussed in a separate section. The discussion is particularly useful because the state and practice of religion do not fit the "normal" Latin American model. It is simply different, a model sui generis—a description that can be applied to many aspects of contemporary Cuba.

The complex question of the Cuban economy—addressed in two divergent views—is the basis for a fascinating discussion. Issues of power, political structure, and control—especially pertinent and, perhaps, the most misunderstood aspect of contemporary Cuba—are addressed in a number of thoughtful essays. Cuba's international relations, with both the United States and the rest of the world, round out the contributions. All of this is set in context by a first-rate overview by coeditor Max Azicri.

Taken individually, each of these chapters provides a useful analysis into key areas of contemporary Cuba. Studied as a group, they constitute a wide-ranging overview of a neighbor in the midst of major flux. It is a case history of a society determined to remain independent and cling fiercely (and proudly) to its revolutionary roots, while at the same time recognizing the need to "move with the times" and to make significant concessions. And all the time, Cuba is faced with the challenge of fostering (clearly limited) change with its self-declared enemy just ninety miles away. It is a heady, volatile mix, replete with major difficulties. The refrain *"no es fácil"* (it is not easy), usually employed by individual Cubans striving to get by despite major daily obstacles, can be employed just as well to refer to the national struggle.

The study of Cuba in many ways is a stroll through magical realism. Some examples illustrate this phenomenon: Washington maintains its Trading with the Enemy Act more than four decades after its passage, yet in the past two years U.S. companies have sold over $500 million in food products to Cuba. Cuba is apparently facing a cash liquidity crisis and yet can pay cash for these goods (current U.S. legislation proscribes any credit for Cuba). The revolutionary government is reputed to be increasingly isolated, and yet over one hundred seventy countries annually condemn the U.S. embargo at the United Nations. And finally, the revolutionary government, it is claimed by government opponents, is about to fall—and yet Fidel Castro has stared down ten U.S. presidents (most of whom have made the same claim). All of this defies logic, and is an implicit demand for informed debate.

This book provides no definitive answers, and indeed several of the academics have clearly different views on current (and future) developments in Cuba. It does, however, make a major contribution to the necessary discussion about this small island of 11 million people, just ninety miles to the south of the United States.

Reference to the United States is pertinent, for this bilateral relationship is the most important external influence on Cuba's survival strategy. For over four decades Cuba has been the focus of bilateral tension and much continuing ignorance. As long ago as January of 1961 Washington broke diplomatic relations, and since then, with a few exceptions, has maintained an official policy of barely disguised hostility. Meanwhile, the rest of the world has moved on, while Cuba itself has clearly changed dramatically. The demographics both on the island and in Cuban American communities have also evolved, and all trends indicate an increased willingness to discuss openly a renewed bilateral relationship. The issues of this decade are radically different from what they were even a decade ago, let alone nearly fifty years. For the logjam to be broken between Washington and Havana, the players need to understand the fundamental dynamics and above all to appreciate the reality of revolutionary Cuba in the middle of this century's first decade—and not to dwell on the Cuba of the early 1960s.

In sum, before any attempt at normalization can occur, it is important to have an informed public debate about the real essence of Cuban society, to understand its idiosyncrasies and its similarities, its successes and failures—and its concerns. This collection of essays provides a basis for stimulating discussion and brings fresh air to some dusty topics. It is a timely, and badly needed, contribution.

John M. Kirk
Series Editor

Preface

The challenges and opportunities facing Cuba in the new century and new millennium are central to this book. The volume was conceived in scholarly panels on Cuba held in two international congresses of the Latin American Studies Association (LASA). Some of the panelists' papers are included here, while other scholars were especially invited to write chapters for the study. It includes specialists from Cuba, the United States, and Canada.

Special thanks go to University of Havana professor Esteban Morales Domínguez. In addition to his scholarly chapter and an economic appendix, he made possible chapters authored by other Cuban academics included in this volume. Our thanks go also to the foreign language scholars who translated the Cuban social scientists' chapters, to Mercyhurst College professor Alice Edwards for her invaluable help in translating manuscripts, and to Edinboro University faculty, staff, and students who provided timely advice and help, notably Cori Dunagan, head of the Learning (Computer) Technology Center, and Paige A. Blakley, student graphic designer. We also thank John M. Kirk, always willing to help in so many ways, and Gary Provost, who kindly reviewed the manuscript twice for the University Press of Florida, as well as the reviewers who chose to remain anonymous. To all of them we are deeply grateful.

From the vantage point of their own specialized fields, the chapter authors provide a unique view of contemporary Cuba. If, thanks to them, this book enlightens and informs the reader of the facts involving the Cuban reality, its major problems and great potential, we will have received the best possible reward for our labor. We would also like to acknowledge our unique opportunity to work together on this book, which evolved from our long scholarly association on numerous projects on Latin American subjects.

Abbreviations

ACP	African, Caribbean, and Pacific
ACRC	Association of Combatants of the Cuban Revolution
ACS	Association of Caribbean States
ALADI	Latin American Integration Association
ANAP	Association of Small Farmers
BD	Biological diversity
BTTR	Brothers to the Rescue
CAME	Council of Mutual Economic Assistance
CANF	Cuban American National Foundation
CARICOM	Caribbean Community and Common Market
CARIFORUM	Caribbean Forum
CC	Central Committee (of the Cuban Communist Party, PCC)
CDA	Cuban Democracy Act
CDR	Committee for the Defense of the Revolution
CEA	Center for the Study of the Americas
CEC	Cuban Council of Churches
CEDEM	Center for Demographic Studies
CEDSI	Center for the Study of Defense and International Security
CEE	State Statistics Committee
CEEM	Center for the Study of the World Economy
CEPDE	Center for Population Studies and Development
CESEU	Center for the Study of the United States
CIEC	Cuban Council of Evangelical Churches
CIMEX	Department of Convertible Currency
CIPS	Center for Psychological and Sociological Studies
CMEA	Council of Mutual Economic Assistance
CPE	Centrally planned economy
CTC	Confederation of Cuban Workers
ENEC	National Cuban Church Encounter
EU	European Union
FAR	Revolutionary Armed Forces
FCMM	Women's Civic Front José Martí
FDI	Foreign direct investment
FDMC	Cuban Women's Democratic Federation
FEU	Federation of University Students
FMC	Federation of Cuban Women

FTAA	Free Trade Area of the Americas
GDP	Gross domestic product
GFR	Global fertility rate
GNP	Gross national product
GRR	Gross reproduction rate
IISS	International Institute for Strategic Studies
IMF	International Monetary Fund
IPS	Investigation Participation Solution
JUCEPLAN	Central Planning Board
MERCOSUR	Southern Cone Common Market
MINFAR	Ministry of Revolutionary Armed Forces
MININT	Ministry of the Interior
MINSAP	Ministry of Public Health
MINTUR	Ministry of Tourism
MOU	United Opposition Women
NGO	Nongovernmental organization
OAS	Organization of American States
OLPP	Local Organs of People's Power
ONE	National Statistics Office
OPJM	José Martí Young Pioneers Organization
OPP	Organs of People's Power
ORI	Integrated Revolutionary Organization
PCC	Cuban Communist Party
PNR	National Revolutionary Police
PSP	Popular Socialist Party
PURS	Partido Unido de la Revolución Socialista
SE	Emerging sector
SELA	Latin American Economic System
SDPE	Economic Planning and Management System
ST	Traditional sector
TRD	Hard currency stores
TTM	Territorial Troop Militia
UBPC	Basic Units of Cooperative Production
UFR	Revolutionary Women's Union
UJC	Union of Young Communists
UMAP	Military Units to Aid Production
UNEAC	National Union of Writers and Artists
WTO	World Trade Organization

I

Introduction

|

Cuban Socialism in the Twenty-first Century

Max Azicri

Outlasting European Socialism

The year 2000 marked the second year of the fifth decade of the Cuban revolutionary government. Ten years earlier many people had thought it could not survive. Without a doubt, the 1990s were its nadir, unexpectedly following a rather creative, contentious, and in many ways unique thirty-year period. Since the demise of European Socialism, Cuba has undergone in rapid succession three sequential stages: first, it endured terrible adversity; next, it relied willingly on its own outstanding survival instincts; and finally, it purposefully charted and followed its own renewal path. All in all, a somewhat transformed Socialist system emerged from this process, seeking to leave behind the years of suffocating socioeconomic despair and moving forward into a new century and a new millennium with determination, expecting better times ahead.

In the first half of the twentieth century the world witnessed the birth of the Soviet Union and other European Socialist regimes and, thereafter, Socialism expanding into other continents. With the 1959 Cuban Revolution, Socialism finally reached the Western Hemisphere. But by the end of the century the tide had turned against Marxist regimes. While Socialism was suffering what seemed a fatal blow, the Western world savored the victory of industrialized capitalism over Soviet Communism. Notably, the People's Republic of China has successfully prevailed over the anticipated collapse of Marxist regimes, and to a lesser degree so have survivors like Vietnam and North Korea. Still, the emerging worldwide post–cold war political and economic order promised a difficult life for Socialist Cuba.

But Cuban Socialism managed to survive. With a population of over 11 million, the Caribbean island-nation continued to endure the enmity of the United States and overcame the nightmarish decade of the 1990s, even as yesterday's problems still lingered and new ones emerged. Throughout this difficult and protracted period, the true national roots of the Cuban Revolution proved strong enough to withstand the most formidable test it has ever encountered.

The severe hardships of the 1990s forced Havana to enforce the austere Special Period in Peacetime program. Originally conceived for wartime conditions, the special period sought to achieve the nation's and the regime's survival. As Cubans framed the discussion, the hardships were not Havana's doing—notwithstanding the mistakes the revolutionary government had made over three decades. The misfortune was caused by the Soviet Union, under the leadership of Mikhail Gorbachev (1985–91), and his perestroika (administrative and economic restructuring) and glasnost (openness in communication) reforms. The island's benefactor collapsed largely under the impact of such policies in 1991, following the disintegration of the Soviet bloc in 1989. The source for the financial, trade, military, political, and ideological support that had made the Cuban Revolution viable had suddenly failed.

Those events and the ones that followed were not helpful to Cuban Socialism and did not augur propitious times ahead. The domino effect of the Eastern European events of the late 1980s seemed unstoppable, prompting a scholar to state, "That communism collapsed in Eastern Europe [1989] is obvious. But will it therefore disappear entirely in the Soviet Union, too?"[1] It did not take long to answer the question: by the end of 1991 the Soviet Union had ceased to exist.

Cuba's response to the discussions and events unfolding in Socialist Europe was to distance itself as much as possible. Refusing to follow the example set by Gorbachev's policies, Havana unfolded instead its own brand of reform, the rectification of errors and negative tendencies. With mixed results, this national program was inaugurated in 1986, following the Third Congress of the Cuban Communist Party (PCC).

No matter how much Havana wanted to insulate itself from what was happening in Socialist Europe, the tidal wave effect reached the island early. Shipments from the Soviet Union and other Socialist countries became scarce, practically cutting off Cuba's supply lifeline. The worldwide Communist movement, including Latin America's, was entangled in controversy and political disarray and faced a crisis of legitimacy and leadership. The future of Marxism and the political left was seriously questioned. Political analysts held academic seminars and media roundtables in Cuba and elsewhere in the early 1990s, pondering the future of Socialism and the effect that the collapse of European Socialism had on Marxism as an ideology and as a political course of action.[2] A student of Latin American politics chronicles it this way: "The fall of socialism is a watershed for the left in Latin America. . . . [T]he debacle in the East at the end of the Cold War constitutes a terrifying blow to the left. . . . The disappearance and discredit of socialism cannot but damage the left in Latin America and elsewhere."[3]

The historic roots of leftist politics originate not in an imposition from above (forced downward by entrenched leaders and political parties), but mostly from below, born as grassroots reactions to social injustice. "The conditions in Latin America that gave birth and recognition to the left in the past are as pervasive as ever and in fact have become more severe with recent trends."[4] Hence, "in order to determine the current status and future prospects of the Latin American Left, both sides of the ledger must be perused: first, those aspects of the present state of affairs that affect the left negatively; then those that might strengthen its prospects, whether directly linked to the end of the Cold War or not."[5]

Partly in response to the adverse effect of neoliberal policies throughout the hemisphere and the political empowerment acquired by the poor, the Latin American Left was coming into office after winning elections decisively: the Venezuelan president Hugo Chávez (1998, reelected in 2000), Brazilian president Luis Inácio Lula da Silva (2002), and Ecuadorian president Lucio Gutiérrez (2002). These were followed by the election in April 2003 of a center-left president in Argentina, Néstor Kirchner.

During his inauguration in January 2003, President da Silva (better known as Lula) had breakfast with President Chávez and dinner with President Castro. Two weeks later, at the inauguration of the new Ecuadorian president, the four leftist Latin American heads of state (Gutiérrez, Lula, Chávez, and Castro) were welcomed at the national congress in Quito. The hemispheric "axis of good" suggested earlier by President Chávez was coming together to Washington's dismay.[6] Also, at the 2003 Rio Group conference held in Peru, President da Silva announced that Cuba would be invited to the 2004 meeting, which he will host as the new president of the organization. "I see no reason for Cuba to be [left] out of the Rio Group . . . next time, [it] will be invited," said the Brazilian leader.[7]

Castro's attendance at President Kirchner's inauguration was a momentous occasion. Following the steps taken by President Eduardo Duhalde (2002–03), Buenos Aires and Havana strengthened their new friendly relations, which reversed years of estrangement under Carlos Menem (1989–99) and Fernando de la Rua (1999–2001). Besides an hour-long meeting with President Kirchner, Castro was treated to a welcoming reception at the University of Buenos Aires Law School. The law school demonstration paralleled the applause that greeted him during the special ceremony honoring President Duhalde. During his short stay, Castro was also received with honors by the mayor of the city of Buenos Aires.[8]

Amid the turmoil affecting the Latin American Left in the early 1990s, the fact that Cuban Socialism had not collapsed was a positive sign at a time when there were not many encouraging developments. Yet, as I have stated elsewhere, "Since 1989 Havana's external and internal politics have revolved around the profoundly disruptive effect that the collapse of European socialism has had on the island."[9]

After the economy started to rebound and the regime's survival was secured, in December 2001 Havana welcomed the Latin American and Caribbean Left for an upbeat celebration of the Tenth Sao Paulo Forum. Founded in Brazil, the forum had been hosted in Havana in 1993, the worst year of the special period, when Castro admitted that his main concern at that moment was safeguarding the revolution and Socialism.

Eight years later regional political prospects were improving, so when Cuba welcomed four hundred delegates from ninety-four leftist organizations and political parties, they had good reasons to celebrate. José Ramón Balaguer, member of the Political Bureau of the Cuban Communist Party and head of its international relations department, noted the large number of guests attending the meeting and stated that such "participation in the forum [was] a recognition that the Latin American and Caribbean left [was] heading up an experience with . . . . results that [were] positive, constructive, and totally free."[10] The Latin American Left had started its political revival throughout the hemisphere.

But the obstacles faced by the island in the early 1990s were enormous. The notion of dependency on Soviet aid for the regime's survival was so ingrained among political and economic analysts that without Moscow's subsidies Cuba appeared incapable of surviving on its own. To Havana's dismay, 87 percent of its international trade disappeared practically overnight; the gross domestic product fell almost 35 percent and imports 75 percent between 1989 and 1993, while the fiscal deficit rose 33 percent in those four years.[11]

Against this adverse backdrop, Cuban leaders took the decision to resist rather than give in, to fight for the survival of the revolution and the Socialist system—which to them meant defending the country's political independence. But in most quarters it was not a plausible decision. Vice President Carlos Lage candidly admitted to a gathering of Cuban émigrés in Havana in 1994: "The situation was so difficult . . . at the time of the demise of the Soviet Union . . . that [our] will to resist was not credible for most people in the world."[12] But with great sacrifice, suffering the social deficits brought by the 1990s, Cubans proved the skeptics wrong.

President Castro became engaged in a worldwide diplomatic campaign. From the Ibero-American Summits to international gatherings in practically every continent, he pursued a personal and almost peripatetic diplomacy. His traveling was central to the revolution's survival objectives. Through his reaching out to the world, he sought to overcome the isolation Washington wanted to impose on Havana. He needed to show that Cuba was ready to have relations with old friends and to make new ones, to establish trade and financial exchange with willing partners, and to have closely scrutinized foreign investors bolster its sagging economy. The result was favorable to the island; it gained an international presence, securing its rightful place in the world scene.

After Cuba's legalization of the U.S. dollar in 1993, a social divide evolved, separating those receiving cash remittances from relatives living abroad and those who had to survive on the pesos paycheck. In turn, the egalitarian revolutionary value system, so well entrenched in the country's political culture since the 1960s, suffered gradual erosion when the need to satisfy the population's basic needs prevailed. This disruptive trend was underlined by the constant pursuit of the U.S. dollars that guaranteed access to well-supplied dollars-only shops.[13]

In the midst of controversies provoked by self-employment *(cuentapropistas)* and the social by-products of the tourist industry—such as the resurrection of prostitution *(jineterismo)* and foreign hotel investors' bias favoring white personnel[14]—the country slowly regained some economic strength. But an onerous social price was being paid. Cuban Socialism had to find ways to inoculate the society against an increasing moral malaise. A sense of despondency, contrary to the regime's long-held vitality and dynamism, was spreading among some sectors of the population.

Serious economic problems continued to haunt Havana through the 1990s. Among the hard choices the regime had to make to regain its financial viability in 2002 was to retrench the sugar industry, the historic mainstay of the economy. Russia, a long-time major customer, was already buying more sugar from Brazil than from Cuba. Economic planners eliminated the least efficient sugar mills, leaving only 85 of the original 156 operating.[15] This action added thousands to the ranks of unemployed workers whose jobs were lost when their work centers were streamlined. Workers received full compensation while being retrained and resettled into new jobs during this time of economic hardship.[16]

The government recognized that tourism had replaced sugar as the main engine of the economy. Despite the sluggishness of the tourist industry since September 11, 2001, 1.7 million tourists visited the island in 2002—only 3 or 4 percent lower than the year before. According to Richard M. Coplan, president of the American Society of Travel Agents, one million American tourists would visit Cuba within one year of lifting the travel ban.[17]

The Cuban travel ban still remains in place. Yielding to White House threats to veto the legislation, behind closed doors and before it could be discussed by the full conference committee, in November 2003 the Republican majority leadership in the Senate and the House stripped the Cuba travel amendment from the Transportation-Treasury Appropriations bill it was attached to. The House had approved by a vote of 227–188 to eliminate funding for the enforcement of the travel ban, which was also authorized by the Senate with a vote of 59–36. While the purpose of the conference committee is to reconcile language differences in Senate and House legislation, the Cuban travel ban amendment needed no reconciliation since both versions had identical language.[18]

The U.S. Embargo and Hurricane Michelle

The revolution's commitment to social welfare was never fully abandoned, and some areas were even improved during the 1990s. The public health system, however, suffered greatly due to medicine and medical equipment shortages, which were in large measure aggravated by the American economic embargo. The easing of food and medicine restrictions from the trade embargo approved by the end of the Clinton administration allowed only sales that met licensing requirements and were paid in cash. Cuban officials portrayed the requirements as onerous.[19]

There were no sales until Hurricane Michelle hit in November 2001. In spite of the worst natural disaster in nearly half a century, Cuba politely turned down a U.S. offer of emergency relief, challenging Washington instead to ease "the red tape on export of U.S. food and medicines to the island." But the State Department refused to accept the Cuban request.[20]

Suddenly, however, the ongoing negotiations took a turn for the better. After the Bush administration approved the sale, the first shipment of U.S. goods destined to the island in over four decades was loaded in Louisiana on December 14, 2001, reaching Havana's port two days later. Seven subsequent shipments of food and other products from Archer Daniels Midland (ADM), Cargill, Stuttgart, and others had arrived by February 2002, for a total of $30 million. Many more shipments followed.

Havana's rejection of the Bush administration's disaster relief offer confirmed Cuba's opposition to the embargo (called a blockade in Cuba). Its willingness to pay for the goods in cash was a way of reaching out to the American anti-embargo business forces (mainly farming and related interests), and contributing its own limited dollars helped to erode the embargo further. It was reported that

> Cuba's surprise decision to buy up to $30 million worth of U.S. farm products was based both on politics and need. [In November 2001], representatives of . . . Archer Daniels Midland; . . . Cargill, Inc.; and Stuttgart . . . signed contracts in Havana to sell hundreds of thousands of metric tons of rice, wheat, soy, corn, soy meal and cooking oil. The sales would be the first direct purchase of US food by Cuba in nearly 40 years. We've made history," said ADM spokeswoman Karla Miller.[21]

The arrival of U.S. goods raised hopes in both countries that the door had been opened to future trade. In his second visit to Cuba in 2002, seeking to promote trade in pharmaceuticals between the two nations, then Illinois Republican governor George Ryan stated, "I would like to see the blockade end tomorrow."[22] However, despite such promising developments, the traditional anti-Castro rhetoric of the Cuban American National Foundation (CANF) in defense of the embargo continued.[23]

Energized by the food sales, representatives from farming, business, politics, and other concerned sectors gathered in Havana to ask that the humanitarian trade exchange be turned into a permanent commercial relationship. Food shipments were arriving regularly when nearly one hundred fifty U.S. companies and agricultural concerns expressed their interest in a five-day trade fair in Havana. The first U.S. agricultural fair in revolutionary Cuba was inaugurated successfully in November 2002.

Addressing the participants at the food fair, Castro said that in eleven months 712,000 metric tons of food and other products worth $40 million had arrived on time from the United States in fifty merchant ships. He noted that contrary to the predictions by opponents of the commercial exchange, Cuba had made the payments on time. He stated that new contracts were signed during the exhibition for $140 million. This figure was estimated differently by other sources.[24] Cuba's standing as a buyer of American food products changed from last position of 228 countries in 2000 to 144th in 2001, and 46th in 2002. Probably by design, the contracts included firms from thirty-four states, which altogether represented 81 percent of the members of the House and 68 percent of the Senate.[25] Besides satisfying its own urgent consumer needs, Havana had managed to manufacture a respectable U.S. anti-embargo constituency.

Twenty-six American businessmen announced in Havana in December 2002 their support for normalizing relations with Cuba, stressing that "nothing could eliminate the confidence and friendship that has developed during the first year of commercial links."[26] In their opinion, trading with Cuba had brought employment to two hundred thousand people in the United States. In the first year, "Purchases from the United States amounted to $253 million USD of which $174 million [had] already been paid and another $15 million [was] forthcoming by the end of December. This represented 1.07 million tons of food, of which 850,000 [had] already been transported to Cuba."[27] Pedro Alvarez, head of Cuba's ALIMPORT (the state trade agency), stated: "This has been achieved through the efficiency of the U.S. companies, through the support of many board members and agricultural association members, like those for cereal, chickens, grains, etc."[28]

The Working Group on Cuba, a bipartisan group of forty members of Congress involved in changing Cuba policy, provoked a rift between the White House and the Republican-controlled House. After defeating a countermeasure supported by the Bush administration in July 2002, the House approved relaxing the economic embargo (allowing trade of food and medicine through U.S. financing), and lifting the travel ban and the limits on the moneys Cuban Americans could send to their relatives. The Senate, however, failed to act on the proposed changes. Given Bush's hard-line stand announced on May 20, 2002 (and his promise to veto any changes to the embargo), the anti-embargo forces faced an uphill battle to end the over-four-decades-old policy against the island.[29]

September 11 and the Afghan War Prisoners

The terrorist attacks of September 11, 2001, against the United States had a bearing on U.S.-Cuba relations. Taking a principled but controversial position against terrorism, Havana condemned the attacks, characterizing them as "insane." But after stating firmly that "under no circumstances should those responsible for the brutal attack against the American people be allowed to go unpunished," Cuba also said it hoped a "peaceful solution could still be possible."[30]

In a letter to Kofi Annan, United Nations secretary-general, Castro said that Cuba was adhering "to the existent 12 international instruments related to terrorism, three of which Cuba ha[d] already approved and ratified." He promised that Havana would "continue its efforts towards the conclusion of a general and comprehensive agreement against terrorism." Castro informed Annan that Cuba was also planning to pay homage to the seventy-three Cubana Airlines passengers who were killed off the coast of Barbados in 1976, victims of an act of terrorism.[31] While condemning the terrorist attacks against the United States, Castro wanted to remind the world that Cuba had been the victim of numerous acts of terrorism since 1959, largely sponsored by the United States Central Intelligence Agency. When the bombing of Afghanistan started on October 7, 2001, Cuba denounced it.[32]

Cuba's stand ran contrary to American policy. But as a country victimized by terrorist attacks for decades, most of which had gone unpunished, Cuba could not favor the bombing of Afghanistan. As Havana poignantly put it, "This is a war of the most sophisticated technology against those who do not know how to read and write."[33] Cuba was performing a balancing act. It denounced the terrorist attack against the United States and deplored the killing of innocent civilians, but also stood in opposition to military actions in Afghanistan.

As the United States was preparing to launch a military attack against Iraq in early 2003, Cuba denounced "the [greatest] imbalance in the military sector ever to have existed on Earth," and opposed Washington's war plans, stating: "The strongest superpower in the world [has] proclaimed its unilateral right to launch its arsenal of the most sophisticated weapons against another country [Iraq], with or without the authorization of the UN Security Council."[34] Cuba's opposition to the war was shared this time by worldwide public opinion and numerous governments.

The war against terrorism returned to the radar of U.S.-Cuba relations when Taliban and al-Qaeda prisoners were transferred to the American Guantánamo naval base in eastern Cuba. Havana's response to the Pentagon's decision included a muted but agreeable "no comment." The foreign ministry stated that it "did not have the elements necessary to make a judgment and because of that has not adopted any position" on the matter.[35] By the time the first prisoners were arriving under extremely tight security on January 11, 2002, the Cuban military seemed to have "warmed up" to the fact of having detainees from the Afghan war incarcerated in uncomfortable cells in Camp X-Ray, as the detention center was called (the detainees were later moved to newly built facilities), on their nation's soil—albeit under American jurisdiction.[36] Also, while "everyone expected the Cuban leader to be the first to protest the Pentagon's decision to use

Guantánamo Naval Base to house the Afghanistan prisoners of war . . . , Castro not only refrained from verbally bashing his historic archenemy, but passed the word down to his troops to cooperate in this potentially volatile operation."[37]

During a six-and-a-half-hour meeting in Havana with two Republican senators, Arlen Specter of Pennsylvania and Lincoln D. Chafee of Rhode Island, Castro stated that he wanted to cooperate with the United States in "drug interdiction efforts and the war on terrorism," and that he "would not oppose the use of the U.S. Naval Base at Guantánamo Bay . . . to house detainees from the war in Afghanistan." Knowing that Cuba is still listed by the State Department as a nation supporting terrorism, Senator Specter said critically that this situation needs to be "examined and reexamined."[38]

Washington had given Havana advance notice that detainees from the Afghan war would be arriving at Guantánamo. The way the prisoners were treated raised serious concerns in Europe. Pentagon photos showed "al-Qaida and Taliban suspects on their knees and wearing black-out goggles" and "masks over their mouth and noses, hats, and mittens on their hands" upon arriving in Cuba, causing an outcry and creating a diplomatic problem for British prime minister Tony Blair and President Bush. Following human rights groups' protests and claims of "torture," Blair insisted that "the prisoners' human rights be guaranteed."[39] England and Spain sided with Washington, but France, Germany, Switzerland, and others joined the growing protest asking that the detainees receive prisoner-of-war status and be treated according to the Geneva Convention.[40]

Senior officials' statements underscored a rift in the Bush administration. Opposing the view of Secretary of Defense Donald Rumsfeld and Vice-President Dick Cheney, Secretary of State Colin Powell favored adhering "to the [Third] Geneva Convention governing the treatment of prisoners in wartime, adopted in 1948."[41] Bush finally decided the "Geneva Convention would be applied to the Taliban captives being held in Cuba but not to Al Qaeda detainees," and that neither group would receive prisoner-of-war status.[42]

Havana did not join the controversy over the treatment of the detainees and whether the Geneva Convention applied to them. However, after being critical of Cuba's treatment of political prisoners, this time Washington came under criticism for the way it was treating Afghan war prisoners. As the terrorist threat to U.S. national security seemed to increase, the policies enacted by the Bush administration to counter terrorist attacks, which prompted civil libertarians to protest the curtailing of individual liberties, moved the country somewhat closer to the internal security controls Havana has enforced to safeguard its Socialist system. Cuba still offered medical attention and other services if needed, and assured that the military personnel stationed around the base would not be increased on account of the prisoners or the newly arrived American troops.[43]

Fearing that Havana-Washington relations could improve, pro-embargo congressional leaders were worried, anticipating a "tougher time ahead on Capitol Hill." Cuban American congresswoman Ileana Ros-Lehtinen (R-FL) said, "It's definitely a threat. There is no doubt that we are losing ground in Congress. If it weren't for the Bush Administration, [the embargo] would not be in good shape."[44]

Fox, Chávez, Carter, Nader

President Vicente Fox

Before a twenty-four-hour "working visit" to Havana in February 2002 aimed at "restoring a century-old diplomatic relationship . . . damaged in recent years,"[45] Mexico's president Vicente Fox was pressured by his own National Action Party and Washington to meet with Cuban dissidents—which he did by the end of his visit.[46] Still, Fox held a cordial meeting earlier with Castro, exploring avenues for increasing trade between the nations.

President Bill Clinton's Cuba policy advisor, Richard Nuccio, stated that "Bush ha[s] filled most Latin American policy positions with hard-[liners] stand[ing] against . . . Castro, and . . . those leaders would feel disappointed if . . . Fox did not make any critical statements about human rights violations in Cuba."[47] Shortly after, Cuban-Mexican relations fell to their lowest point ever, with serious disagreements between Castro and Fox. Jorge Castañeda Gutman, Fox's foreign affairs secretary at the time, acting in tandem with Otto Reich, then President Bush's assistant secretary of state for Latin America, and other Washington officials, was denounced by Havana as the main instigator of the diplomatic quarrel.[48]

At the opening of the Mexican Cultural Institute in Miami in February 2002, Castañeda stated that the "doors of our embassy [in Havana] and the doors of Mexico . . . would be open . . . for any other Cuban citizen . . . in Cuba or in any other country." The U.S.-sponsored Radio Martí repeated Castañeda's statement in its broadcasts to the island. The news inspired twenty-one disaffected youth to crash a stolen bus into the embassy compound after "hearing rumors that the Mexican government was offering asylum."[49] Cuban and Mexican officials blamed Radio Martí's repeated broadcasting of Castañeda's words for the incident and amicably worked out the diplomatic predicament. But condemning Mexico's accommodating behavior, Miami Spanish-language radio stations sponsored a boycott of Mexican products.

The embassy incident was followed by a more serious one stemming from the United Nations Development Financing Conference in Monterrey, Mexico. Before the gathering started, Castro informed Mexico that he was attending, which prompted a telephone call from Fox to Castro. In a conversation later made public by Castro, Fox complained that he had been notified too late of Castro's plans and that they had accommodation problems. Castro responded that he already had reservations at a local hotel and that he was planning to speak at the conference after being invited by United Nations secretary-general Kofi Annan. Fox's real problem was that Bush refused to come if Castro was present. Fox and Castro agreed that the latter would leave after addressing the conference so Fox could play host to Bush without Castro being present. The Cuban leader made clear that, in the spirit of common friendship, he would do so in deference to Fox.[50]

The strained relationship could barely survive the developments in Geneva at the United Nations Human Rights Commission annual meeting. For years the United States had sponsored resolutions against Cuba, but this time it had Uruguay sponsor a resolution against Havana on its behalf. Despite Fox's assurances that he would never do anything against Cuba, Mexico joined six Latin American countries voting in favor of the resolution, which was approved by a one-vote margin, twenty-two to twenty-one, with nine abstentions. If Mexico had voted against the anti-Cuba resolution, the Bush-Reich maneuver would have failed.[51]

Castro's reaction, vented against Uruguay and Mexico in particular, made news throughout the hemisphere. Uruguay responded by breaking off diplomatic relations with Havana, while Fox and Castañeda denied having betrayed promises made in Havana. Also, the latter insisted that the decision to come to Monterrey and leave early was solely Castro's. After denials from Castañeda and warnings from Cuba, Castro made public his private telephone conversation with Fox on the eve of his trip to Monterrey. At home, Fox was humiliated and charged with having lied to the Mexican people. By the end, the best Mexico and Cuba could say was that they still had diplomatic relations.[52]

Mexico's pro-Washington and anti-Castro posture, and especially that of Castañeda, was part of the conservative change sweeping Mexico under Fox. "The opposition hits Fox where it is most effective, in his relations with the United States," said a Mexican official. But Fox's main problem was that after much ado he had very little to show for it. The White House had failed to deliver Mexico's chief requests—especially normalizing the status of illegal Mexicans on U.S. soil. "President Bush," noted an analyst, "has offered very little to his friend [Fox] in need."[53] Recognizing his predicament, Fox stated that "the United States–Mexico relationship ha[d] 'stalled' and . . . that he had paid a political price for aligning Mexico more closely than ever with Washington."[54] By the end of 2002, Castañeda had resigned his post because of the lack of progress in Mexico-U.S. relations. He also left Cuban-Mexican relations at an all-time low.

President Hugo Chávez

Venezuela's constitutional norms were violated: Following a failed military coup d'état in April 2002 that kept President Hugo Chávez out of office for two days, a broad coalition of discontented businessmen, petroleum executives, union leaders and workers, retired military officers, and large sectors of the upper and middle classes started a general strike by the end of the year. The action was ruining the country economically while attempting unsuccessfully to oust Chávez. A major supplier of oil to Cuba and the United States, Venezuela's oil production was lowered about 90 percent for almost two months, from 3.1 million barrels daily to 200,000, but was increased to the million-barrel benchmark by late January, with prospects of doubling production shortly. After two confrontational and intense months, the strike ended in practically all economic sectors but the oil industry.[55] In a short period, it had ended in the oil sector, too.

Washington's support for the military coup included funding anti-Chávez protesters through the U.S. National Endowment for Democracy.[56] The coup sought to isolate Havana by ousting from power Castro's close friend and to close down Cuba's main oil supply. Among the first decisions made by Chávez's replacement, Pedro Carmona, in his short-lived presidency was to end any shipments of Venezuelan oil to Havana, ending a bilateral agreement approved by Chávez in 2000. Carmona also canceled the Constitution, dissolved the National Assembly (parliament), and fired the Supreme Court.[57] Cuba did not receive any new oil shipments until September 2002, only to have them stop again after the strike started. Resuming Venezuelan oil shipments was going to take some time, which aggravated Cuba's economic troubles.[58]

Unlike Latin American countries and the Organization of American States (OAS), which opposed the coup, the White House took a public stance against Chávez when the revolt seemed to be successful. Reich and other U.S. officials had been in contact before and during the coup with opposition leaders.[59] Later, the White House would support the opposition's call for new elections to end the strike. But to Chávez, the strike was a protracted coup d'état seeking to overthrow him by economic and political means.[60] Although Caracas had proposed Cuba's membership in the Friends of Venezuela group, which brokered an ending to the discord, the island-nation was not included among the participating countries.

Behind the rift between Cuba and Mexico, the failed coup first and the strike later against Chávez, the resolution condemning Cuba in Geneva, and other actions, the Bush administration seemed always present. But Cuba managed to survive, and Chávez survived as well, despite the long-drawn-out strike.[61] And with newly installed leftist regimes in Brazil and Ecuador and a center-left president in Argentina, Bush's initiatives were not expected to have smooth sailing in the region.

President Jimmy Carter

In May 2002, Assistant Secretary of State John Bolton, with no evidence to support his charges, accused Cuba of having developed "at least a limited offensive biological warfare research and development effort, and also [of] provid[ing] dual use biotechnology to . . . rogue states" such as Iran and Libya.[62] Former president Jimmy Carter, during a visit to Cuba in that same month, took issue with the Bush administration's charges. Touring the Center for Genetic Engineering and Biotechnology, he told Castro and Cuban scientists that he had "asked White House, State Department and intelligence officials . . . if Cuba was transferring technology or other information that could be used in terrorist activities, [and] there were absolutely no allegations made or questions raised."[63] Castro earlier had offered Carter free access to any place he would like to visit (and to bring with him any experts he would like to inspect any scientific center), and to talk with anyone even if they were opponents of the government.[64]

Bolton's serious accusation unraveled rapidly. In an unexpected rebuke, "Secretary of State Colin Powell cast some doubt on assertions . . . by a senior State Department official that Cuba was making such weapons."[65] Also, "The administration seemed to have forgotten about the matter . . . . A sweeping, 177-page State Department report on trends in global terrorism summed up Cuba in 47 lines, omitting any reference to its biological research." Moreover, on Capitol Hill, "Otto Reich . . . appeared initially confused when asked why the report made no mention of Cuba's bio-weapons research."[66]

Carter's visit (the first by a U.S. president since the 1959 revolution) was highlighted by his asking the United States to lift the over-four-decades-old economic embargo and to end all trade and travel restrictions. Besides having private talks with Castro, he held meetings with dissidents, including proponents of the controversial Varela Project. Signed by 11,020 registered voters, the Varela project is a citizens' legislative petition, which was delivered to the National Assembly in May 2002 by Osvaldo Payá Sardiñas. Taking advantage of a provision in the Cuban Constitution allowing 10,000 citizens (or more) to request legislation, the Varela Project asked for a plebiscite to authorize transformation of the political and economic system. But rather than petitioning regular legislation, the Varela project requested a referendum to authorize modifying the island's charter—which violated the amendment process established in the Cuban Constitution.[67] At the University of Havana, with Castro in attendance, in a speech broadcast live on television and radio to the entire country and reprinted later in its entirety in the official daily *Granma,* Carter asked the Cuban government to democratize itself and to respond positively to the dissidents' Varela Project. (In January 2003, the National Assembly's Constitutional and Legal Affairs Committee ended the project's legal life when the committee decided not to review it further and to notify the project's sponsors of its decision.)[68] He also challenged Washington and Havana to end the old political dispute.

Showing respect for Carter for having agreed to establish a (diplomatic) interests section in each country's capital city and to lift all travel restrictions (reimposed later) when he was president, *Granma* displayed Carter's statement upon arriving at Havana's José Martí Airport: "I have come to learn how to achieve harmonious U.S.-Cuba relations."[69]

Carter balanced his speech at the University of Havana with strong words for the American and Cuban governments. After denouncing American policies punishing Havana and noting American deficits, he criticized Cuban Socialism from his liberal democratic perspective. His message revitalized long-held expectations in different quarters: the Cuban government and the Cuban people, by asking the White House to lift the embargo and end travel restrictions; political dissidents, by supporting human rights and the Varela Project; Miami exiles, by criticizing the Socialist system; and Americans supporting free trade and travel to Cuba, by denouncing Washington's obsolete policies. Carter made his audiences feel that such objectives were legitimate and feasible, so some applauded his remarks opposing embargo and travel restrictions remarks, while others rejoiced in his criticism of Cuban Socialism.[70]

Ralph Nader

Continuing the policy of welcoming visitors who could influence American public opinion, Cuba's National Assembly invited Ralph Nader, the Green

Party presidential candidate in the 2000 elections, to visit the island. In a three-day visit in July 2002, Nader had dinner with Castro twice, spoke at the University of Havana's Aula Magna (Major Hall), as President Carter had, and called on the United States to lift trade and travel sanctions against Cuba. The embargo, he said, "had made it difficult for Cubans to enjoy freedom of speech and due process." He added, "If our country was under that kind of pressure there would not be much left of our democracy." Criticizing what he called America's "corporate oligarchy," Nader stated that "constitutional freedoms and civil rights ha[ve] been seriously restricted in the United States since the September 11 terror attacks." He also recommended improving the "political flexibility" available in the Cuban political system, noting that "any country that chooses to be socialistic or communistic, if it does not leave open options for revision and opportunity for change, it will not last very long . . . . And if it does last long, it will be a terrible price that the people pay."[71]

Historic Constitutional Amendment

Responding to President Bush's announcement of his newly devised hardline policies, and after the dissidents' Varela Project was made public on Cuban radio and television by President Carter, Castro reacted in support of amending the Cuban Constitution to decree that the nation's Socialist system was henceforth irrevocable.

A petition with more than 8 million signatures (99.25 percent of the 8.25 million voting population) and sponsored by several national organizations was presented to the National Assembly in extraordinary session. Recognizing "the will of the people," stated the petition, the Constitution should declare that "the economic, political, and social regime consecrated in the Cuban Constitution—a socialist one—is untouchable" (changed later to "irrevocable"), and should determine that "economic, diplomatic and political relations with any other state can never be negotiated under aggression, threat or pressure from a foreign power."[72]

Addressing the extraordinary parliamentary session, Foreign Minister Felipe Pérez Roque said the amendment is the "key to what we do when the generation that carried out the revolution, and the command of today, of Fidel, of Raúl . . . is no longer with us." Vice President Carlos Lage stated, "True democracy is socialist . . . the only way to defend human rights is in a society of equality and social justice. . . . For our people to return to the past is undesirable, unthinkable, impossible. . . . The homeland is sacred, the revolution is unconquerable and socialism is irrevocable."[73]

Anticipating events that would unfold later, Castro "warned the United States that his government would not allow 'any more violations of its sovereignty by American diplomats even if it would mean shutting down the United States Interests Section in Havana, . . . something we don't want to do.'" He complained that "over the past few months, the head of the U.S. Interests Section in Havana . . . has been vocal in support of the opposition" and that "U.S. State Department people on the island have been handing out shortwave radios tuned to the Voice of America's Radio Marti."[74]

The National Assembly approved the constitutional amendment. An overwhelming majority (96.7 percent) voted in its favor, and people nationwide showed their support for it. Still, only time will tell if this amendment can effectively withstand the challenges awaiting the nation in the future.

President George W. Bush

President Bush was not moved by Carter's appeal to ease U.S. policy. While celebrating the centennial anniversary of Cuba's independence on May 20 in Miami with Cuban American supporters, he unveiled his new Cuba policy—mostly a rehash of long-standing measures, with some minor modifications. Bush demanded that Castro hold free elections in 2003 under international supervision; free political prisoners; open the political and economic system to permit opposition candidates to organize, assemble, and speak in the next elections; and allow free enterprise, before the United States would consider lifting the economic embargo. Bush also promised to maintain travel restrictions to the island and to veto any attempt by Congress to ease trade restrictions.

The media noted the irony in Bush's *"Viva Cuba libre"* speech and in the site itself, Miami: "Cuba mocked America's disputed 2000 election and its chaotic conclusion in Florida, and Cuba's foreign minister once offered to send observers to ensure fair balloting there in the future." Clearly, "Politics loomed large over Bush's [Miami] speech and trip: Cuban-American voters helped carry him to a narrow victory in Florida, the state that decided the 2000 election, and they favor the kind of hard line Bush was espousing."[75] Sen. Christopher Dodd (D-CT) remarked that "[with such demands] President Bush has . . . guaranteed that the current political system in Cuba will remain the same as it has for the last 40 years that the U.S. has pursued this ill-advised policy."[76]

Castro responded in two successive remarks delivered in Plaza Los Olivos, Sancti Spiritus. The first one was directed to the American people, the second to President Bush. They were different in tone and content. With friendly words, Castro said:

> Our struggle is not and will never be, aimed against the American people. Perhaps, no other country receives Americans with the respect and hospitality displayed in Cuba. . . . Neither a single drop of blood has been shed in the United States, nor has an atom of wealth been lost there in the 43 years of the Cuban revolution, due to a terrorist action originated in Cuba. The opposite is true, since thousands of lives have been lost as well as huge amounts of money due to material damages caused by actions against our homeland originated in the U.S. territory.[77]

Castro then responded to President Bush, speaking to a large crowd in a drenching rain:

> The democracy [he] wants to see in Cuba would be a corrupt and unfair system that ignores the poor. . . . For Mr. W, democracy only exists where money solves everything and where those who can afford a $25,000-a-plate dinner—an insult to billions of people living in the poor, hungry, underdeveloped world—are the ones called to solve the problems of society and the world . . . Don't be a fool Mr. W, show some respect for the minds of the people who are capable of thinking. . . . None of our leaders is a millionaire like the President of the United States, whose monthly wage is almost twice that of all the members of the (Cuban) Council of State and the Council of Ministers in a year.[78]

Ricardo Alarcón, National Assembly president, accused Bush "of pandering to Cuban exiles in Miami . . . to thank them for getting him elected," and he "mocked Bush's insistence that Cuba call new elections in 2003, saying: 'You have to have a lot of nerve to go to Miami and speak of honest and clean elections,' referring to the disputed voting results in Florida during the November 2000 presidential balloting." Cuban dissidents were unhappy too with Bush's speech. "Changes have to be made but changes have to be made on both sides," said Vladimiro Roca. He added, "Dialogue, negotiation and reconciliation will help than continued tough U.S. policies."[79]

Midterm Report

By early 2003, opportunities to improve U.S.-Cuba relations were ignored by the White House. Castro had not opposed Washington's using the Guantánamo naval base to house Afghan war prisoners; an increasing number of American citizens were visiting Cuba (despite numerous prosecutions under Bush of those visiting the island without a U.S. license); and many petitions by farming and industrial interests were requesting expanded trade with the island. Also, a Fourth of July (2002) celebration at Havana's Karl Marx Theater featuring music and poetry "in honor of the 'noble' American people," stated that "the cultural, spiritual and moral legacy of the American people is also the patrimony of Cuba and the Cuban people."[80]

Bush's "compassionate conservatism" did not apply to Castro. His hard-line policy was mainly motivated by domestic politics. The close links between the White House and Cuban American Miami and the president's involvement in Florida politics have surpassed the two previous presidents' efforts to gain Cuban American support.[81] After having characterized American food sales following Hurricane Michelle as an "act of kindness," U.S. diplomats still rated Havana's conciliatory stance and its offer to cooperate with measures against terrorism as a "calculated response to the cold front develop[ed] in the White House, where President Bush has filled key Latin policy posts with officials who are known for their hard-line views on Cuba. The lineup—led by Otto Reich as the Latin America policy chief [from December 2001 to November 2002], and subsequently having him appointed to the National Security Council where no congressional confirmation was needed—[made it impossible for] . . . the administration [to] ease trade and travel barriers against [Cuba]."[82]

Subversive Bush-Cason Scheme and Cuba's April Response

In the spring of 2003 President Bush's hard-line policy provoked a major dispute with Havana, with far-reaching consequences. Enforcing the White House's policy since arriving at the island in September 2002 as head of the U.S. Interests Section, James Cason led a well-organized and well-financed opposition movement.[83] Cuba responded forcefully to Cason's actions, which were compounded by the leadership's fear that Bush's preemptive military strike doctrine could be used against the island as it had been in Iraq. Also, Cuba is still listed by the U.S. State Department as supporting terrorism.[84]

In a broad sweep, seventy-five individuals (including long-term opponents, alleged independent journalists, and others) accused of being involved in Cason's subversive scheming were arrested, judged in summary trials, and sentenced in April to prison terms ranging from six to twenty-eight years.[85] Ratified by the Supreme Court, the sanctions appear to have stopped the opposition movement, at least temporarily.[86] Also, after a wave of hijacks of maritime vessels and aircraft early in 2003 (more than seven in only a few weeks), three ferry hijackers who failed in their attempt to reach the coast of Florida were arrested and in summary trials were sentenced to death, which, combined with strict vigilance, promised to stop new hijackings.[87] Havana stated that permitting more hijackings could have unleashed a migration wave, which the Bush administration had warned would be unacceptable (given extant national security priorities following September 11, 2001) and therefore would be understood as an act of war.[88] But despite its own security concerns, Cuba's sanctions received broad international condemnation and were criticized as excessive punishment for opposing the regime.[89]

After having decided in March to discontinue licensing the "people to people" educational exchange program expanded in 1999 by President Clinton, which made it possible for thousands of Americans to visit Cuba, the Bush administration reacted to the crackdown by expelling seven diplomats from Cuba's Mission to the United Nations in New York City and seven from its Interests Section in Washington, and announcing that the Cuba policy was under review.[90] Havana refrained from expelling any American diplomats, knowing that a tit-for-tat response would play into the hands of Washington's hard-liners.[91] But Cuba charged that Washington's paucity of granted visas had contributed to the hijackings.[92] Only about seven hundred visas had been issued at a time when there should have been half of the annual twenty thousand visas agreed upon in the 1994 Migratory Accords. (On a yearly basis, the calendar for issuing visas runs from October to September.)

The Bush White House had devised a double winner in pursuing its anti-Cuba campaign. It confronted Havana with a no-win political and public relations dilemma: Cuba could either allow the existence of a U.S.-directed, antiregime movement (which meant accepting an opposition aimed at subverting the political system), or move to suppress it (as Cuba did) and then face an international outcry protesting major human rights violations (as has happened). The plan included turning the U.S. Interests Section and its chief diplomat's residence into the center of an anti-Socialist movement, organizing an opposition liberal political party, visiting with fellow schemers in their own homes, promoting and financing independent journalists while providing the means to report adverse news abroad, and pursuing other actions against the political system. In carrying out the plan, Cason had knowingly forced Cuba's hand beyond its limits, and the scheme ultimately ended with the execution of three hijackers and the incarceration of seventy-five collaborators identified by undercover agents who had infiltrated their ranks.

Besides their disaffection with the Socialist system, Cason's fellow plotters were lured into action by the favors they received, including dollars, baskets of consumer goods, unlimited access to the U.S. Interests Section and to the Internet services available on the premises, as well as to expensive items like fax machines and electronic gadgets, that were provided to them by the U.S. diplomatic mission.[93] As a group, they were easy prey in Cason's hands. Their opposition to the system was anchored in their having endured years of hardship under a depressed economy.

Cason's actions ended what had been a relatively conciliatory period for domestic dissent. Notably, while the 2002 Varela Project had been repudiated officially, its sponsors had paid no harsh price for their bold action.[94] The U.S. scheme also fractured a period in which independent foreign visitors were being welcomed, as exemplified by President Carter's critical remarks during his visit to the island.

The April events had an impact abroad, especially in the United States, Latin America, and Europe. The head of the Cuban Interests Section in Washington, Dagoberto Rodríguez, stated that while their diplomatic activities were aimed at promoting good will with the American people, the U.S. Interests Section in Havana "is devoted to promoting opposition in Cuba, creating instability and overthrowing the Cuban government. This is the final goal of the Administration." A State Department official said, however, that "U.S. diplomats in Havana aren't calling for Castro's overthrow, but rather for democracy in Cuba."[95]

Several key groups like Amnesty International, the Center for International Policy, the National Foreign Policy Council, and others persisted in urging relaxation of relations with Havana, and the bipartisan Working Group on Cuba in the House and the Senate continued to support legislation that would soften the embargo and other sanctions, but the administration was able to slow the growing domestic dissatisfaction with its Cuba policy. In addition to the Republican-dominated House of Representatives' condemnation of Cuba's sanctions, many events related to the island were canceled, mostly due to the increasing tensions between the countries. The Cuba Policy Foundation, a Washington lobby working to have the trade embargo lifted, disbanded after the "realization that no one in Congress would move to relax sanctions against Cuba given Castro's latest moves."[96]

While attending an OAS meeting in Chile, U.S. secretary of state Colin Powell sought to have the other foreign ministers condemn Cuba for the crackdown. He failed, leaving Santiago with no apparent support for his initiative. Canada's foreign minister stated that many of his colleagues did not see the OAS as the appropriate forum for discussing the crackdown because Cuba did not have a chance to defend itself and appeared as a victim of the long-standing American embargo.[97] Powell's agenda appeared to disregard OAS members' main concerns. Latin American leaders "have [been] complain[ing] . . . that as far as the Bush administration is concerned, they have 'fallen off the map' . . . except in connection with the war against terrorism."[98]

Still, Washington's Cuba policy found support from the European Union (EU). After having opened an embassy in Havana, the EU announced diplomatic sanctions on Cuba for the incarceration of dissidents and the death penalties on the hijackers.[99] Cuba identified Spain and Italy as the culprits behind the adversarial EU position. While Italian prime minister Silvio Berlusconi was denounced for canceling already granted credits to Cuba, the thrust of the attack was centered on Spain's José María Aznar, a conservative opponent of Socialism and the main instigator behind Europe's hardline policy.[100]

Italy and Spain had supported Washington's Iraq war, although it was Aznar who had gained some international prominence. As seen by Havana, Aznar turned the EU against the island, justifying its stance as a way to make amends for the strained relationship between Europe and Washington caused by the Iraqi war. Pleased by the EU's hard stance, Powell announced that the United States would be aligning its Cuba policy with Europe.[101]

The rift with the European Union had serious consequences for the economy. The EU was Cuba's main trading partner, investor, and source for its international tourism. Also, replacing Greece, Italy's Berlusconi assumed the EU's six-month revolving presidency in the second half of 2003.[102]

Cuba warned the EU that it would not tolerate any "provocations and blackmail" and to stop meddling in its internal affairs. In a massive public demonstration attended by Castro, the EU's actions were denounced.[103] Given the role played by Aznar, the permit for Spain's cultural center in Havana was revoked. In its place, a new Hispanic center, the Federico García Lorca Cultural Center, was formed. Underlining its antifascist character (García Lorca had been murdered by Francisco Franco's Nationalists during the Spanish Civil War in 1936), in front of the new center and the Spanish embassy a major billboard portrays an antifascist painting by Pablo Picasso, *Guernica* (which memorializes the Spanish town in the Basque province destroyed by Hitler's air force fighting for Franco during the civil war). The billboard bears an "Antifascist" legend at the bottom. In addition to the statue of García Lorca, there will be statues of the Spanish poet

Antonio Machado and the Cuban journalist and writer Pablo de la Torriente Brau, who died in 1936 in Spain fighting against Franco.[104]

Cuba had to withdraw its application to the Cotonou Agreement, which offers European economic aid and preferential trade to nations in Asia, the Caribbean, and the Pacific.[105] However, it is difficult to know how long the Bush-Aznar-Berlusconi entente can keep a united Europe in the anti-Cuba camp. There are old and new rivalries lurking under the new Europe-Washington common approach, promising troubled times ahead. European domestic politics could undermine the common approach if opposition forces use the Cuba issue against the government for making Washington's policy its own.

European tourism and investment continued to flow into Cuba following the April crackdown. According to a French diplomat in Havana, "There'll be [no] economic consequences, because the EU has issued no economic sanctions . . . so we don't think that anything will change for now." The president of the U.S.-Cuba Trade and Economic Council explained that it was "too early to tell if the stated common EU position will survive individual EU member countries' interests. Traditionally, the EU has made pronouncements relating to Cuba which have generally not been implemented by individual countries."[106] Also, an official of France's Accor Group in Cuba stated that major hotel corporations like "Meliá and Accor look only at the bottom line, and as long as the bottom line is good, there is no problem." He added, "If business was so bad and they were so nervous, they would never sign contracts or invest in Cuba." In preparation for the tourist season, Spain's Pinero corporation had invested $2 million upgrading the former Club Med on famous Varadero beach.[107]

During the celebration of the fiftieth anniversary of the Moncada barracks attack in the city of Santiago de Cuba that launched the revolution (July 26, 1953), Europe's decision against Havana was denounced. Accusing the EU of acting as Washington's "Trojan horse," Castro said that "Cuba does not need the aid of the European Union to survive." He added, "The government of Cuba, out of a basic sense of dignity, relinquishes any aid or remnant of humanitarian aid [$16.4 million yearly] that may be offered by the European Union and the governments of the European Union."[108]

The Washington-EU understanding did not augur well for Cuba. Among other issues, it could complicate even further the problems facing Cuba's troubled economy. Under such conditions, the regime's staying power was being tested and stretched again, perhaps to its very limits.

After this introductory overview examining some of the complex issues and problems confronting Cuba, let's look next at the outstanding studies included in this book, and learn from their invaluable discussions of Cuban Socialism in this new century. As we will see, there is much more to know and understand on this subject.

Some Comments on the Book's Content

Under what conditions was Cuba's halting economic recovery made possible? What kinds of changes were made in the society, the political system, the military, and the economy? What direction is Cuban Socialism taking now? What is the structural nature of the Socialist system today, and what changes should be expected in the future? These questions are addressed in this book, along with many others. Scholars holding diverse and contrasting viewpoints and explanations provide the answers. Their wealth of knowledge is solidly rooted in their having visited the island many times and having studied its affairs for years. Among the contributors born in Cuba, some live fully integrated into the revolutionary society, while others reside in the United States.

This volume includes seven subject areas central to the evaluation of Cuba's standing in today's world: society, religion, economy, politics, military, migration, and international relations. The chapters examine recent and contemporary issues and the objectives the country seems to be pursuing. Altogether, we have a revealing picture of a nation still living under the Special Period in Peacetime, struggling to forge its own destiny; and of a leadership determined to have the revolution prevail above all, even if it means having to live with compromises of early values and objectives.

Society

To understand the events occurring since the last decade of the twentieth century, one must examine what happened to the nation's social fabric, including demographic policies. The society that emerged under the social transformation started in 1959 was cemented by the revolution's political culture. But how much have social and political values changed under the special period?

José A. Moreno claims that the early social and cultural changes sought to establish the foundation of an egalitarian society. Agrarian and urban reform, a literacy campaign, a universal health system free of charge, and the nationalization and collectivization of productive property were among the societal changes. Previous social cleavages were officially ended, whether they were motivated by race, social class, occupation, or gender.

To Moreno, the revolution's goal of creating a "new man" was compromised under the special period when changes were made to rescue the economy. To what extent was the political culture eroded? Will the government be able to halt the trend toward satisfaction of material needs? Could moral incentives be effective instead? Or is it too late to reverse the trend? Responding to this issue, Havana has limited those economic activities that might deepen socioeconomic cleavages to avoid an unchecked mass movement of people seeking hard-currency salaried occupations. Despite extant feelings of frustration and even despair, most Cubans do not want to "go back to a [social] system of differences and exclusions," asserts Moreno.

The family is at the heart of society, cementing it altogether; and women have been the bedrock supporting society's primary cell. Through their multiple roles as mothers, wives, daughters, and sisters, always taking care of the family needs, women have guaranteed the family's sustenance, making sure there was food at the table, no matter how scarce it became in the early 1990s.

Cuban women's revolutionary actions are not new. They have a history filled with sacrifice and heroic actions. Jean Weisman persuasively makes the point that women have been part of Cuba's long political struggle and have paid the price exacted for their commitment. At the time, most women were not focusing on gender issues, she says, thinking instead about overthrowing the brutal Batista regime (1952–58).

Under revolutionary rule, domestic workers, prostitutes, and other destitute women have profited from new social policies. Although the record shows that most women have improved their lives, have become educated, and have found jobs in all fields and professions, there still is frustration among some women that their appointments to senior governmental decision-making posts have been few and far between, reports Weisman. MAGÍN, an informal women's group composed of specialists in communications, was asked to disband and to channel its activities through the Federation of Cuban Women (FMC) to avoid competing with it. (The FMC is the officially recognized women's group and is now rated as a nongovernmental organization.)

How have women fared under the current special period, especially during the first and most difficult years? Norma Vasallo Barrueta answers this question by providing an insightful picture from the island. She chronicles not only the outward manifestations of women's vicissitudes at the time, but the feelings and frustrations pertaining to their inner lives as well.

Vasallo believes the positive changes that have taken place at the objective and subjective levels since 1959 have effectively heightened women's social standing and self-esteem—the social policies have improved their condition objectively and have modified subjectively the way they view themselves. Still, the downward socioeconomic process that started over ten years ago has been particularly stressful to women.

Not all women have been equally affected by the special period, nor were all equally prepared for such a time. But there have been trying times individually and collectively, and women were at the center of the storm, asserts Vasallo. No matter how disfigured Cuban society may have become in the process, women were chiefly responsible for its actual survival.

Given the close relationship between population growth and social and economic development, Cuba must adopt a demographic policy. Havana should not overlook such a vital social issue, asserts Sonia I. Catasús Cervera. At the 1984 Mexico Conference on Population, the alleged link between population policy and development strategy was confirmed, she says. Thus, extant social development programs should also include demographic components, keeping both sides closely linked.

Population growth in the 1960s coincided with social policies redistributing the nation's wealth. Population growth declined noticeably later, as the low fertility rate failed to offset the negative migratory flow in spite of a declining mortality rate. Still, Cuba rated somewhat better demographically in 1963 and 1970 in comparison with some Latin American countries.

While the fertility rate has improved recently, the question remains whether present demographic growth will be sufficient to satisfy Cuba's needs. Although low population growth reduces pressure for social services, given Havana's social and developmental objectives, current growth rates may be insufficient for long-term manpower needs. Demographic prospects and development plans have become intertwined with the potential for affecting each other negatively.

Religion

The easing of official restrictions on religious practice in the 1990s brought a renaissance of faith-based spiritual awareness to Cubans and raised expectations as to how far religious activism would be allowed in social (and political) life. Given the power and position the Catholic Church enjoyed in the pre-1959 period, it is possible that some of the faithful and the clergy would like to regain their previous social standing.

Margaret E. Crahan examines the changing circumstances surrounding religious life under revolutionary rule, particularly since the 1990s. Cuba is no Poland, a fact confirmed by Crahan, so there should be no expectations that the Catholic Church, or the pope's 1998 visit, could bring down the government.

The rivalry between the Catholic Church and the government is compounded with subtexts that muddle the issues involved. According to Crahan, the Church should not pursue an active role beyond its religious domain in the civil society and should not antagonize a regime that has been legitimized as the defender of national sovereignty and identity and the public interest.

The special period has weakened the government's ability to provide sought-after goods and services. Despite the Catholic Church's aggrandized social standing, it still has a weak social base. The Church's operational code has been caution and flexibility in dealing with the government. Caution has lowered the potential for confrontation, while flexibility has made continuing religious life possible, which in turn has made today's more auspicious period possible.

The Economy

Cuba's main concern since the 1990s has been safeguarding the economy. The difficult decisions made to regain economic viability are examined by José Luis Rodríguez. He provides an account of economic decision making at the worst of times, and of the country's strategies for survival in spite of so many problems. Today's economic indicators are below those of the late 1980s, and it will take time before they can reach that level again, but the 1991–94 period, when conditions were at their worst, has been left behind.

Decision makers needed to reinsert the economy into the world market while retaining its Socialist character. They had to bring in foreign investors without turning the economy into a capitalist one, and they had to find trade partners and finance the sugar industry and other economic activity, and use lenders who feared granting interest credit to a risk-rated economy.

The government rejected market and neoliberal solutions. Such schemes would have resulted in "absolute poverty [for] most of the population and the total loss of the [government's] ability to lead the process of development in favor of the national interest," says Rodríguez. Thus the regime would have to keep the economic crisis from becoming a political one. In spite of public protests in Havana, the 1994 rafters' exodus, defections, and other expressions of discontent, most of the population seemed to favor the Socialist project.

Andrew Zimbalist provides a gloomier assessment of Cuba's economic recovery and future prospects than Rodríguez. The economic record today and during the 1990s "leaves much to be desired," according to Zimbalist. While rapid economic decline was arrested, any "substantial structural reform was essentially halted in 1994." Hence, compared to former Socialist bloc members, Cuba's annual recovery rate since 1993 has been better than only Latvia's and Lithuania's. At such a poor growth rate, Cuba cannot return to the 1990 per capita income level until 2005, affirms Zimbalist. Compared to Latin America, Cuba lagged behind economically but was able to avoid the financial collapse and political instability that have affected some countries in the region. Today, he says, Cuba "look[s] increasingly like a class society, defined by access to hard currency through work, politics, or relatives abroad."

Even though they arrive at different, and at times opposite, conclusions, Rodríguez and Zimbalist in practice complement one another. While Rodríguez praises the obvious gains achieved during the 1990s, he refrains from claiming that the economic recovery is complete. Zimbalist evaluates the period discussed by Rodríguez critically, but his study is centered on the problems of today—whether they are lingering issues or new ones.

And yet, not even a stronger economic recovery could have totally avoided the negative effect of the U.S. embargo; nor could it have spared the country from natural disasters like the 2001 Hurricane Michelle, or even insulate the tourist industry from the sluggishness that followed the September 11 terrorist attack against the United States—these were some of the problems taking place while Cuba struggled to improve its economic performance and financial management record.

Politics

Examining the role and significance of the Cuban Communist Party in the political system, William LeoGrande reviews the events that changed the domestic and international context surrounding the PCC and interprets how such events influenced its fortunes and misfortunes. A decade after the PCC's birth, the First Party Congress (1975) inaugurated the process of institutionalizing the regime, which included a new (Socialist) constitution and the first national elections held under the revolution.

As the guarantor of the Socialist system, says LeoGrande, the PCC sought recently to accommodate its leadership to the rapidly changing economic and social conditions. From the Fourth to the Fifth Party Congress (1990 and 1997, respectively) a significant debate ensued within its ranks. While the avowed objective was to safeguard the revolution and Socialism, there still were divergent opinions on how to accomplish this objective economically and politically. Addressing the issue, Raúl Castro took a guarded approach, but he favored adapting to the national economy the successful initiatives of the armed forces' enterprises.

The PCC, states LeoGrande, has already made progress regarding generational leadership succession. The last PCC congresses decided to downsize the high-level party organs' membership and to open their ranks to younger members and religious believers. LeoGrande finds the PCC was stronger than most of the European Communist parties on the eve of transition in 1989. And yet, warns LeoGrande, the PCC is now confronting a period in which the economic reforms "to reenter the global economy are having significant reverberations and changing the political terrain of the future." In sum, pragmatism, accountability, and effective leadership must guide the PCC's performance in the years to come.

Peter Roman has gained invaluable firsthand knowledge of Cuban legislative practices. He attended National Assembly sessions, examined legislative transcripts from an eight-year period, including the Fifth Legislature's committee meeting reports and minutes (starting in 1998), read voters' letters requesting assistance, and attended accountability sessions of municipal assembly delegates, while conducting fieldwork for over three months.

After having observed the functioning of the National Assembly and political dynamics directly, Roman concluded that the Cuban government is not more democratic or less democratic than that of the United States, nor more or less representative. However, when it comes to representing most sectors of society (such as women, youth, religious leaders, workers, doctors, and teachers), the system produces a "legislature that is far more representative of a pluralistic society than, for example, those who serve in the United States Congress."

Roman acknowledges that "the [practice of] noncompetitive [candidates'] nominations and elections are the weakest link in the Cuban parliamentary system." Nevertheless, when deliberating, "[National Assembly] deputies actively oppose parts of proposed legislation, their objections are taken seriously, and there is an attempt to reconcile differences in the final [legislative] versions."

Conducting fieldwork on different occasions, Arnold August witnessed the 1997–98 elections, the 1999–2000 National Assembly electoral legislation, and the 2000 midterm elections. Based on such observations, August discusses Cuba's electoral practices and institutions.

Direct vote is now used at all levels (municipal, provincial, and national) and has been since 1992, but the election of national deputies and provincial delegates lacks electoral competition, notes August. Still, the voter has the choice of approving or rejecting some or all the candidates listed in the official slate of nominees.

According to August, Cubans claim that their system is more open and democratic than most, giving an equal opportunity to all candidates while avoiding the campaign expenses needed in other places. The candidates' personal qualifications determine whether they are nominated and elected. Also, half of the provincial delegates and national deputies must come from the ranks of municipal delegates, and their sole remuneration comes from their regular salary. But today, asserts August, elected officials' budgetary resources are insufficient to satisfy national needs.

The foremost political issue looming in Cuba's future is the presidential succession. Fidel Castro was seventy-seven years old in 2003 and will be eighty-two by the end of the new presidential term. He appears in good health, but his fainting episode during an outdoor rally near Havana in 2001 added renewed significance to this question.

The succession issue is examined by Nelson P. Valdés. He has studied the existing interlocking relationship between the ruling elite and the mechanisms already in place for an eventual transfer of power. Raúl Castro, Fidel Castro's brother, is recognized as the likely successor. Castro has also indicated that he should be his successor. Raúl and his close associates, the Raulistas, have cohesiveness and resources originating in the armed forces that are not rivaled by any other group.

Raúl will be seventy-seven by the time Castro completes the present term. The presidential succession, however, hinges on how long it will take Castro to allow Raúl to take his place. If it takes too long, Raúl may not be at his best leadership capacity, which would disrupt an orderly succession process. Under any circumstances it will be difficult to succeed Castro, but if Cubans look for matter-of-fact guidance with sound managerial skills, Raúl might be the right person. As noted by Valdés, the difference in leadership style between the two brothers would underscore the beginning of a new period under revolutionary rule.

The Military

The Fuerzas Armadas Revolucionarias (Revolutionary Armed Forces, FAR) was born in the Sierra Maestra and has been a pillar of the regime. Under Raúl's stewardship, the FAR has been in charge of national defense, international missions, and economic enterprises, establishing a record of profitable ventures. Hal Klepak provides a detailed study of the FAR, which he rates as "the most effective of all elements of state power in the country." He examines the role played by the FAR in "the politics, internal security, social life, and economy of Cuba."

According to Klepak, since the 1990s the FAR has been streamlined and has lost the international connections that gave it an advantage in past missions. The FAR is now a domestic defensive force; its internationalist days are over. Involvement in economic activities took personnel and resources away from training and other tasks, reducing the FAR's overall military efficiency. Thus priority was given to combat units trained to defeat an invasion, and those units are better off than most.[109]

The FAR's economic activities have provided it with new budgetary sources and financial independence, which may have an effect beyond the special period. In addition to enjoying the respect and affection of the population, it is the single government institution respected by the American military, states Klepak.

Migrating to the United States

The South Florida enclave has set the tone for most Cubans living abroad since 1959. The United States and Cuba have used migration as a tool in pursuit of political goals, but with quite different reasons and objectives. Félix Masud-Piloto examines the Cuban exodus to the United States that started in the 1960s. Since then, Washington has sought to discredit the Socialist regime. "To accomplish that goal, U.S. laws would have to treat Cubans as a privileged immigrant group, at least until the Castro government was overthrown," says Masud-Piloto. The aim was to build a large exile community that would shine for its prosperity, in contrast to life back on the island. Consequently, Cubans have received every conceivable favor from the U.S. government.

A relic of the cold war, the 1966 Cuban Adjustment Act codified the so-called Cuban "exceptionalism": the "right" to enjoy special treatment upon arriving in the United States. However, as of 1994 a new migratory policy has distinguished two types of migrants: the illegals apprehended in open seas (wet feet), who could be repatriated to Cuba, and those arriving on U.S. soil (dry feet), who could ask for asylum and become refugees in good standing.

Masud-Piloto discusses the Elián González case—the seven-year-old boy rescued off the Florida coast on Thanksgiving Day, November 25, 1999. In the media-driven affair, manipulated by his Miami relatives, Elián became a poster child for the anti-Castro cause. Meanwhile, daily rallies in Cuba demanded Elián's reunification with his father and the rest of the family. Finally, the United States recognized Elián's father's right to take his son back to Cuba. The case turned into a winning public relations event for Cuba.[110]

Cuban Americans had defied public opinion and the federal authorities. Their logic, that when Communism is involved normal rules do not apply, failed in this case. The U.S. approach to the Elián affair shocked most southern Florida Cuban Americans. To them, anti-Castroism is more than political attitudes and rhetoric, it is a way of life; but for the first time it did not coincide with Washington's decisions.

International Relations

Since 1959, Cuba has been a small nation with a large-power foreign policy. But how has it been forced to adapt to an inauspicious environment, marked by U.S. hostility? Answering this kind of question, H. Michael Erisman provides a perceptive analysis of Cuba's world policy today. Recognizing three main attributes of the island's foreign policy—effective sovereignty, economic security, and international stature—he examines the way these objectives have been pursued and the changes that have been made to adapt to present international conditions.

Preserving political and economic independence remains the central goal. As Erisman explains it, while the international context has changed, the primacy of safeguarding the nation's sovereignty is very much alive. Even with adverse conditions, developmental objectives continue. The challenge has been to find ways to pursue them while securing the regime's economic and financial viability.

Erisman analyzes the way external policy objectives are pursued in two consecutive periods: the cold war or classical Fidelismo, and the post-Soviet world or new Fidelismo. As he informs us, the policy changes and adaptations executed during the transition from a past national and international reality to a new one have helped define Cuba's ongoing operational role as an international actor.

The radical nature of the Cuban regime provoked Washington's hostility, and its international policies stood contrary to American interests. Still, despite over four decades of reciprocal animosity, Cuba and the United States have also established mutually beneficial agreements.

Esteban Morales Domínguez examines the Cuba-U.S. conflict by looking at three independent variables present in this political phenomenon: the internal Cuban reality, the internal American reality, and the international reality. This way, he asserts, we can examine Washington's decisions, as well as Havana's behavior within the world context in which both function as political actors. Morales Domínguez asserts that in spite of being treated as a political object, Cuba also plays an active role in a conflictive process that is essentially interactive.

"For over forty years," he says, "U.S. policy toward Cuba was and continues to be based on aggression." However, Morales Domínguez admits, the "world stage . . . where the bilateral conflict is acted out, has changed, leading to new situations." Hence, his model includes variables ranging from the domestic Cuban context to the economic embargo and Washington's attempt to internationalize its policy and the world's response. An intervening variable has been that of the American farmers and businessmen who are building on the food sales started in late 2001 by lobbying for increased trade with Havana. But for Cuba to continue playing an international political role, it needs to expand its political impact in the United States and internationally, and also to continue its economic recovery and social project, according to Morales Domínguez.

Conclusion

Cuba traveled a dangerous road in the 1990s and continues to do so today. With more willpower than actual resources, it extricated itself from the abyss it fell into after the collapse of European Socialism. The recovery has been painful and is not over yet, even though the country has already paid a heavy price.

Cuban society is different today than it was before the commencement of the Special Period in Peacetime. Although its policy choices have been limited by domestic and external factors, its record of conquering what appear to be formidable problems tells us not to underrate Cuba's ingenuity, resilience, and survival instincts. Returning to late 1980s Socialism is not possible, but the country is still Socialist. And where is it going from here? Is today's society an indicator of how it will look tomorrow? What will the final characteristics of the island's Socialist system be?

The island-nation is challenging us to learn why and how it refuses to succumb to adversity but chooses instead to chart its own destiny. Addressing the major issues by applying to the task timely and well-balanced scholarly studies, this book provides a comprehensive picture of a multifaceted and by now legendary country.

Notes

1. Daniel Chirot, ed., Introduction to *The Crisis of Leninism and the Decline of the Left: The Revolutions of 1989* (Seattle: University of Washington Press, 1991), ix.

2. For the impact that the demise of European Socialism had on Cuban intellectuals, see "Rethinking the Revolution: Nine Testimonies from Cuba," *NACLA Report on the Americas* 29 (September–October 1995): 25–30.

3. Jorge G. Castañeda, *Utopia Unarmed: The Latin American Left after the Cold War* (New York: Alfred A. Knopf, 1993), 240.

4. Ibid.

5. Ibid.

6. "Representative Henry J. Hyde, Republican of Illinois and the chairman of the House International Relations Committee, warned late last year that Brazil's new president might join Mr. Chávez and Mr. Castro in a Latin 'axis of evil.'" Juan Forero, "Latin America's political compass veers toward Left," *New York Times* (on line), January 19, 2003.

7. Frances Robles, "Latin leaders will invite Castro to '04 summit," *Miami Herald* (on line), May 25, 2003.

8. Victor M. Carriba, "Argentina y Cuba abren nuevo capítulo en sus relaciones," *Granma Internacional* (on line), May 26, 2003; Vicente L. Panetta, "Larga reunión entre Castro y el nuevo presidente argentino," *El Nuevo Herald* (on line), May 27, 2003; "Argentines swoon over visiting Castro," *Miami Herald* (on line), May 27, 2003.

9. Max Azicri, *Cuba Today and Tomorrow: Reinventing Socialism* (Gainesville: University Press of Florida, 2000), 22.

10. José Ramón Balaguer, quoted in Raisa Pages, "Latin America and Caribbean face far-reaching tasks," *Granma International*, December 9, 2001, 7.

11. See chapter 7.

12. President Carlos Lage, quoted in Max Azicri, "Notes about the Normalization of Relations between Cuba and the Emigration," *NOTICIERO* (September–October 1994): 4.

13. See chapter 2.

14. Alejandro de la Fuente, "The Resurgence of Racism in Cuba," *NACLA Report on the Americas* 34, no. 6 (May/June 2001): 29–34.

15. Domingo Amuchastegui, "Cuba downsizes ailing sugar industry: Authorities to close 71 out of 156 mills," *CUBANEWS* 10, no. 6 (July 2002): 1–2; "Downsizing the Sugar Industry," *CUBANEWS* 10, no. 10 (November 2002): 4.

16. Mary Murray, "Bitter Pill for Cuban Sugar Workers," *MSNBC News* (on line), August 23, 2002; "Fidel assures nervous workers that Cuba's sugar industry won't disappear," *CUBANEWS* 10, no. 10 (November 2002): 4.

17. "Tourism Briefs: ASTA president visits Cuba," *CUBANEWS* 10, no. 5 (June 2002): 5; Larry Luxner, "Meliá to Invest Millions in 2 New Resorts; chain already manages 22 Cuban hotels," *CUBANEWS* 10, no. 10 (November 2002): 1–2; Armando H. Portela, "Sugar-producing Ciego de Avila turns to tourism to save its economy," and "Casinos in Cuba's Future?" *CUBANEWS* 10, no. 8 (September

2002): 14–15, 5; Miguel Comellas, "More Than 50,000 Tourists: Unbeaten Record for One Day," *Granma International,* January 12, 2003, 16.

18. "Cuba Travel," Latin America Working Group (LAWG), November 20, 2003 (on line: lawgcubanetwork@npogroups.org); Nancy Mikelsons, "Cuban Amendment Removal," November 14, 2003 (on line: Nancy.Mikelsons@pobox.com).

19. Tim Johnson, "Cuba declines U.S. aid, wants to pay for relief," *Miami Herald* (on line), November 10, 2001.

20. Ibid.

21. Ann Radelat, "Hurricane Michelle is unlikely force that pries open Cuban market for the first time in 40 years," *CUBANEWS* 9, no. 12 (December 2001): 1–2.

22. "Illinois Governor's Second Visit to Cuba," *Granma International,* February 3, 2002, 4.

23. Anita Show, "First U.S. commercial food arrives in Cuba; hopes raised for trade," *Associated Press* (on line), December 17, 2001; Alan Sayre, "U.S. ships to Cuba for hurricane relief," *Miami Herald* (on line), December 15, 2001.

24. It was reported that net sales at the exhibition totaled $95 million. Larry Luxner, "Cuba food expo nets $95m in contracts; U.S. firms say this is only the beginning," and "Rice exporters see tremendous markets in Cuba," *CUBANEWS* (October 2002): 1, 2–3; Fidel Castro, "We must increase trade and development," *Granma International,* October 5, 2001, 7.

25. Luxner, "Cuba food expo."

26. "Purchases from the United States reach $253 million USD," *Granma International,* December 22, 2002, 16.

27. Other sources reported that U.S. food sales to Cuba for the period totaled only $230 million but predicted that they could reach $1.4 billion by 2005. "EU, Canada watch jealously as US food sales to Cuba jump," *CUBANEWS* (December 2002): 4. Also, Cuba reported that U.S. food sales had increased by 40 percent in the first three months of 2003, compared with the same period a year earlier. "Aumentan 40 por ciento ventas productos agrícolas de EE.UU. a Cuba," *Granma Internacional* (on line), May 23, 2003.

28. "Aumentan 40 por ciento ventas productos agrícolas de EE.UU. a Cuba."

29. Ana Radelat, "House votes to weaken Cuba embargo, but Bush veto may derail legislation," *CUBANEWS* 10, no. 10 (August 2002): 10; Ana Radelat, "Chasm widens between White House, Congress on direction of Cuba policy," *CUBANEWS* 10, no. 7 (June 2002): 1–2; Brian Alexander, "*Embargo Update—* What to Expect from Congress regarding Cuba in the Weeks Ahead," Cuba Policy Foundation/Center for Cuban Studies, December 2002.

30. "Castro urges 'peaceful solution' to terrorism," *Associated Press* (on line), September 30, 2001. In a public meeting the government condemned terrorism and repeated its support of the American people. The rally's theme was "Our solidarity with the American people during the national tragedy they are living through." "Cuba rallies against terrorism, supports U.S. people," *Miami Herald* (on line), September 17, 2001.

31. "President Fidel Castro's Letter to H.S. Kofi Annan," October 3, 2001 (New

York: Permanent Mission of the Cuban Government at the United Nations, 2001), http://homepages.about.com/evelio32/Texto-1.

32. "Key Address by Dr. Fidel Castro Ruz, President of the Republic of Cuba, at a Massive Demonstration Commemorating the 25th Anniversary of the Terrorist Act against a Cubana Jetliner off the Coast of Barbados, Revolution Square, October 6, 2001" (New York: Permanent Mission of the Cuban Government at the United Nations, 2001), http://homepages.about.com/evelio32/discurso/123/.

33. "Cuba says: Afghan Bombing 'a Cure Worse than the Disease,'" *Reuters* (on line), October 8, 2001.

34. "In the very US people we can perceive a friend and potential ally of just causes," *Granma International*, February 9, 2003, 4–5. During the blessing ceremony of a Havana convent broadcast nationally on television, flanked by a cardinal from the Vatican and another from Mexico, Castro praised "the pope's efforts to prevent a war with Iraq." The war could "have disastrous human, political and economic consequences in the whole world," he added. "Castro reaches out to Roman Catholics," *Associated Press* (on line), March 8, 2003.

35. "Cuba has no opinion on U.S. detainees," *Miami Herald* (on line), December 31, 2001.

36. "U.S.-Cuba Military Ties Warming," *MSNBC News* (on line), January 11, 2002.

37. Ibid.

38. Nancy San Martin, "Two senators seek Cuba links," *Miami Herald* (on line), January 7, 2002. A national campaign is underway to remove Cuba from the State Department's list of terrorist nations. The campaign, which started with sixteen signatures from policy groups stretching from Miami to San Francisco, continues to gain support, said Anya Landau of the Center for International Policy in Washington. Nancy San Martin, "Cuba Forced to Sell Technology," *Miami Herald* (on line), October 10, 2001.

39. "Guantánamo prisoner photos stir controversy in Britain," *Associated Press* (on line), January 21, 2002.

40. "Germany criticizes U.S. over prisoners' treatment," *Reuters* (on line), January 22, 2002; "Pentagon defends detentions, Afghan pockets aid," *Reuters* (on line), January 22, 2002. For the first court challenge in the United States over Washington's treatment of Afghanistan prisoners in Guantánamo, see "US judge doubts jurisdiction in detainee challenge," *Reuters* (on line), January 22, 2002.

41. Katherine Q. Seelye, "Detainees are not P.O.W.'s, Cheney and Rumsfeld declare," *New York Times*, January 28, 2002, A6.

42. Katherine Q. Seelye, "Bush now decides Geneva rules fit Taliban captives," *New York Times*, February 8, 2002, A1. For a discussion of prison conditions and denial of rights in Guantánamo for detainees from the war in Afghanistan, see Joseph Lelyveld, "'The Least Worst Place': Life in Guantanamo," in *The War on Our Freedoms: Civil Liberties in an Age of Terrorism*, ed. Richard C. Leone and Greg Anrig (New York: Public Affairs, 2003).

43. Gobierno de Cuba, "Declaración del Gobierno de Cuba a la opinión pública nacional e internacional, Enero 11 del año 2002," press release, Permanent Mission

of the Cuban Government at the United Nations, New York, 2002. Havana launched a campaign for the repatriation of five Cubans sentenced in Miami on espionage charges for informing the Cuban government of possible terrorist actions by Cuban American organizations. The Cuban government stated that it would "devote as much energy to the fight for the five agents as it did for the repatriation of castaway boy Elián González." Anita Snow, "Cuba vows to fight for repatriation of spies convicted in U.S.," *Associated Press* (on line), January 2, 2002. The campaign to free the five Cubans imprisoned in the United States includes a Web site with news and opinion largely ignored in the American media. See http://www.antiterroristas.cu, and other Cuban Web sites making reference to this issue. Other Web sites and statements from solidarity organizations denounce what is characterized as a miscarriage of justice in the trial of the "Five" held in 2001 in Florida.

44. San Martin, "Two senators seek Cuba links."

45. Ginger Thompson, "Mexican leader visits Castro to repair damaged ties," *New York Times,* February 4, 2002, A6.

46. Ginger Thompson, "On Cuba visit, Mexico's chief meets quietly with dissidents," *New York Times* (on line), February 5, 2002.

47. Ibid.

48. "The name of the man to blame for what happened in Monterrey is Jorge Castañeda," Editorial, *Granma* (on line), March 26, 2002.

49. David Gonzalez, "Cubans set on asylum crash a bus into embassy," *New York Times* (on line), March 1, 2002; "Who really drove that bus?" *Miami Herald* (on line), March 25, 2002.

50. Fidel Castro, "Declaración política del presidente del Consejo de Estado de Cuba," press release, Permanent Mission of the Republic of Cuba to the United Nations, New York, April 22, 2002.

51. "Human Rights Commission: Made-in-USA resolution passes with only two-vote margin, despite pressure," *Granma* (on line), April 28, 2002. The Mexican ambassador to Cuba, Ricardo Pascoe, was censured by his foreign relations office for having recommended to his government that Mexico abstain in Geneva rather than veto Cuba. "Censura la cancilleria a embajador en Cuba," *T1MSN-Noticias* (on line), April 2002.

52. "'The relationship is dead,' said Lorenzo Meyer, a historian and political analyst in Mexico. 'The embassies are open, but there's nothing beyond that. It is the first time this has happened in 100 years of formal relations.'" David Gonzalez, "Castro defies Fox of Mexico as once-warm ties sour," *New York Times,* April 23, 2002, A11; Tim Weiner, "Castro's attack on Fox places Cuban-Mexican ties in danger," *New York Times,* April 24, 2002, A6.

53. Christopher Marquis, "U.S. hasn't kept promises to Latin America, critics say," *New York Times* (on line), May 19, 2002.

54. Tim Weiner, "Fox's wooing of America brings him woes at home," *New York Times,* April 26, 2002, A3.

55. Ginger Thompson, "As the hardships mount, Venezuelans consider easing strike," and Jennifer Hughes, "Venezuela raises rates as strike hurts Bolivar," *New York Times* (on line), January 13, 2003; "Chávez wins a battle in oil strike, but

difficulties remain," *MSNBC News* (on line), January 29, 2003; "Chávez opponents shift strategy for early elections as strike reaches two-month mark," *MSNBC News* (on line), January 31, 2003; "Venezuelan strike crumbles as Chávez retains power," *MSNBC News/Associated Press* (on line), February 3, 2003; Juan Forero, "Strike frays in Venezuela as foes of Chávez retreat," *New York Times,* February 3, 2003, A9.

56. "In the past year, the United States channeled thousands of dollars in grants to American and Venezuelan groups opposed to President Chávez, including the labor group whose protest led to the Venezuelan president's brief ouster last month. The funds were provided by the National Endowment for Democracy, a nonprofit agency created and financed by Congress." Christopher Marquis, "U.S. bankrolling is under scrutiny for ties to Chávez ouster," *New York Times* (on line), April 25, 2002.

57. Juan Forero, "President of Venezuela resigns under pressure from military," *New York Times* (on line), April 12, 2002; "Venezuelan interim leader resigns in face of protest," *Associated Press* (on line), April 14, 2002; "Ousted Venezuelan president returns," *Associated Press* (on line), April 14, 2002.

58. Admitting how much the increasing price of oil has affected Cuba and, implicitly, the acuteness of the situation created by the interruption of oil shipments from Venezuela, Castro stated that the escalating price of oil was one of the most serious problems for Cuba and the world economically, which would be aggravated by a war with Iraq. Andrea Mitchell, "A Look into Castro's World," *MSNBC News* (on line), January 22, 2003.

59. "Senior members of the Bush Administration met several times in recent months with leaders of a coalition that ousted the Venezuelan president, Hugo Chávez, for two days last weekend, and agreed with them that he should be removed from office, administration officials said today. . . . Mr. Chávez has made himself very unpopular with the Bush Administration with his pro-Cuba stance and mouthing of revolutionary slogans." Christopher Marquis, "Bush officials met with Venezuelans who ousted leader," *New York Times,* April 16, 2002, A1. "A State Department official [said] . . . that Assistant Secretary of State Otto J. Reich phoned Pedro Carmona, the business man who briefly led the new government, on Friday, the very day he took over." Tim Johnson, "No Encouragement Given for Venezuela Coup," *Miami Herald* (on line), April 17, 2002; Juan Forero, "O.A.S. reaffirms support to Venezuelan," *New York Times,* April 17, 2002, A9.

60. Marcela Sanchez, "Bush administration stumbles again in Venezuela," *Washington Post* (on line), December 19, 2002; Karen De Young, "Recent statements muddle U.S. stance on Venezuela," *Washington Post,* December 21, 2002, A20.

61. The Venezuelan opposition has been relentless in its drive to oust Chávez from office. Following a constitutional provision allowing for a recall referendum halfway through the president's six-year term, 3.2 million signatures were presented to the National Electoral Council seeking Chávez's removal. Government officials noted serious problems with the collection of signatures, which prompted President Chávez to say, "Some people who have been buried for a while appeared to have signed. . . . They should do a much more serious job." "Venezuela's Chávez ques-

tions legitimacy of signatures demanding recall vote," *Associated Press* (on line), August 20, 2003; Juan Forero, "Venezuelan opposition files to seek referendum on Chávez," *New York Times* (on line), August 21, 2003. Seeking to undo a cooperative agreement between Cuba and Venezuela, the Venezuelan Medical Federation succeeded in having the country's First Administrative Court rule that about "400 Cuban doctors working in Caracas slums under an official bilateral cooperation program were practicing illegally and should be replaced by local doctors." The government had justified using Cuban doctors, claiming that "Venezuelan doctors were afraid to work in Caracas's crime-ridden slums." "Venezuela court bars Cuban doctors from working," *Reuters* (on line), August 21, 2003.

62. "Carter takes issue with claims Cuba has supported terrorism," *Associated Press* (on line), May 14, 2002.

63. Ibid.

64. David Gonzalez, "Castro says Carter can inspect biotechnology centers," *New York Times,* May 13, 2002, A3; "Carter Given 'Complete Access' to Cuba," *Associated Press* (on line), May 13, 2002.

65. David Gonzalez, "Carter and Powell cast doubt on bioarms to Cuba," *New York Times,* May 14, 2002, A3.

66. Tim Johnson, "Report Mum on Bio-Threat," *Miami Herald* (on line), May 22, 2002.

67. For views supportive of the Varela Project, see Domingo Moreira, "Project Varela Leads Cuba to Freedom," *Miami Herald,* June 5, 2002; Peter Fritsch, "A Cuban Activist Uses the Sysstem in Bid for Freedom," *Wall Street Journal,* May 13, 2002; "A Cuban Petition," editorial, *Washington Post,* May 1, 2002. For further discussion of the Varela Project, see chapters 9 and 10.

68. "Cuban Assembly rejects a reform project," *Agence France-Press* (on line), January 25, 2003.

69. *Granma International,* May 19, 2002, 1.

70. David Gonzalez, "Carter's trip to Cuba raises many hopes from all sides," *New York Times* (on line), May 12, 2002; Michelle Caruso Cabrera, "Is U.S.-Cuba trade freeze thawing?" *MSNBC News* (on line), May 13, 2002; Tom Branden Brook, "Carter criticizes both Cuba, U.S. trade," *USA Today,* May 15, 2002, 1; "Carter speaks on Cuban TV," *Associated Press* (on line), May 15, 2002; Andrea Mitchell, "Carter's Cuba Trip a Work in Progress," *MSNBC News* (on line), May 15, 2002; "Carter to Meet Cuban Dissidents," *MSNBC News* (on line), May 16, 2002; David Gonzalez, "Party organ in Cuba prints speech by Carter," *New York Times,* May 17, 2002, A6. The government's expectations from Carter's visit were complex. Havana knew that Carter would raise the human rights issue and would probably criticize the Socialist system. At the same time, his stature as a former U.S. president and his public opposition to the U.S. embargo and other punitive policies against Cuba were enough to make him welcome as well as to give him the unlimited and unhindered access he enjoyed in Havana. See Tim Padgett, "What Castro Wants," *Time,* May 27, 2002, 8.

71. "Nader says U.S. should trade with Cuba like China," *MSNBC News* (on line), July 7, 2002; "Nader, in Cuba, opposes embargo," "Nader in Havana: U.S.

should let Cubans breathe," *Reuters* (on line), July 9, 10, 2002. For a discussion of the state of civil rights and liberties in the United States under the legislative and security measures enforced following September 11, 2001, see Leone and Anrig, *The War on Our Freedoms*.

72. "Initiative for a Constitutional Amendment Approved," *Granma International*, June 16, 2002, 4. The initiative for a constitutional amendment that was presented to the National Assembly was sponsored by eight mass organizations and nongovernmental organizations: Cuban Confederation of Workers (CTC), Association of Small Farmers (ANAP), Committees for the Defense of the Revolution (CDRs), José Martí Young Pioneers Organization (OPJM), Association of Combatants of the Cuban Revolution (ACRC), Federation of Cuban Women (FMC), Federation of University Students (FEU), and Federation of Intermediate Education Students (FEEM). "Iniciativa de modificación constitucional," press release, Permanent Mission of the Republic of Cuba to the United Nations, New York, June 2002.

73. Raisa Pages, "A Transcendent 'Yes.'" Also, "Washington Ignoring International Law," "Unanimous Support for Socialism," "Lage: The multi-party system is a trick," *Granma International*, June 30, 2002, 1.

74. Fidel Castro, "We show the strictest respect for the rights of other countries; our rights must also be respected," *Granma International*, June 30, 2002, 6–7.

75. Elizabeth Bumiller, "Embargo remains until Cuba alters policy, Bush says," *New York Times* (on line), May 21, 2002. George W. Bush and Jeb Bush were "the guests of honor of a $2 million fund raiser for the Florida Republican Party at the Coral Gables home of Armando Codina, a Cuban-American real state developer and a former business partner of Jeb Bush. Contributors paid $25,000 per couple to attend, and most of the money was expected to go to Jeb Bush's [gubernatorial reelection] campaign. The White House closed the event to the news media." Ibid. Scott Lindlaw, "Bush won't ease hard line vs. Cuba," *Associated Press* (on line), May 19, 2002.

76. Lindlaw, "Bush won't ease hard line."

77. "Key Address by Dr. Fidel Castro Ruz, President of the Republic of Cuba, at the Open Forum Held in Sancti Spiritus Province, May 25, 2002" (Washington D.C.: Cuban Interests Section, May 2002).

78. "Fidel Castro, speaking in drenching rain, rejects Bush['s] ideas of democracy," *Associated Press/MSNBC News* (on line), June 1, 2002.

79. Anita Show, "Cuba official accuses Bush of pandering to Cuban exiles, dissidents fear continued US policies will hurt their cause," *Miami Herald* (on line), May 21, 2002.

80. Jean-Guy Allard, "In spite of Washington's policies—growing number of U.S. citizens travel to Cuba," *Granma International*, January 12, 2003, 16; Ginger Thompson, "Cuba, too, felt the Sept. 11 shock waves, with a more genial Castro offering help," *New York Times*, February 7, 2002, A9.

81. And yet, the White House's Cuba policy was seen in Florida in mid-2003 as not being tough enough and even somewhat conciliatory to Havana. Governor Jeb Bush and Cuban American political leaders criticized the administration for returning to the island twelve Cuban rafters who had been intercepted by the U.S. Coast

Guard in international waters on July 15, 2003. The Cuban government accused the twelve rafters of having hijacked the vessel after tying up three men who had been guarding it. Oddly enough, the political rift pitted Cuban American leaders against the Bush White House, and Governor Bush against President Bush. "[Siding publicly with his Cuban American supporters, Jeb Bush's] criticism of his brother's administration . . . came at a time of mounting tensions between the Republican Party and Cuban exile groups, who say that President Bush has fallen short on promises to ratchet up economic and political pressure on Fidel Castro." Abby Goodnough, "A Bush faults White House on return of 12 Cubans," *New York Times* (on line), August 2, 2003. South Florida Cuban Americans' political frustration was popularly expressed with "[a] song enjoying frequent airtime on Spanish-language radio stations . . . crystalliz[ing] the deepening discontent of Cuban-Americans with the White House. It ends, 'All together, let's sing: Bush is betraying us.'" Moreover, "13 [Florida] Republican state legislators, including 10 Cuban-Americans, sent the president . . . [a letter warning] that if Mr. Bush did not make 'substantial progress' toward fulfilling . . . Cuban-American demands, 'we fear the historic and intense support from Cuban-American voters for Republican federal candidates, including yourself, will be jeopardized.'" Abby Goodnough, "G.O.P. legislators in Florida criticize Bush on Cuba," *New York Times* (on line), August 13, 2003. In an effort to expand the reach of news and talk shows hosted by Cuban American leaders, the Miami-based Office of Cuba Broadcasting was strengthening the signals of Radio and TV Martí using a satellite located over the eastern Atlantic Ocean off the coast of Africa. The plan was seen as an attempt by the administration to stifle Cuban Americans' criticism of President Bush's Cuba policy. Havana called the broadcasts an attempt by the "U.S. government and Cuban exiles to impose their political views." Castro noted that "earlier efforts to thwart the Cuban government's jamming of TV Marti's signals have failed," adding, "up to now, experience has shown that it has gone badly." "Castro: U.S. efforts to broadcast TV Marti will fail," *Associated Press* (on line), August 24, 2003.

82. James Dao, "Bush names veteran anti-Communist to Latin America post," *New York Times* (on line), January 10, 2003. The Cuban media reported President Bush's controversial appointment of Otto Reich in December 2001 (his assignment ended in November 2002) as assistant secretary of state for Latin America, this way: "He did it! By taking advantage of an absurd law that allows him to bypass the Senate during a congressional recess . . . U.S. President George W. Bush named Otto Reich, a man backed by the Miami terrorist mafia, as the White House's number one man responsible for Latin America. As a payback to the Cuban-Americans responsible for the dirty tricks during his controversial electoral 'triumph' in Florida and as an encouragement for them to participate in his brother Jeb's upcoming political campaign, the most powerful head of state on the planet . . . yielded to the most despicable electoral blackmail. Reich . . . must have been quite disturbed by the many articles in the press attacking him [as]: accomplice and protector of terrorist Orlando Bosch, who was one of the masterminds of a sabotage of a Cubana Airlines passenger plane off the coast of Barbados; agent of the also terrorist Cuban American National Foundation (CANF); . . . overt manipulator of public opinion; . . . CIA

collaborator; promoter of arms sales; apologist for tobacco and alcohol sales; and . . . a fervent anti-unionist." Jean-Guy Allard, "Reich Imposed on Latin America," *Granma International,* January 20, 2002, 14. As replacement for Otto Reich as assistant secretary for Latin America, "the White House announced . . . that President Bush [nominated] Roger F. Noriega, the United States representative to the Organization of American States. . . . Aides to Senator Christopher Dodd, a Connecticut Democrat who led the opposition to Mr. Reich, called his nomination 'disappointing.' . . . Like Mr. Reich, Mr. Noriega served in the State Department during the Reagan administration, helping forge fiercely anti-Communist policies toward Latin America." Dao, "Bush names veteran anti-Communist."

83. Fidel Castro, "Special Presentation by Dr. Fidel Castro Ruz, President of the Republic of Cuba, at the Televised Round Table on Recent Events in the Country and the Increase of Aggressive Actions by the United States Government against the Cuban People" (Washington, D.C.: Cuban Interests Section, April 25, 2003); Felipe Pérez Roque, "Press Conference by Foreign Minister of the Republic of Cuba Felipe Pérez Roque on the Mercenaries at the Service of the Empire Who Stood Trial on April 3, 4, 5 and 7, 2003," *Granma Internacional* (on line), April 9, 2003; Robert Sandels, "Cuba Crackdown: A Revolt against the National Security Strategy," *Cuba-L Analysis* (on line), April 25, 2003.

84. "'The Cuban government energetically rejects, once again, our country's infamous inclusion in this [U.S.] unilateral and illegitimate list,' the foreign ministry said in a statement published in the Communist Party daily newspaper *Granma.*" "Cuba rejects its inclusion in the U.S. list of countries that sponsor terrorism," *MSNBC News* (on line), May 8, 2003; "Cuba angrily rejects U.S. terrorist label," *MSNBC News* (on line), May 8, 2003. "Since the United States launched its war on terrorism the government of President Fidel Castro has said it supports the concept, but not U.S. methods. Havana has also insisted that Washington is hypocritical for not rounding up U.S.-based Cuban exiles it says have conducted and planned hundreds of attacks on the island since . . . [the] 1959 revolution. 'President Bush says those who harbor terrorists are as guilty as the terrorists themselves,' [Ricardo] Alarcón said after announcing that Cuba has posted on the Internet a dossier it gave to the Federal Bureau of Investigation in 1998 detailing exile activity against the country." "Cuba accuses United States of aiding terrorism," *MSNBC News* (on line), January 16, 2003.

85. David Gonzalez, "Cuban dissidents get prison terms as long as 27 years," *New York Times,* April 8, 2003, A10; "Some Cuban dissidents now set for trial, wives of arrested say," *Associated Press* (on line), April 1, 2003; David Gonzalez, "Dozens of Cuban dissidents face trial for subversion," *New York Times* (on line), April 4, 2003.

86. Isabel Garia-Zarza, "Cuban top court shows no mercy to dissidents," *MSNBC News* (on line), June 23, 2003. However, it was reported that "as many as 40 independent Cuban journalists, apparently undeterred by an intensified wave of repression, are challenging the government by filing regular news reports to foreign news outlets—the same practice that resulted in long jail sentences for 75 dissidents in April." Nancy San Martin, "Despite recent crackdowns, Cuban journalists persevere," *Miami Herald* (on line), June 9, 2003.

87. But not for long. Three months later, "for the first time since Cuba executed three men who tried to seize a ferry in April, the communist island reported hijacking attempts—one that failed when the gunmen killed each other, and another that may have succeeded. . . . [Cuba] blamed both incidents on the U.S. Cuban Adjustment Act, which makes it difficult to deport Cubans who land in the United States." "Cuba reports hijacking and deadly attempted hijacking," *Associated Press* (on line), July 15, 2003.

88. "[Dagoberto] Rodríguez [head of the Cuban Interests Section] said that his government has been specifically warned in recent days, through the U.S. Interests Section in Havana, that the United States would consider a new wave of migration an 'act of war.'" Karen De Young, "Cuba denounces diplomats' expulsions; official challenges U.S. to show evidence of spying, calls action prelude to attack," *Washington Post* (on line), May 15, 2003; Fidel Castro, "Speech Given by Dr. Fidel Castro Ruz, President of the Republic of Cuba, at the May Day Rally Held in Revolution Square" (Washington, D.C.: Cuban Interests Section, May 1, 2003); Pablo Alfonso, "*La Habana acusa a Washington de boicotear el pact migratorio*," *El Nuevo Herald* (on line), April 10, 2003. "The President of Cuba's parliament [Ricardo Alarcón] said that . . . the sale in Florida of a small plane taken from the island by a defector was just the latest example of the United States aiding and abetting terrorism. . . . [It] is another demonstration of the U.S. authorities' engagement with anti-Cuban terrorism." Moreover, "a Florida court ruled in December [2002] that the [plane] could be sold to help pay a $27 million judgment against Havana in the case of the ex-wife of a Cuban spy who had sued for civil damages. The plane was sold—to the ex-wife . . . for $7,000." "Cuba accuses United States of aiding terrorism." Also, see Rui Ferrera, "A subasta dos aviones cubanos secuestrados," "Presunto secuestrador del avión apoya la subasta," and "Compran los aviones cubanos secuestrados," *El Nuevo Herald* (on line), June 1, 2, and 3, 2003; Wilfredo Cancio Isla, "Acusan a dos balseros de agredir a guardacostas," *El Nuevo Herald* (on line), May 16, 2003.

89. David Gonzalez, "Crackdown in Cuba; harsh repression suggests Castro felt worried enough to risk ties abroad," *New York Times,* April 11, 2003, A9. For an objective scholarly view of Cuba's actions, see John M. Kirk, "Trying to Understand Cuba's Actions: Stepping outside Sarcasm," *The Globe* (Canada) *(Cuba-L On Line)*, April 23, 2003. Also, "according to Dagoberto Valdés, chairman of the Catholic-sponsored [Cuba-based] Comisión Nacional de Justicia y Paz (National Justice and Peace Commission), 'the facts show that [Cason's activities] have been counterproductive, giving justification to those who attack the opposition." Domingo Amuchastegui, "Despite Climate of Fear, Dissent Far from Dead in Cuba," *CUBANEWS* (July 2003): 9. International solidarity with Cuba campaigns and Internet Web sites have sprung up in addition to the ones existing earlier. The newly posted "Pro Cuba" Web site (http://www.porcuba.cult.cu) collected supportive messages and signatures with an initial list of international celebrities headed by several Nobel Prize winners (including Gabriel García Marquez and Rigoberta Menchú). Following their example, thousands of supporters from all over the world have added their names in solidarity.

90. "Cuba sanctions fail to materialize," *MSNBC News* (on line), May 20, 2003. The new techniques used to broadcast radio and television transmissions to Cuba,

including President Bush's address on May 20, created more problems: "On orders from the White House, the Pentagon deployed a special airplane . . . to beam the signals of Radio and TV Marti to Cuba, using a technology that one administration official said 'breached the wall' of Cuban jamming efforts." "Plane beams broadcasts to Cuba," *Miami Herald* (on line), May 22, 2003. In response, "Cuba charged . . . that the U.S. government was stepping up radio and television transmissions into the communist island, saying that the broadcasts violate international law and the island's sovereignty." "Cuba charges that U.S is boosting its broadcasts into Cuba," *Associated Press* (on line), May 23, 2003. Also, see "President Bush denounces Castro in radio address," *Miami Herald* (on line), May 20, 2003; and "Bush sends radio message to Cubans," *Miami Herald* (on line), May 20, 2003.

91. "U.S. expels 14 Cuban diplomats; State Dept. alleges spying," *MSNBC News* (on line), May 13, 2003. Dagoberto Rodríguez, head of the Cuban Interests Section, said, "'We challenge the U.S. government to present one single piece of evidence of any illegal activity' carried out by any Cuban officials in the United States. . . . They know that they are lying like professional Pinocchios . . . because they monitor us physically and electronically 24 hours a day." De Young, "Cuba denounces diplomats' expulsions."

92. Castro said that "the [ferry hijackers'] executions were necessary to stop a mass exodus encouraged by Washington, which he charges with seeking a migration crisis as a pretext for an invasion." Anthony Boadie, "Cuba blames EU chill on European meddling," *Reuters* (on line), May 19, 2003; Castro, "Special Presentation"; Pérez Roque, "Press Conference."

93. Pérez Roque, "Press Conference"; Sandels, "Cuba Crackdown."

94. Oswaldo Payá, organizer of the Varela Project, Elizardo Sánchez Santa Cruz, founder of the Cuban Committee for Human Rights and National Reconciliation (CCDHRN; exposed by Havana as having been a secret state security agent since the 1990s), and other well-known dissidents were not among those incarcerated in the April crackdown. Still, a well-orchestrated campaign turning Payá into an international celebrity and the symbol of a homegrown opposition movement has been at work. Some of the news reports chronicling his deeds include: "Almost unheard of just a few years ago, Payá is today the most celebrated dissident in Cuba. Founder of the Varela Project, the 51-year-old engineer has received the European Parliament's Sakharov Prize for Freedom of Thought, as well as the National Democratic Institute's 15th Annual W. Averell Harriman Democratic Award." Larry Luxner, "Oswaldo Payá, Cuba's top dissident, talks to *CUBANEWS*," *CUBANEWS* (May 2003): 8. "'The dynamic has changed,' says Joe Garcia, executive director of the Cuban American National Foundation in Miami. 'We finally have strong democratic players on the ground in Cuba.' . . . Payá's celebrity is beginning to rival Castro's. . . . Vaclav Havel, who led the 'velvet revolution' that toppled communism in Czechoslovakia, has nominated Payá for the Nobel Peace Prize. Robert De Niro's Tribeca Film Festival . . . canceled its screening of Oliver Stone's documentary on Castro, *Comandante,* and showed instead a film about Payá." Jim Padget, "Who's bugging Castro? Meet the intractable dissident who provoked Cuba's alarming new crackdown on dissent," *Time*, May 19, 2003, 46–47. For a Cuban version of the role

played by Spanish citizens and anti-Castro Cubans to have the Varela Project organized in the island and how Payá's and other names were recommended to lead it, see Pérez Roque, "Press Conference."

95. Larry Luxner, "Cuba's Top Diplomat in Washington: 'We are not spies,'" *CUBANEWS* (June 2003): 8–9.

96. "CPF board of directors resigns in protest," *CUBANEWS* (May 2003): 2; "Many Cuba-related events cancelled in wake of tensions," *CUBANEWS* (June 2003): 2.

97. Originally sponsored by the United States, Cuba was expelled from the OAS in January 1962 after fourteen of OAS's twenty-one members at the time agreed that "Cuba's adherence . . . to Marxism-Leninism [was] incompatible with the inter-American system." However, "Argentina, Bolivia, Brazil, Chile, Ecuador and Mexico abstain[ed] on the grounds that the measure violate[d] the Principle of Non-intervention in the Internal Affairs of another member state, part of the OAS Charter." Jane Franklin, *The Cuban Revolution and the United States: A Chronological History* (Melbourne, Australia: OCEAN and the Center for Cuban Studies, 1992), 50.

98. Larry Rohter, "Latin lands don't share Powell's priorities," *New York Times* (on line), June 10, 2003; Juan Forero, "Latin America's political compass veers toward the Left," *New York Times* (on line), June 19, 2003; "Powell asks OAS to promote democracy in Cuba," *MSNBC News* (on line), June 8, 2003; "Powell OAS Focus: Cuban Repression," *Miami Herald* (on line), June 9, 2003.

99. "In a biting statement issued in Brussels on behalf of the entire 15-nation bloc, the EU said it was 'deeply concerned about the continuing flagrant violation of human rights and of fundamental freedoms of members of the Cuban opposition and of independent journalists.' Among the measures the EU unanimously approved: limiting bilateral high-level government visits, reducing the profile of member states participation in cultural events and inviting Cuban dissidents abroad [and to festivities in their embassies]." Nancy San Martin, "EU Set to Review Relations with Cuba," *Miami Herald* (on line), June 6, 2003.

100. Joaquín Rivery Tur, "La Unión Europea se ha sumado a EE.UU. y alentado sus sueños anticubanos," *Granma Internacional* (on line), June 11, 2003.

101. George Gedda, "Se acercan EEUU y Europa en la postura ante Cuba," *El Nuevo Herald* (on line), June 9, 2003.

102. Rivery Tur, "La Unión Europea se ha sumado a EE.UU."

103. "Huge march in Havana protests European criticism of Castro," *Associated Press* (on line), June 13, 2003.

104. "Colocan hermosa valla antifascista frente a embajada Española," *Granma Internacional* (on line), June 21, 2003; "Declaración del MINREX, comunica Cuba decisión sobre el Centro Cultural Español," *Granma Internacional* (on line), June 14, 2003.

105. Cuba stated in response to the EU's actions: "The unfair and unacceptable statement issued by the Council of Ministers of the European Union, the European Union's shameful alignment with the frustrated U.S. attempt to achieve the condemnation of Cuba at the Human Rights Commission [the Commission approved send-

ing a *rapporter* to examine human rights conditions but Cuba rejected it], and the timorous decision of the European Union to indefinitely postpone consideration of Cuba's application, has convinced the Cuban government that the conditions do not exist to maintain the application for entry into the Cotonou Agreement." "Statement from MINREX, Cuba desires ever-widening relations with the European Union, but they must be based on mutual respect," *Granma Internacional* (on line), May 19, 2003.

106. Larry Luxner, "Fidel's anti-EU outburst has little effect on European trade, investment in Cuba," *CUBANEWS* (July 2003): 1–2. The executive vice president of the Cuban American National Foundation and former Cuba desk officer at the U.S. State Department, Dennis Hays, was actively involved in reinforcing Europe's negative reaction to Havana's crackdown following Cason's antiregime campaign: "[Hays] has been quietly visiting the Washington embassies of European countries in recent months, trying to get diplomats to toughen their attitudes toward Castro." Ibid., 2.

107. Ibid.

108. Anthony Boadle, "Castro rejects EU aid, defends revolution," *Reuters* (on line), July 27, 2003; "EU is U.S. 'Trojan horse'—Castro," *Associated Press* (on line), July 27, 2003.

109. Recognizing these changes, high-ranking U.S. military officers such as General Charles Wilhelm, former head of the U.S. Southern Command, and retired marine general John Sheehan, agree that the Cuban armed forces are no longer a real or potential threat to Cuba's neighbors. They both concur that the FAR has problems keeping itself viable as a defensive force. Azicri, *Cuba Today and Tomorrow,* 161.

110. "The discovery of the Internet's potential hit Fidel Castro's government like an electrical surge in an underground socket during [the] custody battle over Elián González. Hundreds of thousands of new hits appeared daily on the website of the Communist Party newspaper *Granma.* . . . [The daily's] editors were stunned at least twice during the seven-month custody battle when the weekly number of visitors passed two million. For perhaps the first time, the island, isolated for more than 40 years by U.S. trade sanctions, was offering unedited views directly to Americans and others outside Cuba. . . . We are glad about [the Internet] . . . so we can also transmit our truths and our messages, Castro said during his trip to Venezuela [in August 2001]." Anita Snow, "Cuba uses Internet to 'transmit our truths, messages,'" *Miami Herald* (on line), September 9, 2001.

II

Society

2

From Capitalist to Socialist Culture, and Back to Capitalist Values?

José A. Moreno[1]

Structural Changes in the 1960s and 1990s

In the decades of the 1960s and the 1990s, Cuba underwent significant structural changes that transcended the political and economic mechanisms that brought them about. If we look back at the last forty-two years, we can identify some of the most profound and, often, controversial changes introduced by the revolution in each decade.[1]

Agrarian and urban reforms changed the foundations of the class system and provided the basis for more egalitarian living conditions both in the city and in the countryside. The nationalization and collectivization of productive property was aimed at guaranteeing the citizens a more equitable distribution of income, protection against foreign exploitation, and security of employment. The literacy campaign and the expansion of the health system sought to develop the minds and bodies of all citizens so that they could become more productive and enjoy a better life. These and other measures implemented during the 1960s seem to have been oriented toward the creation of a more egalitarian society, shortening the distance between rural and urban, rich and poor, black and white, men and women. In a relatively short period of ten years, Cuba succeeded in eliminating illiteracy and unemployment, in creating universal health care, in reducing the income gap between workers and professionals, and in curbing discriminatory differences stemming from the old hierarchical system.

These structural changes in the productive, compensatory, and distributive systems imposed by the revolution not only paved the way but also required changes in the normative structure of the cultural values that would support and justify the emerging Socialist society.

In the decade of the 1990s, Cuba again experienced drastic structural changes both internally and in its relations with the outside world. Such changes have deeply affected Cuban society both collectively and in the daily life of its citizens. Although significant changes in the political and economic structures were already in progress from the mid-1980s, the disintegration of the Soviet Union and the earlier disappearance of the Socialist bloc in Eastern Europe forced Cuba to reinvent itself.

In the United States, the anti-Castro exiles, supported by conservative American legislators who had enforced an embargo against Cuba for more than thirty years, seized the opportunity to further strengthen the blockade against Cuba. The Torricelli and Helms-Burton bills were considered the executioner's tools to finish a job started in the early 1960s. Cuba in the early 1990s was isolated, without capital, foreign aid, international markets, or credits to purchase consumer goods abroad.

To reinvent itself, Cuba had to restructure its economy and its social organization to meet the challenges of isolation within a new hegemonic power structure in the world and to function in a global economy. In order to reinsert itself into the new global economy, Cuba had to tap new sources of production, find new markets, and experiment with new forms of investment, exchange, and distribution that would allow it to be competitive in a highly restrictive global system.

Tourism has always loomed large in the Cuban economy as an important source of revenue. For social and political reasons, tourism was deemphasized in the 1960s, but in the 1980s some forms of cultural and environmental tourism were developed. In the 1990s, tourism boomed and became the most important source of revenue for the economy. The capital, expertise, and organizational skills needed to develop tourist sites have come from Canada and Western Europe.

To be fully competitive in the global economy, Cuba had to experiment with some forms of capitalist investment and production: joint ventures and mixed enterprises with foreign capital have been allowed. Together with capital, foreign entrepreneurs bring in forms of organization, incentives, compensation, and promotion based on standards and practices used in capitalist societies and until now totally ignored and ideologically condemned by the leading political class.[2]

In order to avoid high levels of unemployment in an economy going through a severe period of crisis (the Special Period in Peacetime), new forms of production incentives for participation and new business marketing strategies were encouraged. Reversing the "revolutionary offensive" of the late 1960s, when all small businesses, from fruit stands to street vendors, were nationalized, in the 1990s private productive work *(trabajo por cuenta propia)* was allowed. Some one hundred fifty thousand different occupations (from cobblers to taxi drivers) have been allowed. Small service establishments such as restaurants, barbershops, and television repair have flourished all over the country. Farmers' markets exist in all cities and villages, where farmers may sell some of their crops to the general public.

For years, Cubans had received dollar remittances from their relatives in the United States. However, they were not allowed to use those dollars even in stores run by the government that only took dollars as exchange. In 1993 the government legalized the use of dollars. With large amounts of dollars circulating freely (from remittances, mixed enterprises, and tourism), there has been an increasing "dollarization" of the economy. The government has established and maintained, through the years, a standard rate of exchange, and banks and currency exchange *casas de cambio* operate freely to do transactions without significant interference from a black market.

It is fairly obvious that these changes in the economy and the social organization could bring about or facilitate a resurgence of the values of dependent capitalism that the decade of the 1960s attempted to eradicate. Among Cuba watchers it was argued that some of the policies and measures of the 1990s counteracted some of the values that were promoted in the 1960s. Research conducted in Cuba by Guillermo C. Milán and colleagues from the University of Havana Institute of Philosophy between 1994 and 1998 explored the reemergence of individualism and suggested that anomie (a breakdown or absence of norms or social values) is growing in some sectors of the population as a result of the sustained economic hardships of the special period. Professor Milán noted that the population has become more tolerant of minor infractions of the norms and laws as an adaptation to the economic pressures. Nonetheless, he concluded that "there remains a genuine ideological vision of an independent country that is searching to reaffirm its identity as a unified nation."[3]

The main objective of this chapter is to examine whether the measures implemented in the 1990s are purely strategic accommodations to insert Cuba into a global system, preventing the Balkanization and the moral and political disintegration plaguing Eastern Europe, or whether such measures necessarily negate the new society programmed in the 1960s.

The Emerging Values of the 1960s

In a study published in 1970, I argued that the drastic structural changes of the 1960s were designed to rid Cuban society of the class system on which dependent capitalism was based. A matrix of social values that established, justified, and reproduced a system of exclusions, differences, and inequalities inherited from the past and fostered by capitalism was identified.[4]

The strategies of the 1960s sought to substitute a matrix of egalitarianism for the old core of elitism and hierarchical values. Agrarian reform eliminated big landholdings and distributed land to the peasants. Urban reform reduced rents and gave tenants a chance to own a home. Distance between rich and poor was shortened. The measures, however, were not intended solely to eliminate economic differences but also to cut social distances in the access to social services between town and country, black and white, men and women. The literacy campaign, building schools in the countryside for urban children, and the construction of new hospitals in small towns and of polyclinic centers in the most remote areas of the country were measures intended to provide equality for all citizens.

To integrate socially the various dimensions of the matrix of egalitarianism, Che Guevara predicated the value of collective consciousness as opposed to selfish individualism. He advocated voluntary work and participation in community activities such as the construction brigades and agricultural work. These activities helped create a new collective identity and civic consciousness.[5] The emerging "new man" began its formation in the day care centers (jardines de infancia) and was further strengthened in the juvenile organization of the pioneros, the school in the countryside, and participation in the Union of Young Communists (UJC), the Committees for the Defense of the Revolution (CDRs), the Federation of Cuban Women (FMC), the militias, the trade unions, and the Cuban Communist Party (PCC). According to Guevara, however, the so-called new man could not be the product of one, but was a process of several generations.

The Challenge to the New Values in the 1990s

This chapter returns to the subject of value change in Cuba some thirty years after the initial study. To all appearances, the changes in values at this time seem to be in the opposite direction. Is Cuban society moving from the value matrix of egalitarianism to a matrix supporting inequality and exclusion? Are the new measures taken by the government pushing Cuba unwittingly back into capitalism? Are such measures just strategic accommodations to salvage the revolutionary process? If they represent purely an adaptation to new structural conditions, what negative impact could they have on the process of creating the new person? Lastly, is it possible to preserve the revolution in the context of a process of globalization dominated by capitalism?

Let us consider some of the most controversial measures taken in the 1990s and examine whether they represent values that are contradictory to those advocated in the construction of the new man. These measures were only introduced after extensive debate at various levels of Cuban society. Despite participation in such important issues by groups and mass organizations, it seems fair to say that the ruling political class handed down the decisions. With the emergence of a civil society within the Socialist framework, some writers began to suggest that broader forms of participation by an autonomous civil society should be more adequate than extant participation modalities for Cuba's present stage of development.[6]

Tourism

The decision to develop and expand tourism as the pivotal component of the economy was a strategy with far-reaching consequences for the society as a whole. Cuba had closed its doors to tourism in the 1960s because Cuba's leaders thought that the ills and moral depravity it conveyed (gambling, drugs, and prostitution) far outweighed the economic benefits it produced. Still, in the mid-1980s Cuba experimented on a small scale with cultural and environmental tourism.

After the disintegration of the Soviet Union and the demise of the Socialist Council of Mutual Economic Assistance (CAME), Cuba was forced to explore other sources of production and new markets for its products. Natural conditions made Cuba an excellent venue for tourism, and in the 1990s Cuba began to build a competitive infrastructure to attract tourists from Europe and Canada. By the end of the decade, tourism had become the most profitable component of the economy. However, even with the limitations and controls exerted by the government, tourism has brought with it some unintended consequences, such as prostitution *(jineterismo)* and other undesirable forms of behavior. Also, some Cubans see foreign tourists as pertaining to an affluent class from which Cubans are excluded.[7]

Many Cubans regard those who work in tourist places as an emerging new class with access to dollars. Tourism has also brought to Cuba new forms of prostitution. Due to their puritanical background and prurient interest in sex, American visitors to Cuba are particularly interested in finding out about the emergence and growth of prostitution. My personal view is that prostitution *(jineterismo, pinguerismo)* is no different in Cuba from such forms of sexual work in other Latin American countries. Whether

Cuban prostitutes are younger, prettier, more exuberant, or more pleasing to their customers is hard to assess. What seems to be different, however, is the kind of people who participate in the sex trade. According to some writers, the *jinetera* is often a woman with a certain level of education, most of the time single and unemployed, but sometimes married and with children. In a society that does not value virginity for entering marriage and where rates of divorce are very high, it is easy for a single woman to offer her services as an escort to a foreigner who can reward her with dollars and desirable but otherwise unattainable things. Most of the time a *jinetera* is only a part- time prostitute. In her own way, however, the sexual worker contributes to the economy by getting dollars for her tricks.[8]

Most likely, the type of tourism that presently exists in Cuba, with its controls and limitations, will continue to be the most profitable source of income for the country. But as the economy enters into a more stable stage and makes way for other productive, adequately compensated activities, the present undesirable and unintended by-products of tourism will tend to disappear.

Tourism developed in the 1990s mostly as joint ventures with capital from Spain, Italy, Germany, and Canada. Joint ventures, or *empresas mixtas,* have also thrived in many other areas of production, such as mining, communications, transportation, and oil exploration. Foreign capital from Canada, Spain, Mexico, and Italy has contributed to strengthening an economic infrastructure oriented to the demands of a global economy. An economy that was bankrupt in the early nineties began to show signs of robust growth by the end of the decade. Still, Cuba has been forced to make concessions to its foreign partners, as have other underdeveloped countries seeking to attract foreign investments.

In this regard, when countries ruled by dependent capitalist regimes have made concessions to foreign capital by opening free zones and *maquiladoras,* freezing workers' salaries and imposing austerity programs, they have not been challenged by neoliberal economists. But when Cuba was forced to introduce similar practices, not only the Left but also neoliberal economists were eager to condemn the practices.

The workers in joint ventures get paid better than workers in national or government enterprises. Workers in joint ventures also receive other benefits and have access to U.S. dollars, which provokes jealousy and anger among the workers of other enterprises. Like tourism, these joint ventures attract professionals and qualified workers who are willing to forego their trade or profession to get a job in a corporation that gives them access to

U.S. dollars. This quest for dollars has created an overall negative balance for a country that has made significant investment in training a highly qualified labor force that now engages in low-level service occupations. For example, I recently interviewed a young engineer who graduated from a technical university in Havana. After graduation, he took a job with a company owned by the state and was sent across the island on different kinds of projects where his skills were needed. After three years in this job, he decided to quit to take a job as an assistant cook in a pizza parlor in Havana where the main waiter would give him a dollar a day for his work. What motivated him to take such a low-paying job was the hope that eventually he could be promoted to be a waiter. In that position he might make five or six dollars a day in tips, a significant increase over his salary as an engineer working for the state.

"Dollarizing" the Economy

Both tourism and joint enterprises have contributed to the "dollarization" of the economy. When the use of U.S. dollars for internal transactions was legalized, a dual market was created: one for dollars and the other for the national currency. Dollars come into the country through tourism, joint enterprises, and family remittances from abroad. Most consumer goods are sold in government stores ("shopping") only in dollars. This is also true of services provided in restaurants, bars, hotels, taxis, and *paladares* (privately operated restaurants, usually in the family's quarters). However, products purchased through the rationing books in government stores are sold in national currency. Drug stores *(farmacias)* and farmers' markets as well as utilities and transportation also take national currency. Peasants, however, when selling their goods in the countryside, prefer payments in dollars, although Cuban pesos are accepted at the official rate of exchange with the dollar. The increasing use of U.S. dollars reinforces the existence of the dollar-peso double economy. When driving along the national highway, one can see peasants by the road, offering to sell chickens, cheese, and vegetables. The price is always in dollars, although, as mentioned before, one may use pesos at the regular dollar exchange rate.

But not everyone in Cuba has dollars, although dollars are needed to get some basic products. Those who do not have direct access to dollars must buy them in banks or exchange houses at the official rate. The legalization of the use of dollars has allowed the government to extract foreign currency from the population to purchase needed products from abroad. However, because of the American blockade, Cuba must pay much higher prices for such products from third-country suppliers. Panama, the Dominican Republic, Mexico, and Venezuela provide Cuba with such American goods as Coca Cola, cornflakes, Nike shoes, and frozen chickens.

With the dollarization of the economy, there is a resurgence of class distinction between those with and those without access to dollars. Those working in tourism and joint enterprises or who receive remittances from the United States have dollars. Others do not, and if their only source of income is in pesos, they face serious economic hardships to acquire basic products that are sold only in the "shoppings" for dollars. To buy those products they must exchange their meager salaries for dollars. If the only source of income for a family is in pesos, even after using the rationing book (at subsidized prices), the family faces serious problems to pay for needed basic consumer goods either in pesos or dollars in the dollar stores or in the black market. It is precisely the need for dollars that forces young professionals such as architects, engineers, doctors, and teachers to abandon their jobs and seek employment as taxi drivers, busboys, or waiters in tourist places. This, indeed, represents a significant loss in the investment made by the society and the individual through the years it took to complete their training in their chosen professions.

Corruption

With the dollarization of the economy and sparseness of many consumer goods, an increase in corruption has been reported. Under different guises, it affects the society at large. Employees of national enterprises steal materials and consumer goods for their own use or to sell in dollars to others. The most common case of stealing from the state is getting gasoline through illegal means. Gasoline is a very scarce product in great demand. The state controls the sale of fuel and dispenses it in gas stations owned by state corporations. The government dispenses coupons to state officials, police, military, and all corporate and state employees and private individuals who need to use an automobile, truck, or tractor in their jobs. Gasoline is sold through the use of coupons only. State employees who are paid in pesos steal coupons or sell their own in the black market to obtain dollars. For someone with dollars or its equivalent in pesos, gasoline is usually available. Government vehicles or those owned by national enterprises are used by individuals for their own families or, even worse, to provide private services for dollars. State inspectors who supervise the businesses of *paladares* and other small shops are paid off in dollars to avoid fines for lack of compliance with the law. Young men and women engage in prostitution and hustling to make a few dollars from the tourists. Customs inspectors are paid off under the table to allow the importation of taxable items.

All kinds of electrical appliances, from hair dryers to radios, TV, and other equipment brought from abroad are subject to excise tax. In 1999, my young daughter was carrying an inexpensive VCR in her luggage. At the airport her baggage was inspected and she was told that she had to pay fifty U.S. dollars. The inspector took the money, put it in his pocket, and allowed her to proceed. No receipt was given. It was clear that he was pocketing the money. With ten passengers like my daughter, this inspector could be making five hundred dollars a day, or nearly ten thousand pesos, which is roughly the wages of three workers for a full year of work.

Decentralizing the Economy

The process of concentrating all productive property in the hands of the state was partly reversed in the 1990s by the reestablishment of the agrarian cooperatives of production and consumption, by the return of the peasant markets, and by allowing workers to develop their own businesses and trades. All these are important measures of decentralization within a communal framework of production and consumption in a highly centralized economy. Controls exerted by the state in the various activities prevent the accumulation of wealth in the Socialist system. On the other hand, it is the small farmers and those working in cooperatives with limited access to dollars who will benefit the most by selling their products in the farmers' markets at a profit even when prices are controlled by the state. The profits will allow them to obtain the dollars they need to buy products in the shoppings. The farmers' markets thus fulfill several functions: they stimulate productivity, supply the market with products in short supply, counteract the emergence of a black market, and also allow peasants to have access to dollars. Finally, despite their capitalist underpinnings of profit orientation, they are a tool of equalization between the city and the rural area.

Traveling through the countryside to visit my relatives in a small town, I noticed that most peasant homes along the road had an array of domestic animals, such as pigs, goats, and chickens. When I asked a relative traveling with me about them, she explained that the peasants use their garden crops and the domestic animals for personal consumption and for sale in the farmers' markets. When I pointed out that most homes had TV antennas, the same relative pointed out that many peasants are fed and dressed better than city dwellers because the sale of their products allows them to obtain dollars to purchase such items.

The centralization of the economy peaked in 1968 with the revolutionary offensive when all small businesses were nationalized. That year Fidel Castro pointed out that the revolution was not made to protect the rights of a small bourgeoisie. The policy was aimed at eliminating the middleman in sales and services. It was thought, prematurely, that the state could provide all those services to the population while avoiding the enrichment of a few. It soon became evident that an underdeveloped, poor country did not have the necessary infrastructure (transportation, storage, refrigeration, etc.) to provide all those services.

The decision in the midst of the economic crises of the 1990s to permit private initiatives was made partly to reverse that policy. The state recognized that it could not maintain total employment for the labor force and that it could not provide many highly necessary services at low-profit margins. It was then agreed that private individuals would be allowed and encouraged to set up and run their own small businesses, from small home-restaurants to taxi driving and various repair shops. More than one hundred fifty thousand workers have obtained state licenses to perform work in areas such as television and radio repair, construction, pastry shops, and *paladares*. As in most Latin American countries, you can now see in Havana and in other cities a motley array of kiosks, stands, and improvised flea markets and businesses, providing services and selling cheap consumer goods to the population. The owner of the business or service is called a *cuenta propista* (a person who owns a business or trade). Such persons must have a business license as in the United States. They are subject to periodic inspection and must provide proof that their license is current and that their business is limited strictly to what the license specifies. If irregularities are found in the license or in the products sold, a fine could be imposed and/or the license suspended. Some of these businesses are also used as an outlet for the black market, to sell products stolen from state stores or from government warehouses. This explains the need for inspectors to hover over the shoulders of the *cuenta propistas*. Of course, the business owner who engages in black market activities earns more, pays off the inspector, and thus closes the cycle of corruption.

There are, however, some important differences between these makeshift businesses in Cuba and those in other Latin American countries. For example, the controls and limitations imposed on merchants in places like the city of Bahia in Brazil are much less rigid. Once merchants set their stands on the sidewalk of a business street, they can sell almost anything they want, from fruits, spices, and underwear to electrical appliances. Little effort is made by the police to verify that the products sold are legal and that health standards are maintained. This is not the case in Cuba.

The main difference between Cuba and other countries stems from the types of people who manage the businesses. In the Brazilian case the owners of the kiosks or stands are mostly unemployed, low-income, or poor people with little or no education. In Cuba, *cuenta propistas* are mostly people who quit their jobs because of low pay and lack of incentives. Often these small entrepreneurs are professionals who moonlight, part time at first and eventually full time, when they realize that they earn more fixing radios, TV sets, or air conditioners than working as an engineer for a government job. A teacher might make more money repairing bicycles than teaching school, and a doctor will have more access to dollars as a taxi driver.

The Cuban state established a set of limitations and controls, such as issuing licenses, inspecting the businesses, collecting taxes, and so on. The individuals who engage in these private activities *(cuenta propistas)* often resist and criticize the government for establishing such controls and limitations. When they break the laws, serious penalties are imposed, including suspension of the licenses to operate their businesses. Criticisms against the government for exacting high fees and taxes are partly due to the fact that for more than forty years, Cubans have not paid business or income taxes, and the *cuenta propistas* assumed that the legislation allowing small businesses to function was the same as opening the doors to a market economy without restrictions. Some entrepreneurs were eager to point out that those with ties to the government or who manage to pay off inspectors were most likely to thrive in their businesses. The government, however, counters that the strict measures are to be maintained and that corruption is to be prosecuted at all levels. These measures, in general, seek to maintain a level of equality, preventing excessive profits and abuses in providing services that are necessary but that the state cannot efficiently provide.

Conclusion

It is possible that the strategies for development and survival implemented in the decade of the 1990s may appear as contradictory to those introduced in the 1960s. The strategies of the 1960s were consonant with the creation of a matrix of values conducive to the emergence of a new man and the creation of a new society. Such values contemplated the disappearance of class distinctions, selfishness, and individualism. The engine to produce those values was *conciencia* (consciousness) or a collective awareness of self-identity within the framework of the community.

In contrast, the strategies of the 1990s seem to allow class distinctions, to weaken previous efforts toward a collective orientation, and to encourage individualism. It is because these strategies not only can be interpreted in this manner but also can produce those consequences, that the Cuban government has established the controls and limitations discussed earlier. By doing so, however, the government opens itself to criticisms from inside and outside the country. Those inside see such controls as curbing their freedom and limiting incentives to produce. Those outside seem to want Cuba to travel the unrestricted/uncontrolled path of development that some countries of Eastern Europe have followed. That would mean paying a social and moral price that Cuban society thus far seems unwilling to pay.

State controls and social pressures were used in the 1960s to implement Socialist values and are being used in the 1990s to protect and safeguard them. Values, however, must be anchored in the minds and emotions of people. The values of egalitarianism, solidarity, and collective orientation predicated by Guevara in the creation of the new man have been, in some measure, internalized and put into practice in Cuba for some forty years. These values, more than external pressures and state controls, are ultimately the safeguard and the defense of the objectives of the revolution. Notably, the acceptance and assimilation of the new values was manifested in the massive support of the Cuban people for the government's demands that Elián González be returned to his father in Cuba. I observed from close range the reaction of the Cuban population to the manipulations by Miami's Cuban exiles to keep the child in the United States. Many Cubans agreed that material things such as toys, pets, or name brand clothes could not supersede values such as parental love, friendship, and solidarity with teachers and classmates. I attended some of the rallies in front of the American embassy in Havana (housing the U.S. Interests Section) and watched on TV the open forums held every night to demand the return of Elián. In my estimation, since 1959, when the rebel forces came down from the mountains, there has not been as much solidarity and support for the Cuban government as there was in 2000 when the Cuban government demanded the return of Elián.

Faced with the serious economic crisis imposed on the whole society by changing international relations and by the American economic blockade, Cubans have had to adapt to available alternatives that often imposed compromise. Many have chosen to work by themselves or open their own businesses, but they continue to use the rationing book and expect subsidized housing. Some have given up their own professions in search of dollars in the tourist trade, but they still see it as a right to send their children to college free of charge. Others prefer to work for foreign companies because of better pay, but they still expect free full medical services. Most Cubans firmly support the achievements of the revolution in establishing an overall welfare system that provides free and equal services to the population on the assumption that all citizens are equal and have equal rights.

Indeed, it would be fair to assume that Cubans today want and demand better living conditions, more comfort in their lives, and more consumer goods from which they have been deprived in part by the American trade embargo. That does not mean that they do not appreciate or are willing to forsake the benefits received and progress made over the last forty years in health, education, quality of life, and social improvements. The support of the government and the overwhelming solidarity with Elián seem to indicate that for the Cuban people certain things in life transcend consumer goods.

Surely, Cuban society does not want to go back to the system of differences and exclusions between black and white, men and women, city and country, rich and poor that prevailed in Cuba before 1959.[9] Probably the most serious mistake one could make would be to assume that once the present government is replaced, the Cuban exile-elite presently ruling South Florida could return to business as usual in a pre-1959 Cuba. It would be a mistake comparable to the one that led to the failed Bay of Pigs invasion in 1961. The way Cuban society reacted collectively in demanding the return of Elián González to Cuba is an example of how solidarity, among other revolutionary values, has been forged in the new Cuban identity in over forty years.

Notes

1. Professor José A. Moreno has visited Cuba frequently throughout the entire period of revolutionary rule and has chronicled these visits in numerous scholarly manuscripts and publications. On such occasions, he has conducted sociological field research not only in Havana and other major cities but also in small cities and towns, sometimes while visiting with friends and relatives. In this chapter he summarizes some of the observations and findings gathered in such trips. (Editor's note.)

2. On the so-called political class in Cuba and its overall influence on society, see Haroldo Dilla, "The Virtues and Misfortunes of Civil Society," *NACLA Report on the Americas* 32, no. 5 (March–April 1999): 30–36.

3. Guillermo C. Milán, "Inequality and Anomie," *NACLA* 32, no. 5 (March–April 1999): 34–35.

4. José A. Moreno, "From Traditional to Modern Values," in *Revolutionary Change in Cuba*, ed. C. Mesa-Lago (Pittsburgh, Pa.: University of Pittsburgh Press, 1970). Also, see a later collaborative study, Max Azicri and José A. Moreno, "Cultura, política, movilización indirecta y modernización: Un análisis contextual del cambio revolucionario en Cuba: 1959–1968," *Revista Mexicana de Sociología* 42, no. 3 (July–September 1981): 1245–70.

5. The study of Ernesto Che Guevara's social, political, economic, and military ideas as expressed in his writings should include *El Socialismo y el hombre nuevo* (Mexico: Siglo XXI, 1979); *Escritos y discursos,* 9 vols. (Havana: Editora Política, 1977); and the well-known *Guerrilla Warfare* (New York: Vintage Books, 1961).

6. Dilla, "Virtues and Misfortunes."

7. Complaints that Cubans cannot enter hotels, restaurants, and beaches reserved for tourists are vastly exaggerated. Indeed there are restrictions (only U.S. dollars are accepted), and guards screen the entrance of those places (as in many other countries in Latin America) to prevent begging, hustling, and prostitution.

8. Rosa Miriam Elizalde, "Prostitution in Cuba: The Truth about Women Called *Jineteras,*" *Granma International,* September 4, 1996, 8–9. On male prostitution in Cuba, see G. Derrick Hodge, "Colonization of the Cuban Body: The Growth of Male Sex Work in Havana," *NACLA* 34, no. 5 (March–April, 2001): 20–28.

9. On the subject of racial and social differences and exclusions in Cuba before 1959, see Alejandro de la Fuente, *A Nation for All: Race, Inequality, and Politics in Twentieth Century Cuba* (Chapel Hill: University of North Carolina Press, 2001).

3

The Continuing Revolution

Jean Weisman

A Long Political Struggle

An evaluation of the liberation of women is a critical element in the analysis of the successes, failures, and challenges of the Cuban Revolution. Fidel Castro's Twenty-sixth of July Movement's manifesto defined its principal ideals in terms of democracy, nationalism, and social justice and stated that "democracy cannot be the government of a race, class, or religion, it must be the government of *all* the people."[1] While the program did not raise explicit demands related to gender equality, the revolutionaries raised many issues, such as distribution of land, employment, adequate food supply, housing, education, and health care, that have a major impact on the lives of women. Many women who fought in the revolution in the 1950s were very concerned about gender issues, which they addressed in the context of supporting the revolution. By becoming active participants and grassroots leaders within the revolutionary movement, they challenged the stereotype of passive women who stayed at home. While men were the directors of the Twenty-sixth of July Movement, the 1959 revolution would not have succeeded without the participation and leadership of women.

Some of the most dramatic changes in Cuba have involved women who were domestic workers before 1959. According to the 1953 census, 32 percent of Cuban workingwomen were employed as domestic workers, the largest single job category.[2] Most of the domestic workers were black or mulatto girls and women who were paid to clean homes, cook meals, wash clothes, and take care of other people's children. They often lived in small rooms in their employers' homes and worked six or seven days per week, from early in the morning until late at night, for extremely low salaries. Two years after the 1959 revolution, the Cuban government and the Federation of Cuban Women (Federación de Mujeres Cubanas, FMC) organized a massive educational program for domestic workers. More than sixty-three thousand women participated in this program.[3] Full-time, live-in domestic service was eliminated. While many women in Cuba are still paid to clean the homes of other people, they receive salaries, and the conditions are very improved from what they were before 1959. Most of the former domestic workers got jobs as bank employees, telephone operators, taxi drivers, and public employees. The women involved in these life changes developed a sense of self-worth linked to the success of the revolution.

After 1959, Cuban women made significant progress in participation in the workforce, in their increased educational levels, in control over their reproductive systems through access to maternity care, birth control, and abortion, and in participation in mass organizations. The 1990s, however, became a severe challenge for Cuban women, with the collapse of the Soviet Union and the Socialist countries in Eastern Europe and the intensification of the U.S. embargo against Cuba, which resulted in shortages of material goods and severe cutbacks in electricity, domestic fuel, and public transportation. Among the issues addressed by the women's studies programs created at universities throughout the island were the challenges facing women during the special period, which refers to the economic crisis of the 1990s. Professional women working in communications created in 1993 a new organization, MAGÍN.

The group raised criticisms about the lack of women in the upper levels of government and the use of images of women as sex objects to promote tourism. Members encouraged a collective, participatory form of organizing and developed strong relationships with feminists in various countries. They also contributed to bringing about some changes in terms of the media and official policies in Cuba. However, in 1996, after the passage of the Helms-Burton law that intensified the U.S. embargo against Cuba and promoted intervention in Cuba through nongovernmental organizations, MAGÍN was denied meeting spaces and officially informed that the organization should disband. MAGÍN members were told that they could continue to raise issues concerning gender at the workplace and through the FMC.

This chapter provides a voice to three different groups of women: participants in the revolution in the 1950s, former domestic workers who attended educational programs and changed jobs in the 1960s, and women communicators who brought about changes in the 1990s. Each group was active during a critical time in the history of the revolution—the underground movement and the political struggle for power in the 1950s; the complete transformation of the political, economic, ideological, and social structures in the 1960s; and the struggle for the survival of the revolution in the 1990s. The information about the first two groups of women is based on interviews conducted in Havana with the assistance of numerous Cuban women and men during the 1990s. The MAGÍN section, comprising the third group of women discussed here, is based on materials written and published by the organization. The women expressing their views in this chapter, through their personal accounts of participation in the revolutionary process and criticism of the lack of progress in various aspects of Cuban society, provide hope for a new version of Cuban Socialism, with greater diversity and empowerment of women and other sectors of the population that as a general rule have so far been excluded from the highest circles of power.

Women's Role in the 1950s

Soon after Fulgencio Batista's military coup in March 1952, a group of women formed a women's organization opposing the dictatorship. The initial organizers were Aida Pelayo, Carmen Castro Porta (no relation to Fidel Castro), and Olga Román, who had been politically active in Cuba for many years. At a meeting attended by more than forty women in November 1952, the formation of the Women's Civic Front José Martí (Frente Cívico de Mujeres Martianas, FCMM) was announced, operating under the principles of collective leadership, discipline, and self-initiative.[4] Most of the leaders were white middle-class women, but the membership also included factory workers, domestic workers, and students. In January 1953, ninety-one women signed a statement published in the daily *Prensa Libre*. They criticized those who had taken power forcefully in March 1952 and encouraged people to carry out José Martí's ideals of economic and political independence.[5]

The leaders of the FCMM became consultants, organizers, and revolutionary combatants, participating in both legal and clandestine activities. Aida Pelayo frequently met with Fidel Castro in the evenings in the home of Carmen Castro Porta. Pelayo stated that Castro was interested in the work of the FCMM and wanted to know more about her participation in the struggle against the Machado regime, back in the 1930s. She believed that Castro's interest was important because "every event is a link in a long chain of events. We learn from past actions, learning from other experiences, which is advantageous in continuing the struggle. What keeps us going is storing the information and leaving a legacy."[6]

On July 26, 1953, Fidel Castro led the historic attack on the Moncada military barracks in Santiago, Cuba. Members of Castro's group of young revolutionaries were killed and others arrested following the attack; Castro escaped initially, but was arrested later. Pelayo was arrested on July 26 and accused of possessing receipt books and checks signed by the leaders of the attack.

Rosita Mier was elected to the city council *(ayuntamiento)* in the capital of Pinar del Rio province in 1951 when she was only twenty-four years old. She successfully supported a group of workers who were demanding subsidies after a rope factory was closed. She pointed out that the employers almost always hired men for factory work. She said, "The women worked in the office, white women because they would not hire black women." When Batista suspended the 1940 Constitution after seizing power in 1952, Mier refused to swear allegiance to the new regime. She circulated a statement criticizing the government, which was signed by all the council members in Pinar del Rio. Mier and others who signed the statement were arrested. Seeing that a pregnant black woman was bleeding after prison guards had beaten her, Mier demanded that the prison guards provide medical attention. After she was released from prison, she began working with a friend, Fidel Castro, distributing literature to members of the city council. She said: "Sometimes I would drive and he would read poems and other times we would do the reverse."[7]

Maruja Iglesias, a member of the FCMM, attended a meeting of about thirty women soon after the attack on Moncada. The women took up a collection of two hundred dollars, and Iglesias and another woman went to Santiago to give money to the archbishop of Santiago, Monsignor Pérez Serantes, who had been providing food, clothing, and medicine to those who were imprisoned. Iglesias said, "The archbishop told us that he was surprised that we would get involved in such dangerous things when we could get married and have a home and children. We weren't thinking about all of that."[8] Women in the FCMM were constantly challenging the roles expected of them in the patriarchal Cuban society.

Hidelisa Esperón began doing political work with the FCMM when she was twelve years old. She was tortured and sexually abused by the Batista regime. She recalled her experience this way:

> After school I would visit the prisoners. When some of the former
> prisoners went underground, they asked me to join them. In October

1958 the house I was staying at was raided. There was gunfire, and they took several of us as prisoners. They knew that I was a commander and that I knew a lot. I told the man who questioned me that he was a murderer. He had a gun and he pulled it out to shoot me, and I grabbed it to shoot him, but the safety was on. He shouted, and they came in and grabbed me. That's when they raped me and beat me in the head. They left me nude in a cell with thirty-two male political prisoners. All of us were beaten to the ground.[9]

After she was released, Esperón immediately rejoined her revolutionary work. In September 1955, once Castro had arrived in Mexico after being released from prison, he sent a letter to Carmen Castro Porta in which he discussed the role of the FCMM in a comprehensive revolutionary plan:

This is the function we have reserved for the FCMM. To affiliate in this organization all the Cuban women who sympathize with our cause and convert it into the women's organization of the Twenty-sixth of July Movement. You can have a very important role in all aspects of the Movement, above all the workers' sector and the ideological camp and revolutionary propaganda. You will have, as is logical, corresponding representation in the national leadership.[10]

Although the FCMM continued participating in legal and clandestine activities in support of the revolutionary movement, they were never represented at the national leadership level. After the triumph of the Cuban Revolution in 1959, the FCMM decided that they were no longer needed as a separate organization, and they decided to disband. While individuals had joined numerous revolutionary organizations after the revolution, the FCMM continued informally in a support network capacity, participating in educational and historical activities.

Many of the women who directly participated in the Cuban Revolution as combatants had no prior involvement in women's organizations. The most famous leaders were Vilma Espín, Haydee Santamaria, Melba Hernández, and Celia Sánchez. Elvira Díaz Vallina, who was a leader of the Federation of University students, decided to join the Twenty-sixth of July Movement:

The first goal of the women and men was to defeat Batista. But the revolutionary women wanted a change in this country that included their rights, the rights of the family, and the rights of men, because poor men faced discrimination in that society—but not only the poor but also the blacks. "We wanted equality for women with men, the right to work, the right to health, the right to a decent home, in short social justice—although sometimes we couldn't conceive of the exact type of government we wanted."[11]

Díaz Vallina pointed out that after the revolution, she realized it was not just a question of honest politicians. She and her fellow revolutionary women had to address the issue of private property, and its divisive influence on society.

Irma Pérez, who had nine brothers and sisters, lived in a rural house with two rooms. Pérez described what made her join the movement and how the women fought for the right to be combatants:

> We didn't have shoes, and we hardly had any clothes. There were no hospitals or schools in our area. When my brother got sick, my mother brought him to a doctor who wanted her to give him her voting card before he would treat him. My mother refused and he died. I joined the movement when I was sixteen because of the poverty I lived in, the exploitation, the torture, and the massacres.
>
> When I first joined the guerrilla movement, we did the washing and cooking. But we insisted on greater participation. First we became guards and messengers, and then we learned how to use weapons and we participated in the combat with arms.[12]

In September 1958, the Mariana Grajales women's platoon was formed in the Sierra Maestra. The members participated in numerous battles and received extensive praise from Castro and other revolutionary fighters.

There are various perspectives on the kinds of feminist concerns expressed during the struggle of the 1950s. In 1995, Elvira Díaz Vallina, Olga Dotre Romáy, and Caridad Dacosta Pérez published an analysis of a survey of 675 female former combatants who were living in the Plaza de la Revolución municipality in Havana. They interviewed 12 percent of the 675 combatants and found that 94 percent of the respondents had not had specific demands related to gender; they fought against dictatorship and for political and social demands for everyone. The participants' memories are substantiated by documents from the 1950s.[13] A journalist, Mirta Rodríguez Calderón, wrote that during the Batista dictatorship the conception was that feminist demands had to be put aside so that all forces could be united to defeat the tyranny.[14] Aida Pelayo, discussing discrimination against women, said, "We lived that experience, and we were and are feminists, but we aided the struggle to defend the Constitution of the Republic and to be granted the same legal rights as men." She distinguished their perspective from those feminists who only addressed women's issues by saying, "Ours is the political, revolutionary struggle of the people."[15]

While the women's demands in the 1950s were not part of a broad feminist agenda, feminist issues were very much a part of the decision by many women to join revolutionary organizations, to urge the leaders to accept them as combatants, and to work for a democratic society with decent health care, education, housing, and employment. Although the survey of combatants found that 94 percent of the respondents had no specific gender demands, in interviews conducted by the author it was found that issues related to work, education, health care, and political participation were very much part of their struggle. While being interviewed, women often mentioned the fact that before 1959 frequently people had to give up their right to vote by turning over their voter cards to a doctor in exchange for medical care or to an employer for a job. Both the doctor and the employer were part of the patron-client network characteristic of Latin American (and third world) politics. They used the voter cards to enhance their own social/political status (probably by turning the cards over to their patrons, who would use them in votes for their candidates). The women pressured male leaders during the 1950s for greater influence in the struggle, but later, with few exceptions, women did not receive upper-level decision-making positions in the revolutionary leadership.

The Federation of Cuban Women

Castro asked Vilma Espín, who is married to his brother, Raúl Castro, to organize the Federation of Cuban Women (FMC). Espín explained her response this way:

> I asked precisely why do we have to have a women's organization? I had never been discriminated against. I had my career as a chemical engineer. I never suffered. I never had any difficulty. . . . I was very poorly read in politics. . . . But Fidel was different. He was much more prepared than any of us. He had read revolutionary materials. I was only beginning to be a revolutionary.[16]

The FMC was officially organized on August 23, 1960. The organization sought to unite women from various groups and to integrate women into the revolutionary process. Vilma Espín became the first president and has continued in that capacity for over forty years, as well as being a member of the Central Committee of the Cuban Communist Party. The first FMC convention was held in 1962. At that time the federation (as it is known) did not discuss women's equality in a feminist sense but emphasized "the effective and full incorporation of Cuban women from all sectors of the population in the construction of the socialist state."[17]

The FMC was very involved in establishing major educational programs for rural women, domestic workers, and former prostitutes. It supported creating new day care centers allowing women to work outside of the home through paid labor as well as to do volunteer work. FMC leaders also encouraged members to become social workers, to help women and young people who were having problems taking advantage of the newly created social opportunities. They organized committees on each block, on various regional levels and nationally. Many of the women who were participants in the revolutionary movement of the 1950s became FMC members and leaders.

Transforming the Lives of Former Domestic Workers in the 1960s

One of the programs initiated by the FMC was the creation of schools for domestic workers. In January 1961 Castro and Espín asked Elena Gil to direct the Plan for the Advancement of Women, which included schools for revolutionary instructors and night schools for women workers. Oria Calcines, director of the Evening Schools for Domestic Workers, explained that Castro favored the creation of schools for domestic workers rather than unionization:

He wanted to open the doors of culture and direct the women to work centers. This is what killed domestic service. All we had to say was "Here is your school." The domestic workers themselves, by getting involved in the schools and their new jobs, eliminated domestic service without the necessity of creating special legislation.[18]

The comprehensive educational program included literacy classes, consciousness raising, and job training. By then economic and political changes had created new jobs for former domestic workers.

In 1993 and 1994, I and Esther María Rodríguez, a Cuban university professor who had been a director and a teacher in these schools, conducted interviews with thirty former domestic workers. Elda Ibáñez, who later became a cook in a workers' cafeteria, began working when she was nine years old. She pointed out that the only jobs open to black women were domestic work and prostitution:

A friend of mine once said, Let's go to the Prado Boulevard so that we can have some fun. We went there and we saw prostitutes, and my friend said, "Look at how nicely they dress. I'm going to quit working as a domestic. I'm not going to clean floors anymore." I told her, "I'm going to go right on cleaning floors because I don't want to throw my life away." My friend did stop doing housework, and I heard she left Cuba.

One day I was cleaning the bathroom in a house, and the husband came in as I was leaving, and [after making sexual advances] he grabbed my arm and said, "No, don't leave." I shook my arm loose right away and I never went back. There were a lot of girls who, well, it could be that they gave in because of necessity.[19]

Severe sexual harassment was a major issue for domestic workers, and in many cases if they wanted to keep their jobs, they had to submit to sexual advances.

María Teresa Hernández, a white woman who later became a bank employee, was very much aware of class and racial differences:

Poor whites and blacks were the same. We were nobodies because we couldn't go to the social clubs. They gave dances in the country but the groups were separated; they put up a rope and blacks were here and whites were there. There was a lot of racism, and it was inconceivable for blacks and whites to be together. The blacks lived in even more inhuman conditions than we lived in.

The revolution made me a person. It gave me all that I have. It gave me a joy for living, despite the fact that I have lost a son. Fidel made a speech during the FMC Congress and I was "in the air." There are things that one doesn't understand, things that aren't done right, but one sees that the revolution's leaders are trying to move things ahead and that if everything were available, Fidel would be able to solve the problems.[20]

The 1959 revolution gave Hernández a new self-identity, a sense of humanity and career confidence. She concluded that Cuba's problems would be resolved through supporting the leadership of President Castro.

Modesta de Armas, a black woman who became a telephone operator, detailed the extensive racism that existed before the revolution and the support she received from revolutionary instructors:

The instructors who gave the operators' course helped us a lot. They'd say you are there, you represent the revolution, you're the daughters of working people. Blacks have the same jobs as whites now. That doesn't mean that there are no racists. There are blacks who don't like whites, who wouldn't want a white for a mate or a friend either. In terms of work, there could be a boss who indirectly doesn't want a black, but she or he couldn't express that. It would have to be on the sly because no law says that a black who is qualified for a post cannot hope to have it.[21]

De Armas pointed out that at her job all the union leaders were women, but the managers were men, and although the Family Code established equality, women still do most of the housework. While progress has taken place under the revolution to eliminate racism and sexism, she explained ways in which prejudice still persists.

María Manuela Blanco-Alonso, a labor judge, attended the FMC-organized schools for domestic workers. She also attended evening school, and earned a law degree from the University of Havana. According to Blanco-Alonso,

The liberation that women reached is the right to hold office, it is the right to have access to culture, to demand that their children won't be raised illiterate, that there won't be racial discrimination and that we all should have equal rights. As in everything, women's liberation is still not complete, and although there exist possibilities, and the country pledged that with the victory of the revolution women would be totally liberated, this doesn't mean that all the women we see are liberated.[22]

Blanco-Alonso emphasized that the struggle for women's liberation is an ongoing struggle. She stated that although the shortages as a result of the economic crisis made daily life very difficult, she definitely preferred Socialism to capitalism.

In these interviews the women described the devastating poverty that forced them to become domestic workers. Many of their fathers were sugarcane workers who worked just a few months during the year, and the women had to work as domestic workers in order to survive. They emphasized racism as a major reason behind discrimination in housing, education, and work opportunities. They were also critical of the pre-1959 society that offered them the choice of becoming domestic workers or prostitutes, and they frequently discussed the sexual abuse the women confronted on their jobs. In discussing the political conditions that existed at the time, they recognized rampant corruption and lack of democracy.

The schools for domestic workers established in the early 1960s and the new economic opportunities created the conditions that allowed women to transform their lives. Through the intensive literacy programs, consciousness raising, job training, and support in their new jobs, they were able to succeed in an array of careers including working as taxi drivers, switchboard operators, bank employees, judges, actresses, poets, and cooks. Some became union leaders in their work centers and FMC representatives in their neighborhoods.

These interviews were conducted during the worst time of the special period (the early 1990s), when severe shortages in the country had resulted from the collapse of the Soviet Union and the Socialist countries in Eastern Europe, the intensification of the U.S. embargo, and various economic problems. In their responses, the women were concerned about the hardships they endured, but this did not translate into anger against the government. They were, however, very critical of the U.S. economic embargo and made it clear that they did not want to return to a capitalist system. Today, the women continue their struggle for social equality and for a system based on equal distribution of wealth and one without any form of foreign domination. They believe that although there are still individuals in Cuba who have prejudices, institutional racism and sexism have been eliminated.

A review of Cuban history during the nineteenth and twentieth centuries shows that the aspirations of the Cuban people for national independence and social justice were repeatedly defeated by measures taken by the Spanish government and, later, by the U.S. government and various foreign corporations and individuals. The revolution of 1959 allowed the Cuban people to develop their human potential, to create new lives, to have dreams and aspire to better lives for themselves and their families. The women we interviewed identify with the revolutionary changes in Cuba on a very personal level, and they view the revolution as part of a process of gaining control over their own lives. However, they would like to see economic changes that would create more material resources (in terms of food, clothing, housing, and transportation), and they firmly believe that this will happen through supporting their government and working together to resolve their problems.

Women Communicators in the 1990s

In 1993, a group of women working as journalists, television, radio, and film directors, psychologists, sociologists, and researchers joined together to form a new organization, MAGÍN, dedicated to developing an understanding of gender in Cuban society. They were critical of the sexist images of women in the Cuban media and the insufficient numbers of women in the government's upper decision-making levels. MAGÍN organized workshops to develop women's self-esteem and empowerment and succeeded in creating TV and radio programs and articles that challenged prevailing sexist views of women. The development of educational work concerning gender and communication had a major impact on Cuba's participation in the 1995 Beijing women's conference and on a National Action Plan issued by the Cuban government.

Mirta Rodríguez Calderón, a retired reporter for the weekly *Bohemia*, was one of the founders of MAGÍN. She described the birth of the organization:

> Women in Cuba have advanced, probably, much more than our sisters in Latin America, due to the laws to benefit us and to provide us with equality and due to the actions we have taken on our own behalf. However, on the subjective plane, women, along with the rest of society, have received little information about the dimension of gender, discriminatory conditioning, notions of empowerment, construction of alliances and the differences between sex and gender.[23]

More than one hundred women professionals in various careers agreed on the need and urgency to develop an understanding of the role of gender in communication, to better understand language that is used in international debates, to develop educational programs that develop self-esteem, and to teach each other about Cuba's political system. The first public activity was held in March 1994. By April 1996, MAGÍN had organized fifty workshops related to various themes involving gender and Cuban society, including gender in social communication, reproductive rights, gender and race in communication, and the dilemma of the fifties.

Sonia Moro, a historian, wrote an article chronicling the invisibility of women in history. In terms of Cuba she wrote:

> In spite of the great advances of women in all aspects of society and the predictions that women will be leaders in the twenty-first century, it is difficult for those who study history books to receive information about this half of humanity, who through centuries continue to be in the shadows.
>
> To be patriotic today one still has to be "virile." . . . Or better yet: "Cuba is a land with tall men." . . . Without recognizing women, who are half of the population, the possibilities of development will always be mediated, incomplete or insufficient and with a sexist slant, which is not only unjust, but irrational.[24]

Carmen María Acosta de Armas, a writer and poet, and Irene Esther Ruiz Narváez, a television production advisor and researcher, discussed in their writing the various meanings of the word gender and its impact on the mass media:

> Many people understand the word gender in terms of grammar, the styles of literary work, or the type of weave of a garment, but ignore . . . that gender is also the social-historical-cultural conditioning that assigns men as well as women specific roles. . . . Gender is also related to the construction of hierarchies, giving more value and status to the work done by men [while] the work of women is devalued or subordinated in most societies. . . . Mass media have an important role in terms of reproducing a stereotypical image of women. Mass media have been perpetuating a feminine model that contributes to subordination and discrimination against women.[25]

Acosta de Armas and Ruiz Narváez noted how the mass media usually portray men as strong and capable, but women appear as weak and hysterical. They also recognized how difficult it is to change ingrained cultural stereotypes and attitudes, and how reducing social prejudice requires a great deal of work.

Nonetheless, MAGÍN influenced the work of many of the women who participated in the organization, and had an impact on programs produced on television and radio. Orietta Cordeiro, creator of a radio show, *Nosotros,* broadcast on Havana's *Radio Progreso,* admitted to journalist Annet Cárdenas Vega the impact MAGÍN had on her program:

> This space was directed fundamentally to women. We have changed the conception that in reality was discriminatory and at times superficial. We discuss images of women in production, defense, and scientific development, using interviews and other techniques that allow us to address women, the family, and the importance of social unity between men and women. We lacked a consciousness of gender.[26]

The program now discusses ways to avoid stereotyping and encourages women to develop their potential, seeking to empower them in decision making.

Maité Vera, a producer of television programs dedicated to the history of men and women in Cuba, confessed to Cárdenas Vega that she felt inferior when she was young. "If I am born again I'd rather be a man," she thought. "[But] now that I am over sixty," she said, "[and after] these months in MAGÍN, I have regained my self-esteem as a woman and as a creator."[27]

Vera produced a telenovela about a woman who at the critical age of forty, still carrying some of the old social prejudicial patterns, nevertheless lives and works through the many changes brought about by the revolution.

Ada Alfonso, a psychiatrist, also applied what she learned at MAGÍN workshops to her own work. She justified her actions to Cárdenas Vega, saying that "we confront the same problem as other *compañeras:* sexism in language, crisis of self-esteem, and ignorance in terms of women's sexuality."[28]

Nora Quintana, a member of the editorial board of MAGÍN, wrote that these are difficult but not desperate times for Cuban women:

Modernity puts us at the doors of a new century. The country is involved in a changing scene and in this process, the challenge is to dynamically integrate cultural diversity in a shared social order. For women, modernity implies closing the distance between having rights and effectively exercising them. What should we do now? Nothing has been lost, friends, these are only transformations. We have to prepare ourselves for new forms and styles.

We are half of the population of the world and the mothers of the other half. Our hands rock the cradles of the men and women of tomorrow. Who protects the family economy for survival? Love yourselves, enjoy yourselves! Don't ever stop being or feeling like a star.[29]

Quintana looks to the future in Cuba where self-confident women who have managed to be creative during difficult economic times become more empowered through exercising their rights.

MAGÍN was also involved in the planning that took place for the International Women's Conference in Beijing. Some of the delegates attending the conference belonged to both the federation and MAGÍN. After the conference, a meeting was held by MAGÍN members and other members of the delegation. They agreed that Latin American women played a key role in having the issue of gender in mass communications included in the final action plan. The Cuban delegation found that compared to other countries, they had a higher level of social participation and progressive legislation. The images of women in tourism and songs were presented as areas that needed work.[30]

As a follow-up to the Beijing conference, countries throughout the world were asked to present national action plans. Cuba's plan discusses areas such as employment, education, health, legislation, access to decision-making positions, and reproductive and sexual rights, and provides a detailed account for the mass media area. Significantly the section on the media reveals the tremendous influence of MAGÍN's literature. The Cuban National Action Plan included the following communication objectives:

> Media: create intersectoral and interdisciplinary working groups that systematically evaluate and make recommendations on the treatment of women in the media, provide gender-sensitive training to persons engaged in communications, promote the inclusion of talented women in complex artistic works, promote dialogue and debates with artists and creators so that they incorporate images of women that are based on the recognition of their positive social value and contribution.[31]

In early 1996, however, MAGÍN found it was increasingly difficult to find meeting space for its gatherings. The Helms-Burton law, passed in March 1996, had intensified the U.S. embargo against Cuba and increased programs designed to intervene in Cuba through peaceful means. Subsequently, leaders of the PCC Central Committee met with MAGÍN leaders and informed them that they had to disband their group as an independent organization. MAGÍN's membership was told that "70 percent of foreign NGOs [presumably operating nationally] had shown subversive motives and always expected political dividends in exchange for their cooperation."[32] The political authorities also stated that safeguarding national unity was a priority and, therefore, MAGÍN could not be recognized as an independent organization. Still, their work was characterized as valuable, and they were invited to continue operating in their workplaces, and especially in the Federation of Cuban Women, by then an officially recognized NGO.

Conclusion

At the beginning of a new century and a new millennium, an analysis of Cuba's record is central to examining whether a Socialist revolution is a proper route to women's liberation. After interviewing numerous Cuban women, reading their writings, and developing strong personal friendships, I developed a deep respect for their commitment to the Cuban revolutionary process. Still, while the revolution opened the doors to begin the process of women's liberation and Cuban women seized numerous opportunities given to them, much work needs to be done for women to achieve actual gender equality in terms of full participation in the upper-level decision-making political structures.

The women who risked their lives in the revolution in the 1950s initially emphasized their goals in terms of defeating the Batista dictatorship. Through in-depth interviews, it became clear that they also had many feminist concerns that were part of their commitment to social change. After 1959, they worked in a variety of important professional and administrative posts, but with very few exceptions they were not appointed to the senior administrative and political government positions that they deserved.

The former domestic workers were especially eloquent in their descriptions of the total positive transformations in their lives as a result of the revolution. They developed a sense of self-confidence that greatly increased their career options, allowing them to become leaders in their unions and community organizations. But by not being involved in major national decision making, they had to wait for the male leaders to make decisions affecting them. In their interviews, however, they did not raise criticisms of the country's leadership. They were mainly concerned about insufficient material resources in terms of food, clothing, housing, and transportation, and blamed their condition on the embargo imposed by the U.S. government, not on the policies of the Cuban government.

The women in MAGÍN were also highly critical of the U.S. government and, blending their nationalist and feminist outlook, called the Helms-Burton law an ill-inspired "macho" law.[33] They believed that women could strengthen the revolution by doing educational work regarding gender issues and encouraging the ultimate empowerment of women. Similarly to the earlier FCMM, they were independent minded and built a collective decision-making structure.

In the 1950s, feminist demands had been put aside so that all emphasis would be placed on defeating the Batista regime. But it was the work of Cuban feminists (whether or not they used the term to define themselves) that was critical to the success of the revolution. Again in the 1990s, MAGÍN women were told that they could not function independently, that their organizational strength had to be consolidated with others, for the sake of national unity, in the fight against the anti-Cuba policies of the United States. In their brief organizational existence, they eloquently wrote about their commitment to the revolution and proposed creative solutions to current social problems. Nora Quintana stressed the need to recognize gender diversity while being integrated into a commonly shared social order and the need to develop ways for people to exercise their rights effectively.

The Federation of Cuban Women (recognized earlier as a mass organization and today technically as an NGO) has played a major role in terms of educating women, encouraging them to work, and developing community-based programs. But the FMC's hierarchical structure and national objectives are not helping women acquire a feminist understanding of gender, nor supporting media programs with participatory perspectives or new modalities empowering women. As more and more Cuban women have participated in feminist conferences abroad and more women with a feminist perspective have visited Cuba to express their solidarity, Cuban activists have become much more accepting of the term "feminism"—which was derided in the past by the FMC leadership. It has become clear to many Cuban women that there are different kinds of feminism and that feminism that supports political, economic, and social equality can be consistent with the goals of a Socialist revolution. It is important that the language used by MAGÍN to change the image of women in the media was used in the action plan presented by Cuba following the 1995 Beijing women's conference. Encouraging the development of independent women's collectives could strengthen the work of the FMC and help them make strides in increasing equality for women.

In looking at Cuba in the twenty-first century, we can see various alternatives. If the Cuban government could listen to such messages as MAGÍN's (which by now appear regularly in the Cuban media), we could witness the development of new alliances and empowerment opportunities, which would allow women and other groups traditionally excluded from effective power sharing to reach the highest level of government and receive recognition as major actors in making history. If MAGÍN and other organizations equally supportive of the revolution are directed to integrate themselves into officially accepted organizations such as the FMC, leaving no room for their own individualized identity, the creation of new forms of social consciousness and political action will remain severely limited.

Finally, the end of the U.S. economic embargo and diplomatic offensive could offer Cubans the possibility of improving their economic conditions and of developing a political agenda that would not be marred by having to offset Washington's hostile actions. In the long term, the success of the Cuban Revolution could depend on the ability of its leadership to listen to the women who for the last fifty years have been dedicated to struggle for their common cause. This issue applies to people of Cuba and to those around the world who hope that Socialism can provide a vehicle for achieving political, economic, social, racial, and gender equality. In sum, the future of the revolution will depend largely on the effective incorporation of all the social forces that brought the Cuban Revolution to power, as well as on the inclusiveness of the political decision-making process that will determine its direction in the future.

Notes

1. "Program Manifesto of the 26 of July Movement (November 1956)," in *The Cuba Reader: The Making of a Revolutionary Society,* ed. Philip Brenner et al. (New York: Grove Press, 1989).

2. Calculated by the author, based on census data cited in K. Lynn Stoner, *From the House to the Streets: The Cuban Woman's Movement for Legal Reform, 1898–1940* (Durham, N.C.: Duke University Press, 1991), 197–200.

3. Oria Calcines, interview by Esther María Rodríguez and Jean Weisman, Havana, Cuba, February 3, 1994.

4. Carmen Castro Porta, *La lección del maestro* (Havana: Editorial de Ciencias Sociales, 1990), 27–30.

5. Ibid., 251–53.

6. Hidelisa Esperón Lozano, "Aida Pelayo: Combatiente de siempre" (unpublished manuscript), 6.

7. Rosita Mier, interview by Jean Weisman, Havana, Cuba, December 26, 1999.

8. Maruja Iglesias, interview by Jean Weisman, Havana, Cuba, December 24, 1999.

9. Hidelisa Esperón Lozano, interview by Jean Weisman, Havana, Cuba, December 26, 1999.

10. Porta, *La lección del maestro,* 95.

11. Elvira Díaz Vallina, interview by Jean Weisman, Havana, Cuba, December 20, 1999.

12. Irma Pérez, interview by Norma Guillard and Belkis Vega, Havana, Cuba, May 10, 1999.

13. Elvira Díaz Vallina, Olga Dotre Romay, and Caridad Dacosta Pérez, "La mujer revolucionaria en Cuba durante el período insurreccional 1952–1958" (paper presented at the Latin American Studies Association Nineteenth Congress, Washington, D.C., 1995).

14. Mirta Rodríguez Calderón, "Cuba: Declasificar la palabra feminismo," *Cuadernos Feministas* (July–August–September 1999): 30.

15. Aida Pelayo, quoted in Jean Weisman, "The Martí Women's Civic Front," *Cuba Update* (June 1995): 19.

16. Sally Quinn, "Vilma Espín: First Lady of the Revolution," *Washington Post,* March 26, 1977, as cited in Max Azicri, "Women's Development through Revolutionary Mobilization," in Brenner, *The Cuba Reader,* 459.

17. Jean Stubbs, "Revolutionizing Women, Family, and Power," in *Women and Politics Worldwide,* ed. Barbara Nelson and Najma Chowdhury (New Haven, Conn.: Yale University Press, 1994), 195.

18. Esther María Rodríguez and Jean Weisman, "From Maids to Compañeras," *Cuba Update* (June 1995): 24.

19. Elda Ibáñez, interview by Esther María Rodríguez and Jean Weisman, Havana, Cuba, December 19, 1993.

20. María Teresa Hernández, interview by Esther María Rodríguez and Jean Weisman, Havana, Cuba, December 28, 1993.

21. Modesta de Armas, interview by Esther María Rodríguez and Jean Weisman, Havana, Cuba, January 13, 1994.

22. María Manuela Blanco-Alonso, interview by Esther María Rodríguez and Jean Weisman, Havana, Cuba, February 6, 1994.

23. Mirta Rodríguez Calderón, "Fraguar alianzas para estrechar brechas de género," in "¡Dí, mamá!: ¿Tu sabes qué cosa es género?" Asociación de Mujeres Comunicadoras, MAGÍN (1996): 5–8.

24. Sonia Moro, "La invisibilidad de las mujeres en la historia," in Dí, mamá, 41–44.

25. Carmen María Acosta de Armas and Irene Esther Ruiz Narváez, Dí, mamá, 15–18.

26. Annet Cárdenas Vega, "Con miradas de mujer," MAGÍN (May 1996): 34–35.

27. Ibid.

28. Ibid.

29. Nora Quintana, "No dejar de ser estrella," MAGÍN, no. 0: 35.

30. "Las cubanas en Beijing," MAGÍN (May 1996): 31–32.

31. Women Watch Web site: The UN Internet Gateway on the Advancement and Empowerment of Women (http://www.un.org/womenwatch/followup/national/latinsum).

32. María López Vigil, Cuba: Neither Heaven nor Hell (Washington, D.C.: ÉPICA, 1999), 178.

33. Carmen María Acosta de Armas, "Una ley a lo macho," MAGÍN (May 1996): 1.

4

Women's Daily Lives in a New Century

Norma Vasallo Barrueta

> Neither words nor homage can reflect fairly the greatness of the
> Cuban woman, a greatness earned through her incomparable ex-
> ample. No one has made greater sacrifices than she in the special
> period that we are still experiencing nor has anyone succeeded so
> much in converting daily struggle into a heroic feat.
> **Call to order for the Seventh Conference of the Federation of Cuban Women**

To speak of the daily life of "the Cuban woman" in the new century is no longer a simple risk but is, rather, bold impudence. Can we speak of the daily life of the Cuban woman in the 1990s, a period of the most profound economic crisis since the triumph of the Cuban revolution, as if the Cuban woman were a single entity and as if daily life were the same for each one?

What happens on the macrostructural level affects everyone, male and female, although not in the same way. The influence of events is mediated by each of the human groups and institutions to which we belong or with which we are acquainted. These are not the same in their economic, social, historical, psychological, or functional peculiarities. I will use myself as an example:

I am a professional woman, a psychologist, who works as a professor at the University of Havana. There, like other female professors, I belong to the women's studies program. Although as professionals and university professors some of us have an additional academic activity, we do not all have equal working conditions.

In addition, each of us has a family, but some have nuclear families and others have extended ones; some women are married, others are not; some have their own home, others do not; some live in distant areas requiring more travel time; some live in traditional family contexts of varying cultural development and income; some represent the highest level of cultural development attained in their family; and some are the major or sole providers in their families.

Could we think that the daily life of each of us is the same? Absolutely not. Could we say that, at present, the daily lives of Cuban women are even similar? Decidedly not. And if economic changes in the country take place, will they reflect equally on each woman? Will their effects be felt in the same way? Surely they will not. It is not the same for a woman to stop buying shoes when she has three or four pairs at home as for a woman who only has those she is wearing.

So to speak of the daily life of Cuban women today and especially of how it was in the 1990s, one must accept the differences among us and the nuances with which each of us perceived life in that time. How such nuances affect the present perception of our lives depends on how we live and also on how we have lived. It also depends on our history, on how we have defined ourselves, not only as women in a patriarchal culture, but—and this is a unique element in the case of Cuban women—on how we have defined our femaleness in a society where important social changes have occurred. Social transformations have called for the participation of women as social subjects but also as social objects.

Cuban Women in the Last Forty Years

For Cuban women 1959 marked the beginning of a gradual yet sustained process of significant social changes that the feminist movement proposed after becoming aware that the right to vote in itself would not produce the necessary changes in women's lives.[1]

In Cuba, unlike in other countries, these social changes came about not as a consequence of feminist struggles but as the result of an intentional movement for profound social transformation. The focus of the Cuban Revolution's social project emphasized the struggle against all forms of discrimination and inequality among persons, regardless of their social origin and ethnic or sexual identity.

In the political and legal discourse of the 1960s, concepts and categories appeared that only a decade later would develop as fashionable scientific constructs; gender perspective and gender equity can serve as examples. Changing the condition of subordination to which a woman was relegated and liberating her from the domestic space in which, historically, she was confined, changing her not only into a recipient of social transformation but also into a participant in the same transformation, was an important objective of the revolution's social project.

In 1953 only 12.3 percent of the workforce was female, the majority in the service sector and a significant number as domestic workers. The "Cuban woman" of that time found herself in a situation of economic and educational disadvantage that made her dependent on the male, and this was evident in any social class, although it was more critical in the case of the poor woman and even more so in the case of the black woman.

Without a doubt, one of the most important campaigns of the early years was the campaign for literacy, from which both women and men benefited, regardless of their age. Later, to assure continuity and to sustain the results of this campaign—the eradication of illiteracy—free educational services were extended to all parts of the country with equal access for girls and boys. Mandatory schooling through the ninth grade was established. Today, the average educational level in the country is the ninth grade, and there are no distinctions between women and men regarding this.

Women's rapid and sustained entry into universities and nontraditional careers was influenced by their access to all levels of education as well as by media encouragement for women's social participation and for fulfilling traditional masculine roles. Today women represent over 60 percent of university enrollment—over 70 percent of all students in medical careers and over 60 percent of all those in natural science, mathematics, and economics, to cite only a few examples.[2]

From the labor point of view, the feminine presence was in demand in the public sphere. Laws that favored women's access to employment were formulated, and such regulations have been perfected. Cuban women now have the right to aspire to any employment position for which they are qualified, and they receive a salary equal to that of men doing the same kind of work.

The National Health System profoundly affected women's lives, providing free access to care and, from the beginning, developing programs that directly benefited women. Her active role in family planning and the right to make decisions concerning her body have given the Cuban woman an important independence and, consequently, have contributed to enhancing her self-esteem.

Related to family planning is the establishment of the Family Code, which ensures equal rights and obligations to men and women in matters of family and domestic life. Equality between the sexes was contemplated in the 1940 Constitution, but only since 1959 has the notion of equal rights become a reality. In 1976 a new constitution was approved, and it was modified in 1992. The text expresses women's right of access to all state offices and positions in public administration and in the service sector.

The National Assembly of People's Power, Cuba's parliament, created the Permanent Commission on Childhood, Youth, and Equal Rights for

Women. In 1997 the National Action Plan for the Continuation of the Fourth United Nations Conference on Women was activated to provide a follow-up by creating government commissions.

All these programs, laws, and regulations were manifested in the definitive development reached by women in diverse spheres of social life. Thus we can say that in three decades (1965–95), the Cuban woman increased her participation in the national economy from 15 percent to over 40 percent, a process through which she passed with both objective and subjective difficulties.[3] The objective difficulties stemmed from the insufficient number of institutions that might have supported her in her household duties, duties from which she was not able to free herself. Gradually, child care centers were created for preschool children, and full- and part-time boarding schools were created for students at various levels of education. The subjective difficulties had to do with family pressure toward a woman's fulfilling her traditional role as homemaker-mother-wife—pressure that is still exerted in the form of social representations that affect her selfhood. Between 1975 and 1985 more than half a million Cuban women entered the active labor force.[4]

The Cuban woman's presence in the workforce has been marked by upward mobility in the occupational structure, which has afforded her a significant presence in technical fields, including the middle and high personnel levels. This is the result of her sustained access to the different educational programs in the country. As beneficiaries of one of the most significant social achievements of the revolution, women constitute two-thirds of the country's qualified workforce and represent over 60 percent of higher education enrollment, a fact that will contribute to sustaining and increasing their presence in those areas.

What Has Happened on the Subjective Level?

While political, legal, economic, and social changes allowing for upward mobility for women were taking place, the women were as much the object of transformation as they were the subject of it, and the impact they suffered was expressed on a subjective (personal) level. However, each person accepts the diversity of social influences in a manner dictated by his or her multiple group associations; therefore, the same social reality is accepted by and influences each individual differently. The resulting response and its effect on individual selfhood and on the formulation of societal identity is also varied.

Women respond to and appraise the value of social participation differently, which makes its subjective (individual) impact difficult to foresee.[5] Personal changes have occurred in those of us who have lived since the revolution, but they have not affected us in the same dimension or in the same rhythm as the social transformation was taking place.

In a study that I directed through two psychology dissertations, it was demonstrated that in three generations of women—grandmothers, mothers, and daughters, born in the 1930s, the 1950s, and the 1970s, respectively—from a subjective point of view there were both differences and commonalities concerning the meaning of "being a woman."[6] This was expressed as follows.

The Grandmothers' Generation

The family, considered the basic unit of society even when it had become both object and subject of the great social transformations, continues to be the most important human group in the perpetuation of the patriarchal culture and in the transmission of the sexist stereotypes that sustain it. Therefore, women experienced the principal molding of their selfhood in families, where they learned to be correct and prudent, developing qualities related to surrender and dedication. Grandmothers, and also mothers, learned to fear the male and became the bearers of myths and taboos concerning sexuality. Their generation made virginity the trophy that would win them marriage, which was the main objective of their lives, a lifetime goal.

This generation, which experienced the Cuban Revolution in adulthood, participated in it but not as actively as their daughters and granddaughters. Women who experienced the revolution when they already had their families saw in it a window of hope for those who were most important in their lives—their daughters.

Motherhood was and continues to be the means of self-realization to which all else is subordinated in these women's lives. Many of them lacked sufficient education, and the majority of the skills that they developed were related to the efficient management of the home—that is to say, the reproduction of the workforce.

The grandmother and mother generation developed obedience, tolerance, and surrender to the husband, on whom they depended economically. They produced the "giving" woman, who did not think of herself and who asked nothing for herself. Although she might not value herself negatively, she did see herself as less than her real potential would allow, and thus only considered herself as a social object. She was unable to see herself actively as a social subject. Internalized (subjective) obstacles in her sense of self did not allow her to effect a transformation of reality or to transform herself. What kind of life, then, did she live?

She remained as she was told to be, as she was ordered to be. One doesn't change identities easily, and it is more difficult when one continues to live in a social context in which the pillars sustaining the patriarchal culture appear to remain, even after they have been torn down.

The Mothers' Generation

The daughters of these mothers, who were little girls or teenagers when the revolution triumphed, are my generation, the one that brings to life the joy of our parents, of our mother, the continual advocate in her role of educator within the family. It became our destiny to grow from girlhood to adolescence to womanhood in a context where social prejudices toward women and blacks (male and female) were expressed in more or less open forms of discrimination.

Cuban society in the 1960s called for women's presence in the public space and even more for their participation in activities that, up to that moment, had been considered masculine; thus, women were tractor drivers, mechanics in factories, and military personnel. In my point of view, the most important phenomenon that has happened to women is that the social project solidified the bases for making a place for women in today's Cuban society that are both supported and sustained. The result has been that, gradually and in great numbers, women began to permeate all levels of education, not only qualifying themselves but also achieving the mental tools for a critical and creative analysis of their reality and of themselves, a necessary basis for gender consciousness.

But all of this affected my generation in diverse ways, depending on how much our own family, as mediator of all this influence, had been changed or on how much we might have separated ourselves from it. Some educational institutions, during this period, encouraged a change in women's situations by supporting their joining and staying in those institutions.

At any rate, the family has remained as the human group that has most significantly influenced the formation of our selfhood and, within it, has continued to promote marriage and motherhood, along with studies, as central objectives in women's lives. The care of the home and the family continued to present itself as women's domain, even when women joined the workforce as professionals, as clerks, or as laborers.

To be a professional woman became an important objective in the lifetime goals of many of the women of my generation. Of course, to be professional gave access to the public sphere, allowing us to respond to the social demands of our times. In addition, we still were effective advocates of our domestic life, a task that was reinforced constantly by the culture: "You must know how to cook and do laundry," "You must clean well," "Your children and husband first," "A good mother sacrifices for her children," and "A good wife is tolerant." How many times have we heard these phrases spoken by our mothers, our grandmothers, and even by our peers who had already made them their own?

We struggled between a social demand (the public aspect) and a cultural demand (the private) so that we are, in this way, the generation that has been most affected by the change. Those women who obeyed the cultural demand and renounced their personal realization did not become professionals nor have they had an important social role, and they feel frustrated. Those of us who acceded to the social demand, who became professionals and moved into the public sphere, are burdened with guilt because we have not been "good wives" or "good mothers"—qualities that, in stereotypical form, our culture, through the family and "others," passed on to us.

We are, definitively, the generation in conflict, although some of us, when we have undertaken gender studies and have become aware of the "why" of our reality, have liberated ourselves from our guilt because we are or have been the "new-era wives and mothers"—neither good nor bad, but simply "others." Perhaps we are representative of a transition toward a new model that may become anchored in our culture, a model that is more equitable for women.

And My Daughter, and Our Daughters?

In some measure, our daughters' generation has been and continues to be influenced by the patriarchal culture through family example, although that example presents differentiated nuances in the 1970s and 1980s. We are, in my generation, the major agents of their education, and, since we have been influenced individually by the transformation, each of us acts and influences in a different way.

Juxtaposed with what has been transmitted by the family in the education of the daughters are the "new" values, which have been incorporated into the process of social change and which have been influenced by the "traditional" values transmitted, reinforced, and controlled by culture. Thus, the rate of subjective value change here lags behind the objective cultural and social transformation.

Self-determination and family independence are important objectives of this generation of young girls, but these objectives include an active search for a stable relationship as the paradigm for reaching womanhood. The traditional role of wife continues without being associated with that of housewife, a role that does not constitute an objective in their lives since they do not express an interest in developing the skills that might allow them to carry out domestic tasks efficiently.

The daughters' generation senses, in the family environment, the demand for mastery of domestic skills as a prerequisite for the development of the female persona. But such an expectation may provoke a contrary effect on an individual level in that, if a young woman fails to master those skills, she does not feel as though she is less than a woman. This motivates young women to accept change according to advanced notions of womanhood. We are in the presence of a generation that is beginning to be the transmitter of subjective changes derived from the objective transformations that have benefited women, but it is a generation that still cannot liberate itself entirely from what constitutes one of the greatest perceived barriers against women's self-realization as human beings—their leading role in domestic life.

In the personal trajectory of these women, their development and professional achievements occupy a more important place than in former generations, but they keep themselves on the same level as the wife, although they perceive relationships sustained only by affection, understanding, and similar interests, not by economic concerns.

The criteria for selection of a partner and for keeping that partner have changed, indicating a greater independence in women who express themselves with self-determined behavior regarding those criteria. Nevertheless, in these generations, the weight of domestic work that falls on them is evaluated not as an objective of their lives as women, but as external pressures from the culture as transmitted by the family.

The demands placed on the Cuban woman by the new social project that came about with the triumph of the 1959 revolution exist alongside the traditional demands, creating an ambivalence in feminine subjectivity. Guilt and anxiety live on in differing personal achievements in the "mother" generation; doubts and fears live on in the structuring of personal goals in the "daughter" generation.

The depth of the changes effected in the legal and political reality in the Cuba of the past forty years does not have a lineal relationship with changes produced in the subjectivity of three generations of women. Without a doubt, great social transformations require more than three generations for the evaluation of their effect on individual and social subjectivity and on the molding of personal trajectories.

How We Live as a Result of the Economic Crisis of the 1990s

The end of the 1980s marked the beginning of the rupture of the Socialist bloc to whose economy Cuba was closely tied, following imposition of the embargo and the economic and political isolation to which Cuba was subjected by the United States. In the 1990s, the Cuban economy suffered a major decrease in its foreign commerce due to the loss of historical markets for its products and for importing raw materials, equipment, and parts that sustained the majority of its productive activity. This caused the closing of some businesses with an accompanying reduction in the workforce and a reduction in the production of food for lack of fertilizers, animal foods, equipment, and necessary parts for development and maintenance.

The reduction in oil imports—the energy basis for industry, transportation, and all of the country's domestic life—affected women in a major way because of their active role in that domestic life. It became necessary to search for alternative fuel for cooking, implying the actual search, plus additional time and effort spent to achieve a similar result with the alternative fuel. As reported in the Cuban media, it has been calculated that petroleum now costs the country $40 million more annually than it would cost under normal conditions without the U.S. embargo.

It became more costly to import primary products such as food and medicines when the historical markets were exchanged for markets more favorable to our commerce. Cuba was obligated to pay an amount equivalent to approximately twenty-three U.S. dollars more for each ton of food purchased, mostly in transportation costs, since the embargo regulations forbade many enterprises to do business with Cuba. The sale of American food, started in 2001, is based on cash payments alone, payable upon arrival of the merchandise to Cuba's ports.

This macroeconomic reality has had a strong impact on the country's daily life and, in particular, on its women, who, as we have indicated, were and are the ones responsible for domestic life, even though they may be heads of household because they have assumed that role as a part of their personal lives and in spite of their professional development.

The impact of the economic crisis on women's lives is reflected in three fundamental aspects: the reduction in oil imports, the reduction in the availability of food, and the lack of or insufficient supply of medicines, medical-surgical material, or medical equipment.

The insufficient supply of oil in the country (especially in the early 1990s) was experienced in the following ways:

By taking maximum advantage of natural light, the citizens were able to use fuel more effectively; nonetheless, there were hours without any electrical supply, but this situation improved as the effects of the economic transformations began to permeate the internal economy. In Cuba, 94 percent of all homes have electricity.

Television programming was reduced to five hours per day. This, too, has subsequently changed in proportion to the improvement in economic conditions.

The fuel supply (kerosene and gas) for domestic use in homes was reduced. In Cuba, approximately 47 percent of the population cooks with kerosene, 17.3 percent with liquid gas, 4.4 percent with propane gas, and 0.1 percent with electricity, coal, or firewood.[7]

By analyzing these facts we can understand the importance that this crisis has had concerning the home and, in particular, concerning food preparation. With a decrease in the amount of accessible cooking fuel, women have found it necessary to ration their use of fuel for food preparation, thus feeling obligated to spend more time on this activity or to search for alternative sources for fuel for the times when there was none; for example, cooking with firewood when electricity was not available.

The scarcity of fuel affected the supply of electricity and with it the already limited refrigeration of foodstuffs, shortening the time for carrying out domestic activities, since one could not count on lighting nor could one use household appliances. Many women had to change their schedules to complete their household tasks in the early morning hours. Since the shortage of fuel and replacement parts affected transportation, women had even less time to perform their household duties, and they ceased recreational activities that required travel to other places.

Considering transportation problems, perhaps television should have occupied a more important place as one of the few alternatives to outside recreation, but with the reduction in programming hours, it was necessary to seek other recreational options, not only for women themselves but for the entire family. In some cases, this important component for individual development and emotional balance was nearly eliminated.

The shortage of food imports obligated women even more to devote themselves to food management, to develop their creativity in order to present high quality meals, and to make sacrifices in the distribution of food within the family. They could not count on processed foods; thus, they had to devote more time to meal preparation and less time to relaxation. Another consideration is that lines in food markets became longer due to the increased demand resulting from the scarcity of many items and the absence of competition.[8]

Within the traditional roles that women fulfill has been the care of the ill, an activity that has become problematic due to difficulties in purchasing some medicines. Also, women have been affected personally; to cite only one example, the production of sanitary pads has been less than the national demand.[9]

We cannot overlook a positive aspect resulting from the special period: domestic work has been redefined; it has acquired more social and political value; it has become more visible as a supplier to the workforce; and, in many homes, all this has contributed to a redistribution of domestic roles with men assuming tasks that previously they did not perform in order to guarantee the survival of the family.

This economic crisis has not had the same impact on the women of Cuba as similar crises have had on women of other developing regions, including Latin America, in general. The following explains this phenomenon.

Feminine Subjectivity and the Economic Crisis

It is well known that, after each economic crisis, adjustment policies are implemented that impact the citizens and, in particular, women. In studies that address this question, three fundamental aspects are generally analyzed: women's role in the employment structure and the relationship of that role to masculine work; the reorganization of family life; and changes in social security.[10]

In other developing countries, the employment structure discriminates against and subordinates women. Women enter the workforce primarily through the informal economy, which implies less social recognition, worse working conditions, less pay, and no social security or other guarantees of protection. Facing the crisis and the economic adjustment with its decrease in actual salary and its increase in unemployment, cost of living, and inflation, women feel obligated to intensify their efforts in order to contribute to the family economy. For this reason, women look for economic alternatives, which they find in domestic production—in the service sphere and as domestic workers—spheres that barely guarantee subsistence, thus producing an occupational segregation. This is the result of disadvantaged young girls' limited access to education because preference has been given to the male who will be the future economic provider for the family that he creates, a situation that further disadvantages the female in terms of her access to qualified positions.

In Cuba, however, women's participation in work outside the home increased from the 1981 figure of 32.8 percent to 42.2 percent in 1990, reflecting an annual growth of 5.2 percent, while the male workforce showed an increase of 2.4 percent, although since 1990 women have suffered the effects of the economic crisis, "in spite of the fact that workforce participation experienced an average annual decrease in both sexes . . . ; in the case of women, this decrease was 0.5 percent, while for men it was 0.7 percent, a figure that indicates that women's participation has been more stable than men's in the labor sphere."[11]

These statistics are indicative of the privileged place held by the Cuban woman in the country's labor structure, since she constitutes 65 percent of the nation's qualified workforce, the sector least affected by the crisis. Women's majority presence in the qualified workforce is the cumulative result of an increasing access to education. Presently, women represent over 60 percent of higher education enrollment, which guarantees their continued participation in that workforce.[12]

In light of the consequences of the crisis, Cuban women have searched for economic alternatives according to their needs and possibilities. In order to compensate for the decrease in real salary, they have either entered or made a lateral move into the economy's emerging sector. For example, they represent 27 percent of the total self-employed workforce, 8.3 percent of independent farmers, 42.85 percent of workers in international firms, and 37.8 percent of workers in associations and foundations.[13]

The economy's emerging sector is the result of an important social recognition, including an acknowledgement of self-employed work that produces important personal economic income, more so than those activities that require greater work qualification such as in the medical or engineering fields. Therefore, women who work in the self-employed sector are neither discriminated against nor undervalued. In fact, a small study that I performed with students from the School of Psychology revealed that these self-employed women began to be more recognized and respected within the family simply for their valuable economic contribution, as a result of which domestic roles were realigned in order to provide women with better conditions for the fulfillment of their work.

The second area of analysis concerns the reorganization of family life. In some developing countries, one observes in the families that the girls feel obligated to do more domestic tasks and thus to support the mother, on whom falls a double workday. This results in the girls' having to forego schooling in many cases.

The Cuban woman continues to hold the major responsibility for household work and consequently must sustain a double workday, now increased as a result of the crisis. These same conditions have obligated the rest of the family, as a survival strategy, to assume some of the tasks whose burden the wife had been bearing. However, there is an important difference with other developing countries: in the Cuban experience, the economic situation does not affect the daughters and their education. In Cuba, as we have indicated, education is mandatory through the ninth grade, and in the subsequent grades, as well as in higher education, girls constitute the majority.

The third aspect has to do with social security, whose policy has been maintained in spite of the new conditions.

As indicated by Cuban economists, "the bases for the social security system established during the revolutionary stage have been, among other aspects, an increase in protection for working women and their children, as well as an increase in disability benefits; the establishment of retirement benefits for all workers; protection for the long-term and short-term disabled, as well as social aid for all persons in need."[14] Moreover, "in spite of the different measures adopted in the 1990s for the reduction of the fiscal deficit, social expenditures have continued to increase." "The major increase in social expenses occurred primarily in the areas of social security and aid."[15] In all this, of course, women have benefited the same as men, but women have also benefited in areas that pertain only to women, such as those concerning motherhood.

On the other hand, the economic crisis has been reflected in the increase in some social ills, as probably happens in all countries where this phenomenon occurs. Delinquency, violence in general, and prostitution are social problems that have become more evident in these times.

I will stop briefly to consider prostitution because it is a phenomenon that might seem to affect mainly women, although we know that a man can prostitute himself in the same way as a woman. We cannot speak of prostitution as if it were the object of a simple study. It has many causes, and its increase cannot be considered solely as an alternative to economic suffering or as a result of the economic crisis.

Without a doubt, the economic crisis makes something even more evident—that the incidence of prostitution can be affected by the role of the family unit as a social mediator and by education offered through socialization in a historical process. We are speaking here of women who have access to education, to work competency, and to employment and who may already have achieved a great deal. We are not speaking of women without culture, without thinking capacity, or without any possibility of employment, as happens in other societies.

From my point of view, it is an analysis that we Cuban women ought to make: how to achieve a greater gender consciousness that functions as a worldview allowing us to raise our self-esteem, and with that self-esteem to reject our being considered and considering ourselves as mere sexual objects.

Crisis, Transformation, and Feminine Subjectivity

Approximately a decade ago, measures of economic transformation were undertaken or intensified to cope with the crisis, but these measures did not affect the entire population in the same way. Some of these measures supported an emerging sector of the economy—a sector of greater personal wealth, whether it be in money or in kind—that contributed to a certain labor mobility toward that sector, regardless of its lesser social standing.

A preliminary study of women in the traditional sector (ST) of the economy, of education, and of health, and with women of the emerging sector (SE), self-employed workers, and those in corporations and mixed enterprises, sought their level of satisfaction with their new jobs, their perception of the crisis and the economic transformations—the study was focused solely on women because they are one of the population groups most affected by the crisis. I will refer briefly to some of the results.

The women of the ST consider their work to be first interesting and second intense; the women of the SE consider their work to be first intense and second productive. Both groups perceive their work as useful. To remain in the position for which they are qualified makes the job that they are doing seem interesting, and for them to have a job that allows for greater earnings makes the job intense, but their jobs seem to be beneath their preparation and therefore do not allow for their self-fulfillment.

Women view the home, food, and clothing as the major problem areas coming from the economic crisis, and there were no differences between the groups in this view. Both groups considered the quality of the home atmosphere to be the most negatively affected, but the women of the ST cited the work atmosphere instead, which constitutes a major criticism of the workplace today, confirming our earlier consideration.

The majority of the women studied see the country's situation since 1993 as "better" and "clearly better." They favorably evaluate economic transformation measures such as the following: the increase in tourism (notwithstanding its decline following the acts of terrorism against the United States in 2001), acceptance of the dollar as currency, and the creation of stores where money can be freely exchanged. They lament the fact that the benefits are not for all, and "equality" continues to be an important value among women, an unquestionable acquisition of the Cuban Revolution's social project.

The perception of how the crisis has affected women varies according to the work sector to which they belong. Thus, the women of the ST consider their domestic life and their personal economy to have been the most affected. Those of the SE, with greater income, indicate improved health and more free time or recreation, since for them domestic life has been better. The tourism workers point to the lack of free time as the most significant factor. They are younger, so this need is more serious. However, as women of lesser means, their other personal needs seem to have been satisfied.

None of the women considers the crisis to have had a positive aspect; nevertheless, they recognize that now they are more creative, organized, and strong. This is the result of the search for alternative solutions to the multiple problems of daily life, and it speaks to the method of confronting reality that has predominated in many of them. They represent women who are the bearers of a social representation of women as capable of fulfilling any function in society, depending only on their developed capabilities and seeing themselves independently of their condition as women, which is an expression of their high self-esteem. They have an optimistic perception of the future; they express personal lifetime goals that are related not to the satisfaction of basic needs but to the attainment of higher goals—for example, to excel professionally, to be promoted to higher job positions, and to provide an adequate education for their children, among others.

Generally, in our research we verified that there were some pessimistic women who did not see a solution to the problems and who are more critical of the adopted measures; nevertheless, the majority of women exhibit a self-esteem that has not been harmed, and it is that self-esteem that has helped them face the crisis without renouncing what they have already gained and even to identify moments of personal growth within that crisis.

In the last days of 2000 and ten years after the beginning of the special period, the situation in Cuba has improved and with it women's daily lives. That the country has increased its capacity for oil production is indicative of the early stages of economic recovery. We still have some social ills, but we know that what has been lost in five to seven years in the subjective and moral sense will take much longer to be reclaimed. Nevertheless, we count on a spiritual development in which important values such as solidarity, equality, and high self-esteem will prevail, values that can serve as a basis for the recuperation of other values that have become blurred under the effects of a material crisis.

Women, stronger after having endured much hardship without renouncing their rightful place in society, have in the main overcome the setbacks posed by the special period. In sum, Cuban women today can look confidently to their future.

Notes

This chapter was translated by Judith D. Gramley, Ph.D., Edinboro University of Pennsylvania.

1. Amelia Valcárcel, *"El techo de cristal: Los obstáculos para la participación de las mujeres en el poder político"* (Madrid: Editorial Instituto de la Mujer, 1997), 38–39.

2. Oficina Nacional de Estadísticas, *Perfil estadístico de la mujer Cubana en el umbral del siglo XXI* (Havana: Oficina Nacional de Estadísticas, 1999), 116–17.

3. C. Aguilar, P. Popowski, and M. Vercedes, *Las Cubanas en los 90, el período especial y la vida cotidiana* (Havana: Editorial Área de Estudios de la Mujer, FMC, 1996), 2.

4. Ibid., 3.

5. Norma Vasallo, "La conducta desviada: Un enfoque psicosocial para su estudio" (Doctoral thesis, Psychology Department, University of Havana, 1994), 60.

6. Tatiana Cordero, "Abuelas, madres e hijas: La subjetividad femenina en tres generaciones" (Ph.D. diss., Psychology Department, University of Havana, 1995); Ricardo Herrera, "Las representaciones sociales de las funciones de género en tres generaciones: Un estudio comparativo" (Ph.D. diss., Psychology Department, University of Havana, 1998).

7. Herrera, "Las representaciones sociales," 12.

8. In 1993 the farmers' markets, having been suspended in 1986, were reinstated, increasing the availability of food items, although the prices were rather high and not within reach of many consumers. (Editor's note.)

9. Aguilar, Popowski, and Verdeces, *Las Cubanas en los 90,* 10–11.

10. Ibid.

11. H. Safa, "Reestructuración económica y subordinación de género," in *El trabajo de las mujeres en el tiempo global,* ed. R. Todaro, *Ediciones de las Mujeres,* no. 22 (Santiago, Chile: Isis Internacional, 1995).

12. Oficina Nacional de Estadísticas, *Perfil estadístico de la mujer,* 144.

13. Perla Popowski, "Estadísticas de la mujer cubana" (Havana: Editorial Área de Estudios de la Mujer, FMC, 1999), 7.

14. Centro de Investigaciones de la Economía Mundial, *Investigación sobre el desarrollo humano en Cuba: 1996* (Havana: Editorial Caguayo, 1997), 40–41.

15. Ibid.

5

Demographic Transition and Population Policy

Sonia I. Catasús Cervera

An important issue in the ongoing international debate about population is the relationship between population development and population policies and how this relationship should be analyzed. There is a close relationship between population growth and demographic tendencies on the one hand, and social and economic development on the other. Economic and social development affects the reproductive behavior of the population and the way it participates in the country's economic activity, while demographic growth has an important impact on development itself.[1]

These principles were closely analyzed in the first two international population conferences that took place in Bucharest (1974) and Mexico City (1984) and were later ratified in the International Meeting on Population and Development held in Cairo in 1994:

> Sustainable development as a medium to guarantee human well-being, shared on equal basis by all in the present as in the future, requires that the relationship between population, resources, environment, and development be truly acknowledged. In order to achieve sustainable development and a better quality of life for everybody, States should reduce and eliminate unsustainable modes of production and consumption, and should promote appropriate policies—population policies among them—in order to meet the needs of present generations without endangering the capability of future generations to meet their own needs.[2]

To achieve the sustainable-development principle as a working objective, the Cairo conference proposed "to fully integrate demographic factors in development strategies, the planning, the decision making, and the distribution of resources for development at all levels and in all regions, with the objective of fulfilling the needs and improving the quality of life of present and future generations."[3]

The Mexico conference on population confirmed that population policy is an organic component firmly linked to development strategy. The conference asserted that the main objective of social, economic, and human development—part of which is population goals and policies—is to improve the standard of living and quality of life. The principle that socioeconomic transformation is the basis for an effective solution to population problems was ratified. Population policies are an integral element of socioeconomic development, not a substitute for those policies.[4]

Population policies should reconcile demographic tendencies with developmental needs. Hence, any reflection concerning population policy must be related to social policy, which should then be examined within the broader context of the population-development relationship. The validity of these principles was again ratified at the Cairo population conference: "Population goals and policies are an integral part of social, economic, and cultural development, and their main objective is to improve the quality of life of all people."[5] These principles and goals, present in the Cuban process of economic and social development of the last decades, are reflected as well in the country's demographic process.

The Cuban Population

The island that is home to the Cuban population is located in the Caribbean Sea at the entrance of the Gulf of Mexico. The Cuban archipelago is made up of the island of Cuba itself, the small Isla de la Juventud, and sixteen hundred very small islands and keys. In total, the Cuban archipelago has an area of 110,860 square kilometers.

Since 1977, for political and administrative reasons, the Cuban territory has been divided into fourteen provinces and 168 municipalities. In addition, there is the special Isla de la Juventud municipality, which is run directly by the central government. The city of Havana is located in the province of Ciudad de La Habana (City of Havana), the capital of the country. The offices and agencies of the state central administration and their main institutions, including the political and mass organizations, and the complex of scientific and industrial research centers are located in Havana.[6]

As in any other nation, important historical events occurring throughout the twentieth century, besides having economic, political, and social significance, have been fundamental in shaping Cuba's demographic growth. This confirms the close relationship between population growth, the tendencies of demographic variables, and social and economic development.

The first sixty years of the twentieth century are defined—in a succinct synthesis—by the following: (1) the end and aftermath of the wars of independence during the last years of the nineteenth century; (2) limits to the Cuban Constitution at the beginning of the twentieth century that prevented Cuba from attaining complete economic and political independence and defined its condition as a pseudorepublic; (3) the period of relative economic prosperity during the first three decades of the century; and (4) the widespread crisis of capitalism in the 1930s coupled in Cuba with increasing foreign economic dependency and adverse conditions in the political and social spheres. Since 1959 Cuba has experienced a transcendental transformation under the revolutionary government, which introduced substantial social, economic, and political structural changes.

From a demographic standpoint, Cuba is now at the end of a transition or at an advanced stage of it. We examine below the most important aspects of this process in its relationship to the nation's economic and social development.

Most Salient Characteristics of Cuban Demographic Growth

Within the Latin American context, Cuban demographic growth has been characterized by its modest rate. During the first fifty years of the twentieth century, the population grew at an average rate oscillating between 2.0 percent and 3.3 percent. The censuses of the years between 1907 and 1953 show the average annual growth rate of the population to be 2.7 percent; throughout this period the population grew from 2,049,000 to 5,829,000 people.

Demographic characteristics of the population during the first half of the century reveal some interesting facts. In 1907 36.5 percent of the population was younger than fifteen years of age, and 4.6 percent was sixty years or older. At that time there were 110.3 men per 100 women; 43.9 percent lived in urban areas while 26.2 percent lived in Havana province, which includes the country's capital. In 1953, when the population had reached 5.8 million people, 36.2 percent were fourteen years of age or younger, and 6.9 percent were sixty years or older. The gender ratio was 109.2 men per 100 women; 57 percent lived in urban areas and 27.8 percent lived in the capital and Havana province.

More than one million immigrants arrived during the first thirty years of the twentieth century. High fertility rates at the beginning of the century, as well as an early decline in the mortality rates, were partly due to the introduction of health measures, which were directed mostly to guarding the health of the foreign elite rather than the native population.[7]

The demographic features at the beginning of the century, when both the fertility and mortality rates were high, made population specialists mark these years as the early phase of demographic transition. During the first three decades of the century, the mortality rates registered a ratio of about 20 per 1,000, while the birthrate suffered a moderate reduction with a rate of 35 per 1,000, which points to 1930 as the conclusion of the first stage and the beginning of the second.[8]

Between 1930 and 1940 the declining growth rate (1.6 percent) became critical basically as a result of a decreasing and even reversed migratory balance. In the 1950s, natural growth became the main factor responsible for population changes. During this period, the population experienced a slight increase in total growth (2 percent). Rather than an increase in fertility rates, the increase was due to a significant decline in mortality rates. Toward the end of the decade, however, the country showed a gross birthrate of 27.3 per 1,000; the mortality rate was estimated at 6.4 per 1,000; and the negative migratory balance was -0.7 per 1,000.[9]

After more than fifty years of Cuban pseudorepublic, the revolution triumphed in 1959. The new revolutionary government promoted its own social agenda by engaging in radical societal change. The nation's socioeconomic and political transformation had a direct and tangible repercussion on the demographic behavior of the population.[10]

In the 1960s, there was initially a significant fertility increase. Then a negative migratory flow began, at times of significant magnitude, while the mortality rate declined rapidly. This led to an average population growth of 1.98 percent between 1958 and 1970. It is important to highlight the years 1963 to 1967 during this period because the growth rate amounted to a birth boom that reached 2.43 percent.

In Latin America, between 1963 and 1970, countries like Argentina and Uruguay had an average population growth of 1.2 percent and 1.5 percent, respectively; Puerto Rico, Chile, and Mexico grew at a rate of 1.7, 2.4, and 3.5 percent, respectively, while Cuba had an average increase of 2.1 percent.

Income redistribution, together with the implementation of other social policies like free education and public health, and the creation of new employment opportunities that ended unemployment, were of great popularity among the people. These policies were aimed at improving the quality of life of the population as well as at eliminating social differences on the basis of race, gender, social class, or area of residence. Altogether, these policies coincided with the increase of the natural population growth rate during these years. But the policy of nationalizing and recovering national property, together with others breaking up the institutional structure of the neocolonial republic, compelled a dissatisfied sector of the population to migrate, showing their disagreement with the emerging social system.[11]

Beginning in 1970, a severe population growth decline became evident. This was the result of a fertility decline that was occurring at the same time that comprehensive health and sanitary measures were having a positive effect on the mortality rate. The annual growth rate for the decade was estimated at 1.7 percent, but when the fertility level became lower than the population replacement in 1978, it caused an overall decrease in population growth. It reached its lowest level in 1981. Besides the fact that life expectancy reached seventy years of age, such developments allow us to place the end of the demographic transitional stage during this period.[12]

Between 1978 and 1984 the population growth rate was less than 1 percent, growing during the six years at an average rate of 0.6 percent. The predominance of people leaving the country since 1960 made the migratory balance negative with rates varying regularly between -9.5 and -0.4 per 1,000. In the 1970s, family members of those who had emigrated in the previous decade as a result of the agreements between the United States and Cuba since 1965 continued to leave the country. It is important to mention here the negative balance observed in 1980, when the rate reached -4.6 per 1,000 as a result of the migration of one hundred forty thousand people in a single year.[13] What affected this balance more than anything else was the departure, motivated by both subjective and objective factors, of over one hundred twenty-five thousand disaffected citizens from the port of Mariel.[14] This migratory flow, in conjunction with low natural population growth, caused a negative overall growth of 0.62 percent in 1980.

As had happened in other periods, important economic and social factors were linked with the patterns of demographic growth starting in 1970. The economic-development process was accelerated, and industrialization came to occupy an important place in the economic activity, combined with a push toward a greater integration in the economy while the infrastructure continued to be expanded. The political system was institutionalized, and many important advances in social areas, including health and education, took place. Also, women's participation in economic, educational, and social activities was promoted.[15]

The population growth rate was modestly up again between 1985 and 1990, reaching slightly above 1 percent as a result of a small recovery in fertility, although not enough to match the level needed for population replacement. During the five-year period the population grew annually at an average of 1.03 percent. Still, the country's total population had reached 10,694,465 by December 31, 1990.

Table 5.1. Main indicators of Cuban demographic dynamics, 1988–2000 (per thousand)

Year	Net growth rate	Gross birth rate	Gross mortality rate	Migratory balance rate
1988	10.8	18.0	6.5	-0.7
1989	10.3	17.6	6.4	-0.9
1990	11.1	17.6	6.8	-0.5
1991	9.2	16.2	6.7	-0.3
1992	7.0	14.5	7.0	-0.5
1993	6.5	14.0	7.2	-0.3
1994	1.9	13.4	7.2	-4.4
1995	3.5	13.4	7.1	-3.1
1996	3.6	12.7	7.2	-1.9
1997	4.9	13.8	7.0	-1.9
1998	4.2	13.6	7.0	-2.4
1999	3.6	13.5	7.1	-2.8
2000	3.3	12.8	6.8	-2.6

Source: Centro de Estudio de Población y Desarrollo, 1998, 2000 (Havana: Oficina Nacional de Estadísticas, 1998, 2000); Anuario demográfico de Cuba, 1997 (Havana: Oficina Nacional de Estadísticas, 2000).

In August 1990 the government implemented the so-called Special Period in Peacetime. This came as a result of the collapse of the Socialist bloc and the Soviet Union, the suspension of trade and financial transactions with Moscow, and the intensification of the economic blockade imposed by Washington more than three decades before. All of these had extremely serious consequences for the Cuban economy. No matter how desperately needed and well intended the Special Period in Peacetime initiative was, the overall process affected the quality of life of the population negatively.

By the end of 2000 the population had reached 11,217,100, of which 21.2 percent were 15 years of age or younger, and 14.3 percent were 60 years or older. The ratios indicated that the Cuban population was in an aging process as a result of a noticeable fertility decline since the second half of the 1970s. The average and median population ages were 35.81 and 33.32 years, respectively. The ratio between men and women was 998 men per 1,000 women. Nearly one-fifth—19.5 percent—of the population lived in the country's capital. (See table 5.1.)

Even though Cuba is underdeveloped economically and faces the serious problems of the current special period, it exhibits demographic indicators similar to those of developed countries. This is illustrated by such facts as its mortality rate, a life expectancy rate of 74.83 years in 1994–95, and an infant mortality rate of 7.2 deaths per 10,000 of infants less than a year old in 2000. The island's fertility level is the lowest in Latin America (0.76 daughters per woman), which sustains an average annual growth rate of 0.33 percent with an urban population rate of 75.3 percent in 2000.[16] During the 1990s Cuba had the lowest demographic growth in Latin America and represented 2.1 percent of the region's population.[17]

What distinguished this process was that the differential among the most significant demographic indicators was very small among different areas of the country. With regard to such indicator differentials, it appears that the socioeconomic factors influencing national demographic behavior changes are more widely spread throughout the country than originally thought.

Cuban official sources have systematically recorded comparative data of some of the most important indicators in the evolution of mortality and fertility during the last decades, given the significance these variables have for evaluating domestic and international population growth. (See table 5.2.)

Mortality

The protracted struggle for the survival of humanity in its healthiest and fullest state has led to the study of mortality, which has been examined by different disciplines that in one way or another have population as an object of study. This kind of research also includes demographers. Mortality is, without a doubt, the indicator par excellence of the status of a population's health and of the degree of development reached by a country. Cuba, since the early 1960s, has been carrying out an ambitious and extensive public health program as part of its overall strategy for social development.

Beginning with mortality patterns for the three-year periods of 1963–65, 1972–74, 1982–84, 1988–90, 1993–95, and 1998–2000,[18] it is reasonable to analyze the most significant changes in mortality rates, quantitatively and qualitatively, that have occurred in the last thirty years.[19]

With regard to the pattern of deaths between 1964 and 1994, there was a significant decrease in the death rate among children less than one year old, from 20.4 percent to 1.8 percent; however, among persons sixty-five years of age or older, the aging ratio increased from 43.5 percent to 67.1 percent. By 2000 these ratios were 1.4 percent and 71.6 percent, respectively, which reflected the increased population's aging process.

An initial view of the evolution of mortality rates during the last thirty-seven years, examined from the perspective of such general indicators as gross mortality rate (without ignoring its possible imperfections), allows us to point out a decrease of 7.8 percent between the first and third selected

Table 5.2. A comparison of selected demographic indicators between some world regions and Cuba, 2000

	Gross growth rate[a]	Global fertility rate[b]	Life expectancy at birth[c]	Infant mortality rate[d]	Urban population[e]
World	1.4	2.9	66.0	57.0	45.0
Developed countries	0.1	1.5	75.0	8.0	75.0
Underdeveloped countries	1.7	3.2	64.0	63.0	38.0
Latin America and Caribbean	1.8	2.8	70.0	35.0	74.0
Central America	2.1	3.1	71.0	34.0	67.0
South America	1.7	2.7	69.0	34.0	78.0
Cuba	0.7	1.6	75.0	7.0	75.0

Source: Population Reference Bureau, *Cuadro de la población mundial, 2000* (U.S.A.: Population Reference Bureau, 2000).
[a]Difference between relative birth frequency and population mortality; rates per one hundred people.
[b]Children per woman.
[c]Average life expectancy in years for both sexes.
[d]Deaths per 1,000 live births.
[e]Percentage of total population.

three-year periods. The slow growth process reached 20.3 percent by the 1998–2000 period. (See table 5.3.)

The tendency toward growth in the gross mortality rate in the three-year periods of the 1980s and 1990s could be attributed to the ongoing population's aging process, although in a fluctuating manner. This can be inferred by observing the annual mortality rates in the 1980s and, more clearly, in the 1990s. The mortality rate increase was the result of the growth of the elderly population, which resulted in a higher ratio for this population group.[20]

The priority given to the reduction of infant mortality within the health system, and to the Mother and Infant Care Program (implemented with the cooperation of the United Nations since the 1980s), led, among other results, to a death rate decrease of 70 percent between the periods 1963–65 and 1988–90. Notwithstanding its underdeveloped economic conditions, Cuba was positioned as having the lowest infant mortality rate in Latin America and as having a rate comparable to those of developed countries, a fact which has been internationally recognized.[21]

The system of universal health coverage has allowed Cuba to lower significantly the gap between the more and the less developed areas of the country. For example, in 2000, when the national infant mortality rate

Table 5.3. Cuban mortality indicators, 1963–65 to 1998–2000, and life expectancy at birth, 1960–65 to 1994–95

Mortality indicators (rates per thousand)

	1963–65	1972–74	1982–84	1988–90	1993–95	1998–2000
Gross rate	6.4	5.7	5.9	6.6	7.1	7.0
Infant mortality rate	37.6*	29.1	16.2	11.2	9.7	6.9

Life expectancy at birth (in years)

	1960–65	1969–71	1982–83	1988–89	1990–91	1994–95
Both sexes	65.10	70.04	74.22	74.75	74.70	74.83
Males	63.26	68.55	72.63	72.89	72.93	72.94
Females	67.05	71.82	75.97	76.80	76.58	76.90

Source: Comité Estatal de Estadísticas, *La esperanza de vida de Cuba y provincias, 1982–1983* (Havana: Instituto Nacional de Estadísticas, 1985); *Anuario demográfico de Cuba, 1990* (Havana: Instituto Nacional de Estadísticas, 1992); *Esperanza de vida en Cuba en el bienio 1988–89, breves comentarios* (Havana: Instituto Nacional de Estadísticas, 1992); Centro de Estudios de Población y Desarrollo (CEPDE), *Anuario demográfico de Cuba, 1997* (Havana: Oficina Nacional de Estadísticas, 1998); *Anuario demográfico de Cuba, 2000* (Havana: Oficina Nacional de Estadísticas, 2001); Eneida Ríos and Arnaldo Tejeiro, "Evolución de la mortalidad Cubana en Cuba analizándo un trienio de cada década del periodo revolucionario," *Revista Cubana de Medicina General Integral* (1987).
*Adjusted, taking into account that until 1965 the law considered an infant alive if he or she survived twenty-four hours or more.

stood at 7.2 per 1,000 live births, the province with the lowest rate had an average of 5.0 per 1,000, while the one with the highest rate had reached 9.1 per 1,000, a figure still close to that of the most developed regions.

The official estimates for life expectancy at birth, from the 1963–65 to the 1998–2000 periods, reflect an increase of 9.6 years in thirty years, and an average life expectancy close to 75 years by the early 1990s. Examined province by province, as in the infant mortality case, the differential in life expectancy at birth is small since the tables on the extremes are 73.86 and 76.57 for the period of 1994–95. Notwithstanding its high life expectancy rate at birth, the Cuban case presents a peculiarity. When the record is examined by gender, the difference of 3.96 years is small when compared to that of countries with similar mortality indicator tables. Among the latter, the difference between men and women is six years on the plus side for women. During the mid-1980s, while the average life expectancy for men was twelfth among the nations with the highest life expectancy at birth, women were in thirtieth place. This suggests that lower female mortality has the potential of increasing women's life expectancy.[22]

An important factor in the study of mortality is the pattern established by the causes of death. By the end of the 1950s, the main causes of death were those related to the degenerative processes of the human body, such as heart disease and malignant tumors. Then, in the first five years of the 1960s, the causes of death signaled a more defined pattern. Influenza and pneumonia and neurovascular diseases occupied third and fourth place, and together they caused 54 percent of all deaths. At the time violent death occupied fifth place, and enteritis and other diarrhetic disorders were displaced to seventh place.

Starting in 1972–74, violent deaths took third place and since then the five leading causes of death have been set in place. The same range continued in the 1970s, 1980s, and 1990s, and in 1972–74 they were already causing 69 percent of all deaths. But in the 1982–84 and 1988–90 periods they increased in this order: heart diseases, malignant tumors, neurovascular diseases, violent deaths, and the flu and pneumonia. In 1991–93 they added up to 68 percent of all deaths, increased to 70.2 percent, and by the end of the 1990s reached 71.4 percent. In 2000, other indicators of mortality such as the mortality rate of children five years or younger and maternal mortality reached 9.1 deaths per 1,000 live births and 21.3 deaths per 100,000 live births, respectively.[23]

These indicators are evidence that Cuba follows a modern pattern of mortality and that it is in an advanced stage of its epidemiological transition. They also validate the advances made in the Cuban health system, which is highly equitable and freely accessible to the entire population. This system has succeeded in maintaining a favorable performance, even during the adverse economic conditions of the 1990s.

Fertility

Fertility is the demographic variable that has exerted the most influence over both the size and structure of the Cuban population in the last decades. As mentioned initially, the country's fertility declined early in comparison with fertility in Latin American countries with already lower rates in the region. Between 1955 and 1960 Cuban women had an average of 1.83 daughters per woman while in Central American countries, Mexico, and Venezuela this factor varied between 3.15 and 3.38; in Panama it was 2.64 per woman, and 1.51 in Argentina.[24]

After a temporary fertility increase between 1961 and 1964, when it reached 2.30 daughters per woman, the rate began a systematic decline that was eventually interrupted in 1971. The fertility decline was associated with the end of an important national agricultural activity, the sugarcane harvest, which required the participation of thousands of men. Still, the decline accelerated in the last five years of the 1970s, placing the island's fertility below the replacement level (0.94 daughters per woman), a condition that has lasted from 1978 to the present.

Territorial homogeneity has been another variable associated with the fertility decline phenomenon, since the different provinces that make up the country experienced similar trends. The country's capital had the lowest ratio (0.80 daughters per woman in 1990), while the province with the highest ratio scored 1.05 daughters per woman, in spite of exhibiting lower economic conditions. But even this higher rate is lower than in the rest of the Latin American countries, including those expected to have lower or moderately low fertility tables, such as Argentina, 1.1, and Costa Rica, 1.5 daughters per woman.[25]

Another characteristic among the fertility variations is a consistent behavior in both urban and rural areas, with the latter having a more pronounced decline. From 1970 to 1987, the nation's fertility pattern for the entire period was set by the falling birthrate in rural areas. For the entire country, for example, the median of daughters per woman diminished by 51 percent from 1970 to 1987 (see table 5.4). In urban areas the fertility rate was 1.42 and 0.85 daughters per woman, while in rural areas it was 2.25 and 0.96 daughters per woman. In seventeen years the urban fertility rate had fallen 40.8 percent, but in rural areas the decline was even higher, 57.3 percent. The gap separating both regions contracted from 37 percent to 14 percent.[26]

We can reasonably infer that the set of socioeconomic factors that conditioned the fertility decline had a stronger and more decisive impact in rural areas, which have traditionally lagged behind. Some of the factors influencing the process were a population increase in medium-size cities and in small localities; the geographic decentralization of economic investment; and above all the national increment in such basic services as education, health, and social assistance, which were emphasized in rural areas.

The urban and rural decline in infant mortality coupled with changes affecting the factors conditioning fertility and the increasing incorporation of women into the workplace contributed to reduce infant mortality. Such developments disturbed rooted reproductive and family traditions among rural women more profoundly than in urban zones. Between 1970 and

Table 5.4. Cuban global fertility rate (GFR)* and gross reproduction rate (GRR),** 1970–2000

Year	GFR	GRR	Year	GFR	GRR	Year	GFR	GRR
1970	3.5	1.80	1980	1.7	0.81	1990	1.8	0.89
1971	3.8	1.88	1981	1.6	0.78	1991	1.7	0.82
1972	3.5	1.80	1982	1.8	0.90	1992	1.5	0.72
1973	3.3	1.61	1983	1.8	0.89	1993	1.5	0.72
1974	2.9	1.42	1984	1.8	0.87	1994	1.5	0.71
1975	2.7	1.30	1985	1.9	0.94	1995	1.5	0.72
1976	2.5	1.21	1986	1.7	0.83	1996	1.4	0.70
1977	1.9	0.95	1987	1.8	0.88	1997	1.6	0.77
1978	1.9	0.95	1988	1.9	0.92	1998	1.6	0.78
1979	1.8	0.88	1989	1.8	0.89	1999	1.6	0.80
						2000	1.6	0.76

Source: For period 1970–74, A. Farnos, "La declinación de la fecundidad y su perspectiva en el contexto de los procesos demográficos en Cuba" (doctoral thesis) (Havana: Demographic Studies Center, 1985), 62. For period 1975–90, Comité Estatal de Estadísticas, *Anuario demográfico de Cuba, 1990* (Havana: Instituto Nacional de Estadísticas, 1992), 129–30. For period 1991–97, Comité Estatal de Estadísticas, *Información Estadística* (Havana: Instituto Nacional de Estadísticas, 1993); Centro de Estudios de Población y Desarrollo, *Cuba: Proyección de la población nivel nacional y provincial. Período 1995–2025* (Havana: Oficina Nacional de Estadísticas, 1996); Centro de Estudios de Población y Desarrollo, *Anuario demográfico de Cuba, 1997* (Havana: Oficina Nacional de Estadísticas, 1998). For period 1997–2000: Centro de Estudios de Población y Desarrollo, *Anuario demográfico de Cuba, 2000* (Havana: Oficina Nacional de Estadísticas, 2001).
*GFR: Children per woman.
**GRR: Daughters per woman.

1981 the rate of work outside the home for urban women age fifteen and older increased by 60.2 percent, but it grew more in rural areas, 87.4 percent. Also, participation in economic activity signals a fertility differential behavior—a lower fertility rate associated with workingwomen. In 1987 the rate was 0.76 daughters per woman for workingwomen in contrast to 0.96 for nonworking women. While both were below the replacement level, workingwomen reached a much lower fertility level.

The variation in fertility levels was also related to age changes in women's demographic structure. The female population underwent a marked rejuvenation process, manifested by a significant increase in the contribution to the fertility levels made by women 15 to 19 years old, and even by girls 12 to 14 years old. The fertility increment accomplished by younger women reduced the ranking of women age 30 or older, which underscored the fact that the fertility decrease had happened mostly among women on the oldest end of the fertile period.

In the final years of the 1970s and the first five of the 1980s, the 15-to-19-year-old group became the second most important contributor to the fertility equation, which defined the fertility behavior peculiarities of the five-year period. At the beginning of 1985 women 25 to 29 years old regained second place; nevertheless, the rate difference between the two age groups oscillated at the time between 3.2 and 19.9 points per 1,000.[27]

Under such conditions, fertility rates among adolescents and their attitude toward reproduction gained special significance. The country experienced a marked increase in teenage pregnancies in the last decades, coupled with attitudinal changes in their own reproductive capacity. During 1985–90, between 20 and 30 percent of the births were to teenage mothers. The average birthrate by adolescent mothers in Latin America was 10 percent, but it had increased by the year 2000 to 13.1 percent.

Fertility specialists point out that the possible factors associated with this phenomenon include having sexual relations at an early age without contraceptives, lack of knowledge about the optimal age to have children, lack of adequate sexual education, and insufficient parental and teacher guidance about sex and parenting. Hence, although the usual way of becoming a couple in Cuba has been through marriage, since the early 1980s there has been a systematic increase of consensual unions, and teenagers are the leading practitioners. To them mutual consent seems the main rationale to form a union. In 1987, 74 percent of the 35.3 percent of teenagers with stable relationships were holding consensual unions, and in the 1990s the majority of births were from consensual-union mothers. In 1985 the ratio of children born of a consensual union was 55.5 percent, but by 2000 it had increased to 66.8 percent.

In 1987–88 a study about single and unmarried mothers focused on women without a legal marital bond.[28] The findings of this research reported that 31 percent of the women interviewed did not live with the father of their child. In addition, 38 percent of these women were under twenty years of age; 69 percent did not work; and among those who gave up on their education, pregnancy was the main reason for it. What also became evident was that as a group they were psychologically poorly qualified for maternity and family life—especially among teenagers—and had little knowledge about stable sexual relations and life as a couple.

Population Development and Population Policy

At the international level, countries stand differently regarding their approach to the interrelationship between population development and population policy. Since the beginning of the 1960s, Cuba has guided its socio-economic and development strategy in agreement with the country's emerging values at the time.

The Cuban delegation stated at the 1974 Bucharest world population conference:

[A]fter the triumph of the revolution, the Cuban leadership's main concern and the most enduring efforts were directed to bringing about those basic structural changes that tended to promote an integral socioeconomic development. They were not directed to interfere with the demographic process because it was considered that the fundamental problems of underdevelopment did not originate in a high population growth rate or in a high rate of urban concentration.[29]

Moreover, the delegation affirmed:

Slowing the rate of demographic growth was not a policy objective. The obvious profound structural changes at work, catalysts of a harmonious and self-sufficient socioeconomic development, would decisively influence the traditional demographic model, which would then respond in a dialectical fashion to the newly created social conditions.[30]

A decade later, voicing the principles sustaining the island's population-development relationship, the Cuban delegation stated at the 1984 Mexico world population conference:

As part of its general strategy on development, and with the fundamental objective of fulfilling the basic material and spiritual needs of the people, . . . the country has put into practice a very clear policy on population, one that, without considering specifically control goals or birthrate limits, seeks to attain a very qualified population. It has already achieved population growth figures compatible with our economic development and our perspectives. For this purpose, measures have been adopted in order to guarantee jobs to all people that are able to work; incorporate women into the country's social and economic activities on an equal rights level; achieve a planned urbanization and regional development; guarantee educational and cultural improvement; as well as a health system that serves all of the population equally.[31]

In other words, it is not feasible to consider population policy as measures simply based on birthrate, or on any other demographic variable, in isolation. That would constitute a population policy void of a needed social context. As part of the country's social and economic development strategy, population policy should then seek to guarantee the country's education and human reproductive capability, as well as the progressive material improvement of people's lives and working conditions.

Cuba has not decided specific population size goals or a desired growth ratio. Until now, economic-development planning has not required such objectives. Hence, the growth rate has been modified depending on the socioeconomic conditions that have necessarily affected the demographic variables at play.

National population policy includes all the different measures that have been stated previously. In a general sense, the policy is framed within the extant political institutions and state documents; the country's labor, social, health, science, and cultural policies are so expressed in the Cuban Communist Party's (PCC) program. Also stated are the thesis and resolutions concerning the education of children and youth; women's full social, political, and economic participation; agrarian issues; and the peasantry's living and working conditions. They are all included in the guiding documents of the PCC's congresses. The concepts underlining the formation of the Cuban family are formulated in the Cuban Constitution.[32]

Considering what has been discussed here, it seems clear that a population policy without birthrate controls or limits has been in effect. The different social measures that have been integrated into the socioeconomic development policy have sought a well-qualified population as a major objective. Consequently, those same measures constitute in practice a real and effective population policy.

Demographic Perspectives on the Cuban Population

Given the prominent role population plays as both producer and consumer of goods and services, the demographic characteristics of the population work as the bedrock upon which economic and social plans can be elaborated. The process, however, can be rather complex. Besides making a prognosis of the country's demographic evolution in the foreseeable future, it is also necessary to evaluate present and future socioeconomic problems so their probable impact on population growth can be properly ascertained. As a country in an advanced-demographic-transition stage, Cuba has exhibited low mortality and birthrates since the mid-1970s, and for the last three decades its socioeconomic conditions have had an impact on its demographic behavioral patterns.

Table 5.5. Current and projected Cuban population, 2000–2025

	2000	2010*	2020*	2025*
Total population	11,187,679	11,560,891	11,793,253	11,823,899
Population structure (% of population)				
Younger than 15	21.4	18.0	16.8	16.4
15 to 19	65.0	65.2	62.9	59.8
60 and older	13.6	16.8	20.3	23.8

Source: Centro de Estudios de Población y Desarrollo, *Cuba: Proyecciónes de la población, nivel nacional y provincial. Periodo 2000–2025* (Havana: Oficina Nacional de Estadísticas, 1999).
*Projections.

Forecasts of the island's population growth in the first ten-year period of the twenty-first century cannot ignore the extremely difficult economic conditions it faced in the 1990s, and still confronts today. The fact that such international events as the collapse of the Soviet Union and the Socialist bloc, the hardening of Washington's long-maintained economic blockade, and an overall difficult external economic environment are the main causes of such internal malaise does not diminish the negative socioeconomic reality they have created domestically.[33]

The Cuban economy, because of these adverse conditions, has undergone a readjustment process that gives priority to such economic activities as tourism, the medico-pharmaceutical industry, and biotechnology, and engaging in joint ventures with foreign corporations to attract needed capital. The criteria guiding this policy have been to revive the economy as much as possible without affecting the main gains achieved under revolutionary rule.

Nonetheless, population specialists have made projections of Cuba's demographic growth for the period 2000–2025.[34] These projections have included the extant economic reality and its possible impact on population growth, particularly in fertility behavior, as well as international migration. (See table 5.5.)

The forecasts anticipate slow population growth, hardly any at all. For the eleven-year period 2000–2010 the median annual growth rate is forecasted at 0.33 percent, and for the six-year period 2020–2025 the estimate is 0.5 percent. It is estimated that by the year 2025 and thereafter the population will still be under 12 million and the number of people per household will continue to fall. The forecasts should include the aging population, a concern of the health authorities that has required expanded medical and social security services to an older population group. It is expected that by 2025 one in every four Cubans will be sixty or older. Moreover, 50 percent of the working-age population will be between forty and sixty years old, which most likely will affect the productive capability of the labor force and the economy at large.

Final Considerations

Every social- and economic-development process should consider population as a central variable. By including population in development planning, demographic policy makes the economic-strategy objectives more concrete and involves the population in an economic process that would directly affect living conditions. Hence, population policy should be considered as a system of governmentally pursued social objectives directed at improving the living standard of the population. It should serve as a means to accomplish such objectives as strengthening the population's right to work, education, and health care, as well as women's equal participation in economic activities, without resorting to control measures limiting population growth.

Cuba has developed for the last decades a system of official measures that—conceived as part of the chosen economic project—have positively affected the population's quality of life. The socioeconomic policies in place have had a strong impact on the demographic process, making it possible for a country such as Cuba, with underdeveloped economic conditions, to show demographic indicators similar to those of developed nations. Moreover, the homogeneity of economic indicators affecting the different population groups and the entire territory has made possible a system of widely distributed and nondiscriminatory access to social services.

Present demographic characteristics include (1) an improved fertility rate that still is below the replacement level and does not permit a forecast of significant gain in the next decades; (2) an aging population and labor force process; (3) a workforce deficit in rural areas; and (4) a systematic increase of life expectancy with guaranteed public access to medical services. Policymakers should relate this demographic pattern to an integral population policy that explicitly includes the demographic dimension. The population policy should consider not only global objectives but also regional and local ones—which should be helpful in effectively harmonizing the population-development relationship at all levels.[35] Given the prevailing economic conditions, population development should constitute a major challenge to Cuba for years to come.

Notes

This chapter was translated by Professor Carlos Mamani, Gannon University, Erie, Pennsylvania.

1. E. Bueno, "Desarrollo y población: El caso Cuba," in Centro de Estudios Demográficos (CEDEM), *Cuba: Interrelación entre desarrollo económico y población* (Havana: CEDEM, 1988), 1.

2. Naciones Unidas, *Informe de la Conferencia Internacional sobre Población y Desarrollo*, A/Conf.171/13 (Cairo: United Nations, 1994).

3. Ibid., 17.

4. United Nations, International Conference on Population. E/Conf.76/L3 (Mexico City: United Nations, 1984).

5. Naciones Unidas, *Informe de la Conferencia Internacional*, 13.

6. *Cuba: Informe sobre la evolución de su población y la interrelación con el desarrollo* (Havana: Documento Oficial a la Conferencia Internacional sobre Población y Desarrollo, Cairo, 1994).

7. O. Rodríguez and E. Hernández, "El crecimiento de la población," in CEDEM, *La población de Cuba* (Havana: Editorial Ciencias Sociales, 1976), 15–16.

8. R. Hernández, *Estudio sobre la formulación, implementación y evaluación de la política de población: El caso de Cuba*, Monographic Series 17 (Havana: CEDEM, 1988), 11.

9. A. Farnós, "La población y los factores socioeconómicos: El caso Cubano, un ejemplo," in CEDEM, *La población de Cuba,* chap. 10 (Havana: Editorial Ciencias Sociales, 1976), 126.

10. CEDEM, *La población;* Colectivo de Autores, *Cuba: Interrelación entre desarrollo económico y población* (Havana: CEDEM, 1988); Hernández, "Estudio sobre la formulación."

11. CEDEM, *La población,* 18–19.

12. Hernández, "Estudios sobre la formulación."

13. Comité Estatal de Estadísticas (CEE), *Anuario demográfico de Cuba, 1990* (Havana: Instituto Nacional de Estadísticas, 1992), 297.

14. S. Catasús et al., "La reproducción de la población y el desarrollo socioeconómico en Cuba," in *Cuba: Interrelación,* 87–88; A. Farnós and S. Catasús, "Las migraciones internacionales," in CEDEM, *La población,* 80; B. Morejón, "Tipos de patrones históricos de la migración Cubana hacia los Estados Unidos y características diferenciales con respecto a otros grupos Hispanos," in *La demografía Cubana ante el V Congreso* (Havana: CEDEM, 1992), 56–70.

15. Cuban Communist Party (PCC), *Primer Congreso del Partido Comunista de Cuba: Informe central* (Havana: Departamento de Orientación Revolucionaria, 1975), 51; *II Congreso del Partido Comunista de Cuba: Tésis y resoluciones* (Havana: Editorial Ciencias Sociales, 1981), 17–18; *Informe central al Tercer Congreso del Partido Comunista de Cuba* (Havana: Editora Política, 1986), 3.

16. In this case I am using the gross reproduction rate (GRR) fertility indicator, which expresses the average number of daughters that a woman has throughout her

reproductive span (from fifteen to forty-nine years of age) according to a theoretical hypothesis used by the author here. This indicator is also a measurement of population replacement.

17. CEE, *Censo de población y viviendas, 1981,* vol. 16 (Havana: Oficina Nacional del Censo, 1984); CEE, *Anuario demográfico de Cuba, 1990; Esperanza de vida en Cuba en el bienio 1988/89: Breves comentarios* (Havana: Instituto de Investigaciones Estadísticas, 1992); *Información estadística* (Havana: Instituto Nacional de Estadísticas, 1993); *Anuario demográfico de Cuba, 1993* (Havana: Instituto Nacional de Estadísticas, 1994; Centro de Estudios de Población y Desarrollo (CEPDE), *Cuba: Proyección de la población: Nivel nacional y provincial, período 1995–2015* (Havana: Oficina Nacional de Estadísticas, 1996); *Anuario demográfico de Cuba, 2000* (Havana: Oficina Nacional de Estadísticas, 2001).

18. E. Rios and A. Tejeiro, "Evolución de la mortalidad Cubana en Cuba analizando un trienio de cada década del periodo revolucionario," in *Revista Cubana de medicina general integral* (Supplement) (Havana: Centro Nacional de Información de Ciencias Médicas, 1987).

19. S. Catasús and M. Monet, "La transición de la salud y de la mortalidad en Cuba," in *Aspectos relevantes de la transición demográfica en Cuba* (Havana: CEDEM, 1994), 18–41; CEPDE, *Anuario demográfico de Cuba, 1995, Anuario demográfico de Cuba, 2000* (Havana: Oficina Nacional de Estadísticas, 1996, 2001).

20. CEE, *Anuario demográfico de Cuba, 1990;* CEPDE, *Anuario demográfico, 1995.*

21. M. Susser, "La salud y los derechos humanos: Una perspectiva epidemiológica," in *Reunión nacional de epidemiología* (Santo Domingo, Dominican Republic: Conference Proceedings, 1991).

22. CEPDE, *La población Cubana en el contexto mundial: Resumen* (Havana: Oficina Nacional de Estadísticas, 1998).

23. Ministerio de Salud Pública, *República de Cuba: Anuario estadístico de salud, 2000* (Havana: Dirección Nacional de Estadísticas, FNNAP, UNICEF, 2000).

24. H. Behm and J. A. Alfonso, *Cuba: El descenso de la fecundidad, 1964–1978* (San José, Costa Rica: Centro Latinoamericano de Demografía, 1981).

25. CEE, *Anuario demográfico de Cuba, 1990,* 134, 310.

26. CEDEM, *Aspectos relevantes de la transición demográfica en Cuba* (Havana: University of Havana, 1994), 52.

27. Farnós, "La declinación de la fecundidad," 80; CEE, *Anuario demográfico de Cuba, 1990,* 130.

28. M. Alvarez et al., *La madre soltera y la atención que recibe el niño durante su primer año de vida* (Havana: Centro de Investigaciones Psicológicas y Sociológicas de la Academia de Ciencias y Ministerio de Justicia, 1987).

29. Cuba, "Intervención del jefe de la delegación de Cuba en el debate de la Conferencia Mundial de Población efectuada en Bucarest en 1974," *Revista de Economía y Desarrollo,* no. 29 (1975): 176.

30. Ibid., 180.

31. Comisión Económica para América Latina y el Caribe (CEPAL), *Conferencia Internacional de Población,* Serie E, no. 29 (Santiago, Chile: CEPAL, 1984).

32. *Cuba: Planificación del desarrollo y política de población* (Mexico: Foro Internacional sobre Política de Población, 1987).

33. A. Farnós, "Cuba: Perspectivas demográficas en el siglo XXI," in *Aspectos relevantes de la transición demográfica en Cuba* (Havana: Centro de Estudios Demográficos, 1992), 80–81.

34. CEE, *Información estadística* (Havana: Instituto Nacional de Estadísticas, 1993); Farnós, "Perspectivas demográficas," 80–81.

35. E. Bueno, "Desarrollo y población."

III

Religion

6

The Church of the Past and
the Church of the Future

Margaret E. Crahan

Anticipation has characterized Cuba since the fall of the Soviet bloc in 1989. Both within and outside the island, politicians, analysts, business-people, and ordinary individuals have speculated about how long the Communist regime of Fidel Castro will survive. The visit of Pope John Paul II in January 1998 increased such discussion, with some suggesting parallels between the contribution of the prelate's visits to the end of Communism in Poland and the eventual demise of the Castro regime in Cuba.

Such speculation is based on the presumption that the Catholic Church in Cuba and Cuban Catholics resemble their counterparts in Eastern Europe and will play a critical role in fortifying civil society to bring down Communism.[1] Cuban realities challenge this thesis. The Catholic Church in Cuba has never had the institutional strength, nor the hold on the population, that Catholicism has in Poland. Major differences include the number of personnel, institutional resources, penetration of rural areas, nature of popular religiosity, and the historical role of the respective churches. Nevertheless, the Eastern European experience is suggestive, in terms of the possible role religion might play in any transition in Cuba. In their recent comparative study of problems of democratic transitions and consolidation in southern Europe, South America, and Communist Europe, Juan J. Linz and Alfred Stepan affirmed that fortifying civil society was a prerequisite for change and that religions could play a crucial part.[2]

> In democratic societies, religion, the churches, and the voluntary groups linked with them play an important role in bringing people together, articulating moral positions (that often have political implications) and helping to organize a variety of interests. In this respect massive secularization may weaken an active society. Communism made a deliberate effort to secularize societies, persecute religious

organizations, control and infiltrate them, and bar from elite positions those loyal to the churches.[3]

In some cases religion has played a crucial role in preparing civil societies to limit the power of governments, as well as forcing them to become more accountable and responsive to popular demands. This is particularly true in societies in which other elements of civil society are weak or relatively ineffective, such as labor, civic associations, and nongovernmental organizations (NGOs). In cases such as Cuba, the identification of mass organizations with a one-party state leaves little room for the development of autonomous sectors. While the proliferation of NGOs, especially those engaged in human rights work, is frequently considered a crucial measure of the growth of civil society, care must be taken in analyzing their degree of autonomy and commitment to democratic paradigms.[4] State subsidies for government-organized NGOs obviously create dependency even among the most change-oriented groups. State and party control of universities, research institutes, and cultural agencies, among others, tends to cause many to carefully calculate the risks to their material well-being of criticizing the existing system.

In such situations, churches are often seen as alternative institutional bases for the strengthening of civil society. However, in Cuba the historical weaknesses of the Catholic and Protestant churches militate against their playing such a role, although the limited options of other sectors such as labor, intellectuals, students, and NGOs have given religions more importance than their actual strength suggests.

In a country such as Cuba, where self-determination and autonomy have been difficult to achieve, any political system that appears to have contributed significantly to the securing of sovereignty tends to be legitimized as fulfilling national interests and aspirations. Hence, institutions or individuals that appear to be challenging that system can easily be characterized as antinationalist. Struggle for regime change therefore raises issues of national identity, patriotism, loyalty, and what it means to be a good citizen. The building of consensus on regime change becomes laden with issues of national identity and pride. In such situations, churches that support substantial modification of the status quo generally act with the utmost caution, which may appear to be the antithesis of the prophetic stances of religions in other contexts.

Polish sociologist Edmund Mokrzycki has categorized Socialism as "a social system in the strong sense of the term; it has its own equilibrium mechanisms, its own dynamics, and the ability to reproduce constitutive characteristics."[5] If a Socialist system has responded to such historical problems as intervened sovereignty, chronic socioeconomic inequalities, and dependent development, significant portions of the citizenry may consider such a system worth retaining, even if they reject Communism. In the Cuban case, the option for Socialism is closely identified with the assertion of national sovereignty in the face of an extended colonial and neocolonial past, as well as with some socioeconomic advances particularly in education and health care. Furthermore, the definition of democracy may be regarded as more closely linked to that of Socialism than that of capitalism. A Cuban government official asserted that true democracy is constituted by national independence, defense of the rights of citizens, equality, and popular participation in political and economic power. Such democracy needs to be defended without risking the nation's independence and socialist economy, and/or the security of the country or the revolution. Hence, the champions of democracy should never place themselves in opposition to national security, Socialism, or the revolution, the requirements for which are determined by the government.[6] That means any claims churches make to be the arbiters of what is moral in politics and society can be potentially dangerous if the churches seek to change the revolutionary order.

The role the Polish Roman Catholic Church played as a societal legitimator, or more accurately delegitimator, was substantially different from that of the Cuban churches. Under Communism the former enjoyed more autonomy than the latter, in large measure because of the greater institutional strength and popular support of the church in Poland. This caused the government in Poland to recognize the Catholic Church as having power to contend with to an extent not true in Cuba. Evidence of this is that in 1956 the Polish Communist government permitted religious education in the public schools, something the Cuban Catholic Church has requested but has been denied. In addition, the religious press in Poland was allowed to operate relatively unfettered, whereas in Cuba it has been restricted. Even in the 1990s when there was greater flexibility on the part of the Castro government, church publications could run afoul of officials if they were regarded as taking positions contrary to the revolution. As Linz and Stepan have noted, the role of religion in the Polish case was exceptional, given that the state conceded ground to it even in terms of ideological hegemony.[7] But with the historically high rates of secularization in Cuba and the weaknesses of the institutional churches, religion has never had the capacity to challenge the consolidation and projection of the Castro regime's political and ideological power.[8]

Even if the Catholic Church were stronger in Cuba, it is unlikely that civil society could play a role comparable to its role in the democratic transition in Poland, where numerous horizontal relationships within civil society were conducive to building consensus around an agenda for change. Not only were students, intellectuals, and professionals highly organized and mobilized, but the independent labor union Solidarity had 10 million members at its height in the 1980s.[9] As Linz and Stepan noted:

> In Poland's self-organized society, people dared to organize, act, think, and live, in the famous phrase of Adam Michnik, "as if they were free." Indeed, the power and legitimacy of Solidarity after one year of existence was such that Stefan Kania, first Secretary after Gierek and before Jaruzelski, took pains to deny that a situation of dual power existed in Poland (i.e., between the collapsing party and Solidarity). In Gramscian terms, Solidarity in the fall of 1981 possessed hegemony in civil society, and the party maintained its power only to the extent that it controlled the coercive forces of the army; and the security services and the shadow of the Soviet Union limited a challenge to the regime.[10]

Nothing comparable to Solidarity exists in Cuba either in the labor sector or elsewhere. While some small groups of workers have organized outside the confines of the state- and party-dominated Cuban Confederation of Workers, their number is infinitesimal compared with Solidarity. With a weak NGO and civic sector, that leaves religion as the strongest element within civil society, albeit with substantial limitations.

This study, as a consequence, discusses the future role of religion in Cuba by first analyzing whether or not the Catholic and Protestant churches in Cuba have the capacity to help promote a democratic transition. Second, it examines the current status of church-state relations in an effort to determine whether or not the churches have sufficient autonomy, credibility, and operational space not only to help determine the nature of any transition but also to contribute effectively to long-term democratization.

In order to accomplish this, this chapter also takes into account the difficulties of even strong churches in promoting democratic consolidation in Communist contexts. A recent study, *Gott Nach Dem Kommunismus*, by Professors Paul Zulehner and Miklós Tomka of the Pastoral Forum in Vienna, Austria, argues that the contribution of religion to democratization is linked to churches having "strong institutional structures closely tied to national identity."[11]

The authors note that churches in Eastern Europe that had vigorous command structures and allowed for less internal flexibility survived Communism better than more adaptable and democratic ones. These same characteristics, however, undercut their capacity to adapt and contribute to democratic consolidation. In addition, limited internal response even to the modernization and democratization stimuli of Vatican II inclined them to continue to look to the state in the post-Communist period to achieve institutional objectives. This tended to undercut the credibility of churches in the newly democratizing, more pluralistic societies of Eastern Europe. Fear of the free play of democracy caused some sectors of the churches to be regarded as antidemocratic, which diminished their influence. Overall, few of the Catholic or Protestant churches were well prepared, institutionally or theologically, to be a major force in the consolidation of democracy, although some, as in Poland, played important roles in the transition. This raises the question of whether further democratization will strengthen the churches or marginalize them. The experience of Eastern Europe highlights the issue of whether the institutional churches in Cuba are equipped not only to promote a democratic transition but also to effectively confront the challenges posed by the arduous process of democratic consolidation.

The Status of Institutional Religion

Prior to the 1959 revolution Cuba had the weakest Catholic Church presence, as well as the highest level of Protestant penetration, of any Latin American country. In addition, a fair proportion of the population practiced spiritism, rooted in African or nineteenth-century European practices.[12] Cuba was also considered the most secular society in Latin America in the 1950s. A 1953 survey found that 72.5 percent of Cubans identified themselves as Catholics with 24 percent attending Mass occasionally. Approximately 25 percent consulted spirits.[13] Church-based priests numbered about eight hundred sixty, while there were over three thousand nuns and priests largely engaged in educational rather than pastoral work. Just prior to the revolution there were slightly more than 9 priests for every 1,000 Cubans; today the ratio is about 1 to 44,000.[14]

At the outset of the revolution in 1959, Catholics reflected generalized support for the government, particularly given widespread opposition to the dictatorship of Fulgencio Batista (1952–58). However, by the middle of that year opposition from within the church was coalescing around three prime issues: land reform, the government's plan to increase its control of education, and allegations of Communist influence within the revolutionary leadership. Tensions boiled over at the National Catholic Congress in November 1959 for which a reported one million people turned out, including Fidel Castro. José Ignacio Lasaga, a lay leader, summed up the sentiments of many when he exhorted the crowd: "Social justice, yes; redemption of the worker, yes; Communism, no!" The crowd responded by shouting *"Cuba si, Comunismo no!"* and the gathering passed a resolution opposing all totalitarianisms.[15]

Thereafter tensions between the Catholic Church and the state escalated, with priests denouncing the revolution from the pulpit, services being disrupted by government supporters, and an increasing number of clergy, religious, and laity leaving the country. On May 1, 1961, private schools were nationalized on the grounds that a number of them had been used to prepare for the insurrection that was supposed to accompany the Bay of Pigs invasion the previous April; this further stimulated the exodus. A 1969 survey of Catholic parishes in urban Havana projected that by 1972, 50–70 percent of parishioners would have left Cuba.[16]

Similarly, Protestants demonstrated high levels of disaffection over the direction of the revolutionary government, and large numbers of pastors and the faithful migrated. In 1958 church officials estimated that there were one hundred fifty to two hundred fifty thousand Protestants in the country, primarily Baptists, Episcopalians, Methodists, and Presbyterians, as well as Quakers. All denominations suffered massive declines in the 1960s, except for the Baptists, who lost fewer of their pastors and hence were better able to maintain their congregations.[17]

As revolutionary fervor increased so did discrimination, particularly in the workplace and schools. The creation of the Military Units to Aid Production (UMAP) in the mid-1960s, a manual labor program for tramps, pimps, homosexuals, common criminals, and conscientious objectors, including seminarians, was regarded by a good number of church people as evidence of the government's antireligious sentiments. In 1966 a Baptist minister, the Reverend Raimundo García Franco, wrote that his experience in UMAP had forced him to call upon all his psychological and spiritual resources and had thereby strengthened his faith. He also stated that it had helped him better understand nonbelievers. García Franco and others reported that they had been dismayed by the failure of church officials to maintain contact with them both during and after their internment.[18] UMAP was disbanded in the late 1960s, partly due to public opposition.

As in Eastern Europe, the onset and consolidation of a Communist regime prompted the Catholic and Protestant churches to retreat into themselves and become marginalized. The exodus of clergy and laity abroad reinforced the churches' sense of being under siege and without influence. This encouraged passivity and discouraged institutional evolution theologically, pastorally, and politically. By the late 1960s, however, pragmatism led church leaders to attempt to increase the influence of the churches on Cuban society, with the Catholic bishops issuing two pastoral letters in 1969 aimed at helping the church shed its counterrevolutionary image and encouraging lay people to involve themselves in community activities that sought to promote the common good. The Protestant churches also sought rapprochement via greater involvement in revolutionary projects and adoption of new theological trends, including liberation theology, that legitimized Socialism. Such efforts were met by positive government responses, including Fidel Castro's raising in 1972 the possibility of strategic alliances between Marxists and Christians, who, he asserted, "both wish to struggle on behalf of man, for the happiness of man."[19]

In September 1972 the Cuban Council of Evangelical Churches (CIEC) sponsored a meeting of Protestant leaders to discuss the role of religion in the revolutionary process. This led to a meeting between CIEC and government officials in an effort to communicate the denominations' interest in improving church-state relations.[20] Some Protestants were critical of such overtures, and this contributed to the 1974 withdrawal of the Episcopal Church from the council. Nor did these efforts eliminate the revolutionary cadres' suspicions of religion. However, there was increased communication between church and state.

The adoption in 1976 of a new Constitution that designated the state as Socialist and propounded a materialist concept of the universe helped clarify the status of religion. While religious freedom was guaranteed, it was to be within the law and could not be used to undercut the revolution. Some church leaders expressed satisfaction that the government's official position on religion was finally spelled out. The rector of the Catholic seminary in Havana, Father José Manuel Miyares, stated that "it is extremely . . . consoling to see that . . . all types of coercion and discrimination against believers [are] clearly proscribed."[21]

The government's attitude toward religion was further elucidated in resolutions at the First Party Congress of the Cuban Communist Party in 1975, the 1978 party platform, the Second Congress of the Cuban Communist Party in December 1980, the party congress in 1991, and the 1992 reform of the 1976 Constitution. In the mid-1970s the official position was that the struggle for a scientific view of the world was subordinated to the task of constructing a new society in which "believers, nonbelievers, members of religious orders, and atheists have participated, continue to participate, and must necessarily participate."[22]

In short, the realization of revolutionary ideals required that all Cubans, whatever their beliefs, participate. The government's desire for ideological hegemony was contextualized into Cuban realities, particularly given the historic tendency toward high levels of religious belief, if not practice. Hence, the dissemination of historical and dialectical materialism had to allow individual religious beliefs. However, membership in the Communist Party and Young Communist League was to be limited to those who accepted Marxism-Leninism. This effectively excluded those who were religiously active from influential roles in government, education, the media, and other value-molding institutions.

The 1978 party platform reaffirmed official acceptance of liberty of conscience and religious freedom within the law and the demands of the revolution. It specifically condemned use of religion to oppose Socialism. While it criticized antireligious and discriminatory actions against believers, it also reaffirmed scientific materialism as the official ideology and proscribed attempts to use religion as a competing ideology. It also praised the increasing involvement of Christians in liberation movements and strategic alliances between church people and Marxists, as did the 1980 Second Party Congress. Both supported increased opportunities for international ecclesiastical exchanges that exposed Cubans to post–Vatican II trends, particularly among progressive sectors in the rest of Latin America.

Such positions allowed for more space for the Cuban churches, which helped them reduce their marginalization and strengthen themselves institutionally. Nevertheless, unlike in Poland, they continued to have no influence over public education, nor did they have access to the media. Hence, the 1970s witnessed a very slow recouping of both the churches' membership and their role within society. In 1979, for example, the Methodist Church stabilized at about two thousand members as compared to 10,347 members in 1960, and recruitment by the Protestant seminary in Matanzas totaled six students.[23]

While some Cuban Christians favored engaging in dialogue and cooperation with the revolutionary government to achieve the common good, there was also a clear ideological divide, and the state by and large exercised ideological hegemony. Nevertheless, many Cubans continued to believe in a supreme being even if they were not, or never had been, churchgoers. A 1988 survey of seven Cuban provinces revealed that three-quarters (75.8 percent) of Cubans continued to hold religious beliefs.[24]

The churches by the late 1970s wanted to play a less marginal role in society, particularly in view of what they regarded as a rise in moral decay and debasement of traditional values related to family and community. As a result, they became increasingly more inclined to criticize societal defects, if not governmental ones, while at the same time reaffirming their support for the revolution. Such attitudes were reflected at the Catholic Church's 1986 National Cuban Church Encounter (ENEC), the first such gathering since the 1959 National Catholic Congress. Rooted in a nationwide process of reflection in local parishes and church groups that got underway in the early 1980s, the meeting reviewed church history and criticized both the institution's failure to support social justice more actively in the pre-1959 period and its counterrevolutionary stance after 1959. Strongly reflecting the mandate propounded by Vatican II (1963–65) and the Latin American bishops' conferences in Medellín (1968) and Puebla (1979) to engage the world more directly, ENEC emphasized the promotion of peace, disarmament, sustainable development, a new international economic and social order, and increased East-West understanding. With respect to Cuba strong concern was expressed over corruption, fraud, theft, abuse of social property, irresponsibility of workers, abortion, sexual license, and alcoholism. Change of both individuals and societies was to be achieved through intense evangelizing. The objective was to make clear to Cubans the relevance of the Scriptures to Cuban realities in order to stimulate dialogue and thereby create a consensus that would lead to increased efforts to improve societal welfare.[25] ENEC asserted the church's commitment to reconciliation, justice, and the perfectibility of the individual within a context in which the task of assuring socioeconomic justice had been appropriated by a Socialist revolution.

Recognizing both the enormity of the church's task and its limitations, ENEC prioritized institutional strengthening and preparation of the laity to participate more actively in society through intensive religious formation. Both tasks were facilitated by a resurgence in membership, increased material and personnel resources from abroad, and a growing disposition on the part of the government to allow the churches more space, particularly as the state required help in providing social welfare assistance. The latter encouraged the 1991 decision of the Communist Party to admit believers and the 1992 reform of the Constitution that defined the state as secular rather than atheist. This did not, however, encourage many church people to join the party, although three prorevolutionary Protestant ministers ran for and were elected to the National Assembly in the 1990s.

Church growth intensified in that decade. Ecclesiastical commentators attributed this to a number of factors, especially the impact of socioeconomic crisis within a spiritual and ideological vacuum. The crumbling of the Socialist world and the revolutionary dream, they felt, created a thirst for spiritual certainties and psychological support. Some new members were searching for alternative spaces for their own well-being and to find more meaning in their lives. A good number wanted to reencounter traditional values and reasons to hope for a better future. Those congregations that offered dynamic liturgies and a strong sense of community grew apace. Among those who filled the pews were some who had previously been churchgoers and with the 1991 and 1992 government reforms felt freer to attend services. Others came from nonreligious backgrounds and included large numbers of young people, educated by the revolution but reportedly frustrated with both its material and ideological limitations. Some migrated from congregation to congregation searching for answers to a persistent sense of anomie.[26] An official of the Communist Party's Office of Attention to Religious Affairs concluded that the main reason for the growth of churches was that "the churches are doing their work and doing it well."[27]

Some new faiths also began operating within Cuba, but it was the historical denominations that reflected the greatest changes. Catholic baptisms increased from 26,534 in 1986 to 70,081 in 1994. By the mid-1990s there were some six hundred fifty congregations and over two hundred mission houses served by two hundred forty priests. The two Catholic seminaries had approximately eighty seminarians, a number that would increase even more by the year 2000. Some four hundred seventy nuns worked in state hospitals, asylums, and orphanages. In 1998 the government issued visas for some forty foreign priests and religious. Lay movements were expanding, but ecumenism less so.[28]

In 1991 the international Catholic charity CARITAS began functioning in Cuba. By the mid-1990s it was providing substantial amounts of medical and food assistance. Another important advance was the creation of a number of Catholic publications and the expansion of diocesan and parish newsletters. Of note were *Vivarium,* established by the Archdiocese of Havana with a strongly intellectual and cultural emphasis, and *Vitral* of the Diocese of Pinar del Rio, both of which focused on the intersection of religious, cultural, and civic issues. The latter was part of that diocese's efforts to strengthen religious formation and disseminate Catholic social doctrine to the ordinary individual. The church in Pinar del Rio also encouraged the formation of professional cadres with religious beliefs who might assume influential roles in any future government.

Protestant churches experienced a similar resurgence. According to ecclesiastical sources, by the late 1990s there were 552 new congregations, together with some three thousand *casas culto* or house churches. These were served by over eight hundred pastors, sixty-four of whom were women. In 1996 there were two hundred Protestant seminarians with another three hundred people taking extension courses.[29] In 1996 Protestant and Catholic leaders toured Cuba together with party leaders to evaluate the state of church buildings, which led to the repair or remodeling of over five hundred of them, largely through foreign assistance.[30] That same year 162,277 Bibles were distributed throughout the island with government permission.[31]

Spiritualism also experienced growth. As the economic situation declined even before the end of Soviet aid, particular attention was paid to the annual predictions of santería leaders, as individuals searched for reassurance that their lives would improve.[32] The Jewish community expanded, even in the absence of rabbis. Interest in religious studies spread, with courses being offered at the University of Havana and research being sponsored by both church and state. Indeed, one expert remarked that religion went from being an underestimated topic in the social sciences in the 1960s and 1970s to being a major interest by the 1990s.[33] A 1998 meeting of religious studies experts in Havana organized by the Center for Psychological and Sociological Studies (CIPS) was attended by over two hundred Cuban specialists from both the churches and secular institutions.

The January 1998 visit of Pope John Paul II highlighted not only the increased strength of the Catholic Church but also of religion generally in Cuba. It also was a clear indication of a conjunction of interests on the part of church and state. A prime reason for the pope's visit was to fortify the Catholic Church institutionally so that it could capitalize on the increased space that government reforms, as well as government weaknesses, had allowed. Prior to the 1990s the church had not felt as ready to assume a major role in the analysis of Cuban problems, nor in the devising of solutions for them. The desire to do so flowed, in part, from fear of increased moral decay and conflict within Cuban society. The Catholic Church was also preoccupied with the possibility of a destabilizing transition, as was the government. In addition, church leaders wanted to promote reconciliation both within Cuba and with the émigré community.

For the government, John Paul II's visit was not only an opportunity to focus attention on Cuba and undercut charges of religious persecution; it was also an opportunity to increase international opposition to the U.S. embargo. The position of the Catholic Church, as well as the Protestant churches and Jewish and spiritualist communities, was that the embargo was immoral and illegal under international law. In addition, the Catholic Church and the government were preoccupied by the growth of nontraditional religions in Cuba, including Pentecostals.[34] Castro appears much more at ease dealing with the highly centralized and hierarchical Catholic

Church than with the diverse, decentralized, and sui generis new churches. His 1985 book, *Fidel y la religión,* also suggests that he believes he has an intrinsic understanding of the Catholic Church and how it operates.[35]

The pope's visit also eased the way for a nationwide Protestant celebration in May–June of 2000. Protestant leaders both before and after the pope's visit made the point to government representatives that their churches deserved as much attention as the Catholic Church. In addition, it was also felt, as one Protestant leader stated, "Without the visit of the pope to Cuba, the Evangelical Celebration would not have been accomplished to the extent that it was."[36] Forty-nine Protestant groups mounted eighteen gatherings all over the island with an estimated five hundred thousand in attendance. The process of putting together the celebrations encouraged cross-denominational dialogue that promoted ecumenism and some consensus building. In addition, it helped reduce misunderstandings between the historical Protestant denominations and newer ones, a factor that strengthened the Cuban Council of Churches (CEC). Like the pope's January 1998 visit, the public impact helped diminish barriers to believers and stimulated considerable curiosity over the churches' agendas. Since the government allowed television coverage, the celebrations were widely viewed, as the pope's visit had been.[37]

Both of these events were aimed at capitalizing on the increased space available for religious activities in order to reassert the churches' role as moral leaders and legitimizers in Cuban society. They were also intended to revitalize the churches institutionally and disseminate their social doctrines and normative values in order to help transform a society in crisis. The Catholic and Protestant churches were intent not only on dealing with the obvious ills of Cuban society but also on playing roles in whatever transition might occur.

In Cuba in the 1990s and since, it has been increasingly clear that as revolutionary support has eroded and the country has become more difficult to govern, Castro has increasingly turned to the churches, among others, to shore up the legitimacy of the state, as well as to assume some social welfare functions. The inability of the Socialist state to meet the socioeconomic needs of all citizens undermined the principal claim to legitimacy of the revolutionary government. In light of this, the opportunity for religions to reassert themselves and offer alternative societal models increased. The degree to which they would be successful in such an enterprise, however, is related not only to the relative weakness of the government but also to the churches' deficits, as well as to their links to other sectors of civil society and the state of the latter. Hence, the capacity of institutional religion to emerge as a major actor in the democratization of Cuba remains problematic.

Religion and Change

In order to effect, as well as affect, societal change, churches must meet certain prerequisites.[38] Prime among these is a clear-cut agenda rooted in a broad-based consensus both within and outside the church. To mobilize support for such an agenda, churches must enjoy sufficient autonomy and credibility to legitimize the agenda; the necessary resources to convince a critical mass, although not necessarily a majority of society, to accept it or at least not oppose it; the expertise to devise tactics and strategies adequate to successfully promote it; and a long-term commitment to it in the face of changing circumstances both within and outside the denomination. The Cuban Catholic bishops, as well as some Protestant leaders, have periodically mentioned the need for a national dialogue to produce such a consensus-based agenda, although it has not yet been accomplished. In cases where a national dialogue has been successful in assisting democratization, such as in El Salvador in the 1980s and Guatemala in the 1990s, there was a strong disposition to communicate seriously and meet with those with whom there were real differences. Such dialogues contributed to peace processes and accords in both countries, with the churches playing substantial roles in using them to build pressure for good-faith negotiations.[39]

To date the Cuban churches have not had the leadership capacity to generate such a dialogue, nor is civil society in a position to take advantage of such an initiative. This obviously impedes the devising of any broad-based consensual agenda. The Catholic and Protestant churches have focused their efforts on the inculcation and nourishing of hope among Cubans. Cuba in the 1990s witnessed not only an economic downturn but also an upsurge in alienation and anomie within society, as well as a crisis of values related to family and community solidarity. The family, which traditionally was a key element of social cohesion, had been eroded by high rates of divorce, generational conflict, and mental health problems. One study suggested that the economic crisis of the early 1990s prompted some families to conceive of themselves as microenterprises in which children became prime instruments of survival, even through illegal activities.[40]

One leading Protestant minister, the Reverend Carlos Camps Cruell, suggested that the role of the churches should be to provide an "oxygenated space" in society to help revitalize people and prepare them to experience hope, so that they could devise an agenda for change. A committed revolutionary, Camps saw lack of hope and lack of vision as the principal deficits in Cuban society. Without hope, he believed, it would be impossible to successfully seek new options and models to achieve justice. It was through the Gospel message, he argued, that hope could be restored by reaffirming the message that in God a full and abundant life is possible.[41] The latter, however, should not be construed as encouraging inertia, but rather an active search for solutions for the ills of society, both spiritual and material.

Camps further explored the role of churches in Cuba by suggesting that like spouses, church and state should be "inconvenient friends." In any country, he argued, religions have the prophetic responsibility of insisting that the state see to societal well-being and justice for all. Furthermore, churches have the responsibility of accompanying and assisting the state in the struggle to achieve the common good. Church and state have the obligation, therefore, of being inconvenient friends and pointing out the other's errors. A principal task of the churches, he insisted, is to help generate concrete visions of the future based on present realities, as well as infusing those visions with the promise of salvation, thereby generating hope.[42]

The agenda of the Catholic hierarchy is more directly critical than the Protestant churches of Cuban society and the government. In the midst of the economic crisis of the early 1990s, the Catholic bishops issued a pastoral letter (September 8, 1993) entitled "Love Hopes All Things." In it they defined the roles of church and state:

> Revitalizing hope among Cubans is a duty of those responsible for the government and the future of Cuba; it is also a duty of the church, which is separated from the state, as it should be, but not from society. Together we can do so with a great willingness to sacrifice by "loving more intensely and teaching how to love, with trust in human beings, and confiding in God's fatherly aid and in the innate power of good," as Paul VI said.[43]

A year later, during a periodic "ad limina" visit to Rome to report to the pope, Cardinal Jaime Ortega y Alamino described the task of the Cuban church as the instilling of love, truth, reconciliation, and hope, particularly in view of the failure of the revolutionary dream. Given that the revolution had raised so much hope, mobilized a people, and awakened dormant consciences, the church recognized a duty to help preserve the advances of the revolution. At the same time it also had an obligation to help the Cuban people transcend their limitations, particularly by increasing popular participation in political and economic decision making. The latter was to be stimulated by intense evangelizing so that the laity would be better prepared to act through a mobilized civil society.[44]

In order to implement the Catholic Church's goal of revitalization of hope, and hence of civil society, the bishops' conference devised a Global Pastoral Plan, 1997–2000. Its principal objectives were:

1. to promote evangelizing via prophetic, participatory, and inculturated communities in order to disseminate the Gospel message and thereby promote human dignity, reconciliation, and contributions to the construction of a society characterized by love and justice;
2. to organize a national plan for Christian formation that, together with the strengthening of church communities, could serve as a promoter of evangelization and sign of love and reconciliation; and
3. to instill greater consciousness that all individuals are children of God, which requires that all be treated justly.[45]

The Global Pastoral Plan set forth a program that included organizing periodic missions and preparing evangelizing agents and materials; developing a catechesis for different stages of belief; mounting dynamic liturgies to demonstrate the insertion of spirituality into Cuban life; developing a theology of reconciliation; educating to encourage dialogue and to search for ways for Cuban society to develop; promoting common actions by diverse sociocultural sectors; emphasizing the service aspect of the church; creating a theological-pastoral commission that would illuminate the content of ecclesiastical goals; studying Cuban culture to discern its values and integrate them into pastoral programs; promoting spaces for church and social participation; and celebrating the faith in a more participatory manner that reflected Cuban realities.[46]

This ambitious plan did not, however, satisfy everyone in the Catholic Church, including some priests who in mid-1999 circulated a strong critique of both the hierarchy and the government. They condemned the latter as totalitarian and the former for not doing enough to challenge it, nor supporting dissidents sufficiently. The priests recommended tackling the Cuban political, economic, and moral crisis by

1. becoming more Christian by living more in accord with the Scriptures;
2. focusing on tensions generated by the increased number of foreign clergy who added to existing issues caused by generational and secular-regular differences;

3. devoting more attention to Cuba's problems;
4. devising a specific agenda to achieve church objectives and depending less on improvisation; and
5. becoming more active in opposing injustice, oppression, and the culture of fear and passivity in Cuba.

In addition, the clerics argued that with the improved economic situation of the Catholic Church came the obligation of administrative transparency and greater participation on the part of the clergy and laity in determining ecclesial economic priorities. Finally, they felt the church's calls over the previous twenty years for a national dialogue were flawed since they were based upon the government's willingness to dialogue. Instead the church should pursue a national dialogue that included civil society sectors such as other churches, fraternal organizations, and autonomous groups.

The priests concluded that while the visit of Pope John Paul II in January 1998 had been a boon for religion in Cuba, the Catholic Church had been unprepared to fully capitalize on it, in large measure because it lacked a plan to do so.[47] Senior church officials were perturbed by the priests' letter and suggested that it was politically inconvenient and reflected the opinions of only a handful of clerics. Nevertheless, on a number of occasions the prelates admitted that fewer advances had been made as a result of the pope's visit than they had hoped.

Indeed, on the second anniversary of John Paul II's visit, the Cuban bishops' conference issued a pastoral letter entitled "A New Heaven and a New Earth," calling for Cubans to mobilize to substantially change their society. The prelates argued that salvation requires the transcending of boundaries and forging ahead in search of new possibilities even without a plan. Cubans, they asserted, were caught between something that was losing meaning and the uncertainty of new beginnings. The pope's call to celebrate the millennium as a new beginning had, they asserted, special meaning for Cubans since it required a more critical look at Cuban realities. The bishops admitted that it was difficult to detach from the past and embrace an unknown future, as well as hard to perceive God's presence in Cuban society. In addition, there existed real obstacles to new initiatives both from within and outside the country. Nevertheless, legal means had to be found to encourage greater popular participation in reforming society. Such a task required the involvement of all citizens in discussing economic, political, social, and cultural issues, which made dialogue and reconciliation to build consensus even more important.[48]

While the enormity of the task was recognized in the pastoral letter, the strategies the bishops opted for were more hortatory than pragmatic. The prelates focused on evangelization to stimulate prophetic communities that would be more participatory and to promote human dignity and reconciliation. In particular, they felt, there had to be a greater integration of evangelization and social commitment, as well as a strengthening of the social welfare activities of the church. The bishops invoked the words of John Paul II during his visit, asserting that "Cuba needs to find a gradual and peaceful way to construct a new society."[49]

What do such exhortations and pastoral plans mean in reality? A brief look at activities in the dioceses of Camaguey and Pinar del Rio suggests some progress in religious formation and generalized outreach. For example, the Father Ramón Clapers Center for Religious Formation in Camaguey organized well-attended courses in the late 1990s for children, youths, and adults, based on materials donated by the Catholic Church in Mexico. In 1999 and after, periodic spiritual retreats were attended by several hundred children and youths. In addition, summer camps, festivals, and sporting events were arranged for young people that combined recreation with evangelization. That same year public processions were held in honor of the patroness of Cuba, La Virgen de la Caridad del Cobre, at which the national anthem was sung, in part to reaffirm that church people were patriots too. Christmas festivities included some public events, and each community in the diocese without a priest received a crèche donated by a German church group. Foreign and Cuban religious were active within the diocese engaging in religious, cultural, and social service activities. Three Passionist novices were consecrated in August 1999, while one Oblate nun was inducted, reflecting a generalized increase in Cuban vocations.[50]

Similar flurries of activity occurred within the Protestant churches, some of which were notable for their focus on infusing Cuban society with progressive social doctrine. Two ecumenical groups were especially active, namely, the Christian Center for Reflection and Dialogue in Cardenas and the Martin Luther King Jr. Center in Havana. Both were supportive of the revolution, with the former directed by the Reverend Raimundo García Franco, the Baptist minister who had been interned in UMAP in the mid-1960s. The King Center was also headed by a Baptist minister, the Reverend Raúl Suárez, who is one of three Protestant clerics serving in Cuba's National Assembly. Both have focused on community organizing and leadership training, as well as on meeting social welfare needs. The Cardenas Center has a large meals on wheels program for the elderly, while the Havana Center has organized grassroots and community organizing programs for people of all ages. Both have also been active in organizing environmental and self-help groups, particularly emphasizing training community leaders including young people. In addition, the centers organized conferences, seminars, and courses focusing on the role of churches and church people in Cuba today. Their publications emphasized related topics.[51]

Such publications took advantage of increased openness since the late 1990s to disseminate church positions to a growing audience. However, there were limits to the freedom they enjoyed, as witnessed by the experience of the periodical *Vitral*, published by the Catholic Center for Civic and Religious Formation of the Diocese of Pinar del Rio. Established in 1994 it undertook to carve out space to disseminate diverse opinions on issues of interest to ordinary Cubans. In particular, it wanted to provide an outlet for articles by individuals who differed in terms of their philosophies, ideologies, and religious beliefs. Most of its contributors were young professionals and artists, as well as some workers, many of whom were not Catholic. By 1997 *Vitral* had come under such strong criticism by local and national government and party officials that a meeting was arranged on May 14, 1997, at the provincial headquarters of the government of Pinar del Rio. Present were the vice president of the provincial government, the secretary of the provincial council, the head of the Communist Party's provincial political-ideological department, the functionary who oversaw religious affairs, representatives of the Central Committee's Office of Attention to Religious Affairs and of the Ideological Committee of the Young Communists, an expert in religious studies, and an economist, as well as the editorial board of the periodical. The purpose was to communicate concern over criticisms *Vitral* had made of government policies. The government and party delegation held that 30 percent of the articles appeared impartial, while 60 percent distorted Cuban realities. They also alleged that the majority of the articles constituted attacks on the government, with the intention of changing it. Furthermore, the officials disputed *Vitral*'s supposed characterization of the Cuban people as enslaved, anguished, and seeking to be free. The officials claimed that the opinions expressed reinforced right-wing opponents of the revolution.[52]

In response, the representatives of *Vitral* insisted that their purpose was simply to fulfill the exhortation of Vatican II to develop pastoral work that reflected the intersection of faith and society, as well as faith and culture. In addition, the 1986 ENEC meeting had encouraged the creation of "a space for transparency and the multicolored light of Cuban culture and society."[53] The publication aspired to reflect the diversity of opinions not only within the Catholic Church but also within Cuban society. It was not intended to be a political or scholarly journal; hence its articles were not written by experts, but rather by ordinary individuals. In fact, it wanted to reach those who did not go to conferences or scholarly seminars. The editorial team made clear that while they published criticisms, their intent was not to oppose the revolution but to make it more responsive to Cuban citizens. Nor were they recommending a neoliberal economic model instead of Socialism, as charged.[54]

The discussion between the officials and the *Vitral* representatives clearly demonstrated the ideological divide between the state and one of the most change-oriented sectors of the Catholic Church. In contrast to the officials, the editorial team regarded the airing of criticisms of the government as making the revolution more democratic and thereby more likely to endure. *Vitral*'s defenders also felt it contributed to civic education, particularly by informing citizens of their rights and duties, as well as the complexities of the problems facing their society. In this way the editorial board felt it was promoting the revolutionary and Christian ideal of seeking the perfectibility of society.[55]

In their hopes of stimulating dialogue and increased popular participation in Cuba, the *Vitral* representatives challenged the ideological and political hegemony of the Castro government in the midst of an economic crisis. They clearly intended to mold opinions and stimulate citizen activism around a change-oriented agenda, albeit the latter was not clearly defined. They offered no specific options but rather called for ordinary Cubans to take their fate into their own hands. In a society with the level of political, ideological, and social control Cuba has, this was remarkable. It also was clearly regarded as threatening the hegemony of the government. While the Castro regime viewed *Vitral* as a dissident and partisan voice, its editorial board felt that by giving space to diverse opinions they were being nonpartisan and were operating within the revolution. The government continued to disagree and in 2000 Fidel Castro publicly criticized *Vitral* for violating the boundaries of legitimate criticism.

The attitude of Cuban church officials to *Vitral* varies, reflecting a lack of consensus within the church over both an agenda for change and strategies to accomplish it. There appears to be satisfaction on the part of some that the publication challenged the ideological hegemony of the government, although they do not publicly support the editorial board. Other senior officials are uncomfortable with the opinions the magazine publishes and regard it as causing unnecessary problems for the church. Still others feel that it is playing a useful role in expanding the boundaries of the political space currently available, especially at a time when the legitimacy of the government has seriously eroded. However, in the increasing competition to define a national agenda, neither the Catholic Church nor the Protestant churches have offered an agenda that is agreed upon by their own institutions, much less that reflects a broad-based consensus within society.

The competition for legitimacy between church and state in terms of representing the aspirations of the Cuban people was further complicated by the Elián González case in 1999–2000. As Castro himself recognized, the situation provided an excellent opportunity to recoup support and to mobilize the entire country in support of the government, as the defender not only of parental rights but also of national sovereignty.[56] In addition, the government gained as a result of increased mobilization of the general public around the issue and the incorporation of many youths and children into the movement. The erosion of popular support for the government and increasing disaffection were somewhat arrested. The churches supported the government on the issue.

But the benefits of the Elián González case faded, and church and state again competed to define Cuba's agenda for the future. While there has been a resurgence of religion in Cuba at a time when the erosion of the government has opened up opportunities, the churches have not, either individually or collectively, enunciated a consensual agenda based on a common strategy. Divisions within churches, such as that evidenced by the 1999 statement of some Catholic priests, or among religions as witnessed by the ongoing tensions between the historical denominations and newer faiths, suggest that it will be difficult to achieve a common agenda beyond the most general terms. Such an agenda might serve to legitimize change, but not to define its nature. The vagueness of church statements is reinforced by the denominations' commitment to the salvation of all. While this has a certain logic, given the churches' transcendental goals, it does not provide a basis for broad-based mobilization of Cubans, most of whom do not identify with the churches. Add to this the concern of virtually all of the denominations with their institutional weaknesses, and consensus building is further hampered. Moreover, the caution of most churches reinforces the passivity of the citizenry. The low level of organization and lack of strong leadership of Cuban civil society, together with the absence of horizontal alliances, undercuts the possibility of mobilization sufficient to effect change.

The Catholic and Protestant churches in Cuba, by and large, do not appear to want radical change. In general, they accept the Socialist option, while rejecting Communism. Thus they avoid identifying themselves with government opponents with a more clear-cut ideological alternative. Given the extent of alienation and passivity in Cuban society today, the likelihood that a strategy based on evangelization could result in substantial mobilization is unlikely. In short, the situation is unlike that which existed in Poland where a strong church joined with mobilized civil society led by a large labor movement to undercut a Communist regime. Even with those advantages, the consolidation of democracy in Poland has been difficult.

In Cuba the possibility that religion can play a major role in democratization is even more limited. Change may come more as a result of circumstances than as a result of the actions of churches. The question that remains is to what degree they will be able to influence, as well as adapt to, change. Given weak churches and a frail civil society, strategic alliances would be necessary but also possibly unstable if no strong leadership emerges. In such a situation, the churches would require a great deal of skill to infuse society with their values and social doctrine. In addition, while more and more people are joining the churches in the new century, there is no strong evidence that the efforts at religious formation are creating the cadres necessary to mold a new government. This suggests that religion in Cuba may facilitate change but not channel it to the degree the churches hope. Nor does it guarantee that the churches will be well prepared to adapt to a more participatory, conflictual, and democratic society.

Notes

1. For reasons of space this chapter focuses on institutional religions in Cuba, primarily the Catholic Church, which has historically predominated, and second on the Protestant churches. The role of santería and other forms of spiritism in Cuba is difficult to quantify given their decentralized, noninstitutional nature. The Jewish community, numbering between twelve and fifteen hundred, is mentioned only briefly.

2. Juan J. Linz and Alfred Stepan, *Problems of Democratic Transition and Consolidation: Southern Europe, South America, and Post-Communist Europe* (Baltimore: Johns Hopkins University Press, 1996).

3. Ibid., 245.

4. Margaret E. Crahan and Ariel Armony, "A Note of Caution on Civil Society and Transitions from Authoritarianism" (paper presented at the conference "Rights vs. Efficiency in a Globalized Era: Citizenship and Governance in Latin America and Southern Europe Project," Universidad di Tella, Buenos Aires, Argentina, August 27–29, 1998).

5. As quoted in Linz and Stepan, 246.

6. Juan Valdés Paz, as quoted in Rafael Hernández, "¿Hacia una nueva sociedad Socialista?" (unpublished manuscript).

7. Linz and Stepan, 256.

8. On the weakness of the Catholic and Protestant churches in prerevolutionary Cuba, see Margaret E. Crahan, "Cuba," in *Religious Freedom and Evangelization*

in Latin America: The Challenge of Religious Pluralism, ed. Paul E. Sigmund (Maryknoll, N.Y.: Orbis Books, 1999), 87–92.

9. Linz and Stepan, 262.

10. Ibid., 263.

11. John L. Allen, "Structure meant survival: Study finds Catholicism outlasted liberal Protestantism in Iron Curtain countries," *National Catholic Reporter* 8 (October 1992): 12.

12. Ileana Hodge Limonta and Minerva Rodríguez Delgado, *El espiritismo en Cuba, percepción y exteriorización* (Havana: Editorial Academia, 1997).

13. Pedro Monomé Moreno, Gustavo Véliz Olivares, and Zeida Sánchez Alvisa, "Social Functioning and Evolution of Catholicism in Cuban Society," *Social Compass* 41, no. 2 (1994): 263.

14. Enrique López Oliva, "Evolución de la religión en las condiciones sociales Cubanas" (paper presented at the conference "Retos y desafíos para Cuba contemporánea," Kellogg Institute, University of Notre Dame, 1998), 23–24.

15. Alfred L. Padula Jr., "The Fall of the Bourgeoisie: Cuba 1959–1961" (Ph.D. diss., University of New Mexico, 1974), 459.

16. Mateo Jover, "The Cuban Church in a Revolutionary Society," *LADOC* 4, no. 32 (April 1974): 27.

17. Margaret E. Crahan, "Salvation through Christ or Marx: Religion in Revolutionary Cuba," in *Churches and Politics in Latin America,* ed. Daniel H. Levine (Beverly Hills, Calif.: Sage Publications, 1980), 245.

18. Raimundo García Franco, "Pastores en la U.M.A.P.: Diálogo en la U.M.A.P." (unpublished manuscript, October 2, 1966), 1–8.

19. Fidel Castro, "There are no contradictions between the aims of religion and the aims of Socialism," *Granma,* November 20, 1977, 5.

20. Jim Wallace, "Christians in Cuba," *Cuban Research Center Newsletter* 3, no. 1 (April 1973): 10.

21. Elmer Rodríguez, "Cuba: Who said there is no religious freedom in Cuba?" *Prensa Latina News Service,* no. 168 (November 1, 1977): 2–3.

22. Center for Cuban Studies Archives, New York, "Resolution on Religion: First Party Congress of the Cuban Communist Party, December 1975," D888, 35.

23. B. H. Lewis, ed., *Methodist Overseas Mission, 1960: Gazetteer and Statistics* (New York: Board of Missions of the United Methodist Church, 1960); Paul Jeffrey, "'A Fully Cuban Church': New members flock to evangelical churches, but some leaders are questioning the rapid growth," *Latinamerica Press,* 31, no. 45 (December 6, 1999): 4.

24. Jorge Ramírez Calzadilla, "Religion, cultura y sociedad en Cuba," papers, no. 52 (Barcelona, Spain: Universidad Autónoma de Barcelona, 1997), 147.

25. *Encuentro Nacional Eclesial Cubano* (ENEC), *Documentación Final* (Miami: ENEC, 1987), 99–100.

26. Carlos M. Camps Cruell, "El papel de la iglesia en la sociedad Cubana actual," *Revista Reflexión y Diálogo* (January–March 2000): 8–16; Rafael Cepeda, Elizabeth Carillo, Rhode González, and Carlos E. Ham, "Causas y desafíos del crecimiento de las iglesias Protestantes en Cuba," *Temas,* no. 4 (October–December

1995): 56–60; Carlos Manuel de Céspedes García-Menocal, "¿Puede afirmarse que el pueblo Cubano es Católico o no?," *Temas*, no. 4 (October–December 1995): 20–22; Conferencia de Obispos Católicos de Cuba, "Un cielo nuevo y una tierra nueva: Mensaje de la Conferencia de los Obispos Católicos de Cuba con ocasión del jubileo del año 2000," *Enfoque, Año 2000*, 69 (January–March 2000): 6; López Oliva, "Evolución," 22; Jorge A. Pomar, "El renacimiento religioso en Cuba," *Revista Encuentro de la Cultura Cubana*, no. 12/13 (spring–summer 1999): 67.

27. As quoted in Jorge Ramírez Calzadilla, "Religión, cultura y sociedad en Cuba," papers, 25; López Oliva, "Evolución," 5–7, 26, 32.

28. Ibid., 7, 25.

29. Ibid., 7.

30. Caridad Diego, chief, Office of Religious Affairs, Government of Cuba, interview by author, July 2, 1998, Havana, Cuba.

31. López Oliva, "Evolución," 7.

32. Pomar, "El renacimiento," 60–62.

33. López Oliva, "Evolución," 3.

34. Crahan, "Cuba."

35. Fidel Castro, *Fidel y la religión* (Havana: Oficina de Publicaciones del Consejo de Estado, 1985).

36. Rodolfo Juárez, "La celebración evangélica: Su posible impacto social y religioso," *Revista Reflexión y Diálogo* (January–March 2000): 22–24.

37. Ibid., 28.

38. These prerequisites are derived, in part, from analyses of how other institutions promote change. See, for example, H. E. Chehabi and Alfred Stepan, eds., *Politics, Society and Democracy: Comparative Studies* (Boulder, Colo.: Westview Press, 1995); Ruth Berins Collier and David Collier, *Shaping the Political Arena: Critical Junctures, the Labor Movement, and Regime Dynamics in Latin America* (Princeton, N.J.: Princeton University Press, 1991); Peter B. Evans, Dietrich Rueschemeyer, and Theda Skocpol, eds., *Bringing the State Back In* (New York: Cambridge University Press, 1985); Albert O. Hirschman, *The Rhetoric of Reaction: Perversity, Futility, Jeopardy* (Cambridge: Harvard University Press, 1994); Peter Katzenstein, *Corporatism and Change: Austria, Switzerland and the Politics of Industry* (Ithaca, N.Y.: Cornell University Press, 1984); Scott Mainwaring and Timothy Scully, eds., *Building Democratic Institutions: Party Systems in Latin America* (Stanford, Calif.: Stanford University Press, 1995); Angelo Panebianco, *Political Parties: Organization and Power* (New York: Cambridge University Press, 1988); Theda Skocpol, *States and Social Revolution: A Comparative Analysis of France, Russia and China* (New York: Cambridge University Press, 1979); Charles Tilly, *Big Structures, Large Processes, and Huge Comparisons* (New York: Russell Sage Foundation, 1985).

39. Margaret E. Crahan, "Religions and Conflict Resolution: The Case of the Guatemalan Peace Process" (paper presented at the Seventeenth Annual Conference of the Association of Third World Studies, November 18–20, 1999, San José, Costa Rica).

40. Patricia Arés Muzio, "Familia, ética y valores en la realidad Cubana actual," *Temas*, no. 15 (September 1998): 61; Matilde Molina Cintra and Roda T. Rodríguez

Lauzurique, "Juventud y valores, ¿crisis, desorientación, cambio?" *Temas*, no. 15 (September 1998): 65–73.

41. Camps Cruell, "El papel de la iglesia," 12–14.

42. Ibid., 15–17.

43. Cuban Episcopal Conference, "A Call for True Dialogue," *Origins* 23, no. 16 (September 30, 1993): 279.

44. Jaime Ortega y Alamino, *Discurso de Mons. Jaime Ortega y Alamino: Visita ad limina de los obispos de Cuba, 25, VI. 94,"* Rome, June 25, 1994.

45. Conferencia de Obispos Católicos de Cuba, *Plan Global de Pastoral, 1997– 2000* (Havana: Secretariado General de la COCC, 1996), 2–4.

46. Ibid., 6.

47. "Cuba, Its People and Its Church," LADOC, no. 30 (July/August 2000): 11–17.

48. Conferencia de Obispos Católicos de Cuba, *Plan Global,* 10, 4–11.

49. Ibid., 9.

50. "Resumen de noticias de la Arquidiócesis de Camagüey," (2000): 1–7; "Actualidad diocesana," *Boletín Diocesano,* Camagüey, no. 39 (January 20, 2000): 21.

51. For descriptions of their activities see the *Revista Reflexión y Diálogo* of the Christian Center for Reflection and Dialogue and *Caminos* of [Havana's] Martin Luther King Jr. Center.

52. "Memoria: Transcripción del diálogo efectuado entre representantes del gobierno y del partido y miembros del consejo de redacción de la revista Vitral del Centro de Formación Cívica y Religiosa de la Diócesis de Pinar del Río," May 14, 1997, 1–8.

53. Ibid., 18.

54. Ibid., 18–24.

55. Ibid., 28–34.

56. "Key Address by Dr. Fidel Castro Ruz, President of the Republic of Cuba, to the Rally Held at 'Commander Ernesto Che Guevara' Square in Villa Clara Commemorating the 47th Anniversary of the Attack on the Moncada Barracks on July 26, 1953. Villa Clara, July 29, 2000" (press release, Permanent Mission of the Republic of Cuba to the United Nations, New York, July 29, 2000), 1, 17.

IV

The Economy

7

The Road to Economic Recovery

José Luis Rodríguez García

It has been more than ten years since Cuba first had to deal with the most profound economic crisis of its history. After overcoming the initial and most serious impact of the crisis, a phase of gradual economic recovery began in 1995. In this chapter we will share some reflections about those factors that established the basis for a successful economic recovery within a Socialist context and some reflections about the main defining characteristics of the recovery up to the end of the 1990s.

The Preamble of the Recovery

An analysis of the causes that made it necessary to decree the present special period leaves no doubts about the reasons for its implementation. External factors forced the implementation of the special period in September 1990 in order to face the sudden and irreplaceable loss of the thirty-year-old commercial and financial relations with the European Socialist countries and the USSR and to face the toughening of the economic blockade by the United States.

In those critical moments, when many considered the disappearance of the Socialist system in Cuba inevitable and when neoliberal readjustment measures were being imposed throughout the world, the country chose to defend the Socialist model. Cuba made the necessary changes in order to adapt the Socialist model to the difficult conditions it was facing. Cuba was convinced that it was possible to achieve efficiency and equity without embarking on the road to a market economy.

An emergency economic program was put into effect, supported by a strategy whose fundamental objectives were to resist and overcome the effects of the crisis with as little social cost as possible. At the same time, conditions were created to reinsert the Cuban economy into the world economy, counting on the essential political consensus to carry out such a program.

In that regard, it is important to point out that to be able to apply such a strategy, the country had already created a significant potential of natural and human resources. This is conveyed, in the first place, by an average annual growth of 4.6 percent of the gross domestic product (GDP) for the years 1959–89.[1]

Moreover, the concept of development applied by the revolutionary government during these years always conceived economic growth as indivisible from progress in basic social services. Thanks to the advances attained in education, public health, social security, culture, and sports, the country had accumulated invaluable human capital to confront the crisis.

The added creation of a humanistic and solidaristic political conscience in a people with a profound concept of freedom and national sovereignty placed the population in an exceptional position to successfully defend the Socialist project against the adversities of a crisis with potentially severe consequences.

Furthermore, in the mid-1980s a process of correcting mistakes and negative trends had started with a goal of improving the Cuban Socialist model. The result of this process, up to 1989, created better conditions to begin a quick reorientation of the economic policy once the special period was implemented.[2] Still, the impact of the crisis was without a doubt brutal, as illustrated by the statistics. The gross domestic product fell almost 35 percent between 1989 and 1993; the fiscal deficit rose to 33 percent of the GDP in 1993, and imports at current prices fell 75 percent in those four years.

To confront the difficult situation, certain measures were put into place at the beginning of the special period. This process of transformation in the economic paradigm would, without renouncing its Socialist essence, open considerable space to market mechanisms in order to reactivate production and services, a course with considerable complexities.[3]

Nevertheless, this process always had clearly defined conceptual and political objectives and limits for the direction of the country. Above all, it was essential to maintain power and to do everything that could be useful for the nation and the people in situations where it was essential to resist in order to save the country's independence and to make only concessions that were unavoidable to achieve its goal.[4]

Thus by recognizing a greater economic role of market mechanisms, one was merely accepting the real presence of factors—amid the crisis—that

had motivated economic development.[5] However, it is important to emphasize that this growing importance was always seen as contradictory to the
interests of a Socialist society such as Cuba's. This perception has had a
strategic importance for the survival of the Cuban revolutionary project.
Misunderstanding about this position caused many specialists and supporters of capitalism to believe that they saw in the initial changes of the special
period the unavoidable transition to a market economy.[6] That misunderstanding also produced the thesis of the "deceleration" of economic reform
and other similar ideas.[7]

The decisive factors, in order to resist and then to overcome the effects of
the crisis, are, in the first place, the Cuban people's great capacity to endure,
a capacity based on the political and moral values created by the revolution
throughout many years. Second, a fundamental factor is the revolutionary
leadership's clear political understanding of the new economic phenomena,
and basically, its understanding of the contradictory essence of monetary-
mercantile relationships in a Socialist economy, as well as the necessity of
creating the conditions to prevent its unchecked development.[8]

It is only when these elements and their role in the gradual recovery of the
economy are taken into account that it becomes possible to adequately
frame the transformation in economic policy that took place, especially
beginning in 1993.

The Road to Recovery

From a macroeconomic point of view, the Cuban economy had to face,
from 1990 to 1993, a growing internal imbalance, beginning with the sudden aggravation of external economic imbalances.[9] In other words, the balance of available resources was reduced as a consequence of the country's
export of goods and services. This affected the levels of consumption and
investment in the economy, beginning with a heavy fall of the GDP. Nevertheless, the damages to investment, especially to consumption, have in
Cuba unbreachable social and political limits. Thus it was necessary to
obtain essential financial resources to cover those gaps.

The manner in which this objective was accomplished constitutes another unique characteristic of the Cuban economy of this decade. Resources
were not obtained by opening of the economy to market forces, or by priva-
tizing government property, or by trimming social expenditures. Different
from other readjustment cases, it was not acceptable to apply market and
neoliberal laws to restrict without limits the levels of consumption and in-

vestment. Such actions would have resulted in the absolute poverty of most of the population and total loss of the ability to lead development in favor of the national interest.

For Cuba, a readjustment of this type would have meant the destruction of the revolution's work and the loss of independence and national identity. The Cuban people had to face difficult times, made more difficult by the economic blockade of the United States.[10] Cuba had to achieve its goals without giving up its principles and by testing the capacity of its people to resist.[11]

The recovery process started under these conditions. Cuba was striving to guarantee access to maximum possible resources in order to secure survival, holding consumption to a minimum and reorienting investment toward sectors that would contribute most to short-term recovery. In 1990, the necessity to reform first the external economic policy seemed obvious, given the unfavorable changes in the international economic spheres. Reform was necessary to prevent a collapse that for many seemed inevitable.

It was then that access to direct foreign investment accelerated as a complement to the investment of national resources, and as a means for alternative access to new markets, technology, and financing.[12] Therefore, from only four joint ventures in 1990, with an investment volume of less than $100 million mainly concentrated in tourism, by the end of 1999 there were 370 joint ventures with a volume of committed investment of more than $4 billion, basically concentrated in tourism, the nickel industry, oil prospecting and extraction, and telecommunications.

Furthermore, a restructuring of foreign trade began. The state monopoly disappeared from this area, according to constitutional changes introduced during the summer of 1992. Cuba went from having 50 companies operating in a centralized manner in 1989 to more than 350 working free from centralization in 1998, carrying out a geographical rearrangement that favored Latin America, the Caribbean, and Canada as well as Western Europe and China.

Exports grew at an average annual rate of 2.9 percent between 1994 and 1999 (at constant or adjusted-for-inflation prices, this rate reached 7 percent), reflecting the significant exporting efforts of the country.

Considering the rate of exported goods and services at constant prices, the positive economic influence of tourism is verified by its annual rate of growth of about 10 percent in the last five-year period. This sector increased in the number of tourists at an annual average rate of 21.7 percent from 1994 to 1999, generating income that grew 2.3 times during those years. At the same time, tourism had a significant multiplying effect in the internal economy, consuming nationally produced goods for 51 percent of its input in 1999. All of this allows us to describe tourism as the most dynamic sector in the economic recovery process because it generated more than 50 percent of the currency that entered the country at that time.

Imports of goods and services were also rising in the economic recovery process at an average annual rate of 15.7 percent between 1994 and 1999, at current prices. This figure demonstrates a high degree of elasticity of imports in comparison to the growth of the gross domestic product. The imbalance of current prices between imports and exports reflected among other things the deterioration of the terms of exchange, which are estimated to be 28.5 percent between 1995 and 1999. Nevertheless, when comparing the current accounts balance in the balance of payments to the GDP, there is evidence of a gradual financial recovery. This balance, even though it was negative between 1993 and 1999, declined from 2.5 percent to 1.3 percent during those years.

The process of substituting imports also contributed to the gradual improvement of the external financial imbalance. The biggest advances were observed in the generation of electric energy. From generating less than 20 percent of electricity in 1995, the national production of electric energy increased to 41 percent in 1999. In addition, the presence of Cuban products in the hard currency stores (*tiendas de recuperación de divisas*, TRD), which sell mainly to tourists, increased to 47 percent in 1999.[13] The efforts to close the foreign financial gap through the promotion of exports, the substitution of imports, and direct foreign investment have been decisive elements in the road to economic recovery.

However, the volume of income produced has not allowed Cuba to completely address the demands of foreign financing. The adverse international commercial and financial situation, the negative effects of the American economic blockade, and the shortage in the production of important exportable resources such as sugar have had an impact on the ability to resolve such demands—sugar production declined from an already depressed production of 4 million tons in 1994 to only 3.8 million tons in 1999, and gross export earnings declined to a low 38 percent. Therefore, it has been essential to confront an increasing volume of short-term financial obligations and high interest rates, practically the only ones available. Foreign financial dynamics, while they have not affected the economy's solvency, have forced Cuba to confront increasing pressures in their short-term liquidity.[14] Today, one can affirm that the lack of hard currency is the main obstacle to a faster economic recovery. Hence, a structural solution to these financial problems, which have not prevented the sustained economic recovery since 1995 but have seriously limited its rate of progress, lies in the solution to the fiscal imbalances in the national economy.[15]

The most significant changes in economic policy took place in 1993, when they could not be delayed any longer. It had been necessary to delay them in order to assimilate the new economic reality that Cuba had to face. While great efforts were made to affect the population as little as possible, changes had to be made in a situation where production and consumption suffered more and more from the impact of the crisis.[16]

The changes in the internal economic policy can be grouped for analysis according to different criteria. To examine the policy's effects on the process of recovery, it is necessary to look at those measures whose impact was greatest in the short term in currency circulation. Around 1993, it was precisely in that area that imbalances in the real economy were expressed with greatest clarity and sharpness. Cuba came to a point where the excessive liquidity in the hands of the population brought about an accelerated monetary depreciation as well as increasing inflationary pressures. A tendency to barter instead of using the universally accepted exchange of money also manifested itself.

Additionally, the circulation of hard currency was increasing in the informal economy. This currency arrived in Cuba via clandestine remittances, tourism, and foreign investment. Facing a sharp shortage of hard currency due to the decline by more than 38 percent of export earnings on sugar, the country needed to attain as much convertible currency as possible in order to meet its international financial obligations. Besides, tourism and foreign investment operations were becoming very difficult to carry out properly with a depreciated currency, making necessary new monetary arrangements.

Therefore, Law Decree No. 140 was adopted in 1993. This legislation legalized the possession of six different kinds of foreign currency and authorized their use for transactions by individuals as well as in the business sector. A dual monetary system was created. The decree also authorized the entrance of foreign currency remittances destined for the population.[17]

These currencies are secured by a network of foreign currency collection stores (the TRDs). These stores only accept foreign currencies at prices that already include high taxes. This allows part of the population to improve its standard of consumption, and it allows the state to secure hard currencies that are already circulating in the country. Also, they presumably are increased by remittances that are redistributed in order to meet the obligations of social consumption and the investments needed for the recovery of the economy.[18]

At the business level this measure defers the need to readjust the rates of exchange of the Cuban peso by allowing investors and handlers of the foreign sector to work directly with freely convertible currencies. Thus, there is no need to resort to the dangerous resource of a monetary devaluation.

The negative social effects of the decriminalization of hard currency possession were confronted immediately. Compensatory measures were adopted to use hard currency as a work incentive in key sectors of the economy, bringing about a jump in productivity with a minimal expenditure of resources. The process was expanded quickly, going from 115,368 workers covered by the system who received an incentive of US$3.1 million in 1994, to 1,079,566 workers in 1999 who received an incentive of US$52.3 million and represented 32 percent of workers employed by the state.

In short, the so-called dollarization process, while having social and economic costs that should be taken into account, has been without doubt a catalyst in the process of economic recovery. It incorporated additional financial resources into the internal currency circulation, and it brought faster and more efficient mechanisms to commercial and financial transactions with the international economy. However, it should be considered a temporary measure to solve a problem that requires the gradual adjustment of the rate of exchange whenever the necessary conditions arise.

The relief that the decriminalization of possession of foreign currency meant for internal financial tensions could not have materialized if a set of measures to restore the internal financial balance had not been put in place. These measures triggered the gradual recovery of production and services, stopping the depreciation of the national currency in order to restore the functions of money in the economy. The complexity of this process involved measuring popular economic participation for several months, which delayed the approval of such measures pending subsequent analysis and support by the National Assembly in May 1994.

The program for the stabilization of internal finances sought to confiscate goods obtained through speculation (Law Decree No. 149), including increasing prices and tariffs of nonessential goods and services, elimination of improper gratuities, and approval of a new tax system. A restrictive budgetary policy was also adopted, but basic social services were not affected.

Between 1994 and 1999, these measures allowed the state to reduce the quantity of currency in the hands of the population by 17.7 percent and to reduce the budget deficit from 33 percent of the GDP in 1993 to 2.4 percent in 1999. It also allowed the revaluation of the national currency against the

U.S. dollar, which reached 150 Cuban pesos per dollar in February 1994 and finished at 21 pesos per dollar in 1999.

Solving the external and internal financial imbalances made possible the consolidation of the economic and social recovery that began in 1995 after the fall of the economy was halted in 1994. In this way, beginning with 1993, measures were adopted to improve financial efficiency.

Regarding property, government farms were turned into cooperatives through the creation of a system of Basic Units of Cooperative Production, UBPCs. This process was justified by the lack of imported material resources needed by the sizable state farms and the substitution of available natural and human resources in the country. At the same time, the cooperative option would be an incentive for the producer because of his direct participation in the distribution of earnings. However, given the degree of decapitalization suffered in the farm sector, results from the UBPCs will take years to show, and the UBPCs will face many difficulties in the process. Still, budget subsidies for losses in the agricultural sector were reduced by 75 percent between 1993 and 1999, and government help to the UBPCs was reduced by 28.2 percent from 1995 to 1999.

The opportunity for self-employment raised employment levels and increased the availability of products to different segments of the population. Also, workers attained substantive income gains given the prices received for their products and services during the compounded situation of excess cash and limited supply that has characterized the special period. At the end of 1999, the number of self-employed persons reached 165,400. While they have played a minor role in the economic recovery, the level of control that the state has achieved over activities that previously existed in the informal economy resulted in a positive balance in the initial stage of the special period.

Complementing the decisions mentioned before, by the end of 1994 markets were approved for the sale of agricultural and industrial products and handicrafts. Private producers as well as cooperatives and state enterprises used the newly available markets to sell their surplus at market prices. By the end of 1999 the private sector represented 54.3 percent of total agricultural sales, while its participation in industrial market sales was only 9.3 percent. Sales in both markets have continued to grow modestly during these five years, although the growth is relatively stronger in the industrial products and handicraft markets due to the growing participation of the state in their transactions.

A consistent declining tendency in the agricultural market saw prices fall an average of 51 percent between 1994 and 1999. The prices were still relatively high because the state's and cooperatives' supplies were still insufficient to affect prices decisively. The market's contribution to foodstuffs during the years of economic recovery has been essentially complementary and has covered only a segment of the population. Also, as a consequence of the measures adopted during the five-year period, it is estimated that the role of the informal economy in the population's consumption has been greatly reduced. There was a 65 percent reduction in average prices between 1994 and 1999.

While the measures examined up to this point draw together essential changes in the internal economic policy, it is still necessary to point out the profound transformation that began in the state's management system. In effect, in April 1994, a restructuring process of the state's central administrative bodies began. This process reduced the number of ministries and bureaus from fifty to thirty in 1999, along with the corresponding reduction of administrative personnel, who left to cover other more useful social functions.

In the enterprise area management decentralization together with reorganization and resizing has resulted in a very different socialist enterprise structure in the last five years. At the end of September 1999 there were 134 major enterprises, among them 32 corporations and 59 associations; and 5,279 ventures, including 1,975 enterprises and 1,312 affiliates. Under the category of corporations, 251 state enterprises were established. In the agricultural sector 6,449 entities included 1,143 agricultural production cooperatives, 2,530 credit and service cooperatives, and 2,666 UBPCs. There were also 19,821 usufructs that permitted work on unused state land.

By reducing subsidies attributable to state enterprise losses, the internal economic readjustment process contributed to a restructuring of internal finances.[19] Furthermore, decentralization of resource management, including hard currency, increased administrative efficiency, resulting in higher levels of economic efficiency in production and service organizations from the bottom up. Meanwhile, it was necessary to give more participation in the decision-making process to worker representatives in each entity, within the context of their capabilities and function. All of this forced Cuba to adopt a modified financial planning system in order to maintain social coherence and control of the economic development process at the macroeconomic level.

The favorable conditions created by the restructuring of the financial and banking system permitted the government to plan more profound changes. In May 1997 this restructuring resulted in the division of functions between the central banking system and the commercial banking system.

Consequently, the Fifth Cuban Communist Party Congress, held in October 1997, decided to apply the enterprise improvement experience developed by MINFAR (Ministry of Revolutionary Armed Forces) to the entire country's enterprise system for ten years. In August 1998, Law Decree No. 187 was approved. This legislation set down the general regulations needed for the enterprise improvement movement.

The last step in the enterprise improvement movement was the beginning of a new stage in the change process that has been developing in the economy for many years. This phase entails an integral transformation of enterprise management methods, in order to increase the efficiency and competitiveness of state enterprises.[20]

The Necessary Balance, 1995–1999

Although the Cuban economy has been subjected to all kinds of tensions, it has not only resisted the impact of the crisis but has begun to overcome its negative effects as well, which is shown by the advances made in economic and social development during the last five years, and which places the economy in an irreversible recovery stage. This is not to say that every year there will be a high level of profit or even that there could not be a situation that could lower these rates at any given moment. Still, the most important results obtained from 1995 to 1999 strongly guarantee the continuity of the economic and social recovery trend. In recent years Cuba has experienced growth in several economic indicators.

1. Cuba's GDP grew at an average annual rate of 4 percent while it is estimated that the Latin American and the Caribbean GDP grew at an average rate of 2.5 percent. Taking these figures to the per capita growth level, Cuba grew 3.6 percent, while Latin America and the Caribbean grew .06 percent per year. By 1999 Cuba had reached a GDP equivalent to 80 percent of that of 1989.

2. Efficiency indicators show a positive tendency. Productivity increased 3.3 percent annually; energy intensity decreased 7.7 percent; and investment performance improved 74 percent.

3. The industrial sector grew at an annual average rate of 6.2 percent while agriculture grew 6.9 percent.

4. Growth in the economic indicators occurred within a noninflationary context.

Therefore, the total cash liquidity's participation in the GDP was reduced from 42.6 percent to 38.5 percent; the budget deficit, in relation to the GDP, declined from 3.5 percent to 2.4 percent; the consumer price index was reduced by 3 percent; and the informal average annual exchange value of the Cuban peso per dollar declined from 32.1 to 21.1.

These economic growth rates were accompanied by significant social advances. Hence, between 1995 and 1999:

1. The people-per-doctor rate declined from 193 to 175 in 1998; the infant mortality rate of children under one year of age declined from 9.4 to 6.4 per 1,000 live births; and public health expenditures increased from 5.1 percent to 6.3 percent of the GDP.

2. The level of schooling for children five years old and under increased from 89.8 percent to 98.5 percent, and for children 6–14 years old it increased from 97.5 percent to 98.2 percent. Additionally, the average education level of the population increased from eighth grade to ninth grade of schooling, and the education budget increased from 6.3 percent to 7.3 percent of the GDP.

3. The average salary grew from 190 to 223 pesos a month; hard currency in the hands of the people increased from 44 percent to 62 percent of the total population; and the unemployment index fell from 8.3 percent to 6 percent.

4. The rationing system was preserved in order to maintain an equitable access to foodstuffs by the entire population, and the regulated consumption of milk per capita increased by 26 percent, rice by 23.3 percent, beans by 34.8 percent, and eggs by 18 percent. Also, the consumption of macronutrients increased by 10.6 percent in terms of calories and 7.2 percent in terms of protein.

The results discussed in this chapter do not reflect everything the Cuban people have achieved during the long hard years of the special period, thanks to their daily heroism and their unyielding stoicism. These are transcendental achievements because they confirm the validity of the most revolutionary concept of how to achieve authentic development, especially when compared with the neoliberal capitalist model that was presented to the world as the only possible alternative, and when Cubans stood alone holding the flag of Socialism.

More than ten years have passed and the Cuban revolution has not crumbled; it has endured countless hardships, it has been harassed without rest. It has confronted the challenges of American imperialism and with the calm conviction of victory, it has reorganized its forces and begun the long road to economic recovery. (See appendix A.)

Notes

This chapter was translated by Professor Amanda Frantz-Mamani, Edinboro University of Pennsylvania, and Professor Carlos Mamani, Gannon University, Erie, Pennsylvania.

1. José Luis Rodríguez García, "La experiencia Cubana en el enfrentamiento a la crisis de los años 90" (paper presented at the Second Ibero-American Meeting of the Ministers of Finance and Treasury, Havana, 1999), 2. Unless otherwise indicated, the statistics cited in the paper are based on the author's calculations using information provided by the Office of National Statistics, the Central Bank of Cuba, and the Ministry of Finance and Planning.

2. Regarding the basis of the rectification process, see *Informe central, III Congreso del Partido Comunista de Cuba (PCC)* (Havana: Editora Política, 1986); and also Fidel Castro's speech at the closing session of the Third Congress of the PCC, December 2, 1986, *Cuba Socialista* 25 (1987).

3. These complexities were already perceptible when the Fourth Congress of the Cuban Communist Party was taking place in October 1991. At this occasion it was stated that it was a necessary to "modify and accelerate as much as possible to plans anticipated beforehand and to adopt as a strategy the concentration of available efforts and resources in a set of programs of greatest priority, and to inevitably restrict, in an organized and fair manner, the population's level of consumption and the levels of economic activity in diverse spheres." At the same time still more complex situations with extraordinary serious effects on the economy were prevented, such as the interruption of important economic and social activities and a greater reduction in the standard of living of the people. See Resolution about the Economic Development of the Country, in *IV Congreso del Partido Comunista de Cuba: Discursos y documentos* (Havana: Editora Política, 1992).

4. With respect to that, Fidel Castro, the commander in chief, would express in August 1999 fundamental ideas about these topics when he stated: "Who has the power? That is the key, because if the people have it, if the workers have it, and not the rich, the millionaires, then we can have a policy in favor of the people, respecting the agreements made with particular foreign companies, respecting everybody and the interests of all, because we are not planning on nationalizing anybody." He also illustrated the difficulty of the decisions to be made when he stated: "We cannot guide ourselves by the criteria about what we like or dislike, but rather by what is useful and what is not useful for the nation and the people in these very decisive moments in the history of our country." Within the framework of this strategy, the concessions that had to be accepted were understandable. He added: "We have said that we are introducing elements of capitalism in our system, in our economy, that is a fact; we have talked even of the consequences that we see from the use of such mechanisms. Yes, we are doing it." Fidel Castro, "Mientras el pueblo tenga el poder lo tiene todo" (speech, *Cuba Vive* International Youth Festival, August 5–6, 1995) (Havana: Editora Política, 1995), 31, 45, 50.

5. The persistence of monetary-mercantile relationships in Socialism has been the cause of important debates for many years. Nevertheless, the objective existence of

these relations was only scientifically explained at the end of the 1960s, when it was demonstrated that the specifically social characteristic of labor did not attain an adequate level of expression in Socialism. This was expressed by a relative economic isolation that needed market categories to measure it within the context of the social division of work, even when the means of production were socially owned.

6. See, for example, Carmelo Mesa-Lago, *Are Economic Reforms Propelling Cuba to the Market?* (Miami: University of Miami, 1994).

7. See M. Pastor and Andrew Zimbalist, "Has Cuba Turned the Corner? Macroeconomic Stabilization and Reform in Contemporary Cuba," *Cuban Studies* 27 (1997); and Instituto de Relaciones Europeo-Latinoamericano, "40 años de revolución en Cuba: ¿Transición hacia donde?" Dossier no. 68, chap. 2 (Madrid, 1999).

8. Che's premonitory criticism about the reason for the noncontradictory action of the law of value in Socialism maintains all its validity for Cuba during this stage. In this respect, Che wrote in 1964: "We deny the possibility of the conscious use of the law of value based on the nonexistence of a free market that automatically expresses the contradiction between producers and consumers." Ernesto Che Guevara, "Sobre el sistema presupuestario de financiamiento," in *Obras, 1957–1967* (Havana: Editorial Casa de la Américas, 1970), 273.

9. These imbalances were present even before the special period, but the external economic flows based on more just economic relations with the USSR and the European Socialist countries lessened them substantially. The level that these imbalances reached is not the object of this discussion. However, it is important to point out that it is not possible to begin a development process without incurring a certain level of external financial imbalance, which has to be covered by the corresponding credits.

10. The American economic blockade has cost the Cuban economy more than $67 billion since its inception at the beginning of the 1960s. See "Demanda del pueblo Cubano al gobierno de los Estados Unidos por los daños económicos ocasionados a Cuba," *Granma*, January 5, 2000.

11. To consciously take on that attitude is only possible when there is a high degree of identification between individual and collective interests, based on the understanding of political and social objectives shared freely. See Dario Machado, "Hablemos de gobernabilidad, el caso Cubano," *Cuba Socialista* 4 (1996).

12. The weight of Cuba's resources in the total of investments continues to be predominant, averaging 64 percent for the period of 1994–98, a figure higher than the estimated 48 percent in 1989.

13. The presence of these products in the internal market in easily convertible currency—this includes basically tourism and hard currency stores (TRDs)—is characterized by a level of competition that allows them to compete in equal conditions with imported products. This level of competition, while it cannot be compared to what is required when one attempts to export, has created an incentive to improve financial efficiency.

14. The necessity of financing investment that cannot be quickly recovered with short-term loans has without a doubt increased their cost and forced Cuba to successively renegotiate the debt. The fall of the price of exports, as in the case of sugar and

nickel for long periods, has had an impact on that necessity because of the decrease in resources needed to expand the country's ability to borrow. Nevertheless, the renegotiations of the official short-term debt have been successfully accomplished with important creditors such as Italy, Japan, and Great Britain, and contacts have been initiated with the Paris Club in order to begin a dialogue on restructuring the official debt to the countries that make up that group. See Central Bank of Cuba, *Informe económico 1998* (Havana: Central Bank of Cuba, 1999), chap. 5.

15. Clearly, the solution to the foreign financial gap can be found essentially in the solution of internal imbalances. However, that does not mean a mutually exclusive solution of both levels but rather their interrelationship. See Alfredo González, "Economía y sociedad: Los retos del modelo económico," *Temas* 11 (July–September 1997); and "El nuevo modelo de análisis de finanzas internas," *Cuba: Investigación Económica* 2 (April–June 1999).

16. See José Luis Rodríguez, "Cuba: 1990–1995: Reflexiones sobre una política económica acertada," *Cuba Socialista* 1 (1996): 22–23.

17. This measure was probably the one with the greatest political impact. The country was forced to adopt it when facing the critical economic situation happening during the worst moments of the special period.

18. These revenues, while important, are not comparable to those that are obtained from tourism and other sectors of the economy in terms of net revenues. The remittances that the population receives constitute an important source of income to be spent at the TRDs, but not their only source. One should not forget that the incentive system, tourism, and the sale of hard currency in exchange for national currency also constitute additional sources of income available to the population. Additionally, it should be emphasized that there is not a precise total of the sum of remittances that enter the country because this money does not usually circulate through the banking system. However, some estimates tend to exaggerate their volume when compared with what is sold internally in hard currency to the people. Last, it should be recalled that the remittances go directly into the hands of the population; they are not the state's revenues. The state retains only part of that income when the population uses hard currency to buy at the TRDs. Therefore, to maintain that the remittances constitute the most significant source of hard currency revenues of the country is absurd and baseless.

19. This process was initiated in 1996 in the textile industry. It led to favorable results and full labor guarantees for those workers who became available.

20. "The improvement of the government enterprise has as its objective to increase to the maximum its efficiency and ability to compete by granting the authority and establishing the policies, principles, and procedures that will facilitate the development of initiative, creativity, and responsibility among all managers and workers." See Executive Committee of the Council of Ministers, "General Guidelines for Enterprise Improvement" (Havana: Council of State Publications, 1997), 1.

8

Measuring Economic Performance

Strong and Weak Prospects

Andrew Zimbalist

This chapter traces Cuba's economic policies and performance from 1990 to the present. After reviewing current economic conditions, I consider Cuba's new development strategy based in tourism and make some concluding remarks about the country's economic prospects.

Cuba's economic record since the collapse of the Council of Mutual Economic Assistance (CMEA) in 1990 leaves much to be desired. With the exception of Latvia and Lithuania, the Cuban economy fell more precipitously than that of any of the thirteen former Soviet bloc countries and USSR republics.[1] The speed of its recovery since 1993 at an annual rate of 4.2 percent has only been average in this group. Were Cuba to maintain this growth rate over the next four years, it would finally return to its 1990 level of per capita income in 2005.[2] However, prospects for growth in 2002 and 2003 were poor due to the recessed international economy and the ongoing effects of Hurricane Michelle.

If Cuba's economy is compared to the economies of Latin America, its performance during the 1990s lags considerably. Nonetheless, it has avoided the financial collapses, political instability, and economic catastrophes experienced by many of its Latin neighbors in the first years of the twenty-first century.

The Cuban economy experienced a massive external shock with the dissolution of the Soviet trading bloc twelve years ago. In response, the economy began to decentralize and Cuba's precipitous economic decline was arrested, but the process of substantial structural reform was essentially halted in 1994. Today, Cuba is left with a slowly recovering economy and uncertain prospects.

Undoubtedly, the Cuban Revolution has made enormous and impressive strides since 1959 in providing basic social services to all its citizens as well as in establishing certain norms of equity and equality. While Cuba's social safety net has been diminished and its provision of universal, free medical care has been compromised, the society's norms of equity and equality have also been challenged.[3] Cuba has come to look increasingly like a class society, defined by access to hard currency either through work, politics, or relatives abroad.[4] According to one study based in part on data from the Cuban government's Instituto Nacional de Investigación Económica, the share of income going to the top 5 percent rose from 10.1 percent in 1986 to 31.0 percent in 1995.[5] Another Cuban study found that the share going to the bottom 20 percent fell from 11.3 percent in 1986 to 4.3 percent in 1999, while the share going to the top 20 percent rose from 33.8 percent in 1986 to 58.1 percent in 1999.[6] Equally problematic, material rewards in Cuba today do not correspond in any meaningful way with one's economic contribution.

Present Economic Reality

The basic outline of Cuba's economic predicament is clear. During 1988–89 Cuba received 85 percent of its imports and several billion dollars in subsidies annually from the Soviet bloc. Also, Cuba received 12–13 million tons of oil from the former USSR. By 1994 overall imports of Russian oil had fallen to below 2 million tons. Cuba's total goods imports fell from $8.1 billion in 1989 to under $2.0 billion in 1994, and all sources of aid had dried up.

Unlike 1959–60, when U.S. trade disappeared and the USSR was there to bail Cuba out, since 1990 there has been no one to rescue Cuba. Indeed, under pressure from an ardent, well-organized, deep-pocketed, and conservative Cuban American lobby, the United States has only moved to tighten its embargo, which the Cubans estimate to have cost them over $60 billion to date, with annual costs of over $1 billion in recent years.

A vicious cycle set in. Without foreign exchange, output fell rapidly and shortages became ubiquitous. The government response was to give priority to maintaining basic social services and near full employment. This policy, while helping to prevent the potentially devastating social consequences of shock economic policies, led to a 90 percent increase in the government budget deficit (reaching 5.05 billion pesos in 1993).

Such deficits in Cuba, without an independent central bank and without a bond market, have traditionally been financed directly by printing money.[7] This leads to a magnifying problem of excess liquidity.[8] Indeed, by the end of 1993 the Cuban economy had an accumulated liquidity of 11.04

billion pesos, more than three times as large as the amount the Cuban government estimated at that time to be the desirable level. The money supply excess was compounded by the growing goods shortages engendered by the precipitous drop in Cuban imports and the tightening of the U.S. embargo. Thus, the Cuban money supply increased from 23.9 percent of GDP in 1990 to 66.5 percent in 1993.[9] The upshot was that there was too much money chasing too few goods, and increasingly Cuban workers were being paid in pesos that they could not spend. Workers lost any monetary incentive to work, which was only exacerbated by the growing difficulty in getting to work with a dysfunctional public transportation system and by the absence of necessary raw materials and spare parts at their workplaces. A black market developed where prices, due to the pent-up demand from excess money balances, were out of the reach of most budgets. Workers in the state sector connived to divert raw materials and goods to the black market, further undermining the state sector's capacity to produce.

Financing from the CMEA (the former Soviet trade bloc) was cut off. Also, Cuba had stopped paying its medium- and long-term hard currency debt in the mid-1980s, and anything but begrudging and expensive short-term trade financing was impossible to obtain.[10] In this circumstance, Cuba turned to foreign capital to establish tourist and export enclaves.[11] Here some improvements were made, but the flow of foreign investment was too slow and too small to make a significant dent in Cuba's economic free fall. By the end of 1993, according to official Cuban statistics, the Cuban economy was producing approximately 35 percent less than it did in 1989, or roughly about 40 percent less in per capita terms.

The Cuban government had little choice but to take some significant reform measures. To deal with excess liquidity, it followed a four-part program to reduce gradually the supply of excess money balances beginning in mid-1994, including price increases of several consumer goods and services, abolition of certain free services, introduction of new taxes, and reduction of subsidies to state enterprises.[12] These policies, along with increased sales of cigars and alcoholic beverages to the public, achieved some modest initial success, as excess liquidity was reduced by around 25 percent by mid-1995.

These fiscal reforms were combined with such substantial structural changes as the depenalization of the use of dollars in July 1993,[13] as well as the expansion of self-employment opportunities and the cooperativization of most state farms beginning in September 1993, reopening of the farmers' markets in October 1994, introduction of industrial and craft markets in December 1994, and the opening of CADECA hard currency exchanges in mid-1995.[14] Each of these reforms was a step toward promoting decentralization, individual initiative, market incentives, and greater efficiency. The fiscal and structural reforms, together with the rapid development of Cuba's tourism industry and its linkages to other sectors of the economy, an inflow of approximately $2.5 billion in foreign investment, and growing remittances from Cuban exiles, were sufficient to thwart the economic downturn and initiate a modest economic recovery.[15]

Three Distinct Economies

Cuba today has three distinct economies. First, there is the traditional public sector with state ownership, fixed prices, and central administration. This sector still accounts for more than three-fourths of the official labor force. At least two hundred thousand workers have been laid off from jobs in this sector over the last four years. To be sure, this is a large number of layoffs, but capacity utilization in the state sector is around 35 percent.[16] The Latin American Economic Council (CEPAL) estimates that the government would need to lay off another four hundred thousand or more to put these enterprises on a competitive basis in terms of productivity.[17]

Second, there is the export enclave sector with state and state/foreign ownership, producing with the aid of foreign technology, capital, management, and marketing skills. This sector caters to the international market. It encompasses tourism, nickel, tobacco, citrus, fishing, and biotechnology. With the exception of biotechnology, which has held steady, each of these sectors is experiencing modest to good growth.

Third, there is the informal and market sector, which consists of self-employment, production above state quotas, and production destined for the export sector, hard currency shops, farmers' markets, industrial and craft markets, and black markets. These markets in general have been dynamic. By way of example, in 1996 in hard currency shops Cubans spent $627 million, 18 percent more than in 1995 and equal to approximately 13.8 billion pesos at the parallel market rate of exchange, or 54.8 percent of official, current price GDP (25.2 billion pesos). In 1996, Cuban families spent at least two-thirds of their budgets on informal and free markets. According to government figures, hard currency shop sales grew another 17.8 percent in 1997 and 15 percent in 1998.[18]

The growing importance of hard currency has obligated the Cuban government and foreign companies operating in Cuba to use hard currency bonuses to motivate workers.[19] In March 1998, 1.5 million workers received hard currency incentives or payments in kind (averaging fifty-three dollars each per year, which in parallel market pesos is worth more than five months of average wages).[20] In 2000, 1.7 million workers, or 42.5 percent of the economically active population, received part of their income in U.S. dollars (although the yearly average appears to have fallen below forty dollars per worker). In Cuba's perverse economic environment, these hard currency rewards are constructive because they help mitigate the distorted incentives that prevail wherein hotel chambermaids, bellhops, taxi drivers, prostitutes, and others can earn several times as much as engineers, doctors, or manufacturing workers. Unfortunately, while reducing the distortion, they are insufficient in magnitude to reverse the trend for doctors to become cabbies or lawyers to move into retailing, or the lack of incentive for students to stay in school to increase their human capital. Nor will it diminish the pervasive rent-seeking behavior practiced throughout the Cuban economy, such as when buyers for state companies demand a 3 percent commission from the foreign company before signing an import contract.[21]

Fiscal and Monetary Imbalance

While it is true that the Cuban government has made significant strides toward fiscal and monetary balance, there is still a long road to travel.[22] And monetary balance is necessary if Cuba is to restore the peso as the economy's currency. Although the central budget deficit, after growing to 30.4 percent of GDP in 1993, was reduced to 1.9 percent of GDP in 1997 and remained between 2.2 and 2.5 percent during 1998–2001, and the money supply has been cut by some 42 percent, these figures understate the extent of the problem. First, CEPAL suggests that a significant part of the deficit reduction is, on the one hand, due to substituting central bank loans and growing accounts receivable for budget subsidies to state enterprises and, on the other hand, due to shifting some central expenditures to local governments.[23]

Second, some imbalances are still huge. Whereas the Cuban government has estimated that the appropriate level of liquidity is 3.5 billion pesos, liquidity at the end of 2001 was 11.82 billion pesos (that is, over 3.3 times its desired level). And matters are still worse: with hundreds of millions of dollars circulating in Cuba, at the parallel market rate of exchange (roughly twenty-six pesos to the dollar in mid-2002) the total liquidity represented by the dollar is 130 percent that of the peso. Further, the current account deficit is large and growing. It grew from $308 million in 1994, to $419 million in 1996, to $830 million in 2001.

Thus, Cuba needs to push forward more aggressively in its pursuit of economic balance. It is necessary to further reduce the government deficit, and to do this will entail massive layoffs of state sector workers. The only way to cushion this blow socially is through the expansion of other sectors.

For other sectors to expand, in turn, there must be new investment, and this brings us to the third salient feature of the Cuban economy today, the lack of investment.

Lack of Investment

The ratio of investment to the GDP in Cuba was 24.3 percent in 1989 and 21 percent in 1991; it fell to an average of 6.3 percent during 1994–96. Since the GDP was lower during 1994–96 than in 1989, the absolute drop in investment spending is even greater than these proportions suggest (in the neighborhood of 80–85 percent). It is reasonable to expect that depreciation or capital consumption allowances would be in the neighborhood of 8 to 14 percent of the GDP; hence, at the 1994–96 investment rate, Cuba was actually being decapitalized.[24]

Investment spending picked up in 1997 and 1998, but most of the growth was related to hotel construction in the tourism industry, and the aggregate amount of gross fixed capital formation was still well below the level of 1990 (5.04 billion pesos in 1990 versus 1.91 billion pesos in 1998). Of the 1.91 billion pesos invested in 1998, only 0.67 billion was in machinery and equipment. Since 1998 investment has grown at approximately the same rate as the GDP. In 2001, the gross investment ratio had increased to 11.1 percent of the GDP, but this is hardly a basis for long-term growth. Cuba has to increase its capital stock if it hopes to sustain economic growth.[25]

Cuba's capital shortage is still more grim because of its increasing demographic maturity. In 1960, 8 percent of its population was over sixty years of age; in 1990, 12 percent of its population was over sixty; and by 2015, due to its low birth rate and growing longevity, 18 percent of its population is projected to be over sixty. Since individuals over sixty tend to not to save, this will create a downward bias in the savings rate for Cuba, and capital formation will become more difficult.

Consider Cuba's recent investment experience. With a few exceptions, such as tourism, there has been little investment in the traditional state sector, and the state's fiscal situation makes this condition unlikely to change much.[26] The other two options are the informal sector and foreign investment.

While private activity in the informal sector had been flourishing until 1998, it has been tightly circumscribed by government policy that basically proscribes capital accumulation in this sphere. Consider, for instance, the treatment of *paladares* (private family-run restaurants). First, as is true throughout Cuba's private sector (with a few puzzling exceptions), the *paladares* are not allowed to hire outside labor.[27] Second, the owners must provide government agents with receipts to prove that they obtained all their food through legal channels. Third, they must pay a monthly license fee of $375, plus 1,500 Cuban pesos to the government.

Fourth, they pay a progressive income tax with top rates of 50 percent on all revenues after deducting 10 percent for costs, making the tax rates on actual net income confiscatory. For instance, suppose there is a *paladar* with revenues of 1,000 pesos and actual costs of 500 pesos. According to the government tax policy, this *paladar* would be allowed to deduct only 10 percent of its revenues, or 100 pesos, as its costs, and would have to pay a 50 percent tax on 900 pesos (1,000 pesos of revenue minus 100 pesos of reportable costs). Thus, the tax would be 450 pesos on an actual net income of 500 pesos (1,000 pesos of revenue minus 500 pesos of actual costs). This amounts to an effective tax rate of 90 percent. Fifth, restaurants are limited to twelve seats, and only seated customers are allowed to be served; take-out customers are not permitted. Under conditions like these, it is hard to imagine any capital accumulation occurring in the private sector. The few private operators who have significant after-tax income generally find ways to transfer their capital outside Cuba, since accumulation inside the country is only permitted in low-yielding savings accounts. It was no surprise, then, when the government reported that retail food sales fell 14.7 percent in 1998.[28]

Officially sanctioned self-employment reached over two hundred thousand, but many operators have gone underground to avoid onerous state taxes and regulations, and other have been closed down by the government. By late 1998 the number was below one hundred sixty thousand.[29] A clear indication of the declining importance of this sector is given by the government's figures on the amount of taxes collected from workers on their own account. This sum fell from 173.3 million pesos in 1998, to 155.7 million pesos in 1999, to 135.4 million pesos in 2000 and 132.7 million pesos in 2001.[30] This is especially problematic because the private service sector is labor intensive and would provide an excellent absorption area for the half million or more excess workers in state enterprises.

Existing controls spawn under-the-table payoffs to government monitors and encourage black market transactions. Regulations here need to be liberalized, and wholesale markets need to be legalized and allowed to flourish.

Foreign Investment

It is apparent that Cuba has benefited significantly from the foreign investment that has occurred to date. To be sure, foreign investment has provided the catalyst for much of the productive activity in the present economy, namely, the rejuvenation in agriculture and industry to supply the bustling tourist and hard currency markets. Foreign investment has also been a catalyst in transforming Cuba's business culture from one rooted in the complacency and waste of central planning to one that is oriented toward competition and efficiency of the market.

Officially it is claimed that more than $2.5 billion has been invested in the island since 1990.[31] Many claim that this is an inflated figure, but official data (from balance of payments statistics) show that net foreign direct investment (FDI) flows between 1993 and 2000 amounted to $1.93 billion, which would suggest that the $2.5 billion figure may be accurate.[32] It is not known, however, to what extent the official FDI flows actually represent new capital as opposed to offsets in debt-for-equity swaps or imputed value from management contracts with foreign companies.

By the end of 2001 there were 405 "active foreign agreements" (supposedly involving both joint ventures and management contracts), representing an increase from just one contract in 1988 to 31 contracts in 1993, 261 in 1997, and 395 in 2000. The most important contracts so far have been for mining, oil exploration, telecommunications, and tourism. The investors come primarily from Spain (23 percent of the contracts), Canada (19 percent), Italy (9 percent), France (4 percent), the United Kingdom (3.5 percent), and Mexico (3.5 percent).[33]

Paradoxically, FDI flows have increased in Cuba since Clinton signed the Helms-Burton law in March 1996. Among other things, this bill was intended to make it increasingly difficult for foreigners to invest in Cuba. Foreign companies under Helms-Burton can now be sued in U.S. courts if they are found guilty of "trafficking in U.S. property in Cuba." Helms-Burton notwithstanding, FDI flows increased from $82 million in 1996 to $442 million in 1997, before declining to $207 million in 1998 and to $178 million in 1999, but then increasing again to $400 million in 2000.

Although it is clear that there have been substantial FDI flows to Cuba during the last decade, it is also clear that they are far from sufficient to compensate for the lack of state investment. FDI flows during the period 1993–2000 were approximately $1.9 billion. Total gross investments in the same period amounted to around 13.7 billion pesos (in current prices). At the official parity exchange rate of 1:1, the FDI share of gross capital formation in the period was around 14 percent. This is a reasonably high share in comparison to that of other Latin American countries, but it should be recalled that the Cuban investment rate is still low, having increased from a mere 6.4 percent in 1993 to 11.1 percent in 2001.

In his speech before the National Assembly of People's Power in December 1998, Carlos Lage affirmed the difficulties Cuba is having in attracting foreign capital, even to the tourism sector: "Until now foreign investment [in tourism] has been very reduced, coming via management contracts, and the remodeling of some of the hotels where there are management contracts."[34] Cuba's inability to attract more foreign investment is particularly notable given the rapid increase of the same throughout Latin America during the 1990s, where yearly foreign investment rose from $8.4 billion in 1990, to $30.2 billion in 1994, to $50 billion in 1997. Considering the Caribbean alone, foreign investment in 1997, for instance, grew by 25 percent to $4.5 billion.

The problem is, in part, Helms-Burton; in part, it is Cuba's labor costs and government-controlled labor market for foreign companies; and there are other factors as well. There is also an issue regarding the tendency until now for foreign investment to concentrate in natural-resource-intensive sectors (e.g., tourism and agriculture) and energy-intensive sectors (e.g., nickel). With a shortage of energy but an abundance of highly educated labor, Cuba's long-term development needs seem to require investment in certain technology-intensive sectors—areas where Cuba had been developing a specialization within CMEA trade.

Lastly, Cuba's experience with foreign investment since 1993 has been during the initial tourism build-out and mostly during a period of strong growth in the world's markets. Cuba's tourism industry, which had been growing at close to 20 percent annually, saw its revenues fall by 10 percent in 2001. The pace of foreign investment in Cuba slowed in 2001, and it shows no signs yet of picking up. It is difficult to believe that under current circumstances Cuba can rely on foreign investment to generate the basis for sufficient capital accumulation to promote sustained economic growth.

Cuba's New Growth Engine

Import Substitution Based on Tourism

Cuba's tourism-based strategy is aimed at both upgrading local industry and substituting imports.[35] The argument for focusing on tourism is twofold. First, tourism tends to require relatively large amounts of imports from diverse economic sectors. It therefore opens up many import substitution possibilities. Second, tourism is an area where Cuba should have clear comparative advantages ("sun, sand, and salsa"), with additional opportunities to develop other segments such as health tourism, ecological tourism, and cultural and historical tourism.

During the 1990s Cuba's tourism industry experienced steady and rapid growth. The number of foreign tourists increased from 370,000 in 1990 to 1,774,000 in 2000. The number of visitors, however, remained practically stagnant in 2001, as a result of the decline in worldwide travel following the terrorist attacks of September 11, 2001, and recessionary economic conditions in Europe, the United States, and Latin America. Tourism is by far Cuba's largest source of hard currency earnings; its proportional contribution grew from 4 percent in 1990 to 43 percent in 2000. Gross income from tourism in 2000 was estimated to be $1.9 billion, compared to a total of $1.5 billion from exports of goods (primarily sugar and nickel) in that same year.

Gross investment in the tourism industry accounted for almost 20 percent of all investments in Cuba during the 1990s.[36] The number of people employed in the sector is estimated between one hundred and one hundred fifty thousand, and some additional two hundred thousand people are estimated to work in industries that supply inputs to the tourist sector.

In the early nineties, the development of international tourism was understood to be little more than a temporary solution to Cuba's intensifying hard currency shortage. What was an ad hoc solution initially has since become enshrined as a purposeful development strategy. Because the tourism industry has many linkages to other sectors of the Cuban economy, many domestic factories have been upgraded and modernized by replacing imports. New and more efficient production and management systems have been put in place, often in collaboration with foreign partners. The upgraded companies supply goods not only to the tourism sector itself but also to the so-called dollar shops, where most of the customers are Cubans who have access to dollars.

Tourism requires the production of hundreds of basic items, including bedsheets, towels, carpets, mattresses, wallboard, glass, kitchen equipment, elevators, televisions, telephones, VCRs, furniture, bathroom fixtures, food, liquor, and much more. It has been estimated that only 12 percent of goods and services consumed by the tourism industry came from local producers in 1990. As can be seen in table 8.1, this proportion is estimated by Cuban scholars to have risen steadily to 65 percent in 2001.

Most production for the tourist sector is performed by Cuba's holding companies. Although the holding companies are state owned, they operate

Table 8.1. Cuban tourism indicators, 1990–2000

	Tourists (1,000)	Rooms (1,000)	Gross income ($ million)	Income per tourist ($)	Local sales* (%)
2001	1,775	37.2	1,900	1,070	65
2000	1,774	34.7	1,948	1,098	61
1999	1,603	32.3	1,901	1,186	53
1998	1,416	30.9	1,759	1,242	49
1997	1,170	27.4	1,515	1,295	**
1996	1,004	26.9	1,333	1,328	**
1995	746	24.2	1,100	1,475	**
1994	619	23.3	850	1,373	**
1993	546	22.1	720	1,319	**
1992	461	18.7	550	1,193	**
1991	424	16.6	402	948	**
1990	340	12.9	243	715	12***

Source: Claes Brundenius, "Whither the Cuban Economy after Recovery?" (paper presented to Symposium on Tourism Services, World Trade Organization, Geneva, Switzerland, February 22–23, 2001), 383.
*Local sales in foreign currency to the tourism industry as share of total goods and services consumed by the tourism industry.
**No available data.
***Estimate based on Miguel Figueras, "International Tourism in the Cuban Economy" (paper presented to Symposium on Tourism Services, World Trade Organization, Geneva, Switzerland, February 22–23, 2001).

relatively free from government interference and are expected to respond to conditions in the domestic and international market. These companies are linked to local state industries, which, in turn, are upgraded and modernized in order to be able to compete with and ultimately substitute for imports. The local upgraded industries are encouraged to deliver high-quality, competitive goods to the tourism sector, the local dollar shops, and, eventually, export markets. Collaboration with foreign companies is central to this endeavor.

While it is clear that Cuba's recovery since 1993 owes much of its success to the growth of the tourism sector, it is less clear that this sector can be expected to serve as an engine of growth for the future. One problem is that the income per tourist has been declining steadily since 1995, from $1,475 in 1995 to $1,070 in 2001. If the "income per tourist" level of 1995 had been maintained, then gross hard currency income would have been $2.6 billion in 2000, instead of $1.8 billion.

The decline is a by-product of visitors taking shorter trips to Cuba (the average length of stay in Cuba declined from 10 days in 1993 to 7.8 days in 1999) and tourists spending less money during their visits. The latter results from a shortage of activities and goods on which tourists can spend their money while in Cuba as well as the tendency for tour operators to require use of all-inclusive packages that seem to discourage tourists from spending money outside the hotels. Further, the appreciation of the dollar against the Euro through 2001 made travel in Cuba more expensive for Europeans, and this too may help to account for the lower dollar spending per visit.

A related issue is the rapid growth of Caribbean tourist destinations relative to demand. Expansion of tourism in Cuba and elsewhere in the Caribbean is forcing prices down and vacancies up. Thus, while Cuba has hundreds of miles of beautiful coastline still to develop, it is not clear that demand will warrant its development in the near future.

In contrast, one area of success is Cuba's ability to increase the share of local value-added in the tourism sector. According to official data, the domestic share of deliveries to the tourism industry increased from 12 percent in 1990 to 65 percent in 2001, and the national participation in the sales of the dollar shops increased from 29 percent in 1996 to 51 percent in 2000.[37] These shares look impressive, especially having increased over such a short period, but it is not clear how they are calculated. One important issue is the extent to which the imports of raw materials by local tourism-supply industries are deducted to arrive at a net, local contribution.

To ascertain this, it would be necessary to have access to an input-output matrix for the Cuban economy. The last such matrix was constructed in 1987 and is thus of little relevance today. Work on a new input-output model covering all economic activities is not a priority in Havana at present (apparently on economic grounds). Instead the Ministry of Tourism, together with the National Statistics Office, is working on so-called satellite accounts, that is, an input-output model that relates to the tourism industry alone. Such a model would indeed facilitate monitoring the impact of the "engine of growth." The model has, however, not been published. Apparently, the model's results are contradictory and difficult to interpret. Among other reasons, this is due to complications connected with Cuba's dual economy (e.g., an official rate of one peso to one dollar and a parallel market rate of twenty-six pesos to the dollar).

Final Thoughts: Economic Outlook

Although the tourism-based strategy may ultimately prove somewhat successful in the Cuban context, it clearly contains many limitations. First, many of the segments of a typical tourist package to Cuba (or any other tourist package, for that matter) are appropriated by other "players," outside Cuba. It has been estimated that out of the total spending by a typical tourist on a package tour to Cuba, the tour operators get 20 percent and the airlines 40 percent; the remaining 40 percent is spent in Cuba (equivalent to "gross income" in table 8.1).[38] The big winners seem to be the tour operators, and a major problem is that they can, on short notice, decide to shift destinations. They very seldom make long-term commitments. The decisions are probably rational from their own point of view, although they seem irrational and sometimes turn out to be disastrous for the abandoned destinations. Nonetheless, it is possible for Cuba to capture new segments. The national airline (Cubana de Aviación) can try to compete with the international airlines, and the national tourist agencies can try to compete with the big tour operators. But that is an uphill, costly, and risky competition.

Second, there is a question about the adequacy of demand. Not only has the increase in supply been outstripping the growth in demand, but tourism can also be very volatile. Changing world political and economic conditions or shifting personal preferences and fads can occasion sharp increases or decreases in the demand for tourism in Cuba. Cuba experienced such a turnaround following the September 11, 2001, terrorist attacks in the United States.

In this sense, just as is the case with other mono-export, natural-resource-based economies, it is important for Cuba to diversify. Fortunately for Cuba, its economy does have other irons in the fire already (such as nickel, sugar and its derivatives, oil, biotechnology, tobacco, citrus, and fishing).

The island also stands to benefit from the prospective gradual lifting of the U.S. embargo. In September 2002, the Republican-controlled U.S. House of Representatives, under strong pressure from the U.S. farm lobby, voted by nearly a three-to-one margin (more than enough to override a threatened veto from George W. Bush) to allow U.S. banks to finance farm exports to Cuba and to reopen U.S. tourism. But the Senate failed to vote on the proposed changes, and the long-standing restrictions remain in place.

There is also the question about whether the linkages to tourism will lead Cuba to develop higher value-added, technologically upgraded industries that are based on Cuba's relatively skilled labor force. Simple linkages to light industry and some agricultural sectors will tend to lock the economy into low productivity sectors. Certainly, there are some linkages to high productivity sectors (such as telecommunications), but it is too soon to assess how far these will carry new investment and development.

Tourism has had a clear impact in smoothing Cuba's transition out of the inefficient, protected CMEA market into the world market economy. Through the dollar economy, it has provided sufficient stimulus to work for a significant share of the economy. However, the bulk of the economy remains in the state-administered sector. In the end, Cuba's ability to rationalize its internal economic organization will have as much to do with its future performance as its selection of a sectoral development strategy. (See appendix A.)

Notes

1. See Claes Brundenius, "Whither the Cuban Economy after Recovery?" *Journal of Latin American Studies* 34 (2002): 389.

2. The Cubans have kept their real GDP series in constant prices of 1981. This presents the well-known index number problem: growth rates are higher when the base year of prices employed is earlier. In this case, Cuba's base year is twenty-one years old, and this raises a red flag about the estimated rates of Cuba's economic recovery. As Brundenius has elaborated based on the *Anuario estadístico de Cuba* for 1996 and 1999 and updates from official data, when 1981 constant prices are used, by 2000 Cuba fully recovered its level of 1989 industrial output; however, when 1995 constant prices are used, by 2000 Cuba's industrial output was only 53.5 percent of its 1989 level. Brundenius, "Whither the Cuban Economy," 386.

3. It cannot, however, be argued that the Cuban government has not made serious efforts to maintain its social safety net. For instance, in the 1998 state budget, expenditures on social assistance rose by 32.6 percent, on housing and community services by 16.8 percent, on public health by 7.1 percent, on social security by 5.3 percent, and on education by 3.9 percent. In contrast, spending on defense and civil order fell by 1.3 percent. For 1999, social spending increased by 13.2 percent, constituting 43.2 percent of the total budget. For 2000, social spending increased another 8.9 percent and rose to 43.3 percent of the total state budget. See Cepal, *Balance preliminar de las economias de América Latina y el Caribe, 1999,* 77–79, *2000,* 76–78; speeches by José Luis Rodríguez, Osvaldo Martínez, and Carlos Lage before the National Assembly of Popular Power on December 21, 1998, *Granma,* December 1998; and Claes Brundenius, "Cuba: Retreat from Entitlement?" in *Exclusion and Engagement: Social Policy in Latin America,* ed. Chris Abel and Colin Lewis (London: Institute of Latin American Studies, 2002). According to official data, life expectancy in Cuba rose slightly during the 1990s (from 74.6 years in 1990 to 74.8 years in 1999) and infant mortality continued to decline (from 10.7 per 1,000 in 1990 to 6.4 per 1,000 in 1999).

4. Another area wherein the Cuban revolution has made impressive gains is in the economic condition of blacks. Unfortunately, Cuban blacks have been hit hardest by the economic collapse. In large part this is because they have disproportionately remained in Cuba and have few relatives abroad who send them hard currency remittances. For this and other reasons, racial disparities and tensions have grown in Cuba in recent years.

5. Rikke Fabienke, "Income and Wealth Distribution in Cuba after 1989" (paper presented to the conference "Globalization, Changing Paradigms and Development Options in the Third World," Centre for Development Research, Copenhagen, June 11–13, 1998). Fabienke also finds that the Gini coefficient increased from 0.22 in 1986 to 0.48 in 1995. The estimated Gini coefficient in 1953 was 0.55.

6. Lia Ane, "Cuba: Reformas, recuperación y equidad" (paper presented to the Second Symposium on Economic Reform and Social Change in Latin America and the Caribbean, Cali, Colombia, November 2000), 23–24. Cited in Brundenius, "Cuba: Retreat from Entitlement?"

7. With an independent central bank and bond market, the government would typically finance its deficits by selling bonds to the public, not by printing money. Although this may have inflationary implications under certain circumstances, there would be no direct connection to excess liquidity.

8. Liquidity refers to the amount of assets that are available for the purchase of goods and services. Most frequently, it refers to funds in checking accounts and cash in the hands of the public.

9. See Ana Julia Jatar-Hausmann, *The Cuban Way: Capitalism, Communism and Confrontation* (West Hartford, Conn.: Kumarian Press, 1999), 77.

10. Because of risk, foreign currency cash flow issues, and the length of time between the placing of an order for internationally traded goods and delivery, virtually all foreign trade is financed, that is, bank credits make it possible for the producer to be paid in local currency before the good is delivered.

11. An export enclave is a sector that is largely detached from the rest of the economy and produces for the export market.

12. The majority of state enterprises in Cuba run a deficit. This deficit is traditionally covered by funds from the state budget.

13. Dollar use was already rampant at the time. By depenalizing the use of dollars, the Cuban government was hoping to bring the dollars out of the underground economy and into open trade activity where they could be captured by the government. See Jatar-Hausmann, *The Cuban Way,* for a tactful discussion of the dollar depenalization and its effects.

14. CADECA is the acronym for *cajas de cambio,* or exchange houses. Cuban citizens can exchange pesos for dollars or vice versa at these exchange offices. The rate of exchange fluctuated between 20 and 22 pesos to the dollar until 2002, when the peso depreciated to approximately 26 to the dollar.

15. Such remittances are estimated to have reached nearly $1 billion annually by the end of the nineties. They have grown as the economic situation of Cuban Americans has improved and that of Cubans on the island has deteriorated.

16. Economist Intelligence Unit (London: EIU), 62. The low rate of capacity utilization is due to the shortage of inputs and the lack of demand.

17. CEPAL, *La economía cubana: Reformas estructurales y desempeño en los noventa,* (Mexico City: United Nations CEPAL, 2000), 253.

18. CEPAL, *Balance preliminar* (2000), 76.

19. A useful discussion of hard currency and related bonuses with extensive examples from the foreign enclave sector is provided in Philip Peters, "A Different

Kind of Workplace: Foreign Investment in Cuba," Alexis de Toqueville Institution, Arlington, Va., March 1999.

20. Cuba maintains an official exchange rate of one peso equal to one dollar. Cuba uses this rate for trade accounting and for certain transactions, such as exchanges with foreign companies of foreign currency for pesos to pay their Cuban workforce. The parallel market rate, the rate used at CADECA outlets, is set to approximate the market supply and demand for pesos and dollars. As such, it is expected to eliminate, or at least sharply reduce, interest in currency trading on the black market. By attracting the dollars from remittances and other sources into the state-run CADECA chain, the government is able to capture a greater share of the hard currency entering Cuba. Of these 1.5 million workers in 1998, 1.13 million received these incentives in cash form, representing a 21 percent increase over 1997. Rodríguez, speech, December 21, 1998.

21. Rent-seeking behavior refers to a situation wherein a person, because of a political appointment or role in a monopolized market, can take advantage of his or her position. As a result, the individual can personally profit, but prices are altered to lower efficiency.

22. Fiscal balance generally refers to a balanced budget, and monetary balance refers to a situation wherein, given the institutions and practices of the financial system, the population is holding neither too much nor too little money to purchase the goods being produced.

23. In some cases, an enterprise's cash flow can be jeopardized because it does not receive punctual payment for goods shipped. On their books the money they are owed is called an account receivable. Since the Cuban state owns most enterprises, it can shift the accounts receivable among enterprises instead of making cash infusions (subsidies). This will lower the apparent budget deficit. The government can also arrange for the central bank to loan enterprises money instead of taking it out of the government budget. This too will lower the apparent budget deficit. At least until their switch to the western System of National Accounts (SNA) in the early 1990s, the Cubans kept a single consolidated government budget. However, if they did not switch to keeping separate local and central government budgets along with the adoption of the SNA, then this CEPAL observation would appear to be erroneous. If they did switch, then the observation would appear to hold.

24. All machinery and equipment depreciates over time. A country's capital stock (the value of its machinery, equipment, and infrastructure) grows only if the new investments in a particular year exceed the amount of depreciation in its existing capital stock.

25. Oficina Nacional de Estadísticas, *Cuba en cifras, 2000* (Havana, 2001), 30–31; CEPAL, *Cuba: Evolución económica durante 2001* (Mexico City: U.N. CEPAL, 2002, LC/MEX/L.525) (on line), 1–41.

26. The state sector comprises over three-fourths of all official employment in the country. It includes almost all industrial, mining, transport, military, and utility production. These branches constitute the traditional state sector, along with state farms in agriculture. The state sector also includes most tourism and finance as well

as a substantial share of services. Other sources of employment include coopera-tives, paladares, and international tourism in hotels.

27. The proscription on hiring "wage labor" has been common to all Socialist economies and derives from the Marxist notion of exploitation. More practically, the Cuban government limits the hiring of outside labor because it fears the conse-quent growth of a powerful private sector.

28. Martínez, speech, December 21, 1998.

29. There is an excellent discussion of the self-employed sector in Jatar-Haus-mann, *The Cuban Way*, chaps. 6 and 7.

30. *Cuba en cifras, 2000,* 34; Cepal, *Cuba: Evolución,* 2.

31. With commitments included, the total amount reportedly reached over $5 billion. *Cuba: Country Report; May 2001* (London: EIU, 2001).

32. See, for instance, María Werlau, "Update on Foreign Investment in Cuba: 1996–97," in *Cuba in Transition,* vol. 7 (Washington D.C.: Association for the Study of the Cuban Economy, 1997).

33. *Cuba: Inversiones y negocios, 1998–2000* (Havana: Centro de Estudios de la Economía Cubana, 2000), 42–43. Detailed data (for instance, invested amounts cross-classified by country and sector) are not published in Cuba, reportedly as a way to safeguard company secrets in order to avoid retaliation by the United States. According to estimates by Pérez-López, the total amount of delivered FDI as of May 2, 1998, was $1,757 million (in contrast to an announced total of $5,636 million). Jorge Pérez-López, "Foreign Direct Investment in the Cuban Economy: A Critical Look" (unpublished manuscript, July 1998).

34. Lage, speech, December 21, 1998. Translation is by the author.

35. The argument in this section follows in part that in Claes Brundenius, "Tour-ism as an Engine of Growth: Reflections on Cuba's New Development Strategy" (working paper, Center for Development Research, Copenhagen, 2002).

36. Miguel Figueras, "International Tourism in the Cuban Economy" (paper presented to Symposium on Tourism Services, World Trade Organization, Geneva, February 22–23, 2001).

37. Marquetti and Garcia use a figure of 18 percent, not 12 percent, for 1990. They also cite the proportion of 61 percent for 2000. Hiram Marquetti and Anicia Garcia, "Cuba's Model of Industrial Growth," in *Development Prospects in Cuba,* ed. Pedro Monreal (London: Institute of Latin American Studies, 2002).

38. Estimates provided by Miguel Figueras, advisor to the Cuban Ministry of Tourism (MINTUR).

V

Politics

9

The "Single Party of the Cuban Nation" Faces the Future

William M. LeoGrande

"Men die, but the party is immortal," read the 1973 banner headline in *Granma*, official organ of the Communist Party of Cuba. As suggested by the article that followed, at a time when the party was being strengthened as part of the "institutionalization" of the revolution, the Communist Party is intended to be the organizational guarantor of the continuity of Cuba's Socialist system.[1] But the history of the Cuban party has always been atypical among fraternal Communist parties elsewhere in the Socialist world. It did not lead the struggle against Fulgencio Batista's dictatorship in the 1950s; it did not direct the political system in the 1960s and 1970s; and since the collapse of the Socialist camp, the Cuban party has looked and sounded more like the party of the Cuban nation (and Cuban nationalism) than the vanguard of the revolutionary working class.[2] The party's challenge in the years to come is to find a way to accommodate its leadership of Cuban politics to the island's rapidly changing economic and social reality.

Origins of the Communist Party of Cuba

Inaugurated in 1965, the Communist Party of Cuba (Partido Comunista de Cuba, PCC) was the first Communist party created after the triumph of the revolution it was intended to lead. Built during the 1960s from among the veterans of three revolutionary organizations that fought against Batista's dictatorship, the PCC did not preside over Cuba's transition to Socialism or direct the new political system that followed.[3] During the revolutionary regime's critical early years, it was the Rebel Army (later, the Fuerzas Armadas Revolucionarias, FAR) that provided the political apparatus through which Fidel Castro and his closest compatriots governed the nation.

Creation of the new Communist party followed Castro's declaration of the Socialist character of the revolution during the Bay of Pigs invasion, and it had both domestic and international purposes. Domestically, Castro sought to forge a political instrument that would unify the fractious revolutionary family and mobilize supporters; internationally, he sought to demonstrate to the Soviet Union that Cuba was, indeed, a member in good standing of the Socialist camp, worthy of Soviet economic assistance and military support. But the party-building process got off to a rocky start. The first effort, the Integrated Revolutionary Organizations (Organizaciones Revolucionarias Integradas, ORI), was dismantled in early 1962 after a faction of old Communists from the Popular Socialist Party tried to capture control of it by filling its ranks with PSP members to the virtual exclusion of veterans from Castro's Twenty-sixth of July Movement.[4]

The second attempt, the United Party of the Socialist Revolution (Partido Unido de la Revolución Socialista, PURS), was shaken by another crisis when two leading members of the former Communist Party were implicated in the infamous 1957 murder by Batista's police of revolutionary students at 7 Humboldt Street. The subsequent trial became a political airing of animosities among the veterans of the PSP, the Twenty-sixth of July Movement, and the student-based Revolutionary Directorate. Only Castro's intervention prevented the revolutionary leadership from shattering into warring factions.[5] Yet another crisis erupted in 1968, when a small group of party members (a "microfaction") was caught conspiring with Soviet-bloc diplomats to replace Castro for not conforming to Moscow's economic views.[6]

As a result of this turmoil, the leaders of the revolution were reluctant to turn over too much authority to the new party apparatus for fear that their efforts to institutionalize Fidel Castro's charismatic authority might dissipate it instead. Castro and a small circle of trusted lieutenants, most of whom had fought together in the Sierra Maestra during the struggle against Batista, continued to make major policy decisions. When the new Communist Party was finally inaugurated in 1965, this inner circle became the party's Political Bureau, but the change was more a matter of name than process. Castro continued to make major policy decisions in consultation with the same people. The more elaborate decision-making machinery of the party, including the one-hundred-member Central Committee, remained unused for most of the next decade. The PCC did not convene its first congress until 1975, before which it had neither a program nor statutes. Its small size (just 55,000 members in 1969, or 0.6 percent of the population) made it the smallest ruling Communist party in the world by a wide margin, and it had party organizations in only 16 percent of the nation's work centers, covering less than half the labor force.[7]

Only in the 1970s did the PCC develop into an organization strong enough to assert real direction over the Cuban political system. The "institutionalization" of the revolution, commenced after the failure of the ten-million-ton harvest in 1970, brought major changes to all of the island's political structures, but the party benefited most from this decision to replace the ad hoc, fluid political processes of the 1960s with more formal, permanent institutions. The PCC's founding congress was held in 1975, by which time it had grown to 202,807 members (2.2 percent of the population). Its organizational apparatus was stronger and more elaborate. Party bodies at all levels, including the Central Committee, began meeting regularly. In short, by the late 1970s the PCC had taken on the leading role in politics typical of ruling Communist parties elsewhere.[8]

The years 1975–86, from the First Congress to the Third Congress of the Communist Party of Cuba might be called a period of routine or "normal" politics. Except for internal turmoil sparked by the Mariel crisis in 1980, the domestic political scene was relatively quiet. Dramatic events tended to be concentrated in the international arena—Cuba's involvement in Africa, its chairmanship of the Nonaligned Movement, its confrontation with the United States over Central America, its defeat in Grenada. During these years, the PCC grew in size, organizational capacity, and administrative authority. Membership grew substantially, from 211,642 members in late 1975, to 434,143 in 1980, and 523,639 in 1985. Party bodies met regularly, and the apparatus developed a system for controlling the appointment of cadres to all major posts in the government and mass organizations.[9]

The dominant theme at the PCC's Second Congress in 1980 was continuity. The Second Congress reaffirmed the validity of the program adopted at the First Congress and most of the supporting resolutions. The bulk of the discussion both before and during the congress focused on social and economic development.[10] The party's work, as Castro noted in his main report, had been "directed towards boosting and consolidating the Economic Planning and Management System, improving the mechanisms of economic leadership, and raising the quality of production."[11]

In the mid-1980s, Mikhail Gorbachev's perestroika and glasnost stimulated more open debate about the future of state Socialism throughout the Communist bloc, and Cuba was no exception. Party ideological chief Carlos Aldana would later confess to being among those smitten by Gorbachev's ideas, until he was set straight by Fidel.[12] Castro, too, saw the economic failings of the Soviet planning model—the inefficiency, the tendency to produce corruption, the erosion of ideology by the individualism of material incentives. But where Gorbachev saw the need for more radical economic restructuring to give fuller scope to the market, Castro saw the limited market reforms of the 1970s as the source of the problem, not the solution. Thus the Cuban version of perestroika was to reverse course, limiting and scaling back the use of market mechanisms and emphasizing, once again, the political-ideological element of voluntarism and moral incentives within the broader system of economic command.

The Third Congress in 1986 marked the launch of the rectification campaign, a major retreat from the Soviet-sponsored Socialist economic management system (Economic Planning and Management System, SDPE) installed in the mid-1970s and praised during the Second Congress. Criticizing the SDPE for fostering inefficiency, corruption, and profit-minded selfishness, Castro called for the "rectification of errors and negative tendencies" in the economic management. The campaign focused on recentralizing economic planning authority, dismantling SDPE material incentives and market mechanisms, and combating corruption.[13] The free farmers' markets launched in 1980 were closed, wage inequalities were narrowed, and voluntary labor was touted once again—all echoes of the radicalism of the late 1960s. Che Guevara assumed a new prominence as his views on the superiority of moral over material incentives gained new currency.

By putting politics in command over economic policy, the rectification campaign implicitly meant a more assertive role for the PCC. At the outset of the campaign, for example, principal responsibility for economic policy was moved from the Central Planning Board (Junta Central de Planificación, JUCEPLAN) to a special Central Group of the PCC's Political Bureau.[14] Such a major reversal in policy produced some political casualties among the elite. The foremost was the top planning official, Humberto Pérez, president of JUCEPLAN, who was dropped from his alternate membership in the Political Bureau at the Third Congress. Also dropped from that body were full members Ramiro Valdés (replaced as minister of the interior), Sergio Del Valle (replaced as minister of health), Blas Roca (replaced for health reasons), and Guillermo García. Three other alternate members were dropped as well. In the PCC Central Committee, 37 percent of the full members and 47 percent of the alternate members were replaced—the largest turnover in the party's elite bodies since its founding. The new leaders promoted to the Political Bureau included the leaders of mass organizations and provincial PCC secretaries, in line with the rectification theme of focusing on ideological work led by the party.[15]

The rectification campaign can be traced to both political and economic origins. Politically, the regime suffered from reduced legitimacy in the early 1980s, beginning with the Mariel exodus and aggravated by the alleged corruption scandal of Luis Domínguez, a protégé of Fidel's who was caught amassing a small fortune in hard currency. The debilitation of the Communist Party, its neglect of political work, and the erosion of Socialist ethics due to the incursion of the market all weakened the regime's capacity to mobilize support. On the economic front, the regime suffered a severe hard currency shortage in the 1980s due to having borrowed excessively from Western sources in the late 1970s. As domestic production stagnated in the early 1980s, the only hope of servicing the external debt was to reduce domestic consumption in order to boost exports. Thus the return to moral over material incentives had an underlying economic logic—domestic austerity was a necessary corollary of Cuba's economic stabilization progress.[16]

The Communist Party in the Special Period: The Fourth Congress

Over the next several years, the Cuban regime was rocked by a bewildering rush of events, both domestic and international. At home, the arrest, trial, and execution of General Arnaldo Ochoa and his coconspirators for cocaine trafficking, and a subsequent series of corruption trials, struck a heavy blow to regime legitimacy. During a period when the standard of living for ordinary Cubans had been falling and Fidel Castro had been exhorting people to emulate the selflessness of Che Guevara by working harder for less, the scandals revealed that significant numbers of senior officials were living luxuriously through corruption.[17]

Abroad, the European Communist states were experiencing a flowering of economic and political reform spurred by Gorbachev's policies of glasnost and perestroika, which ran directly counter to the retreat from market mechanisms represented by Cuba's rectification campaign. Jorge Domínguez notes that there was a vigorous, albeit somewhat veiled, intellectual debate in Cuba over the merits of Gorbachev's reforms until the summer of 1989, by which time Castro's negative verdict on the experiments had been registered unequivocally.[18] Then, the sudden collapse of European Communism triggered an economic cataclysm in Cuba, prompting an uncharacteristically vigorous debate within the Cuban political elite over the future of the revolution.

Held at the beginning of Cuba's special period, the PCC's Fourth Congress endorsed a series of economic and political reforms designed to bring Cuba safely through the trauma of the demise of the Socialist bloc. The special period's economic measures were analogous to a wartime economic crisis plan; its political measures went under the general rubric of "perfecting" and "revitalizing" Cuba's political institutions.

As in 1970, after the failure of the ten-million-ton harvest, the Cuban leadership reacted to the crisis both by revising economic policy and by trying to rebuild regime legitimacy by making political institutions more responsive to popular demands. From the outset, however, the basic strategy was to undertake only the reforms absolutely necessary to guarantee the survival of the existing order, although the political leadership did not always agree about the extent of the requisite reforms. A transition away from either Socialism (i.e., state control of the commanding heights of the economy and maintenance of the welfare state) or Leninism (one-party rule with limited freedoms of expression and association) was never seriously contemplated, as symbolized by Castro's slogan of the time, "Socialism or death!"[19]

In the economic realm, the leadership's initial plan was a short-term strategy for surviving a transition during which Cuba would reorient its international trade relations and adjust to the loss of Soviet subsidies, but not fundamentally alter its centrally planned economy. In addition to emphasizing self-sufficiency (especially in food) to reduce the need for imports, the strategy called for increasing foreign investment and exploiting the potential of the tourism sector.[20] By 1993, however, it was clear that these measures were inadequate. From 1989 to 1993, Cuba's GDP (gross domestic product) fell by 35 percent, according to official figures, and by as much as 50 percent, according to unofficial ones.[21] The resulting political discontent produced serious antigovernment disturbances and growing pressure for emigration, culminating in the so-called rafters crisis of 1994 when tens of thousands of Cubans set off for the United States on flimsy rafts.

Starting in late 1993, the government adopted a series of structural domestic reforms that amounted to a de facto acknowledgment that changes in the external sector of the economy were not sufficient to meet the crisis. Among the reforms were reintroduction of free farmers' markets, transformation of most state farms into cooperatives (*unidades básicas de producción*, UBPC), legalization of self-employment in most occupations, reduction of subsidies to state enterprises, reduction of price subsidies on nonessential consumer goods, and legalization of ordinary citizens' possession and use of dollars.[22] Together, these reforms fueled a gradual economic recovery beginning in 1994, and by the end of 2000 the economy had recovered to about 88 percent of the 1989 GDP. Outside analysts disagree as to whether the limited reforms made thus far are sufficient to produce stable, long-term growth, but the success of the reforms at reversing the slide in the GDP meant that Cuba's political leadership was able to forego more drastic changes, such as the legalization of small and medium-sized private enterprises—a step the leadership debated during the middle of the decade.[23]

In the political realm, reforms have been less dramatic and can be seen as an extension of the changes initiated earlier as part of the rectification process. Fidel Castro's diagnosis of the regime's political problem was that it had copied the economic and political models of the European Socialist states too closely. Thus, Cuba reproduced a form of Socialism that was highly bureaucratized and apolitical, in the sense that the party focused its efforts too much on economic management and not enough on the "political work" of sustaining its ideological hegemony.[24] This was Castro's rationale for rectification, his explanation for the eventual collapse of the European regimes, and his motive for limiting political reforms during the special period.[25]

To counter the political weaknesses they saw in Europe, the Cuban leaders sought to reform their political institutions by making them more responsive—a process very similar to the "new phase" of "institutionalizing" the revolution that followed the 1970 economic debacle. For the PCC, the first wave of change was the introduction of secret ballot elections for party leaders at the base (in the workplace "nuclei") in early 1990. Prior to that, elections had been by open nomination and a show of hands. Subsequently, new municipal and provincial leaders were elected (in the usual way, from slates of preselected nominees), producing a 50 percent turnover in municipal leaders and the replacement of two of the fourteen provincial secretaries.[26]

Next came a major downsizing of the party bureaucracy preceding the Fourth Party Congress. The number of departments in the Central Committee staff organization was reduced from nineteen to nine, and the staff was cut by 50 percent. The Party Secretariat was abolished as a separate organization, with its organizational responsibilities distributed to individual members of the Political Bureau. Provincial committee staffs were cut as well, and overall, some two-thirds of the positions in the PCC's paid apparatus were abolished. In the posts that remained, a significant number of the incumbents were replaced.[27]

The March 1990 call for the Fourth Party Congress sought an unprecedented openness in debate, not just among party members but among the entire populace, so as to foster greater participation and build "the necessary consensus" for the government's policy response to the special period.[28] But the call was so extraordinary that people did not know how to respond, and the leadership halted the discussions after just a few weeks because the grassroots meetings were producing little more than hortatory praise for the party and the revolution. "We're just not used to debating," explained party ideological chief Carlos Aldana.[29]

In June, debate resumed under the guidance of a new Political Bureau statement emphasizing the virtues of open discussion: "The quality of these meetings can't be measured—as we mistakenly have, at times—by the unanimity reached, or by the absence of points raised that could be considered problematic or divergent." But even then, it was clear that some in the leadership were worried that excessive democratic debate might get out of hand. The revised call also set limits, noting that the discussions were intended to provide "political clarification" and that the Socialist character of the Cuban system and leading role of the party were not open to debate. The first round of discussions, the June document noted candidly, had produced "a worry among some party leaders and cadres about what are the limits of debate." The answer: "An undeniable value that is not open to question is, of course, the Socialist option. . . . Equally, we reaffirm fully the idea of a single party [that is both] *martiano* [following José Martí's ideas and example] and Marxist-Leninist."[30] Party conservatives thought the debate process, despite its limitations, was still too vigorous. Political Bureau member José Machado Ventura complained publicly that debate on the economy had been "improper and hypercritical . . . incompatible with our principles and likely to sow confusion."[31]

Eventually, some three million people participated in the precongress debates, producing over one million suggestions.[32] There was sharp debate on issues such as whether to allow religious believers to join the Communist Party and on whether free farmers' markets, abolished during rectification, ought to be resumed.[33] The principal political criticisms voiced in the discussions concerned the sclerotic bureaucratism that had overtaken local government and the mass organizations, especially the Federation of Cuban Women (FMC), which some people argued should be disbanded or merged with the Committees for the Defense of the Revolution (CDR).[34]

The local Organs of People's Power (OPP) were widely described as ineffective, largely for lack of resources and insufficient authority in dealing with the government's administrative bureaucracy.[35] People in the precongress meetings also criticized the National Assembly of People's Power for holding superficial and pro forma debates and for being little more than a rubber stamp for government proposals. One of the more popular suggestions was to have provincial assembly delegates and National Assembly deputies directly elected rather than picked by the municipal assembly delegates.[36]

Debate continued at the Fourth Congress itself when it opened in October 1991, and for the first time some votes on proposed resolutions were not unanimous. The party underwent significant changes at the Fourth Congress. Its statutes were amended to redefine the PCC as the party of the "Cuban nation" rather than the party of the working class, and the new statutes emphasized the ideological roots in the ideas of Martí, Marx, and Lenin.[37] The prohibition on party membership for religious believers was lifted, and the process for choosing new party members was simplified so that more members could be drawn from work centers based on a vote of their coworkers (rather than requiring sponsorship by existing members or prior membership in the Youth Communist Union).[38] Over the next five years, these changes produced a flood of new members as the PCC's ranks grew from 611,627 at the Fourth Congress to 780,000 in 1997 on the eve of the Fifth Congress. By 1997, 232,000 people, one-third of the PCC's total membership, had joined the party since the beginning of the special period.[39]

The Fourth Congress also adopted the suggestion that all delegates to OPP assemblies be directly elected by their constituents, and it called for the strengthening of the National Assembly's work commissions.[40] But it rejected proposals made in the precongress meetings that candidates be allowed to campaign and thereby present contrasting policy views. Nor did it endorse the idea of allowing competing policy views in the state media.[41] On the economic front, the congress endorsed a liberalization of rules governing foreign direct investment and the legalization of self-employment, but it rejected reopening the free farmers' markets (although, as the economic crisis deepened, this decision would be reversed in 1994).[42]

Divisions in the Party: Reformers versus Hard-Liners

The limited reforms produced by the Fourth Congress were the result of an internal struggle in the PCC between a reform faction, led by party ideological chief Carlos Aldana, UJC (Union of Young Communists) first secretary (later foreign minister) Roberto Robaina, and economic manager Carlos Lage, on the one hand, and a conservative faction ("*los duros,*" or "hard-liners," as they are known in Cuba) led by José Ramón Machado Ventura and José Ramón Balaguer, on the other. The reformers pushed for the use of market mechanisms to speed economic recovery, and greater political space for dissenting views that were not manifestly counterrevolutionary. The conservatives argued that rapid economic change would undercut the party's political control and that any political opening in the midst of economic crisis risked setting off a torrent of criticism that might sweep away the regime, as had happened in Eastern Europe and the Soviet Union.[43]

Initially, the reformers seemed to have the upper hand. In early 1990, the Central Committee's announcement of the campaign to "revitalize" the party was accompanied by a call to create "a climate favorable for the development of creative thinking and fertile debate." At the same meeting, Robaina was elevated to alternate member status in the Political Bureau.[44] The call for the Fourth Congress followed shortly thereafter, stimulating unprecedented discussion, as we have already seen. Yet the call also contained a warning that the right to debate and criticize would not extend to regime opponents. "Counterrevolutionary and antisocial elements . . . should be warned that acting at this time as the puppets of imperialism will mean the[ir] becoming the biggest traitors Cuba has ever had and that is how the law and the people will treat them."[45]

A delay of several months in convening the Fourth Congress was attributed to the unresolved internal debate between reformers and conservatives. "There is a major struggle between the forces represented by Aldana and those of Machado Ventura, and Fidel hasn't decided between them," explained an unnamed Cuban government official.[46] When the congress did convene, radical reform proposals, particularly that of creating a prime minister position separate from the first secretary of the party, thereby devolving some of Castro's authority to other decision makers, were not on the agenda. The leadership had decided that major political changes were too risky in light of Cuba's economic problems. "For the revolution to be perfected, it must first close ranks," Carlos Aldana explained after the close of the congress. "For us to develop new democratic processes and apply economic recipes . . . that lead to an improvement in our standard of living—for all of that to happen in 1994, we have to close ranks now."[47] Nevertheless, the reformers fared reasonably well in the new leadership lineup; Carlos Lage and Abel Prieto, head of the National Union of Writers and Artists (UNEAC), were added to the Political Bureau, joining Aldana and Robaina. After the congress, the locus of debate between reformers and conservatives shifted to the local and national OPP elections scheduled for late 1992 and early 1993.

The cause of party reformers was dealt a severe blow in September 1992 when Carlos Aldana, the most powerful Cuban politician besides the

Castro brothers, was dismissed from the Political Bureau, ostensibly for involvement in illegal financial dealings.[48] Regardless of the real reason for Aldana's dismissal, it changed the balance of power within the top echelons of the party in favor of the conservatives. Aldana's position as chief of ideology for the Central Committee was taken over by conservative José Ramón Balaguer, who was also promoted to the Political Bureau.[49]

As the economy deteriorated in 1992 and 1993, the Cuban leadership's tolerance for political dissent contracted along with it. Raúl Castro emerged as the pivotal figure in the regime's response. Despite being hostile to the idea of political liberalization, he was a persistent advocate of economic reforms, applying the management experiments underway in the armed forces since 1986 to the state sector of the civilian economy. These reforms, adopted under the rubric of the Enterprise-Perfecting Plan *(Perfeccionamiento Empresarial)*, involved significant decentralization of management authority and increased use of market-based incentives.[50] In 1993, as food shortages worsened, Raúl finally convinced Fidel to allow the reopening of private farmers' markets as a means of stimulating food production. Providing enough for people to eat had become a matter of national security. "Beans are more important than cannons," Raúl argued.[51]

But on political issues, Raúl was intransigent. In the midst of a government crackdown on the small dissident movement that followed the Fourth Congress, he warned that the government might revive the Revolutionary Tribunals used to try accused counterrevolutionaries in the early 1960s.[52] As the economy continued to decline, political discontent grew, culminating in popular disturbances with political overtones: in the summer of 1993, in Cojimar; in August 1994, on the Havana waterfront; and in the so-called rafters crisis of September 1994. By 1995, the leadership's tolerance for voices favoring even modest political change had evaporated.

In March 1996, Raúl Castro presented a report from the Political Bureau to a plenum of the Central Committee in which he outlined, with considerable candor, the political and ideological challenges posed by the collapse of European Communism, Cuba's terrible economic decline, and the regime's necessary concessions to the market and private sector. All this had created "feelings of depression and political confusion," he acknowledged. The party needed to wage a "battle of ideas" to explain these events, lest people lose faith in Socialist values and be seduced by capitalist consumerism. "We must convince the people, or the enemy will do it."[53]

As a negative object lesson, he singled out the Central Committee's own research centers, especially the Center for the Study of the Americas (CEA), which had fallen prey to U.S. efforts at "internal subversion." Moreover, he extended his critique to every institution of intellectual pursuit. "Within the universities, in film, radio, television and culture in general, both types of behavior exist: behavior which is faithful to our revolutionary people; and the minority with an annexationist orientation, far removed from the patriotic conduct of the majority of our intellectuals." He warned against the mass media's taking an overly critical attitude—an error that eroded party authority in Eastern Europe and the Soviet Union, paving the way for the restoration of capitalism. The party would need to "examine" all these institutions, he concluded, in order to thwart U.S. schemes to turn them into "fifth columnists."[54]

The subsequent investigation of CEA and the other research centers was directed by the conservative faction of the party, despite opposition from the reformers. Resistance to the political purge within the Political Bureau itself blunted its impact.[55] Although the research team at CEA was dispersed to other research centers, its members were exonerated of any counterrevolutionary activity. Other research centers escaped largely unscathed, except for the chilling effect of the investigations.

Party conservatives were able to gain the upper hand because of heightened tension between Cuba and the United States. Raúl's March 1996 speech came just a few weeks after the Cuban air force shot down two Brothers to the Rescue planes, which prompted the quick passage of the Helms-Burton bill, further tightening the U.S. embargo and writing it into law. But even before the planes were shot down, Cuban leaders had been increasingly concerned that Washington might exploit the ongoing debate in Cuban society to subvert the revolution. Discontent and demoralization were real, for all the reasons Raúl Castro outlined, and the proliferation of groups and social sectors not directly under party control—small farmers, entrepreneurs, the churches, NGOs (nongovernmental organizations)—created openings that the enemy might exploit. Dissident groups, albeit small and isolated, were proliferating and trying to forge a coalition, Concilio Cubano, which the government quickly broke up by arresting its most prominent instigators.

The one element of Cuban civil society that seemed relatively insulated from the closure of political space in 1995–96 was the Catholic Church. But conservatives in the PCC were unhappy with the degree of latitude the church was allowed. Some spoke against opening the party to believers during the debates leading up to and during the Fourth Congress. Others reportedly opposed inviting the pope to visit the island, a visit that took place in 1998.[56] In 2001, the Havana provincial party, led by hard-liner Esteban Lazo, produced a report that called for a counteroffensive against the church's growing role as a provider of medical and other social benefits.[57]

Stabilizing the Status Quo: The Fifth Party Congress

The Fifth Congress of the PCC, held in 1997, offered an opportunity to assess the effectiveness of the party's and government's response to the crisis of the special period. Two main resolutions were discussed in the preparatory meetings leading to the congress—one on economic policy and one on politics. Together, they demonstrated the limits of adaptive change. The economic resolution called for greater efficiency and continued growth of the tourist sector as the leading source of hard currency; it offered no new reforms.[58] The political resolution, entitled "The Party of Unity, Democracy, and the Human Rights We Defend," constituted a manifesto against political liberalization. It argued in defense of Cuba's one-party system led by the Communist Party, in favor of Socialist democracy based on mass participation rather than the bourgeois "liberalism" of contention among diverse interests, and for human rights based on social justice rather than unfettered political liberties. In short, it presented a brief for the political status quo. The document portrayed the revolution of 1959 as a direct continuation of the struggle for independence and national sovereignty stretching back to 1868, and the Cuban Communist Party as the "legitimate heir" of José Martí's Cuban Revolutionary Party. Disunity among the revolutionary forces led to defeat in 1878, to U.S. domination after 1898, and to the collapse of the 1933 revolution. "Hence, the great lesson has emerged out of our own historical experience: without unity, revolutionaries and the people can achieve nothing in their struggle," and unity required, as in the time of Martí, a single party to prevent the United States from reimposing neocolonial capitalism on Cuba.[59]

Interestingly, the Fifth Congress elected a new Central Committee of only 150 members, far below the 225 elected at the Fourth Congress. The downsizing was intended to make the body more efficient and to prevent it from being infected with any "ideological viruses," explained Raúl Castro, who apparently had a major role in the selection process. "What happened to the socialist countries of Eastern Europe and the Soviet Union is not going to happen here," he added.[60] Apparently, the diversity of views inside the party that produced differences between reformers and hard-liners, although submerged since Aldana's dismissal, persisted. Reformers suffered yet another blow, however, when Foreign Minister Roberto Robaina was fired for poor performance in 1999 (although his termination coincided with a corruption inquiry into a firm where his wife was a top official). He was replaced by Felipe Pérez Roque, Castro's chief of staff, a reputed ideological hard-liner.[61]

The reaffirmation of the limited-reform strategy made at the Fifth Party Congress suggested that Castro and his top lieutenants were generally convinced they had weathered the worst of the economic and political maelstrom following the Soviet Union's collapse. The gradual recovery of the economy and the absence of further outbreaks of public disorder after 1994 served as evidence of their strategy's success.

Toward the Future

Despite the changes forced on the Cuban Communist Party over the past decade, it is still led by the charismatic founder of the revolution, who keeps alive the flame of radical nationalism and social justice. As founder, Fidel Castro's authority has been unassailable within the revolutionary leadership. At moments when the revolution has been riven by sharp cleavages, Castro's authority has provided the glue to hold the elite together—through the conflicts between the urban wing of the Twenty-sixth of July Movement and the Rebel Army, between the veterans of the Sierra and the old Communists, between the armed forces and the Interior Ministry in the aftermath of the Ochoa affair, and between reformers and hard-liners during the special period.

Since Castro can reach out and resolve any policy issue he chooses, elite decision making inevitably involves lobbying Fidel. Other leaders must compete for Castro's time and attention, striving to get him to focus on their priority issues and to decide in their favor.[62] Proximity to Castro is the most precious political resource, and it is perhaps no coincidence that younger leaders have risen to prominence by serving as his aides (for example, Carlos Lage and Felipe Pérez Roque). Policy conflicts among elite factions are thus channeled upward to Fidel for resolution, rather than causing permanent splits or expanding in scope to draw in potential allies from state and party institutions or the mass public.

When Castro departs, this will all change. Raúl Castro will almost certainly assume the formal mantle of leadership as head of the party and government.[63] On a number of issues, the post-Castro leaders will undoubtedly be in accord. They will be determined to maintain Cuba's independence and national sovereignty—that is, to prevent the island from falling once again into political and economic dependence on the United States. They will also agree on the need to maintain the social achievements of the revolution, especially the ones that enjoy the highest level of popular support, the advanced systems of health care and education. But as the new leadership faces tough policy choices, debate will surely intensify, spurred by those who favor more thoroughgoing economic reforms and greater political liberalization. After winning some key battles in the early 1990s, the reformers have been frustrated by Fidel's intransigence. Pent-up demands for further change will be hard to contain when Castro no longer stands as an insurmountable bulwark against it.

For Castro's heirs, the situation will be reversed; their right to govern will derive from the legitimacy of the institutions over which they preside, not from their personal virtues, which can only appear weak and pallid in comparison to Fidel's. Without Castro's charismatic authority, those institutions will have less legitimacy and hence less claim on people's unquestioning obedience. The global failure of Socialism, Cuba's subsequent economic crisis, and the reappearance of allegedly capitalist vices such as crime, corruption, and prostitution, have already seriously eroded the regime's legitimacy in the past decade.[64]

To meet the challenge of diminished legitimacy, Castro's heirs might well follow the pattern set by the successors to regime founders in Eastern Europe, appealing to culturally resonant themes, especially nationalism.[65] In Cuba, of course, the party and the revolutionary government have steeped themselves in the symbols of Cuban nationalism from the very beginning. It was no coincidence that Fidel chose the moment of the 1961 Bay of Pigs invasion to declare the Cuban revolution Socialist. The invasion gave him the perfect opportunity to wrap Socialism in the Cuban flag, making it a nationalist project. In recent years, nationalist themes featuring José Martí have gotten greater play than Leninist ones. The Elián González affair in 1999–2000 demonstrated that nationalism remains a potent political force, regardless of how disheartened ordinary Cubans may be about the decline in their standard of living. Nonstop political mobilizations demanding Elián's return gave the regime an opportunity to reignite the nationalist fervor of the revolution's early years for a new generation of Cubans.[66]

The Cuban Communist Party has already made significant progress in addressing one succession issue that stymied both the Soviet and Chinese regimes for years—the issue of generational leadership succession. The first hint of change came at the PCC's Third Congress, which for the first time removed a number of "*los históricos*" (the historic leaders of the revolution) from the Political Bureau and Central Committee. The Fourth Party Congress went even further in this regard. Of the 11 new people added to the 25-member Political Bureau, all were under fifty years old. The new Central

Committee of 225 was made up of 126 new members and 99 incumbents, only 23 of whom were members of the founding Central Committee in 1965. The average age of the new Central Committee was just forty-seven.[67] The Fifth Congress elected a Central Committee that was younger still, and only half the size of the previous body.[68] On the new Political Bureau, Fidel Castro was the oldest member, and the average age was just fifty-three. The National Assembly has experienced a similar process of incorporating younger leaders. The 1993 election produced an Assembly with 83 percent new members, with an average age of forty-three, which remained unchanged through the elections in 1998.[69] "There has already been a tangible transfer of power [to the next generation]," explained Foreign Minister Felipe Pérez Roque, "and that has been done by Fidel."[70]

Organizationally and ideologically, the PCC is stronger than most of the European Communist parties were on the eve of transition in 1989. During the decade of the 1980s, the legitimacy of the European parties was so badly eroded that they steadily lost members, even though membership was necessary for career advancement. In Cuba, by contrast, the party has grown rapidly throughout the special period, at almost double the rate of the decade before. In a time of serious economic dislocation, the Cuban leadership has tried to bolster the main instrument of ideological mobilization and motivation by widening its nationalist appeal as the party of the Cuban nation, by opening its doors to religious believers, and by making admission to party membership contingent on a vote of confidence from one's coworkers. That the party has grown as much as it has is a sign of its resilience. To be sure, there are tangible material benefits attached to being a member of the PCC (although they are relatively few for the rank and file), but that was even more true of the Eastern European parties, yet it did not halt the exodus of the disaffected.

Interviews with several hundred Cuban voters in 1989 local delegate elections found that people tended to vote for candidates based on positive personal characteristics like honesty, civic-mindedness, and so on. Many voters did not even know whether candidates were PCC members, and only 10 percent said that they took party membership into account in casting their ballots. Yet most candidates nominated and elected by their neighbors are, in fact, PCC members, suggesting that the party is successfully incorporating people at the grassroots who are engaged and active and have both respect and credibility among their fellow citizens.[71]

Additionally, polls taken over the past few years among both Cubans on the island and recent émigrés to the United States consistently indicate the existence of what Mahr and Nagle call a "socialist value culture."[72] Large majorities of respondents cite the education and health care systems as major achievements of the revolutionary regime and want them to be retained.[73] A 1994 Cid-Gallup poll conducted on the island asked, "In a society, what do you consider most important for everyone? Should the law promote economic and social equality, or should the law promote individual freedom?" Half the respondents said equality; 38 percent said freedom. When asked, "Who should run the farms and factories of Cuba," 51 percent said the government should, and 36 percent said they should be run privately.[74] The prevalence of such values indicates that a significant constituency exists in Cuba for the core social policies of the Cuban party.

Finally, the regime's response to the Varela Project's petitions for a referendum on changing the political system demonstrates the party's continuing ability to mobilize people. The regime-sponsored constitutional amendment declaring Socialism "irrevocable" may not necessarily be a true barometer of popular sentiment (it was not adopted by secret ballot, for example), but the fact that the party and its affiliated mass organizations could turn out eight million people to sign petitions on very short notice is indicative of considerable mobilizational capacity.[75]

Despite these organizational and ideological advantages—and the top leadership's preference for the political status quo—the Cuban Communist Party is faced with a polity in flux. Even the limited economic reforms forced on the regime by the need to reenter the global economy are having significant social reverberations and changing the political terrain of the future. As market reforms weaken the Communist Party's control over the economy, its political monopoly becomes frayed as well. Emergent entrepreneurs, both farmers and small businessmen, depend less and less on the state for their well-being. As they accumulate wealth and grow increasingly indispensable to the health of the economy, their desire for less government interference is certain to take a more explicitly political direction. Fidel Castro clearly dislikes and distrusts this emerging entrepreneurial class, but the government cannot do without its productivity, its expansion of employment opportunities, or its tax revenues (all of which the state sector fails to provide). Thus the regime must put up with people whose self-interest places them in conflict with it—over tax rates, regulations, supply distribution, and, ultimately, fundamental ideology.

As Cubans increasingly interact with populations abroad, through tourism, family visits, and professional cooperation (all of which the government promotes for economic reasons), the danger of "ideological contamination" increases. And as regime legitimacy erodes because of the failure of Cuba's Socialist model, ordinary Cubans are bound to ask (as Cuban intellectuals already do) whether there shouldn't be more open debate about alternative futures. The proliferation of nongovernmental organizations in recent years has created social networks independent of party supervision and direction. Even those that have been spawned by the government itself for the purpose of soliciting hard currency from foreign NGOs create mechanisms through which a growing number of Cubans will come into contact with people—and ideas—from abroad.

The government can try to quell these stirrings but it cannot eliminate them, because they are the unavoidable by-product of the economic concessions that Cuba has been forced to make to capitalism. The market has eroded the scope of state and party control, creating what an observer of Eastern Europe called "islands of autonomy" in civil society that serve, albeit fragilely, as "safe spaces" within which people forge new social relationships and networks of communication, acquire consciousness of their common interests, and develop the capacity for politics outside the regime.[76] The future of the Cuban Communist Party will depend on whether it takes the leading role in adapting itself and the Cuban polity to these emerging social forces, or is swept aside by them.

Notes

1. Castro first used the phrase in his July 26, 1973, speech commemorating the attack on Moncada barracks (which produced the headline quoted, in *Granma Weekly Review*, August 5, 1973), and he has repeated it frequently in the years since, most recently in a speech on February 23, 2001 (speech, celebration of the fortieth anniversary of INDER and dedication of the International School of Physical Education and Sports, text at http://www.cuba.cu/gobierno/discursos/2001/ing/f230201i.html).

2. The characterization of the party in the title of this chapter as the "single party of the Cuban nation," is from Alberto Alvariño Atienzar, "The Cuban Nation's Single Party," *Granma International*, May 13, 1997.

3. The three organizations were Fidel Castro's Twenty-sixth of July Movement, the student-based Revolutionary Directorate, and the old Communists of the Popular Socialist Party.

4. Castro's denunciation of the ORI was delivered in three speeches, on March 13, March 18, and March 22, 1962, reprinted in Fidel Castro, *Fidel Castro Denounces Sectarianism* (Havana: Ministry of Foreign Relations, 1962).

5. Fidel Castro, "Declaración del primer ministro en el juicio contra el delator de los mártires de Humboldt 7," *Obra Revolucionaria* 7 (March 24, 1964), 5–47.

6. Raúl Castro, "Report to the Central Committee on the Activities of the Microfaction," *Granma Weekly Review*, February 11, 1968.

7. For a more detailed discussion of the PCC's weakness in the 1960s and early 1970s, see William M. LeoGrande, "Party Development in Revolutionary Cuba,"

Journal of Interamerican Studies and World Affairs 21, no. 4 (November 1979): 157–80.

8. William M. LeoGrande, "The Communist Party of Cuba since the First Congress," *Journal of Latin American Studies* 12, no. 2 (November 1980): 397–419.

9. Communist Party of Cuba, *Second Congress of the Communist Party of Cuba: Documents and Speeches* (Havana: Editora Política, 1981), 77–84; Marifeli Pérez-Stable, "'We Are the Only Ones and There Is No Alternative': Vanguard Party Politics in Cuba, 1975–1991," in *Conflict and Change in Cuba*, ed. Enrique A. Baloyra and James A. Morris (Albuquerque: University of New Mexico, 1993), 67–85.

10. Almost half of Fidel Castro's "Main Report" to the congress focuses on economic and social development plans, and the congress resolution on this subject is 123 pages long. Communist Party of Cuba, *Second Congress of the Communist Party of Cuba.*

11. Ibid., 80.

12. Mimi Whitefield and Andres Oppenheimer, "No. 3 man in Cuba is booted," *Miami Herald*, September 24, 1992; Howard W. French, "Cuban's exit hints at trouble at top," *New York Times*, September 27, 1992.

13. Sergio Roca, "The *Comandante* in his Economic Labyrinth," in Baloyra and Morris, *Conflict and Change in Cuba*, 86–109. A less frequently articulated but no less important goal was to bring the burgeoning trade imbalance under control by stabilizing export production and reducing imports. Jorge F. Pérez-López, "The Cuban Economy: Rectification in a Changing World," *Cambridge Journal of Economics* 16, no. 1 (1992): 113–26; Susan Eckstein, *Back from the Future: Cuba under Castro* (Princeton, N.J.: Princeton University Press, 1994), 73.

14. Fidel Castro, *Main Report: Third Congress of the Communist Party of Cuba* (Havana: Editorial Política 1986), 38–39.

15. Jorge I. Domínguez, "Blaming Itself, Not Himself: Cuba's Political Regime after the Third Party Congress," in *Socialist Cuba: Past Interpretations and Future Challenges*, ed. Sergio Roca (Boulder, Colo.: Westview, 1988), 3–10; Rhoda Rabkin, "Cuba: The Aging of a Revolution," in Roca, *Socialist Cuba*, 33–56.

16. As Susan Eckstein points out, antagonism to the market did not extend into the external sector of the economy, where the government was suffering from a serious shortage of hard currency. Foreign investment, especially in tourism, was encouraged during rectification rather than discouraged. Eckstein, *Back from the Future*, 73.

17. Juan M. del Aguila, "The Party, the Fourth Congress, and the Process of Counterreform," in *Cuba at a Crossroads: Politics and Economics after the Fourth Party Congress*, ed. Jorge F. Pérez-López (Gainesville: University Press of Florida, 1994), 19–40.

18. Jorge I. Domínguez, "The Political Impact on Cuba of the Reform and Collapse of Communist Regimes," in *Cuba after the Cold War,* ed. Carmelo Mesa-Lago (Pittsburgh: University of Pittsburgh Press, 1993), 99–132.

19. Castro first used the slogan in January 1989 in two speeches commemorating the triumph of the revolution, but it only became a routine closing to his speeches in December after the collapse of the Eastern European Communist regimes.

20. Comisión Económica para América Latina y El Caribe (CEPAL), *La economía Cubana: Reformas estructurales y desempeño en los noventa* (Mexico City: United Nations CEPAL and Fondo de Cultura Económica, 2000), 15–16, 44–45.

21. Jorge F. Pérez-López, "The Cuban Economic Crisis of the 1990s and the External Sector," *Cuba in Transition* (Association for the Study of the Cuban Economy) 8 (1998): 386–413; CEPAL's estimate of the decline, 32 percent in real terms, is among the lowest. CEPAL, *La economía Cubana*, 44.

22. Externally, the emphasis on attracting foreign investment and expanding tourism continued. For an overview of Cuban reform measures, see Omar Everleny Pérez Villanueva, "Cuba's Economic Reforms: An Overview," in *Perspectives on Cuban Economic Reforms*, ed. Jorge F. Pérez-López and Matías F. Travieso-Díaz (Tempe: Arizona State University Center for Latin American Studies, 1998). The texts of the decree laws legalizing dollars, legalizing self-employment, creating the UBPCs, and reorganizing the state bureaucracy are in Instituto de Relaciones Europeo-Latinoamericanas (IRELA), *Cuba: Apertura económica y relaciones con Europa* (Madrid: IRELA, 1994), 233–44.

23. For a pessimistic view on the long-term viability of the current reforms, see Andrew Zimbalist, "Whither the Cuban Economy?" in *Cuba: The Contours of Change*, ed. Susan Kaufman Purcell and David Rothkopf (Boulder, Colo.: Lynne Rienner, 2000), 13–30. For a more optimistic, although not uncritical view, see CEPAL, *La economía Cubana*, 14–42. GDP data for 1989 to 1999 are from CEPAL, *La economía Cubana*, table A-10; data for 2000 are from CEPAL, *Statistical Yearbook for Latin America and the Caribbean 2001* (Mexico City: CEPAL, 2002), table 54.

24. According to the "Resolution on the Program of the Communist Party of Cuba," adopted at the Fourth Party Congress in 1991, under the SDPE, "the political work and the actions of the revolutionary vanguard were reduced to mere formalities." The text of the resolution is in Gail Reed, *Island in the Storm: The Cuban Communist Party's Fourth Congress* (Melbourne, Australia: Ocean Press, 1992), 101–10.

25. On the origins of rectification and the collapse of Socialism in Europe, see Castro's opening address to the Fourth Party Congress in Reed, *Island in the Storm*, 25–79.

26. "Asambleas de balance en las organizaciones de base del partido," *Granma*, January 6, 1990; Marifeli Pérez-Stable, *The Cuban Revolution: Origins, Course, and Legacy* (New York: Oxford University Press, 1999), 169.

27. Eckstein, *Back from the Future*, 114.

28. Pérez-Stable, "'We Are the Only Ones,'" 81; "Llamamiento del partido," *Granma Resumen Semanal*, March 25, 1990.

29. "Se require una participación consciente y activa," *Granma*, April 13, 1990; Reed, *Island in the Storm*, 14–15.

30. "Acuerdo del Buro Politico sobre el proceso de discussion del llamamiento al IV Congreso," *Granma*, June 23, 1990.

31. Roca, "The *Comandante*," 102.

32. Reed, *Island in the Storm*, 17.

33. Eckstein, *Back from the Future*, 115.

34. Reed, *Island in the Storm*, 17–18; Eckstein, *Back from the Future*, 115.

35. Haroldo Dilla Alfonso, Gerardo González, and Aba T. Vincentelli, "Cuba's Local Governments: An Experience beyond the Paradigms," *Cuban Studies* 22 (1992): 151–72; Carollee Bengelsdorf, *The Problem of Democracy in Cuba: Between Vision and Reality* (New York: Oxford University Press, 1994), 155–65; Communist Party of Cuba, "Resolution on Improving the Organization and Functioning of People's Power," in Gail Reed, *Island in the Storm*, 120–26.

36. Reed, *Island in the Storm*, 17.

37. Compare "Statutes of the Communist Party of Cuba," in *Second Congress of the Communist Party of Cuba*, 128, to the "Resolution on the Rules of the Cuban Communist Party," in Reed, *Island in the Storm*, 88.

38. Reed, *Island in the Storm*, 88, 89, 94.

39. Max Azicri, *Cuba Today and Tomorrow: Reinventing Socialism* (Gainesville: University Press of Florida, 2000), 338 n.18; Fidel Castro Ruz, *Informe central, discurso de clausura: V Congreso del Partido Comunista de Cuba* (Havana: Editora Política, 1997), 68.

40. Reed, *Island in the Storm*, 122.

41. Jorge I. Domínguez, "Leadership Strategies and Mass Support: Cuban Politics before and after the 1991 Party Congress," in Pérez-López, *Cuba at a Crossroads*, 1–18.

42. Ibid.

43. A number of analysts have described the factional cleavages in the PCC: Eckstein, *Back from the Future*, 257–58; Reed, *Island in the Storm*, 21; Oppenheimer, *Castro's Final Hour* (New York: Simon and Schuster, 1992), 379–80; Edward Gonzalez, *Cuba: Clearing Perilous Waters?* (Santa Monica, Calif.: Rand, 1996), 39–42.

44. "Pleno extraordinario del Comité Central," *Granma Resumen Semanal*, February 25, 1990.

45. "Llamamiento del partido."

46. Pablo Alfonso, "Dispute delays party session, official says," *Miami Herald*, March 29, 1991.

47. Oppenheimer, *Castro's Final Hour*, 383–99.

48. James Canute, "Top Cuban ideologue dismissed over scandal," *Financial Times* (London), October 13, 1992; "Aldana says business gaffe led to ouster," *Miami Herald*, September 29, 1992.

49. Andres Oppenheimer, "Cuban expelled from party," *Miami Herald*, October 27, 1992; Reuters, "Cuba replaces official with close Castro ties," *Los Angeles Times*, September 24, 1992.

50. Oppenheimer, *Castro's Final Hour*, 385–86.

51. Larry Rohter, "Cubans find the army rising as the party sinks," *New York Times*, June 8, 1995.

52. Lee Hockstader, "Cuba steps up intimidation of dissidents," *Washington Post*, January 21, 1992.

53. Raúl Castro, "The Political and Social Situation in Cuba and the Corresponding Tasks of the Party," *Granma International*, March 27, 1996.

54. Ibid.

55. On the opposition of reformers in the party leadership, see Maurizio Giuliano, *El caso de CEA: Intelectuales e inquisidores en Cuba* (Miami: Ediciones Universal, 1998), 54. This account includes many of the internal party documents related to the investigation of CEA.

56. Serge F. Kovaleski, "Castro, Catholic Church both appear to gain from John Paul's visit," *Washington Post*, January 26, 1998.

57. Zenit News Service (Italy), "Cuban Communists want to erase traces of papal visit," February 27, 2001.

58. "Resolución económica del V Congreso del Partido Comunista de Cuba," http://www.cuba.cu/politica/webpcc/resoluci.htm.

59. "The Party of Unity, Democracy and the Human Rights We Defend," *Granma International* (on line), May 1997.

60. Serge F. Kovaleski, "Castro appears strong, Cuban economy weak," *Washington Post*, October 11, 1997; Juan O. Tamayo, "Raúl Castro takes on a higher profile," *Miami Herald*, December 17, 1997.

61. Serge F. Kovaleski, "Cuba replaces foreign minister with top aide to Castro," *Washington Post*, May 29, 1999.

62. Reformers in the PCC acknowledge as much with the refrain "With Fidel, everything; against Fidel, nothing." Quoted in Eusebio Mujal-León and Joshua W. Busby, "Much Ado about Something? Regime Change in Cuba," *Problems of Communism* 48, no. 6 (November–December 2001): 6–18.

63. In a speech on January 21, 1959, Castro designated his brother as "second in command," to take over in case he himself were killed by the enemies of the revolution. "Castro speaks before Havana rally," Foreign Broadcast Information Service, *Latin America Daily Report*, January 22, 1959. At the close of the Fifth Party Congress, he referred to Raúl as his *"relevo"* ("relief") when he passes away, and after Fidel's fainting spell in July 2001, he said, "If I go to sleep for eternity, Raúl is the one with most authority and experience." Juan O. Tamayo, "Raúl Castro takes on a higher profile," *Miami Herald*, December 17, 1997; Andrew Cawthorne, "Castro says his health 'better than ever' after fainting at recent rally; brother confirmed as his successor," *San Diego Union-Tribune*, June 30, 2001.

64. Raúl Castro was candid in acknowledging that these problems posed a serious ideological challenge for the revolution and that the party needed to wage a "battle of ideas" in response. Raúl Castro, "The Political and Social Situation in Cuba and the Corresponding Tasks of the Party," *Granma*, March 27, 1996.

65. Korbonski, "Leadership Succession and Political Change in Eastern Europe," *Studies in Comparative Communism* 9, nos. 1–2 (Spring–Summer 1976): 3–22.

66. David Gonzalez, "Cuba sees fervor over Elián useful in other battles," *New York Times*, July 5, 2000.

67. Domínguez, "Leadership Strategies and Mass Support"; Juan M. del Aguila, "The Party, the Fourth Congress, and the Process of Counterreform," in Pérez-López, *Cuba at a Crossroads*.

68. Mark Fineman, "Castro points to his brother as successor," *Los Angeles Times*, October 12, 1997.

69. David Clark Scott, "Castro's Foreign Office Choice: Sign of a New Generation?" *Christian Science Monitor*, April 1, 1993; Interview with Ricardo Alarcón in Cynthia Tucker, "Communism after Fidel Castro," *Atlanta Journal and Constitution*, July 8, 2001.

70. Scott Wilson, "The Face of Cuba's New Generation," *Washington Post*, September 12, 2000.

71. Dilla Alfonso, González, and Vincentelli, "Cuba's Local Governments: An Experience beyond the Paradigms," *Cuban Studies* 22 (1992): 151–72; Dominguez, "Leadership Strategies and Mass Support," 1–18.

72. Alison Mahr and John Nagle, "Resurrection of the Successor Parties and Democratization in East-Central Europe," *Communist and Post-Communist Studies* 28, no. 4 (1995): 393–409.

73. For details on the polling results, see Dario L. Machado, "¿Cual es nuestro clima socio-politico?" *El Militante Comunista* 9 (September 1990): 2–12, quoted in Domínguez, "Leadership Strategies and Mass Support," 1–18; Dario L. Machado, "Democracia política e ideología: Una opinión despues del V Congreso del partido," *Cuba Socialista* 9 (1998), quoted in Azicri, *Cuba Today and Tomorrow,* 120–22; Mimi Whitefield and Mary Beth Sheridan, "Cuba Poll: The Findings," *Miami Herald*, December 18, 1994; "How Cubans Responded to Questions," *Miami Herald,* December 18, 1994; Churchill Roberts et al., *Measuring Cuban Public Opinion: Project Report* (Miami: University of Florida, 1999).

74. Whitefield and Sheridan, "Cuba Poll"; "How Cubans Responded."

75. Details on the constitutional revision are in Raisa Pages, "A Transcendent Yes: Cuban deputies approve constitutional reforms making Socialism irrevocable," *Granma International,* June 24, 2002.

76. The concept of "islands of autonomy" is from Valerie Bunce, *Subversive Institutions: The Design and Destruction of Socialism and the State* (Cambridge: Cambridge University Press, 1999). For a discussion of how economic reforms in a centrally planned economy can lead to social pluralism, setting the stage for political change, see David Stark, "Entrepreneurs on the Road to Post-Communism," *Contemporary Sociology* 18, no. 5 (September 1989): 671–74. The most detailed study of the evolution of Cuban civil society in recent years is Damian J. Fernández, *Cuba and the Politics of Passion* (Austin: University of Texas Press, 2000).

10

The National Assembly
and Political Representation

Peter Roman

This study analyzes and evaluates the Cuban National Assembly, determines its role within the Cuban government, and studies the contributions made by the National Assembly deputies. My research has focused on the electoral process, the law-making process, National Assembly and commission debates, the work of the commissions, oversight of governmental ministries and agencies, responses to complaints emanating from the population, the accountability of deputies and their contact with constituents, and the role of the Communist Party (Partido Comunista de Cuba, PCC).[1]

I conducted fieldwork in Havana from October 5 to December 29, 2001. During this time I was provided with materials I requested: transcripts of all National Assembly sessions from 1992 to the present (Third, Fourth, and Fifth Legislatures); commission documents, reports, and minutes and/or recordings of commission meetings and activities during the Fifth Legislature (starting in 1998); and letters from the population requesting assistance. I interviewed, among others, National Assembly president Ricardo Alarcón, National Association of Small Farmers (Asociación Nacional de Agricultores Pequeños, ANAP) president Orlando Lugo Fonte, Economic Affairs Commission president Osvaldo Martinez, the president of a municipal candidacy commission, National Assembly deputies, and municipal assembly delegates. I attended commission meetings and the National Assembly session in December 2001. I attended meetings of deputies in the provinces, a municipal assembly plenary session, and accountability sessions of municipal assembly delegates with their constituents. I recorded over fifty hours of tapes.

To evaluate the deputies' contributions and influence in shaping legislation and policy, including the economic plan and budget, I studied transcripts of all the National Assembly plenary session debates from 1992, and commission minutes from 1998. Following the process of how a bill becomes a law, I attended meetings of deputies in Pinar del Rio, Matanzas, Havana, and the City of Havana province, as they discussed pending legislation on agrarian cooperatives and antiterrorism. Subsequent commission meetings sought to integrate the changes suggested by the deputies and to reach consensus.

My initial premise is that the Cuban government is not necessarily more democratic or less democratic than that of the United States (I hesitate to use the word democratic because of the difficulty of defining this concept), or more or less representative. It is a different system of government, legislating for a socialist rather than a capitalist economy, and therefore should not be studied by using the U.S. system as a model.

The Local Organs of People's Power

The three levels of the Cuban system of representative government, known as the Organs of People's Power (Organos del Poder Popular, OPP), are the National Assembly, the provincial assemblies, and the municipal assemblies. The latter two are known as the Local Organs of People's Power (Organos Locales del Poder Popular, OLPP).[2]

The term of office for municipal assembly delegates is two and a half years. Municipal delegates are elected in competitive elections separately from the deputies and provincial delegates. Except for the officers, municipal assembly delegates serve without pay and continue to work at their regular jobs, as is the case with National Assembly deputies and provincial assembly delegates.

The municipal assemblies control and monitor all economic, social, educational, and public health activities in the municipality and oversee consumer affairs and public services, mainly through assembly commissions. The delegates hold weekly office hours for constituents, and twice a year they hold accountability sessions for groups of around fifty constituents, during which delegates report on their activities, answer constituents' concerns *(planteamientos)* recorded at the previous session, and hear new *planteamientos,* usually regarding local problems.

The people's councils bring municipal government closer to the neighborhood level in the cities, and in the rural areas they make the municipal government more accessible to isolated locations. They are formed by the delegates from approximately ten adjoining municipal assembly electoral districts, plus the directors of the main economic and social activities in the territory as well as local representatives of the Federation of Cuban Workers (Confederación de Trabajadores de Cuba, CTC) and mass organizations such as the Federation of Cuban Women (Federación de Mujeres Cubanas, FMC), Committee for the Defense of the Revolution (Comité para la Defensa de la Revolución, CDR), and, in rural areas, ANAP. Since the presidents and vice presidents work full time for the people's councils, they are constantly on the scene to assist the delegates, sometimes applying pressure to solve problems. They also oversee local economic activity and monitor local administrators, root out petty corruption, and mobilize the citizenry around local projects and issues.

The National Assembly

National Assembly deputies and provincial assembly delegates serve for five-year terms and are nominated and elected together during the same electoral process. Candidacy commissions select the candidates, and the elections are not competitive. Municipal delegates may also be elected as National Assembly deputies or provincial assembly delegates, and constitute up to 50 percent of the deputies and delegates in these bodies (they are referred to as *diputados de base*).

Only the National Assembly has legislative powers. This includes approving the economic plan and budget each year. It meets in regular plenary sessions twice a year for approximately two days each time. Extraordinary sessions may be called at any time. Most of the work is done by the Assembly commissions between sessions. The Council of State, consisting of thirty-one National Assembly deputies, carries on the official work of the National Assembly between sessions.

There are ten permanent commissions with about twenty-five deputies on each: Constitutional and Judicial Affairs; Productive Activities; Local Organs of People's Power; Education, Culture, Science, and Technology; Economic Affairs; Health, Sports, and Environment; National Defense; Services; Youth, Child Care, and Women's Rights; and Foreign Relations. During the year the commissions (and subcommissions) meet, usually with high government officials present, draft legislation, review pending legislation, carry out inspections, do studies, respond to citizen complaints, conduct public hearings, and periodically report to the National Assembly plenary regarding their audits of government organs and ministries. Not all deputies are members of commissions (for example, those in national leadership positions are usually excluded).

Prior to each regular session of the National Assembly, all the commissions meet, followed by two days during which four ministers report to the deputies regarding the activities of their ministries and then are subject to questions posed by the deputies.

Defining the Cuban Socialist Parliament

Based on the evidence gathered, preliminary findings indicate that what is perceived as defending the Cuban Revolution, that is, supporting Socialism and the basic needs and welfare of the population, has been the stated motivation and purpose guiding most of those who founded, lead, and participate as deputies in the Cuban National Assembly. The Assembly operates on the basis of five principles: first, it must be representative of Cuban society, and as a result there are deputies from most sectors of society and walks of life, including experts in economics, farming, health, education, sports, and other areas under the purview of the National Assembly. Second, it must have close contact and connection with the population, realized in great part by having almost half of the deputies also be municipal assembly delegates. Third, it must consult with constituents, deputies, experts, interested parties, government officials, the PCC, the CTC, and mass organizations regarding proposed legislation, and to formulate lists of candidates. Fourth, it must express critical opposition with regard to measures under discussion, such as items within proposed legislation, but not as an organized political opposition or an opposition attacking the system. And fifth, its goal is to reconcile differences in order to reach consensus prior to presenting measures to the Assembly plenary sessions.

The Communist Party and the National Assembly

The Communist Party is not an electoral party. It does not officially nominate or approve candidates on the municipal, provincial, or national level, and there is no party or Union of Young Communists (Unión de Jóvenes Comunistas, UJC) official on the candidacy commissions at any of these levels. Certainly it is clear that at the municipal level the party has no formal role in selecting candidates, although I encountered isolated incidents where the local party attempted to influence voters to nominate and vote for the candidate the party wanted to become the municipal assembly president.[3] For the provincial and national candidate selection process, the party probably serves mainly as a veto for candidates selected by the candidacy commissions. The party selects the candidates for leadership positions in the National Assembly, for the Council of State, and Council of Ministers.

Regarding legislation, the party programs passed at the congresses are supposed to set the parameters for government policy.[4] However, these parameters are very broad and general. In some cases, for example, they set limits, such as the economic resolution passed in the Fifth Party Congress in 1997. Referring to private economic activities among Cubans, the resolution did not mention middle-sized enterprises, which were not included in the subsequent legislation on the economy.[5] People's councils for isolated rural areas were called for in the program of the Third Party Congress in 1986, and subsequently pilot projects were set up in a few locations in 1989.[6] When they were established throughout all of Cuba in the early 1990s, though, they bore little resemblance to what had been proposed in the Third Congress, and Castro said as much during the debate on the People's Council Law in the National Assembly in 2000. The constitutional amendments, passed in 1992, came in great part from the program passed in the Fourth Party Congress in 1991, after much debate and many changes made during the Assembly plenary session. However, none of the laws passed in the 1990s and up until 2002, including the 1992 Electoral Law, were written by the PCC or originated from the party programs. For example, the People's Council Law was written by members of the Assembly Commission on Local Organs of People's Power, and the proposed law on agrarian cooperatives was written by ANAP. All proposed legislation is sent for consultation to government bodies, mass organizations, specialists, National Assembly deputies, sectors of the population, and the party.

The percentage of deputies who are party members ranges from 80 to 90 percent, and for municipal assembly delegates it ranges from 60 to 70 percent. However, these figures are not greatly important. It would be very difficult to tell the difference between a deputy or delegate who is or is not a party member, and the party does not tell representatives how to vote.

The party controls how the OPP functions, making sure the procedures are followed and rooting out corruption. For example, when a dissident was not allowed to propose himself as a municipal assembly candidate, he complained to the party, which ordered a new nominating session for that neighborhood. There, his name was proposed by another person, but he lost the vote to become a candidate.[7] When a municipal candidacy commission ignored the advice of a people's council to drop a candidate being proposed, the candidacy commission was criticized by Castro in a subsequent municipal party meeting.

The question of the role of the party is a bit confusing, because the national leadership and the party leadership are practically identical. National Assembly president Ricardo Alarcón is a member of the party's Political Bureau (which underlines the importance of the National Assembly and gives the Assembly a voice on this body), and he is also a member of the Council of State. To be sure, about half the members of the Council of State are also members of the Political Bureau. When Alarcón operates as Assembly president and when as a party leader is perhaps not a relevant question, or one that can be answered easily; the functions of the party and the Assembly are different.

Elections and the National Assembly

Candidates for National Assembly deputy and Provincial Assembly delegate are proposed by candidacy commissions at the municipal, provincial, and national levels. Neither the party nor the UJC have seats on these commissions. There are 609 seats in the National Assembly. The deputies represent municipalities, or in the case of large municipalities, districts within the municipalities, and are elected by voters who reside in these municipalities or districts. Most deputies have no residency requirements, but the *de base* deputies reside in the district they represent.

Many of the deputies are national figures who currently reside in Havana but are elected by municipalities in other provinces. For example, Fidel Castro is elected in Santiago de Cuba, and Osvaldo Martínez is elected from Holguín. But if the deputies who reside in Havana had to represent Havana, there would not be enough National Assembly seats from the municipalities within the City of Havana to accommodate all of the national leadership. This is especially so because *de base* deputies (including those from Havana) do have residency requirements, and therefore must live in the city.

Candidates are divided into two categories: *de base* (up to 50 percent of the candidates), who are also municipal delegates, and *directos,* who encompass the country leadership and the rest of the deputies. The candidates representing leadership ranks are selected mainly by the national and provincial candidacy commissions. The municipal candidacy commissions choose the *de base* candidates and most of the other *directos* candidates in consultation with the provincial candidacy commissions. Aside from the *de base* candidates and the national leadership candidates, the rest of the *directos* are selected to ensure representation from most sectors of society (women, youth, religious leaders, workers, doctors, teachers, and so on), which results in a legislature that is far more representative of a pluralistic society than, for example, those who serve in the United States Congress.[8] It also means that the presidents and members of Assembly commissions will most likely be experts in the area over which the commission has jurisdiction. For example, Osvaldo Martínez is director of the Center for the Study of the World Economy (Centro de Estudios de la Economia Mundial, CEEM) and presides over the Economic Affairs Commission. A medical doctor and an educator are secretaries of the Public Health Commission and Education Commission, respectively.

Nominations controlled by the candidacy commissions help alleviate the fear that anti-Cuban groups based in the United States and aided and financed by the U.S. government would attempt to inject their own candidates into the race, with the intent of paralyzing, sabotaging, and tearing down the Socialist political and economic system.[9]

During the neighborhood encounters I attended in Havana in the 1998 electoral campaign, one candidate (usually the one best known) and someone from the area usually gave speeches extolling the virtues of all the candidates and urging everyone to vote for the entire slate (voto unido), which is possible by checking off the slate box at the top of the ballot. I did not witness anyone asking the candidates policy questions. The political rally ambiance did not seem to lend itself to this possibility (although I was told of instances of sharp questioning of candidates during such encounters in the 1992 electoral campaign).

The elections are noncompetitive: the number of candidates equals the number of seats to be filled.[10] Alarcón, in an interview with me in 1994, explained the system of the voto unido and the noncompetitive elections as necessary. They permit the candidates who are also municipal delegates, and thus unknown outside of their districts, to have a chance to be elected.[11] Voting is secret and voluntary, although some told me they feel social and political pressure to vote.

The noncompetitive nominations and elections are the weakest link in the Cuban parliamentary system, in that they result in many candidates who lack independence and/or close links to and contact with the population. However, among the most outspoken deputies are the de base deputies, since they have their own independent electoral base and they are in close contact and communication with their constituents. And these are the candidates, according to Alarcón, who benefit most from noncompetitive elections.

Contacting the Population

Most citizens I spoke with in Havana did not know who the deputies from their municipalities were (which may not be the case regarding deputies from rural areas and small towns). This can be attributed, in part, to candidates running as a slate rather than as individuals, and many *de base* candidates being unknown outside of their municipal electoral district.

After the election, except for when deputies consult sectors of the population regarding pending legislation (such as farmers regarding legislation on agrarian cooperatives), little opportunity exists for regular contact between the deputies (in their role as deputies) and the population, and for citizens to relate directly to their delegates their opinions regarding issues before the National Assembly. I did attend municipal delegate accountability sessions of *de base* deputies, and sessions where deputies attended accountability sessions within the municipalities they represent. However, little mention was made regarding pending legislation and policies before the National Assembly or activities of the deputies present, and those attending asked no questions regarding those issues.

The deputies must also give an account of their activities once during each five-year term to the municipal assembly in the municipality from which they were elected. However, after reviewing these reports, I found them to be formalistic, with little substance or content. National Assembly deputies attend municipal assembly sessions in the municipalities from which they were elected but do not seem to serve as a link to the National Assembly, since municipal assembly delegates do not usually ask their deputies to bring up their concerns to the National Assembly.

One important point of contact with the population can be attributed to the Cuban parliament's unique characteristic of currently having up to 50 percent of the deputies also be municipal assembly delegates, a good number of whom are also presidents of their people's councils. Their knowledge and awareness of the population's needs and desires, based on their intimate and daily contact with the people in their districts and their people's councils, is clearly manifested in National Assembly plenary and commission debates.[12]

During the National Assembly deliberations on the 1992 Electoral Law, deputies argued that to keep the percentage of *de base* deputies from decreasing, the term of office for municipal delegates should be increased to five years (equal to that of the deputies). Since the municipal and national elections take place within a few months of each other, the shorter municipal term means that after two and a half years, some *de base* deputies choose not to run again for the position of municipal delegate, or may not win the election if they do. Thus, for the following two-and-a-half-year period, these deputies, who were previously *de base*, continue serving as deputies without also being municipal assembly delegates, thus decreasing the percentage of *de base* deputies in the National Assembly to much less than 50 percent.[13]

There is also direct contact with the population through the Office of Attention to the Population (Oficina de Atención a la Población), which receives complaints directly from citizens regarding personal problems (mainly housing) by letters or through interviews. Furthermore, President Alarcón also receives letters from the population, which he usually forwards to this office, and the National Assembly commissions receive complaints from citizens regarding the areas of concern of the commissions. (For example, complaints regarding schools are usually sent to the Education, Culture, Science, and Technology Commission, and complaints regarding transportation are sent to the Services Commission.) The commissions usually attempt to investigate and find ways to resolve these complaints.

How a Bill Becomes a Law

Bills, or *proyectos de ley,* are initiated and/or written by mass organizations, the National Assembly leadership, National Assembly commissions, government ministries, and the PCC. In some cases the National Assembly conducts public opinion surveys to determine public attitudes toward the need and premises of proposed legislation. In some cases, when it was determined that the public was not ready (not supportive enough yet), such as implementing contributions to social security and income taxes, new legislation has been held up. After the first version is written, the process of consultation and revision is directed by the relevant Assembly commission, together with the Constitutional and Juridical Affairs Commission, whose role is to check its legality and constitutionality. For example, the trajectory for the proposed law on the environment was directed by the Health, Sports, and Environment Commission; the bills on foreign investments and on taxes were led by the Economic Affairs Commission.

Whatever its origin, proposed legislation goes through a lengthy process of gauging and preparing public opinion, and a process of consultations in Havana and all the provinces with government officials, experts, mass organizations, citizens who would be affected, deputies, and other National Assembly commissions. Based on these consultations, extensive changes are incorporated and the bill usually goes through many drafts. A bill will not be presented before the National Assembly until a consensus has been reached; and if no consensus can be reached, it will either be withdrawn or be sent out for more consultations to iron out the differences. Once it is presented to the National Assembly plenary, it is subject to extensive floor debates where important changes may be made. After a law is passed, the Council of Ministers draws up regulations for implementing the new law; and these are then approved by the Council of State.

The exceptions to this lengthy process involve the national budgets and economic plans, which must be approved by the National Assembly at plenary sessions held in December. The Economic Affairs Commission meets with the minister of finances and prices, the minister of economics and planning, and other officials from these ministries during the year to monitor the budgetary and planning process; but according to the minutes of the meetings I reviewed, the commission makes few concrete contributions to these processes. The annual budget and plan are not usually finished until a few days before the National Assembly meets, which leaves little time for the other deputies to study them. Prior to leaving for Havana for the plenary session, deputies are briefed regarding how the plan and budget will affect their provinces, and the same ministers and ministry officials address each commission meeting just prior to the plenary session, regarding how the budget and plan will affect their particular areas.

According to political analyst Alan Chartock, in New York state (which has about twice the population of Cuba), most state legislators see the budget only just prior to voting on it. "It should always be remembered that a vast majority of the [New York] legislators have almost no idea of what's going on until the final document is shoved in front of them, with little or no time for analysis and intelligent debate."[14]

The proposed legislation regarding people's councils was debated in the National Assembly plenary session in 2000, but its origins can be traced to the Third Party Congress of 1986.[15] By 1989 a few pilot projects were started. In 1990 they were constituted in the City of Havana, and mentioned in the revised 1992 Cuban Constitution. By 1993 they were constituted in the rest of the country. In July 1993 the people's councils were discussed in the National Assembly, and a document was written establishing guidelines as to how they should operate. In 1997 a subcommission of the OLPP Commission was established to draw up new regulations for the people's councils.

In 1998 the president of the National Assembly created a working group, consisting of OLPP and Constitutional and Juridical Affairs Commission members and legal advisors, to write a new law based on these regulations. The first version was written in February 1999, and the working group traveled to the provinces to meet with experts on people's councils. One hundred sixty-four opinions were given and incorporated into a second version in June 1999, which was discussed by the Assembly leadership and deputies familiar with the people's councils and legal codes. Based on these contributions, a third version was written in September 1999.

The working group took this version to the provinces for discussion with the presidents of all the people's councils, provincial representatives of mass organizations, and the leadership of the municipal assemblies. It was also sent for comments and opinions to the national leadership of the mass organizations, to all the professional deputies working at the National Assembly, and to those in the PCC directly linked to the OPP. During this round 674 opinions were collected. Version four was issued on November 8 and discussed with all the deputies in the provinces, resulting in another 305 contributions.

In December 1999, version five was presented to a joint meeting of the OLPP and Constitutional and Juridical Affairs Commissions; and as a result of the analysis made, version six came out in February 2000. The working group made another round to the provinces to meet with municipal assembly secretaries, people's council presidents, and representatives of mass organizations, during which time they gathered yet another 222 opinions. In April 2000 they wrote version seven, which was discussed in meetings with all deputies in each province and with experts and academics, among others, which resulted in 286 opinions. Version eight was presented on June 8, 2000, to the National Assembly leadership. The working group was expanded and came out with version nine on June 13 based on the discussion during the June 8 meeting. Version ten was presented on June 22 to the expanded group to work on style, vocabulary, uniformity, and some new modifications. This resulted in version eleven, which was presented on June 23 to a joint meeting of the OLPP and Constitutional and Juridical Affairs Commissions, attended by President Alarcón, along with other experts and high government officials. This version was presented to the regular session of the National Assembly, where further modifications were discussed during the debate. In all, 1,661 opinions were considered (many of which were included in the final version) during the process of developing a consensus regarding this pending legislation on the people's councils.

The legislation on agrarian cooperatives was proposed by ANAP during its congress in 2000. It was sent for opinions to the Ministries of Agriculture and of Sugar, and to legal and agricultural experts. The National Assembly leadership decided to present it to the National Assembly for approval during the December 2001 regular session. The process was led by the Productive Activities and the Constitutional and Juridical Affairs Commissions. It was then sent to mass organizations and to the PCC for consultation. The version that emerged was sent to deputies in all the provinces, to give them the opportunity to consult with their constituents, especially with farmers belonging to agrarian cooperatives. In subsequent meetings presided over by National Assembly officials, held in every province, deputies raised concerns expressed to them by their constituents.

At the conclusion of this process, the leaders of both commissions, ANAP president Lugo Fonte, and legal advisors met at the National Assembly headquarters for two days on December 13 and 14, to try to include the opinions expressed in opposition to certain parts and to reconcile the differences. However, this proved to be impossible because of disagreements that could not be reconciled, especially regarding policies related to housing and to hiring outside labor. One deputy from Matanzas stated that if the bill were presented to the National Assembly session it would be a bombshell. At the Productive Activities Commission meeting held just prior to the December 2001 session, the latest version of the bill was read including all the changes made, but then Lugo Fonte announced that the bill would not be presented in December due to lack of consensus. Subsequently the project was sent to the general assembly of every agrarian cooperative in the country for consultation, followed by further consultations with government officials and leaders of mass organizations, and a second round of meetings in every province with deputies, in order to have the legislation presented in the regular summer 2002 National Assembly session.

Another example of consultations that influenced pending legislation is the workers' parliaments that were held in every work center throughout Cuba during 1994. The opinions expressed by the population influenced subsequent legislation dealing with the economic crisis of the early 1990s and with the reestablishment of the private peasant markets.[16]

The National Assembly plenary session debates at times are perfunctory but often are meaningful, leading to major changes. Examples of the latter include the debates on the tax law, where the CTC leaders were influential in staving off an income tax and a provision for worker contributions to social security; on the law on foreign investments, where the CTC deputies managed to guarantee workers' rights when working for foreign firms; and on the penal code, where the penalties on rape and the definition of a minor were changed. Fidel Castro usually speaks more than other deputies, but many times he plays the role of devil's advocate, attempting to stimulate debate, asking questions of the deputies who have spoken. Interestingly, during the debate on the People's Council bill, Castro stated that he had not even had a chance to read the bill. When an amendment to the law against acts of terrorism was being voted on, Castro at first did not vote. He then asked Alarcón how he should vote, because he said he did not fully understand what was being proposed.

A provision in the Cuban Constitution allows ten thousand citizens to petition to bring up proposed legislation for a vote in the National Assembly. According to a report from InterPress Third World News Agency (IPS), "A coalition of 119 political opposition groups in Cuba are near their goal in collecting enough signatures to convene a referendum on freedoms of expression and association, a new electoral law, general elections and amnesty for political prisoners." The Cuban government claims that these groups are directed by and paid by the U.S. Special Interests Office in Havana.[17] After the coalition (known as the Varela Project) delivered eleven thousand signatures to the National Assembly on May 12, 2002, Alarcón replied on CBS *Evening News* on that day that the Cuban government would deal with the petition by strictly following the Cuban Constitution. In an exchange on May 14, 2002, between former president James Carter and students and faculty of the University of Havana, José L. Toledo, dean of the Law School and president of the National Assembly Commission on Constitutional and Juridical Affairs, pointed out that Article 88, Part g, of the Cuban Constitution allows for legislative initiatives by citizens' petition. However, the Varela Project was not proposing legislation but rather constitutional changes, which, according to Article 137 of the Cuban Constitution, can only be done by a two-thirds vote of the National Assembly. "One cannot try to take shelter behind legislative initiative in order to subvert the legal order of the country."[18]

Opinions and Consensus

While no organized opposition exists in Cuba, it is clear from the lawmaking process that deputies freely express their opposition to sections of pending legislation with which they disagree, their opinions are heard and taken into account, and, based on these opinions, changes are made. Deputies who disagree with items do so with the goal of improving rather than opposing the final product, and are active participants rather than adversaries in the lawmaking process. It is clear that until differences are reconciled, measures are not brought to the floor of the National Assembly.

This explains, at least in part, why all votes have been unanimous in the National Assembly. The leadership simply will not bring an item to a vote if there is not a reasonable assurance that the vote will be unanimous. Yet in 1991 the Fourth Party Congress rejected "false, mechanical, and formalistic unanimity," and former National Assembly president Juan Escalona told me in an interview in 1992, "It is absurd—the country of unanimity."[19]

But all subsequent votes have been unanimous. There seems to be pressure to conform. Escalona told me that unanimous votes show respect and confidence in the "historical leadership" and recognize its prestige, and will probably continue as long as it remains in power.[20] During the debate on the 1992 Electoral Law, some deputies opposed the noncompetitive elections and the method for electing municipal assembly presidents and vice presidents. When disagreement was expressed as to whether the term of the municipal delegates should be five years or two and a half years, President Castro asked all the deputies to support the latter position in a show of support for the country's leadership. Despite opposing points of view on these items, the vote for the law was unanimous. A deputy told me that although opposition was expressed in the hallways outside the main chamber, there was pressure to approve the law unanimously. During the debate on the penal code, Pastor Raúl Suárez of the Martin Luther King Center stated that he could not vote for the bill since he opposed the death penalty. However, he ended up voting for it. I asked him why, and he replied that he had voted for it because he agreed with the rest of the legislation and also to show unity. He told me that Fidel and Raúl Castro had sent him a note prior to the vote stating it was all right for him to vote against the measure. During the debate on foreign investments, Deputy Agustín Lage opposed the part that allowed Cubans in the United States to invest in Cuba. However, he ended up voting for the bill. When I asked him why, he responded that he had been convinced by the arguments on the other side and that he wanted to preserve the consensus. It seems that unanimous votes also can be attributed to what deputies have told me is a show of respect and deference to the "historical leadership," and will continue as long as that leadership remains in power.

Conclusions

The ingredients for a legitimate parliament are present in Cuba. While the National Assembly may not be the most important power center in Cuba, there is no denying its authority and influence within the government. Major legislation cannot go forward without its approval. While at the end of the legislative process the votes may be unanimous, certainly the deputies, working in commissions, participating in the writing and consultation process, and engaging in plenary session debates, have a major impact in shaping the final version of laws. Furthermore it is clear that lawmaking is an extremely participatory procedure.

The fact that the National Assembly meets in plenary session only twice a year for two days each time does not reveal the real work performed by the Assembly, its leadership, the commissions, and the deputies. Commissions initiate, write, rewrite, and revise pending legislation, and guide it through the consultative process. They oversee government ministries, monitor the economic plan and budget, inspect domains under their jurisdiction, and attend to citizen complaints. The importance of the commissions is underlined by the fact that important government ministers, other national leadership figures, and Assembly leaders attend and participate in their meetings. The president of the Productive Affairs Commission has a notebook filled with business cards from representatives of American firms who want to sell goods to Cuba and who recognize the importance of the National Assembly.

While most people, especially in cities, do not know who their deputies are, nonetheless, deputies have meaningful interaction with the population in several ways. First, *de base* deputies, by the nature of their position as municipal assembly delegates, almost by definition are in constant contact with the citizens they represent in their electoral district and people's councils. Second, deputies certainly must interact with the population during the consultation process for pending legislation. Third, deputies have contact with citizens when National Assembly commissions perform inspections. (For example, deputies from the Services Commission interviewed passengers as part of the inspection of transportation facilities.)

While elections are not competitive, the nomination process is consultative. While the PCC undeniably is an important force in Cuban society, it does not determine who will be nominated. Furthermore, the party does not replace the government, nor does it make the National Assembly superfluous. Finally, deputies actively oppose parts of proposed legislation, their objections are taken seriously, and there is an attempt to reconcile differences in the final versions. It is not an organized opposition. It is not a systematic opposition, but rather a temporary one depending on the issues at hand. Those who oppose certain items most likely will end up supporting the finished product, and other deputies will similarly question portions of other bills. Those who express such differences are usually effective, and in any case are loyal to the system.

Notes

1. An early version of this chapter was presented by the author at the Cuba Seminar, Bildner Center for Western Hemisphere Studies, City University of New York Graduate Center, April 26, 2002. (Editor's note.)

2. For a detailed analysis of the municipal assemblies, see Peter Roman, *People's Power: Cuba's Experience with Representative Government,* updated ed. (Lanham, Md.: Rowman and Littlefield, 2003).

3. Ibid., 108–9, 117–18.

4. Ibid, 92.

5. "Resolución económica del V Congreso del Partido Comunista de Cuba," *Granma,* November 7, 1997, 1–8.

6. *Resoluciones aprobadas por el III Congreso del Partido Comunista de Cuba* (Havana: Editora Política, 1986), 18–21.

7. Roman, *People's Power,* 112.

8. Pluralism is defined as "a condition of society in which numerous distinct ethnic, religious, or cultural groups coexist within one nation." *American Heritage Dictionary of the English Language,* 3rd ed.

9. The two parties in the United States without question support the capitalist political and economic system, and in the candidate selection process neither party would tolerate someone whose goal was the destruction of the U.S. government and economy. Furthermore, the April 2002 attempted coup in Venezuela demonstrates the destructive and antidemocratic behavior and goals of a disloyal opposition allied with the United States. Christopher Marquis, "U.S. bankrolling is under scrutiny for ties to Chavez ouster," *New York Times,* April 25, 2002; Christopher Marquis, "Bush officials met with Venezuelans who ousted leader," *New York Times,* April 16, 2002. "*EE.UU. metido hasta la médula en el golpe en Venezuela,*" *Granma* (on line), April 17, 2002.

10. One should keep in mind that in the U.S. House of Representatives elections, of the 435 races in November 2002, only about two dozen were expected to be truly competitive contests. Ronald Brownstein, "Close House races go the way of rotary phones, Newt Gingrich," *Los Angeles Times,* April 15, 2002. Alison Mitchell, "Redistricting 2002 produces no great shakeups," *New York Times,* March 13, 2002.

11. Roman, *People's Power,* 139–40.

12. Peter Roman, "Focus on Cuba: Manifestations of Democracy," *Washington Report on the Hemisphere* 20, no. 4–5 (April 15, 2000): 11.

13. Jesús Pastor García Brigos, "People's Power in the Organization of the Cuban Socialist State," *Cuba in the 1990s: Economy, Politics, and Society, Socialism and Democracy* 15, no. 1 (spring–summer 2001): 113–36.

14. Alan S. Chartock, "They blew the budget process yet again," *West Side Spirit,* May 23, 2002, 39.

15. The information presented here is based on an interview with Tomás Cárdenas, president of the National Assembly Commission on Local Organs of People's Power, in November 2001.

16. Roman, *People's Power,* 245–57.

17. Patricia Grogg, "Dissident initiative seeks vote on rights for all," International Press Service, March 23, 2002.

18. "Es necesario encontrar las vías para el entendimiento, la tolerancia y la paz," *Granma* (on line), May 16, 2002.

19. Roman, *People's Power,* 86–87.

20. Ibid., 88.

11

Socialism and Elections

Arnold August

In addition to my earlier field research of Cuban electoral practices, the midterm elections of March–April 2000 provided me with factual information on municipal elections. Combined with the extraparliamentary activities of December 1999 and May and July 2000, and the 1999 and 2000 laws covering the functioning of the political process, the new findings have motivated me to examine further some of the points raised in a previous study.[1]

The lack of a well-documented study of the Cuban notion of democracy and elections became evident during the course of seminars and in different book reviews. What really seemed necessary was objective information about the actual workings of the electoral system, including the historical background against which the current process is playing its role. It was startling to realize how many academics specializing in Latin American and even Cuban affairs were poorly informed of Cuba's electoral process. Although this subject is debated among students of international affairs, it is not well known. All in all, the educational objective behind my initial work remains valid.

By presenting here new insights on the electoral system, this chapter upgrades previous studies and summarizes the historical background process discussed in an earlier account and analysis.[2]

Past Electoral Experience

The first step in understanding Cuba's experience with democracy and political processes is to recognize the major transformation that was accomplished by the 1959 revolution. The struggle for national and social emancipation that started in the last third of the nineteenth century finally culminated in 1959, when the populace at last gained political power. The forms and structures that this power took were never perfect and still are not. However, their aims are diametrically opposed to those that existed before 1959. Historically, Cuba, its people, and its resources had mostly functioned as an appendage of political and corporate interests of Spain and, later, the United States. A powerful minority of U.S. businessmen, including members of the criminal underworld and their Cuban partners (particularly under the Batista regime in the 1950s), played a part in ruling Cuba. (Regrettably, the well-known Elián González case revealed that the Cuban American political right today is not that different from what it was in the 1950s.)

In the political process initiated in 1959 and implemented throughout the 1960s, many of the major orientations and even decisions regarding the nation were agreed upon in open mass assemblies. One major decision was the rejection of elections at that time. Was this because the Cuban people and their leaders were antidemocratic? Actually, Cuba's experience with democracy and elections should take into account the 1902–58 period, when a U.S.-style, multiparty political process was put into effect. The grievances generated by the badly copied U.S. political and electoral process contributed to the decision to reject elections after 1959. So when Castro asked a mass assembly whether to hold elections in the near future, the people responded negatively. The only electoral experience they had had was one in which corruption reigned, while U.S. business concerns and government officials manipulated the various political parties (and strongmen) in order to maintain their political and economic control over the island.[3]

The Revolution's Electoral Process

It was not until 1974–76 that the regime proposed and involved the people in establishing an electoral system, one that has evolved and changed over time. A modern view of the system can be gained from a study of the general elections of 1997–98 (following a five-year cycle, the next ones took place in 2002–3), plus the municipal elections held in 2000. However, municipal elections take place every two and a half years, alternately coinciding with the general elections (1997–98 and 2002–03). The municipal elections held in the spring of 2000 were followed by new ones in the fall of 2002.

There are three levels of elected state officials: municipal, provincial, and national. The concept of municipality in Cuba is different from the one used in North America and Europe. The City of Havana (Ciudad de La Habana) province, with a population of more than two million people and the size of a typical American city, is divided into fifteen municipalities. Therefore,

Havana, in terms of economic entity and political process, is not a city as such. The fifteen municipalities included in it comprise one of Cuba's fourteen provinces, and they are jointly known as City of Havana province (each municipality has its own level of distinct economic and political responsibilities). A typical municipality in this province is Plaza de la Revolución, which includes 104 wards. During the 1997 general elections, the twelfth ward had 1,291 voting citizens. Although it includes an area of only two city blocks by four blocks, it represents one of the building blocks of the entire electoral process since the electoral system is built on the "bottom to top" principle.

Still, the series of small municipalities that comprise the sprawling cities are not miniature cities in appearance only. Each municipality is the locus of juridical, economic, and social power in its area. Although the municipality lacks legislative powers, the municipal delegates have the responsibility to supervise, inspect, and monitor all the social, economic, judicial, and political affairs in their area, including the local budget and economic plan, as well as to adopt regulations governing their cultural and social life. The delegates can fire and hire administrators of local enterprises located in their jurisdiction, and have a say in provincial and national enterprises operating within their borders.

Municipal Elections

In many ways, local elections are the most important ones, since they affect the composition of the higher levels of political power, the provincial and national assemblies. Up to half of the delegates to the fourteen provincial assemblies and to the National Assembly must by law be composed of municipal delegates in good standing—nominated and elected through established municipal elections procedure.[4]

Voting registration is nearly a two-month process preceding the first step in the electoral process, the nominations. With very few exceptions, such as the severely handicapped and criminals, everyone sixteen years and older has the right to vote. A register of eligible voters is maintained for this purpose, and preelection registration is used to update and verify it to safeguard its accuracy. There are no encumbering obstacles; everything is facilitated so that all citizens of voting age are on the list. Everything is done within a block or two of the resident's home. If the citizen is not mobile for health or other reasons, the registration is done at the person's home.

For the purpose of nominating candidates, the already compact municipal ward is further divided into nomination areas. Following our case study, the twelfth ward of the Plaza municipality is divided into seven nomination areas. Each of these areas contains about one hundred fifty voting citizens. In geographical terms this would encompass about one or two sides of one street block per nomination area. On successive evenings or on Sunday mornings, one after the other, the local elections committee convokes a nomination area assembly of the one hundred fifty or so citizens living in the area. These meetings normally take place in the street situated on the block where the people live. While only those people who are registered voters and who live in the nomination area have the right to nominate, the meetings are public. Citizens are called upon to propose the nomination of any citizen who lives in the ward. There is no limit to the number of people proposed for nomination—the proposed nominee does not have to live in that area but must reside in the ward. My observations in 1997 and 2000 have shown that nomination proposals are always made by individual citizens. People speak on their own behalf as voters, so anyone may propose candidates and may also be nominated. For this purpose, the citizens' names are included in a voters' list that is inclusive and made available to the voters. The overall procedure is spontaneous, not orchestrated.[5]

The Communist Party does not participate either formally or behind the scenes in preparing the nominations, nor do the Comités de Defensa de la Revolución (Committees for the Defense of the Revolution, CDRs), nor mass organizations such as the Cuban Confederation of Workers (CTC) or the Federation of Cuban Women (FMC), which is today regarded as a nongovernmental organization. The person proposing a candidate must give reasons for his proposal. They are always based on the nominee's experience, personal integrity, and qualifications. Political affiliation (party membership) is not a consideration, but the person being proposed must formally accept the nomination. The proposed nominee does not, and by law cannot, make any speeches promising to do such and such a thing to gain support from the voters.

I attended one of the nomination area assemblies in March 2000, held for that year's municipal elections. Something that I had barely noticed during my observations of the 1997 municipal nominations and elections became clear. No one, neither the proponent nor the proposed nominee, used the future tense. This might seem at first glance to be a banal observation, but not so: virtually everything is based on what the person has already accomplished in terms of efforts to contribute toward the better economic and social functioning of the ward and municipality. The citizen's personal and political integrity based on a publicly verifiable evaluation is what counts; there are no empty words. The simplicity of the nomination system is startling.

Once the nomination proposals are completed, a vote takes place by show of hands for each proposed candidate by his or her neighbors. The votes are counted and the person who receives the most votes is the candidate in that area. The same procedure takes place in the other six nomination area assemblies of our case study ward. It often occurs that a person nominated in one area assembly is also proposed and then wins the nomination in another area. One has to keep in mind that while only those living in the nomination area can propose candidates for elections, a nominee can live anywhere in the ward. Some people are thus nominated by several nomination assemblies because people at times build up a reputation as a result of their work and become locally known social and political personalities. A minimum of two and a maximum of eight citizens per ward are then nominated. In a nutshell, nominations for the municipal elections are based on the involvement of neighbors who in the main all know each other.

A similar procedure takes place simultaneously throughout the country in more than 37,000 nominating assemblies with a participation rate usually close to 90 percent. Although quite different from most liberal democratic electoral systems, the Cuban nomination procedure is as valid as others.

The question remains as to whether this system of nomination is based on the right of every citizen to nominate candidates without any interference by the Communist Party or any other organization. My own observations of the Cuban electoral process show that while there have been some violations of the principle in past elections since they were established in the 1970s, the matter has since been properly settled. The Cuban theory on open nominations is mostly carried out in practice. Still, there may be some exceptions whereby party cells get together for informal nominations during the nominating area assemblies period. However, this is not tolerated either by the party or the electoral commissions that oversee the elections. The issue of strengthening the notion both in theory and in practice that it is the people who are sovereign and that no organization can or should usurp this sovereignty has as its main source such leaders as Castro, Ricardo Alarcón, and Raúl Castro.

It was noticeable in my field research that the older leaders were many times the most resilient and the most willing to be innovative and open minded in their thinking. The party and the leadership that came out of the 1950s were in the forefront of ensuring that the political system live up to its commitment of making the citizens truly sovereign in the full constitutional meaning of the term. The nomination procedure became a crucial test of the validity and legitimacy of the political system.

Once the nominations are over, the municipal elections begin across the island. Whether they are part of the general elections, as was the case in 1997, or the partial elections of March 2000, the electoral system at the municipal level remains the same.

Elections, Campaigning, and Requirements

There are no election campaigns as we know them in North America or Europe. One does not need to spend money to be nominated or elected in Cuba. Anything resembling a traditional election campaign, including the use of funds or any other material tools, violates the law. Such a practice would also be contrary to the revolution's political culture. The local electoral commissions put together short biographies and photos of the candidates, all of equal size. The candidates' biographies are posted together in such public areas as local markets, stores, clinics, and schools. The objective is to provide an opportunity for the people to know who the candidates are so they can make their decision privately. In most cases, however, even the posting of this information is a mere formality since the citizens usually know the nominee as a neighbor. Still, some changes were introduced in the 2000 elections to improve the electoral process. Since all the neighbors are not always familiar with all the nominees, the 1992 Electoral Law provision allowing meetings between candidates and the electorate was applied in 2000 for the first time in many wards across the country. The candidates must meet the voters at the same time; no individual meetings are allowed between one candidate and the voters. After about one month, during which citizens get to know the candidates through the posted biographies and more recently through meet-the-candidates information meetings, secret ballot elections take place on the basis of universal suffrage.

While all the different organizations and the leadership call massively on the people to vote, voting is not obligatory, and no one is in any way punished or discriminated against for not voting. The designated voting areas in the city are usually situated a block away or a short distance from each voter, and in the countryside it is almost the same. The electoral commission verifies first that the voter is on the list and then hands the voter a ballot listing the names of the candidates. The voter has complete secrecy to vote for one of the candidates, to spoil the ballot, or to leave it blank. There is no police presence during the elections, which are most peaceful. The ballot boxes are watched over by young school students. After the vote, held on a

Sunday in order to provide the opportunity for all to vote, the ballots are counted on the spot and in public. Any citizen or even a foreigner can attend the public counting.

In order to be elected, the candidate needs more than 50 percent of the vote. For those not receiving the designated minimum, a second round is organized for the following Sunday between the two candidates who received the most votes. During the municipal elections held in the spring of 2000, of the 14,686 wards in the 169 municipalities in the country, 13,853 delegates were elected in the first round. In 833 wards another round had to take place. For the first time in municipal elections, in one ward even a second round was not conclusive. In this case both candidates won the same number of votes. In the specially organized third round, one candidate finally came out on top.

The voting rate in the first round of the 2000 municipal elections was 98.06 percent of eligible voters. This was up from the 97.59 percent in the 1997 municipal elections, which were held as part of the general elections. While Cubans put a lot of emphasis on the high percentage of people voting, what is particularly significant is how people vote. (The voting rates and results of the 1998 National Assembly elections will be dealt with below.)

Once the municipal elections are completed, the municipal assemblies are then constituted across the country. The first act is the nomination and election by the delegates, voting by secret ballot, of the president and vice president of each municipal assembly. When the municipal elections do not coincide with the provincial and National Assembly elections, such as those held in 2000, then the electoral process ends with the election of the municipal assemblies' leading officers. But for the general elections held every five years, the conclusion of the municipal elections signals the beginning of the elections to the two higher levels, provincial and national.

Electing National Deputies

The focus here will be on the elections of national deputies since the procedure is similar to the one used for provincial assembly delegates. How do nominations and elections to the highest level of state power take place? Both nominations and elections are different from the process at the municipal level. Havana attempted to apply the municipal level's direct nomination principle as closely as possible to the national level. This was done while taking into account the major differences between a local assembly responsible for a limited area and the national legislature responsible for the entire country. The latter is designed to mirror the nation as a whole, including in its ranks people from all geographical areas and from all walks of life.

For the last general election, as is always the case, candidacy commissions were formed at the national, provincial, and municipal levels including representatives from mass organizations, as well as farmers, students, trade unions, women's organizations, and so on. Presided over by the trade union representative, the commissions' mandate is to propose candidates for election to the provincial and national assemblies, a process close to what is done at the municipal level. For this purpose, during the fall of 1997, citizens were consulted at the national, provincial, and municipal level through their respective mass organizations. By the end, commission members went to the place of work or the neighborhood of the proposed candidates to verify that people at the base believed that the nominees were really worthy of occupying a position of state power.

The consultation at the local level is important, since it is a source of potential candidates for the provincial and national levels. According to the law, as mentioned above, up to half of the provincial and national assemblies' composition must be made up of municipal delegates. The National Candidacy Commission is also charged with searching for potential candidates from among the public. It seeks out those citizens whom the voters would find appropriate for the National Assembly, including political, cultural, and sports personalities, and those who are not well known outside their place of work or neighborhood but who are considered able to make valuable contributions to national political life.

In a long process, about 1.6 million people were consulted as to why a candidate should be nominated for the elections. An initial list of sixty thousand potential candidates was then drawn up after the consultations ended. For the National Assembly elections, through another series of consultations, a shorter list of 609 candidates was established. Each of the individuals suggested as candidates was proposed for a definite municipality or a district within a municipality.

Deciding who should be a candidate for which municipality is a complicated process. If everyone were placed for elections in their respective cities, Havana and other large cities would have far more candidates than outlying regions. Hence, the municipality is divided into districts when the population exceeds one hundred thousand, with a maximum of four districts per municipality, depending on the number of residents.

The densely populated City of Havana's Plaza de la Revolución is divided into three districts, so a total of nine citizens were nominated to run in this municipality. Five candidates were well-known notables while, applying the rule that up to half of the national candidates should come from the municipal base, the other four were municipal delegates (see table 11.1).

Table 11.1. Electoral districts in Plaza de la Revolución municipality

Plaza de la Revolución	Notables	Municipal Delegates
District 1	1	2
District 2	2	1
District 3	2	1

Source: Plaza de la Revolución Municipal Electoral Commission, 1997.

Each National Assembly deputy is elected by voters from a definite municipality, or if the municipality has a relatively large population, from a district. Once elected, the deputy represents the entire municipality as well as the overall national interests; the districts into which the municipality was divided for electoral purposes no longer exist after the elections.

The number of 609 proposed nominees coincides with the number of seats in the National Assembly. The final say as to who the candidates should be, whether they are from the public or from the municipal assemblies' elected delegates, belongs to the municipal assemblies. Another important issue is whether the municipal assembly agrees with having a candidate represent their municipality. In 1997, the municipal assemblies rejected four candidates proposed by the candidacy commissions because they felt that the nominees were not appropriate for state duty. The candidacy commissions then had to propose new candidates chosen from their list of potential nominees.

Once the municipal assemblies approve the proposed list, a period is allowed for the citizens to get acquainted with the candidates. This is far more crucial than in the lower level where virtually everyone knows each other. Half of the candidates are chosen from the general population, but while some are not well known, others may be nationally famous. To bridge the name recognition gap, several meet-the-candidates meetings were organized in December 1997 and January 1998. Their purpose was twofold. First, they allowed the citizens to get to know the candidates, and second, they allowed the candidates to familiarize themselves with the municipality and its economic and social problems, so as to better represent the population in that area.

This was noticeable in Abreus municipality, Cienfuegos province, in the countryside, where the candidates visited workplaces, sugarcane fields, and economic institutions. In the urban Plaza de la Revolución municipality, candidates visited hospitals, schools, and government offices and held open discussions with the administrators and employees about different issues,

Table 11.2. Spoiled, blank ballots cast in national elections, 1993/1998

| | National Elections Year | |
	1993	1998
Spoiled ballots	3.99%	1.66%
Blank ballots	3.28%	1.65%

Source: Cuba National Electoral Commission, 1998.

including hospital problems, their expectations regarding health services, and the quality of education.

After the "familiarization period" lasting from November 29, 1997, to January 10, 1998, the elections took place on January 11, 1998. As in the lower-level elections, voting was secret and based on universal suffrage. While a candidate must always garner more than 50 percent of the votes to be elected, the main difference is that while there is only one candidate for each seat in the National Assembly, at the local level a minimum of two to a maximum of eight candidates must run for a delegate seat. This is a controversial fact in Cuba, but more so overseas among students of the island's political system. (This debate is dealt with below.)

The results of the national elections, in terms of the proportion of eligible people voting and how they actually voted, are significant, especially since the January 1998 elections were held under U.S. political and ideological pressure, seeking to discredit the electoral process. Official sources revealed in 1999 that U.S. sympathizers in Cuba had pursued tactics of a massive boycott and a nullified ballot campaign in the 1998 national elections.[6]

A recurring question is whether issues have a place in the electoral process. Do citizens ever take a stand on an issue or series of issues? In the 1997–98 elections a major issue faced the electorate: whether people preferred the extant political system, or the political system that critics, opponents, and the United States had been pressuring Cuba to adopt.

The results of the 1998 national elections in the context of the boycott and nullified vote campaign showed a reversing trend. Of the total number of eligible voters, 98.35 percent voted. While this was slightly down from the 99.6 percent vote cast in the 1993 national election, the figure was a clear defeat for the opposition (that is, dissidents). A decrease of barely more than 1 percent is an indication of the failure to make a breakthrough in the campaign to discredit the Socialist system. The U.S.-sponsored campaign supported spoiled and blank ballots as an alternative for those who wanted to express their opposition, rather than a boycott. The antigovernment campaign was discussed in meetings attended by candidates and vot-

Table 11.3. Spoiled ballots cast in Ciudad de La Habana province, 1993/1998

	National Elections Year	
	1993	1998
Spoiled ballots	10.43%	3.42%
Blank ballots	4.17%	4.00%

Source: Cuba National Electoral Commission, 1998.

ers, especially in places like Havana, where Ricardo Alarcón led a debate on the issue. While not all spoiled and blank ballots represent an opposition statement since some are caused by voter error, the 1998 national-level results, in contrast to 1993, were significant, representing a decrease of approximately two-thirds in the spoiled and blank votes (see table 11.2).

Moreover, the results for the national elections in City of Havana province, which has a concentration of political dissidents and U.S. anti-Castro pressure and is the province with most problems with day-to-day economic and social life, shows a decline of spoiled and blank votes from 1993 to 1998 (see table 11.3). The two-thirds decrease trend in spoiled ballots repeated itself. Besides the usual task of choosing well-qualified candidates, in 1998 there was the already mentioned issue of rendering judgment on the political system and its electoral process. In reality the elections turned out to be a plebiscite on the legitimacy of Cuba's democracy. Recognizing the dissidents' defeat, one of their best-known leaders, Elizardo Sánchez, stated that the 1998 national elections "signified the renovation of the mandates and the legitimacy of the government."[7]

However, critics of the regime have argued that the opposition has no other choice than to boycott the elections or spoil the ballots to express their disagreement with present-day policies. But there is no legal or administrative impediment for a member of the opposition to propose a candidate or to be nominated with the municipal assemblies. At least in principle, opposition members can be nominated and elected to the lower level, and subsequently move upwards into positions from which they can plead their case. In practice, however, they are not nominated due to such factors as the political isolation from revolutionary politics in which the dissidents and their policies find themselves.

Once the elections to the provincial and national levels are over, the new legislatures are established. After the 1998 elections, the new legislature of the National Assembly was convened a month later. The Assembly president, vice president, and secretary were elected after all the elected deputies were called upon to propose candidates to the National Candidacy Commission, which in turn whittled down the list of nominees to three. The Assembly then adjourned for a secret vote. After being reelected president, Ricardo Alarcón and his two fellow elected officers were responsible for presiding over and conducting the business of the Assembly. Their first responsibility was to lead the nomination and election of candidates to the State Council.

Organizing the *Consejos Populares*

The *consejos populares* (popular councils) are formed at the local level after the municipal assemblies have been constituted, following the elections of municipal delegates. The *consejos* were suggested in 1986 to support the work of municipal delegates and to strengthen citizens' participation in local affairs. For this purpose each municipality is divided into smaller units; for example, the Plaza de la Revolución municipality is divided into eight *consejos populares,* which involve the municipal delegates included in their jurisdiction. The delegates are responsible for electing the president and vice president of the *consejo* from among themselves—who may or may not be professionally paid, full-time officers.

Besides the elected membership, nonelected representatives from mass organizations, economic corporations, factories, hospitals, and hotels are also included, as long as the number of nonelected representatives does not surpass the number of elected ones. Becoming president or vice president of a *consejo popular* enhances a municipal delegate's social standing and may motivate the delegate to run for elections and occupy higher-level positions. This is most evident in rural municipalities like Abreus, Cienfuegos province, where rural and town workers have been able to become local leaders. Thus the *consejos populares* have provided a needed administrative and political training ground for common citizens.

The *consejos populares* were institutionalized in the 1992 Constitution, after having been spread across the country and following a trial period in Ciudad de La Habana province. In the session of July 2000, the National Assembly enacted a new law on the *consejos populares* that served to clarify and reinforce their role at the local level in the political system.

Accountability of Elected Officials

The accountability of elected officials to the citizens is an important part of the electoral process and takes two forms: the "rendering accounts" sessions, and the right of citizens to recall an elected person and have his mandate revoked for good cause.[8] The most important sessions take place at the local level, where every six months the delegates have to report on their work on behalf of the citizens who nominated and elected them. In May 1998, six months after the 1997 municipal elections, the local delegates dutifully faced their electorates. The twelfth ward in Plaza de la Revolución municipality was divided up into smaller areas for this purpose. In order to increase the citizens' control over their delegates, the areas are smaller than those used for the nomination of candidates. Neighbors' participation along with the delegates in the governance of their own area forces the delegates to focus on solutions to the problems facing the locality. When local administrators attend such meetings, they not only explain the reasons for shortcomings but also become involved in finding possible solutions. There are times when delegates cannot find a viable answer to a known problem, but the meeting still remains spontaneous, provoking a lively interaction between electors and elected officials. When the problem calls for another meeting, administrators at the ministerial level are called to provide solutions. The intense give-and-take of these meetings once prompted a reporter from *Granma*, the official Communist Party daily, to title her article, "Una reunion caliente" (A sharp debate).[9] As expected, since the system's institution in 1976, the delegates have faced the electors every six months during the two-and-a-half-year mandate. Following the new assembly elected in April 2000, the first rendering-accounts sessions started in the fall of 2000.

Rendering accounts is a process that takes place at different levels of the government system. National Assembly deputies render accounts periodically to the municipal assembly delegates who approved their nomination for elections. Also, the Council of State, responsible for running the state between parliamentary sessions, is accountable to the National Assembly and periodically has to provide a report on its work.

The Revocation Process

If 25 percent of the voters registered locally sign a petition for revocation of the municipal delegate's position, then the revocation process is initiated. After going through the municipal assembly, the revocation request is presented to all voters in the municipal ward to decide by secret vote, similar to the procedure followed in the elections. If more than 50 percent of registered voters favor revocation, then the delegate is removed and a new election is held, providing the period is far enough away from the next municipal elections to merit such an election in only one ward.

Revocation of the provincial delegates and National Assembly deputies takes place in a similar way; however, in this case the elected officials initiate the revocation procedure. In September 1999, during a regular session of the National Assembly, a law on revocation was presented and finally adopted, articulating in more detail the procedures to be followed.

The Fairness of the Electoral System

Among the objections about the electoral process is the lack of competitive election between two or more candidates at the national level, where there is only one candidate per seat. The right to elect deputies to parliament exercised by the municipal assemblies was taken away in 1992, when direct elections were adopted. Differently than at the municipal level, which has conducted direct elections for local delegates all along, the 1976 charter established indirect elections for National Assembly deputies and provincial delegates, until it was modified by the 1992 Electoral Law. Still, some analysts argue that the 1992 constitutional reforms and the Electoral Law did not go far enough, that they should have included competitive elections at the national level.

While not entirely without merit, the objections are not serious enough to invalidate the electoral system. To say that elections at the municipal level are competitive and others are not applies a notion that may be relevant to electoral politics elsewhere, but not in Cuba. In reality, the municipal elections are not competitive in the way the term is generally understood. People who run for local office are often neighbors and friends and colleagues; the usual competitiveness that characterizes elections in most places is not present here. The electoral choice is left up to individual citizens while candidates to municipal office carry on their normal personal, family, and professional lives as they do throughout the year.

The assertion that competing elections with two or more candidates per seat are necessarily more democratic than one per seat runs contrary to basic principles of Cuba's participatory democracy, which came into practice in 1959 under the revolutionary government. While supporting a system that is by no means perfect, revolutionary values recognize that people's sovereignty is effectively exercised when the will of the majority is democratically expressed. Besides, in addition to electoral practices, this brand of democracy manifests itself through other structures and modalities. In 1993, at the height of the economic crisis following the collapse of the Soviet Union and the tightening of U.S. punitive policies over Cuba, the National Assembly called for workers' parliaments to be held all over the island. They were organized in the workplaces and neighborhoods to discuss ways of confronting the ongoing crisis. Over the course of four months thousands of assemblies took place with millions of citizens participating. Later, many of the proposals were brought to the National Assembly where they were legislated upon.

Cuban democracy also expresses itself through the readiness of elected officials to respond to people's demands. In December 1999, following the request of Elián González's father, Juan Miguel González, to have his son returned to him, the National Assembly adopted a resolution demanding the boy be returned to his father in Cuba. Following this, the entire body of deputies took to the streets and headed a demonstration of thousands of people to the U.S. Interests Section in Havana. The 2000 May Day parades were also turned into massive demonstrations across the island, demanding the return of Elián to his family.

Other political activities have taken the form of governmental decrees. Amendments to the Penal Code were adopted, imposing harsher penalties for such social crimes as engaging in underage prostitution, pimping, and so on. This was in response to people's demands for firm action addressing the criminal behavior that erupted in the 1990s during the special period. Whether from the workers' parliaments, myriad mobilizational marches, or governmental decrees responding to people's demands, these actions involve the elected representatives, who exercise their leadership democratically.

Electing Women

Cuban women have historically been victims of discrimination and were not highly regarded in society for their potential contributions outside the traditional roles assigned to them. In the 1997 municipal elections, about 18 percent of the chosen delegates were women, and in the April 2000 elections about the same percentage of women were elected. But the percentage of women sitting in the National Assembly is 28 percent as compared to 18 percent at the municipal level.[10] How to explain this disparate electoral outcome?

On the municipal level, where citizens propose candidates directly, the reality is that in many cases the citizens are still acting out traditional prejudices and therefore are less prone to nominate women. On the national level, however, mass organizations and their membership are involved in the nomination process. They are more aware of historical social inequalities facing the system (as gender-based prejudice) and take action decisively to remedy the situation. The end result is more women are being nominated and elected at the national level than at the local one.

Weaknesses of the Electoral System

What are the main weaknesses of the Cuban electoral system? It is far from perfect, and the Cubans are aware of this. They are the first ones to recognize its imperfections and also to take action to improve the system. The 1992 reforms introduced direct elections for the first time at the national level; the latest laws on revocation of elected officials (1999) and on *consejos populares* (2000) are cases in point. However, a potential major problem is the increasingly uneasy relationship between elected officials and the newly emerging economic actors, more so than any weakness in the electoral system itself. Once nominations and elections are completed, what power do elected delegates and deputies actually have over the new interests and forces growing in a society with an increasingly diversified economy? Expanded foreign investment and tourism have become the main sources of foreign currency, and the U.S. dollars in circulation are central in today's economy. In many ways, the economy and society that existed in the late 1980s are there no longer. The resources available to the emerging economic actors are considerable, while the people's representatives, especially at the local level, seem limited in terms of resources and capacity to act.

After following a rigorous nomination and electoral procedure, municipal delegates must still keep their regular jobs while carrying out their new responsibilities on a voluntary basis—mostly after work in the evenings or on weekends. This helps to ensure that elected representatives keep close ties and do not distance themselves from the electors. But it also puts a strain on the delegates and limits their capacity to act as representatives of the citizens in their ward. Also, they must offer time-consuming renditions of accounts every six months in open sessions.

Municipal delegates are reelected quite often; those who are not are replaced by newly elected ones. In the 2000 elections, as in 1997, more than 50 percent of those elected were first-time delegates. While the electors showed their confidence by reelecting half of the delegates, the question remains as to why so many delegates do not run for reelection. Municipal and provincial delegates, as well as national deputies, are always busy, selflessly going about their tasks without receiving any substantial reward for their efforts. The work of elected officials at all levels means thankless sacrifice compounded by lack of needed resources to accomplish their work. Comparing their resources with those of the new, lower-level technocrats (mostly those working for foreign investment corporations in partnership with the government, or in the tourist industry), shows that the difference is out of proportion. Personal observation and research show that seldom would the newly emerging technocrats need to wonder if they could accomplish their work or find themselves compelled to forget their responsibilities for lack of time or resources. Even though the upper levels of government, including state enterprises, joint ventures, and the party as a general rule honor the characteristic revolutionary honesty, institutionalized corruption is increasingly happening at state enterprises (nationally owned or joint ventures) and lower levels of the tourist industry. Sometimes the same corrupt individual occupies a low-level party post, and some tourist technocrats rake in hundreds of U.S. dollars in one or two days of underhanded activity.[11]

Still, in theory the new technocrats are accountable to elected officials. Whether it is a hospital administrator catering to foreigners or the head of a construction company building sites for foreign consumption, all are equally accountable for their activities, and in the process the public could find their actions to be insufficient or harmful. In practice, however, the elected delegates are the ones who are on the defensive, seeking patch-up solutions to insurmountable problems. Hence, to what extent are these technocrats really accountable, and what portion of their mistakes remains hidden from public scrutiny? For municipal and provincial delegates and national deputies striving to carry out their responsibilities after their normal working day, the double workload makes life increasingly difficult, particularly since the economy relies heavily on foreign investment. The free circulation of dollars combined with the fact that some people are seemingly more capable than others of acquiring them has created an irritating divisive feature in today's society.

According to the Cuban minister of audit and control, Lina Pedraz, "Corruption is not a major social problem in Cuba."[12] And yet, the economic power accumulated in the hands of this newly emerging privileged class constitutes a potential threat to the exercise of political power by the people and their representatives. This contradictory situation is not an unusual anomaly in capitalist economies, where even though the very wealthy comprise a small portion of the population, they still retain most if not all power. Today, however, there is no guarantee that the traditional praiseworthy attitude of Cuban elected representatives, from the municipal to the national level, can prevail over the newly created economic forces, whose interests obviously lack the ideological collectivist objectives of those who are entrusted to occupy positions at different levels of state power.

The policy that elected officials should maintain their jobs while carrying out their functions has been a key ingredient in their keeping close ties with the electors. But under those conditions, what chance do they have to prevail over the new economic actors? As the economy develops and becomes more complex and involves more individuals linked to foreign capital or tourism, the troublesome relationship between elected officials and new technocrats is bound to become more problematic. It seems that the full weight of state power, assuring that the economy really works for the people, especially at the local level, will be needed.

The presidents and vice presidents of municipal assemblies have been full-time professionals whose salaries are paid by the municipality, but according to a 2000 law, the leading executive personnel of the *consejos populares* no longer have to be full-time workers. This is a well-intended law; still it should prevent any bureaucrat working alongside elected representatives from controlling the electoral, representative structure. And it should release elected officials from time-consuming jobs, so their political and administrative authority will efficiently be used to satisfy the populace's needs and expectations.

As the Cuban economy continues its present path, the door for some individuals to acquire more economic clout and standing than others remains open. The political system must rise to the occasion, ensuring that the electoral process will allow elected officials to effectively prevail over the growing technocratic cadres and any other serious obstacles, while defending the people's best interests.

Notes

1. This chapter is partly based on the author's study, *Democracy in Cuba and the 1992–98 Elections* (Havana and Montreal: Editorial José Martí and Canada-Cuba Distribution and Publishing, 1999). It is also the result of additional field research and seminars and book presentations that took place from 1999 to 2001 in Canada, the United Kingdom, and the United States.

2. August, *Democracy in Cuba.*

3. Louis A. Perez Jr., *Cuba: Between Reform and Revolution* (New York: Oxford University Press, 1988), and *Cuba under the Platt Amendment: 1902–1934* (Pittsburgh, Pa.: University of Pittsburgh Press, 1986); Enrique Meitin, "De los partidos en la primera etapa de la Cuba neocolonial," *Bohemia* (January 24, 1975): 67; Jorge Ibarra, *Cuba: 1898–1921, partidos políticos y clases sociales* (Havana: Editorial de Ciencias Sociales, 1992); Enrique Cirules, *El imperio de La Habana* (Havana: Casa de las Américas, 1993); Antonio Ramos, *Manual del perfecto fulanista: Apuntes para el estudio de nuestra dinámica político-social* (Havana: Editorial Jesús Montero, 1916).

4. See the 1976 Constitution of the Republic of Cuba as amended in 1992, Article 87.

5. Author's personal observations during the 1997 and 2000 municipal nomination area meetings in Plaza de la Revolución municipality, City of Havana province, and the Albreus rural municipality, Cienfuegos province. For a critical scholarly study of Cuban politics that reaches similar conclusions, see Peter Roman, *People's Power: Cuba's Experiment with Representative Government* (Boulder, Colo.: Westview, 1999), 105–12.

6. Grupo de Trabajo de la Disidencia Cubana, "Call to the Cuban People." The basis for the appeal could be seen in Grupo de Trabajo de la Disidencia Cubana, *La patria es de todos* (Havana: n.p., June 27, 1997).

7. Cited in Dalia Acosta, "Cuba: Nuevo parlamento revelará el rumbo de Fidel Castro," *Inter Press Service,* February 23, 1998; Roman, *People's Power,* 146.

8. Nonelected officials are also accountable. For example, members of nonelected positions in the Council of Ministers, municipal and provincial administrations, and ministries have to render accounts to their respective assemblies.

9. Maria Julia Mayoral, *Granma,* November 4, 1998.

10. National Electoral Commission, 2000.

11. A criminal underground has emerged throughout the island, not just in major cities like Havana and Santiago but in relatively small towns as well. Rather than holding a regular job, these individuals belong to prostitution and theft networks, sometimes coordinating their actions with lower-level technocrats working in the tourist industry. Seemingly acting with impunity, they manage to accumulate sizable fortunes (by Cuban standards) in U.S. dollars, while the police seem reluctant to take action against them.

12. *Radio Habana Cuba,* May 31, 2001.

12

Presidential Succession
Legal and Political Contexts and Domestic Players

Nelson P. Valdes

This chapter describes the context within which a post–Fidel Castro transfer of power will likely take place, based on the way in which power has been exercised, the interlocking nature of the Cuban ruling elite, and the institutional mechanisms that are in place to ensure a peaceful transfer of power.[1]

Raúl Castro, if alive, likely will succeed his brother, but his exercise of power will necessarily imply a different style of government.[2] Raúl Castro and his close associates (the Raulistas) have attained a degree of control, cohesion, and resources not found among other sectors of the society. If only domestic forces are taken into account, the outcome of the succession is already secure.[3]

Even though a succession at first may require greater cohesion and unity at the top, the progressive transformation of Cuba's economic policy, practice, and institutions eventually could lead to the appearance, development, and strengthening of multiple sources of economic power. The post–Fidel Castro regime could, if economic performance improves, postpone any significant political openings. In that scenario, the sectors that gain in economic ascendancy would fail to assert themselves in politics. Nonetheless, new economic sectors could, in time, contribute to a diverse socioeconomic system.

The Historical Context

It is widely assumed that if Fidel Castro dies, then the social, economic, political, and cultural institutions created under his leadership will come to an end. Such assumptions may well be invalid. There are domestic institutions, institutional procedures, and vested interests in place that will play a significant role in shaping the island's future even in the absence of Fidel Castro.

The succession question has been a central concern of the Cuban government. The very fact that the U.S. government and the exiled opposition is counting on Fidel Castro's death to bring about a political and economic restoration has been more than sufficient incentive for Castro and his associates to take the necessary institutional precautions. The critical question is whether the succession will be peaceful and without trauma. For that to happen it will be necessary for the ruling elite to preserve its cohesion and unity.[4]

On the basis of the country's history, the revolutionaries who seized power in 1959 learned not to split the political and military leadership of their movement. Past struggles for independence ended in failure because the political and the military leaders clashed with one another.

The revolutionary movement against Batista already had Fidel Castro as its political and military leader. However, in the early months of 1959 neither Fidel Castro nor his brother held numerous or interlocking positions within the Cuban government and state.

Fidel Castro, as early as May 1, 1960, when a concerted campaign of assassination attempts against him began, publicly selected his brother Raúl as his heir apparent. His brother had been the leader of the Cuban military since late 1959. Selecting his brother was more than an expression of nepotism. Raúl Castro had shown significant administrative and organizational skills. He had earned recognition from his peers on the basis of merit. Thus, in the early years, through political practice, the two brothers arrived at a unique division of labor—one handled political matters, the other military ones. But either could assume both roles, if necessary, at exceptional times. Political practice and necessity evolved into an informal network of interlocking but separate powers and responsibilities occupied by both brothers and their appointed close associates.

The Succession Context

An analysis of the probable Cuban succession raises, at the very least, two very complex issues. First is the issue of the time it will take after the death of Fidel Castro for a successor or successors to emerge. Second is the political posture and program that such person or persons will defend in a post–Fidel Castro Cuba. In any case, one should consider as a critical factor the existing political system as well as the concrete and specific moment and context when the succession question becomes a real issue. One is a question that deals with the formal institutional structure and process; the other is a substantive political issue.

If the succession takes place immediately or within the next five years, there is no serious threat to the ability of the ruling elite to exercise its power and to govern. There are several reasons for such a state of affairs:

First, the ruling elite has a strong sense of its mission and role within Cuban society. There has been no indication of self-doubts or even cleavages within that ruling elite, perhaps with the seeming exceptional circumstances surrounding the Ochoa–La Guardia affair of 1989 (see chapter 9). Moreover, in the last several years numerous measures have been taken in order to maintain and in some cases increase the control the ruling elite has over the society (for example, the appointment of more military personnel to administrative positions within the state and government entities).

Second, there are no publicly organized political tendencies within the ruling elite. One could point to some diversity of opinions of Communist Party members on particular issues or methods. Up to this point opinions are not articulated as representing specific, concrete, material interests. In the official Cuban political game it is unacceptable to represent or organize "factions." Consequently, it is quite possible that specific material and institutional interests are expressed as if they were the mere perspective of a given individual. Nothing else is allowed. For over forty years the political, economic, social, and cultural regime has functioned with a rigid bureaucratic and autocratic logic; there has been no space for the articulation of diverse perspectives.

Third, the ruling elite has enormous resources at its command compared with the rest of the society. Among these resources can be mentioned the following:

(a) a unified military force
(b) an economic machine controlled by the state that, although inefficient, nonetheless monopolizes a significant portion of the country's economy
(c) an effective and efficient security machine controlled by the Interior Ministry (Ministerio del Interior)
(d) mass organizations that serve as transmission belts between state and citizens
(e) a Communist Party with over seven hundred eighty thousand members found throughout the society and constituting the only politically organized force
(f) a hegemonic control over the mass media, culture, and ideology
(g) control over more than 50 percent of the country's employment

Fourth, although the degree of socioeconomic differences in Cuban society has increased since 1991, there are no real sources of independent social, economic, or political power that could contribute to alternative perspectives or organizations with clearly discernible political and economic goals. (The independent opposition is made up of individuals and numerous small organizations with little if any real organic ties to the population. The opposition, in other words, has not been able to tap any significant source of support within the society.)[5] The new sectors that have appeared as a result of economic reforms—the self-employed, commercial intermediaries, Basic Units of Cooperative Production (UBPCs), mixed enterprises, foreign investors, people living on money transfers from abroad, and so on—do not constitute a class with its own identity or organization.

Fifth, the population tends to hold views that help the ruling elite exercise its power. Among these views can be mentioned:

(a) Involvement in politics does not pay.

(b) The drastic and abrupt reduction in consumption experienced after 1991 has been managed and the worst of the crisis is now behind, or, at least, the best solution is to try to find one's own way of "making it."

(c) Political opposition is not viable, and if one's situation becomes unbearable, then one should migrate.

(d) Cuba's is a highly atomized society in which primary ties (family, neighborhood, and friends) are central and all others are secondary.

(e) There exists a "double morality" that makes it difficult to know who, outside of one's own primary circles, stands for what.

Assuming that the disappearance of Fidel Castro occurs within the conditions mentioned above, and if those variables remain constant, then there is a very high probability that the successor of Fidel Castro will be his brother, Raúl Castro. The reasons for this likelihood are woven throughout the Cuban political, military, and societal structure.

Constitutional Provisions

Council of State

Fidel Castro holds the position of president of the Council of State. Article 74 of the Cuban Constitution establishes that the Cuban National Assembly elects from among its members all the members of the Council of State. In other words, to be a member of the Council of State, one has to be an elected deputy of the National Assembly. The Constitution further states that the president of the Council of State and head of the Council of Ministers presides over the Cuban state and government.

The Council of State must report to the National Assembly when the latter is in session. The Council of State is made up of a president, a first vice president, five vice presidents, a secretary, and twenty-three other members. Fidel Castro occupies the position of president of the Council of State (legislative branch) and head of the Council of Ministers (government and administrative structures). The Council of State, according to Article 89 of the Cuban Constitution, represents and acts on behalf of the National Assembly when the latter is not in session—which is most of the time. Its president can remove and appoint new members of the Council of Ministers when the National Assembly is not in session. Article 94 establishes that "in the absence, due to illness or death of the president of the Council of State, the first vice president will assume those functions." Hence, if Fidel Castro as president has to be replaced (whatever the reason), constitutionally the presidential mantle falls to his brother. As interim president of the Council of State, Raúl would become the head of the government as well. As interim president, Raúl Castro could propose to the National Assembly the new first vice president, all the vice presidents, and other members of the Council of Ministers.

The Cuban Constitution of 1992 grants the Council of State the power to "suspend decisions made by the Council of Ministers and the agreements and decisions of local assemblies if they are not in accordance with the Constitution or the law, or when they may affect the interests of a particular locality or the general interests of the country." Moreover, the Council of State has the authority to seize the "direction of any ministry or state institution" when deemed necessary. The president, as head of the Council of State, has the power to be in control of all military institutions and can determine its military organization. The president has authority over the Council of National Defense and is empowered to declare a state of emergency. This could be done without consulting the National Assembly, if circumstances required it. However, the members of the Council of State need to be informed of any such measures.

Council of Ministers

Fidel Castro, as president of the Council of State, is also the president of the Council of Ministers. The first vice president is Raúl Castro, his substitute. The Council of Ministers functions as the government of Cuba. In the absence of Fidel Castro as president of the Council of Ministers, his position will be taken by the first vice president, in this case his brother.

When the Council of Ministers is not meeting, its work is performed by an executive committee. This committee has Fidel Castro as its presiding officer, Raúl Castro as his second. Carlos Lage is the secretary of the Executive Committee of the Council of Ministers. Article 97 of the Cuban Constitution states that the Executive Committee of the Council of Ministers is appointed by its president. The Executive Committee can make decisions when the Council of Ministers does not meet.

Constitutionally, Raúl Castro is in a position to take command of the leading posts within the executive (within the Council of State and the Council of Ministers). In order to challenge such procedure it would be necessary to act outside the mechanisms and framework of the Constitution.

The Communist Party

First Secretary

By the late 1990s the Communist Party's membership numbered approximately 780,000 members out of a population of over 11 million. The number of Communist members increased twenty times in slightly more than three decades, including the 232,000 members who joined during the last few years. The Central Committee (CC) is made up of 150 members of the party leadership. Usually the party congress brings together approximately fifteen hundred congressional delegates who constitute the very core of the ruling system.

Fidel Castro has occupied the position of political leadership since 1959. At present he has the post of first secretary of the Communist Party of Cuba (the PCC). Formally he holds that position because the party has congresses every so many years (usually every five or six years), where he has been elected. The party membership selects delegates (approximately fifteen hundred) to attend the party congress. The congress, in turn, selects from within its ranks 150 persons who constitute the Central Committee until the next party congress.

Political Bureau

The Central Committee members set the overall policies of the country and also choose a body that will serve as its executive committee when the 150 members are not meeting. That executive committee, chosen from within the Central Committee, is called the Political Bureau. Fidel Castro is the first secretary of the Central Committee and of the Political Bureau. Raúl Castro occupies the position of second secretary of the CC and second secretary of the Political Bureau. Thus, in case Fidel Castro dies or is unable to function, the second secretary is given that responsibility during the interim period when the party congress is not meeting.

Raúl's position is further strengthened by the composition of the Political Bureau. At the Fifth Party Congress (1997), the Central Committee selected twenty-four persons to be members of the Political Bureau (counting Fidel Castro and his brother).[6] The Political Bureau has five high-ranking division generals and eight Communist Party functionaries, two having nationwide functions and the other six having responsibilities within the confines of their specific provinces. The rest hold posts within the Council of State (one), the Council of Ministers (five), and such other institutions as the National Assembly, research centers, and the labor movement. Obviously the military presence within the Political Bureau would offer Raúl Castro an overwhelming influence if he had to take over his brother's responsibilities. Raúl could command the heights of the party leadership with the assistance of important military commanders.

The Military

Fidel Castro is the commander in chief of the Cuban armed forces because that is the power granted by the Cuban Constitution to the person who holds the position of president of the Cuban state (the same power granted by the United States Constitution to the U.S. president). Fidel Castro, of course, commands the Cuban military due to historical circumstances, as well as formal ones. Out of a guerrilla army, the Cuban military became a professional institution and a regular force.[7]

In the absence of Fidel Castro, the symbolic and political post of commander in chief will have to go to the next president of the Cuban state. It so happens that Raúl Castro is constitutionally in line to fill the post of interim president. Moreover, Raúl is also general of the army (the only person occupying that rank), which makes him chief of the Ministry of the Armed Forces. Raúl Castro, then, has the constitutional right to succeed his brother, but he also has control over the institution that would be critical in any future history of the island: the Cuban military.

General Raúl Castro, minister of the Revolutionary Armed Forces, is followed in rank and within the Cuban military high command by men who have been closely associated with him. The first vice minister of the MINFAR and chief of the Joint Chiefs of Staff, Division General Alvaro López Miera, recently was promoted to that position when his predecessor was given the post of minister of sugar.

Below López Miera are three deputy ministers of the Ministry of Revolutionary Armed Forces (MINFAR): Division General Julio Casas Regueiro, Brigadier General Rubén Martinez Puentes, and Rear Admiral Miguel Peréz Betancourt. These high-ranking officials have been closely associated with both Fidel and Raúl Castro for more than forty years, particularly with Raúl. One of Raúl's men, General Abelardo Colomé Ibarra, now heads the Ministry of the Interior—in charge of internal security and the police. There are others in important posts within the state machine, the Communist Party, and the economy.

The Economy

The process of economic reform was begun in 1976 within the Cuban armed forces. The first experiments with capitalist management methods took place in the military, particularly in the arms industry. In those years, only the military dared to experiment with capitalist methods and management techniques. Those early experiments were unknown to most Cubans. It was only the economic, political, strategic, and ideological crisis produced by the demise of the Soviet bloc after 1989 that created the conditions to adopt and experiment with capitalist methods. By 1991 MINFAR had its own management schools and began transforming its rest-and-recreation facilities into hotels, administered by a private corporation, Gaviota. MINFAR's management skills and experienced personnel have since been transferred to other sectors of the state-run Cuban economy.

The military actually initiated the market reforms in the Cuban economy. The process has been slow. This was particularly the case over the issue of turning state farms into private farms. Raúl Castro presented the argument as a matter of national security, because it was necessary to have *"fusiles y frijoles"* (rifles and beans) if the revolution was to survive. The need to increase agricultural output, particularly food production, finally persuaded those who wanted to maintain the state monopoly over agriculture to relent. (Fidel had been a staunch opponent of privatization.) However, it had to be done by using the argument of national security.

Today, many retired or inactive military personnel hold management positions in mixed enterprises and autonomous state corporations. Consequently, MINFAR or persons who have been involved with it are found in every facet of management and the economy. Military men loyal to Raúl Castro, whether retired or active, are found in influential institutions.

Private foreign corporations and semiprivate enterprises, conglomerates, and holding companies have made their presence and growing numbers felt throughout the country. In addition to CIMEX (Department of Convertible Currency), three major conglomerates could have an impact beyond their economic and managerial activities; they are Cubalse, Cubanacán, and Gaviota.

Moreover, each ministry within the Cuban state has begun to follow MINFAR's lead and has joined the process of setting up its own state-owned private corporations.

Interlocking Power Network

Besides the constitutional provisions and overwhelming organizational control, there seems to be a consensus within the ruling elite that Raúl Castro, despite his lack of charismatic qualities, enjoys unqualified support from the ruling elite. Given a stable political scenario, the fundamental key of a political succession will depend on the behavior of that ruling elite. It does not appear that the elite will go in different directions. The Communist Party, the Council of Ministers, the Council of State, the National Assembly, the military, the mass organizations, and those in charge of state-run sectors of the economy probably will hold rank in order to preserve their power and influence.

The Cuban revolutionary regime from the standpoint of power is a unique network of interlocking spheres and positions in which a number of people occupy several offices at the same time.

Within those interlocking spheres of power, Raúl Castro occupies a most unique position. First, he is the heir apparent. This has been made known on numerous occasions. On October 10, 1997, at the Fifth Communist Party Congress, Fidel Castro announced the decision of the Central Committee to ratify Raúl Castro Ruz as first vice president and minister of the Revolutionary Armed Forces, as well as the second secretary of the party. Fidel Castro went on to note that such a decision was "just and fitting" and added, "You know how much it means for our party and revolution to have a second secretary, a leader, a relief [relevo] for everyone and especially for me, as comrade Raúl. He earned that responsibility solely on the basis of history and of pure merits. This gives much security and confidence to all of us, especially to me."

Raúl Castro knows Fidel Castro and his style of exercising power and authority better than anyone else. There is probably no one else who understands the inner workings of power as he does. Moreover, Raúl has at his command resources that no one else possesses. He has the institutional claim and the resources to control the military, the Communist Party, the state and the government. And with those mechanisms he can wield much control over the rest of the society and the population. Moreover, Raúl Castro is further enhanced in his position by a consistent history of personal ties and numerous forms of interaction and support with men and women who owe all that they have to him. They are the men and women who often have been described as Raulistas. There is no other person within the ruling elite or within Cuba, outside of Fidel Castro, who has organized men and women and shares a unique esprit de corps and identity with them. This, of course, seems to be more so among those who have been in close association with Raúl for more than thirty years.

Raúl Castro, obviously, cannot just replace Fidel Castro. The successor will not be able to replicate the unique qualities of the founder. But there is no other person within the island whose relationship with Fidel resembles that of Raúl with his brother. There is no "equivalent Raúl" for Raúl Castro. That means that Raúl will have to find many persons to perform different roles and responsibilities; the interlocking network of power in the hands of just two persons will become ever more collective and decentralized. Fidel Castro on October 10, 1997, acknowledged as much when he stated that "we will increasingly yield our roles, our duties to collective work and effort."

Separation of roles and powers and the broadening of the interlocking network does not imply sufficient room for open dissent or even factionalism. Due to the hostilities remaining between the United States and Cuba, there remains a strong sense among those who exercise power of the need for national unity, particularly within the ruling elite, to avoid their downfall. Instead of being replaced, the ruling elite might, in time, transform itself as the Chinese or Vietnamese political elite have done.

The political succession probably will elicit, at least in the short term, a closing of the ranks around the designated successor, a degree of caution, and even an absence of initiatives.

Once the initial fears and concerns of exercising power without Fidel Castro have passed, the ruling elite might begin to move toward greater diversity of opinions and even clearly defined alternatives, even with Raúl Castro in command.

Other factors, not discussed here, will be U.S. reactions to the new regime as well as the response of the "exile" element.

Conclusion

Outlining the most probable scenario of a post–Fidel Castro succession is always a difficult task, more so when substantive information on the distribution of power within the society is not readily available.

It seems that the conditions are present for Raúl Castro, due to his numerous roles and resources, to succeed his brother. It is safe to assume that those closely associated with Raúl for more than forty-odd years will be in the inner circles of the ruling elite. While the leaders answer to Raúl Castro, and the Raulistas are found throughout the military, it would be an error to assume that every member of the military is a Raulista, or to overlook the complexity of the military as an organization.

MINFAR as an institution probably will continue to be involved in the management and transformation of inefficient administrative and entrepreneurial organizations. MINFAR has found a mission going beyond defense, national security, and the preservation of order; it now speaks the language of self-sufficiency and profitability.

The role of the Communist Party as an institution receives little attention from commentators and analysts, whether foreign or domestic. Although the Communist Party continues to function, its importance in the economic arena has been overtaken by events. The party will remain an instrument of the ruling elite, but it is doubtful that in the foreseeable future it will claim a more activist role. There are multiple perspectives within the party membership and even among the professional cadres, but its rank and file are hindered by party statutes from open discussions or from organizing factions. The Communist Party's legitimacy and authority has been eroded by the collapse of European Socialism, as well as by the absence of open debate within the country. Many loyal party members, in a sense, appear to have withdrawn into apathy or simply quit, or they eagerly await retirement. The young within the Union of Young Communists do not seem to have a clear idea of what a post–Fidel Castro future will bring.

Within the rank and file of the Communist Party there had been hope that Cuba could experience a version of Gorbachev's perestroika, which began in 1991 with the planning of the Fourth Congress of the Cuban Communist Party—combining economic changes with some degree of political democratization. The removal of Carlos Aldana and the beginning of the special period put an end to that option. But it remained an appealing alternative to younger cadres within the Communist Party and among many who worked with mixed enterprises, autonomous state enterprises, and the labor movement, young managers and economic bureaucrats as well as intellectuals. That was not the case among party leaders and officials.

In order to rearticulate a social and political consensus, Raúl Castro and his associates will have to improve the economy's performance and the standards of living of the population, or at least permit greater autonomy to those who wish to succeed on their own.

Fear of social upheaval and the unwillingness to pay the political and social costs of more rapid economic openings certainly play a part in holding back the process of change. Technocrats, enterprise managers, individual entrepreneurs, and all those sectors identified with the so-called "emerging modern economy" certainly favor a greater liberalization. What role some of the civilian personalities (Carlos Lage, Osmani Cienfuegos, Abraham Masiques, Eduardo Bencomo, and so on) involved in some key sectors will play within the new situation is difficult to project or imagine. Probably, state-owned capitalist enterprises that answer to the Council of State or to the different ministries, and foreign investors will have a significant role to play.

International pressure and demands from below could infuse the perestroika option with new energy and support. What role, if any, some of the present-day political figures could play is anyone's guess. Although some names have been offered at times, there is not much conclusive evidence—at least public evidence—that some of the members of the Council of State or the Council or Ministers will favor such a route. (The names of Ricardo Alarcón, Carlos Lage, and Abel Prieto, among others, have been mentioned by the international media. Yet, none of them control any significant resource to challenge the power of the Raulistas.)

Finally, there is always the possible (but not probable) scenario of a defeat of the revolutionary model (in any of its manifestations) by an extrasystemic force, such as an invasion by the United States. But even in such a case, there would have to be a readjustment of forces after the fact, with a broad range of options going above and beyond an initial "second invasion" from Miami. That particular scenario has not been considered in this chapter.

The present situation suggests that Cubans from all walks of life are attempting to find some new niche within the emerging economy, one in which the logic of the dollar and the market are dominant. To find a job that generates foreign exchange now seems to take precedence over other concerns.

The new rulers in Cuba consequently may not face an immediate political or systemic crisis, and they may gain in time and maneuverability if they offer the hope that the future prospects of the nation will be secure and the time of sacrifices soon will be left behind.

Notes

1. "[Castro] told ABC reporter Diane Sawyer on *Prime Time* in 1993: 'I hope that my *compañeros* will not demand from me in five years that I again become a candidate to deputy of the National Assembly' (a necessary condition to be elected head of the Council of State, which by making him president of the Council of Ministers would make him the country's president). [He has occupied the presidency since 1976.] Asked if he would like to retire if the embargo were over and Cuba were advancing economically, he said: 'More or less. I cannot say exactly what I think about this. One is not free, and I am not here for pleasure. I am a soldier in the struggle at this difficult moment, and it would be cowardice to retire.'" (Castro was reelected National Assembly deputy in the 1998 and 2003 elections and, immediately after, Council of State president as well as the country's president.) "Elecciones: ¿Se retirará Fidel Castro?" *Contrapunto* 8 (August 1997): 5–6, as cited in Max Azicri, *Cuba Today and Tomorrow: Reinventing Socialism* (Gainesville: University Press of Florida, 2000), 8–9. (Editors' note.)

2. After completing his fifth five-year term in March 2003, President Castro was 76 years old, and his brother, Raúl Castro, 72. By the end of his sixth presidential term in 2008, Castro will be 81 (but if the presidential term extends beyond the summer, he will be 82) and Raúl 77 (or 78). (Editors' note.)

3. "Speaking for the first time about a possible successor since his fainting spell [Castro passed out in June 2001 while addressing an outdoor rally near Havana] . . . Fidel Castro told NBC . . . *that his brother Raúl remains his likely replacement.* 'Raúl is very healthy . . . . Undoubtedly, he is the comrade who has the most authority after me,' Castro said. . . . 'And he has the most experience. . . . Therefore, I think he has the capacity to succeed me. . . . It is not something that I am worried about, succession.' *During the Communist Party's Fifth Congress in 1997, Fidel Castro described his youngest brother as his "relevo"—a Spanish military term for changing of the guard." Miami Herald (on line), June 29, 2001. (Emphasis added.) (Editors' note.)

4. Forecasting who will be Fidel Castro's successor has been the subject of media speculation for some time. *MSNBC News*'s "Waiting in the Wings: Ready to Step into Castro's Shoes" provides a short list (including brief biographies) of potential successors. As expected, Raúl Castro is listed first, followed by two well-known leaders: Carlos Lage (Council of State vice president) and Ricardo Alarcón (president of the National Assembly), in that order. *MSNBC News* (on line), April 2002. However, for an in-depth discussion of a potential successor, Walter Russell Mead's profile of Ricardo Alarcón ranks first among most media renditions to date. Alarcón is portrayed as the Cuban leader with the needed international experience to lead a post-Castro Cuba—particularly his detailed knowledge of American politics and society after having lived for years in New York City as the island's ambassador to the United Nations. In the last years, as head of the National Assembly, Alarcón has

gained the domestic political exposure and experience he lacked before, including his tenure as the government minister in charge of international relations. Walter Russell Mead, "Profile Castro's Successor?" *New Yorker*, January 26, 1998: 42–49. (Editors' note.)

5. For a discussion of the Varela Project and the actions of other political opposition groups, see chapters 1 and 10 in this volume. (Editors' note.)

6. The PCC's Sixth Congress has been delayed; as of early 2004 the exact date has not been announced. (Editor's note.)

7. See chapter 13 in this volume. (Editors' note.)

VI

The Military

13

The Armed Forces Today and Tomorrow

Hal Klepak

The last thirteen years have arguably been some of the most extraordinary Cuba has known since independence in 1898 and certainly the most challenging in over four decades under President Fidel Castro Ruz.[1] Cuba has endured the collapse of the external pillars of support of its economic, political, and military structures, which it had relied upon since the triumph of the revolutionary Twenty-sixth of July Movement, headed by Castro, in January 1959.

These blows to the island's Communist government have sent the country reeling but have neither brought it down nor changed many of the basic tenets of its foreign and domestic policy. While Communist governments have been swept from power in Eastern Europe and many other parts of the world, the Castro government has survived shattering changes and continues to rule. In the view of some observers, Cuba is on more solid ground at the dawn of a new century than in the last decade.

Crucial to an understanding of this state of affairs are the role, structure, and belief patterns of the Cuban armed forces, the Fuerzas Armadas Revolucionarias, or the "FAR," as they are universally known. The FAR has not only been the bulwark of the government but has surely been the most effective of all the elements of state power in the country. This chapter provides an overview of the role of the FAR in the politics, internal security, social life, and economy of Cuba, and discusses the FAR's place in the external defense of the island. The chapter also discusses the FAR's potential to play a key role in any transition the country will face in the future.

The chapter first presents a historical look at the Cuban armed forces as they existed under Spain and the U.S. occupation and in the half century of formal independence the country knew before Castro's 1959 victory. It then highlights key elements of the early years of the FAR's reorganization as the formal armed forces of the new revolutionary government and ends with a discussion of its more traditional roles in later years.

An analysis of the FAR's situation during the years of the special period offers insight into the likely role the FAR will play in the transition from the present leadership or government of the country, as well as some wider conclusions about its future status.

The History of the Cuban Armed Forces

The First Four Centuries

Cuba was a highly prized strategic asset for the Spanish Empire. It served Spain well as a base for other early conquests, which gave the world the first empire "on which the sun never set." Its excellent and well-protected harbors at Havana, Santiago de Cuba, Cienfuegos, and elsewhere provided a firm base for continental expeditions, and one much closer than Santo Domingo on Hispaniola. Soon well fortified, these ports were to be linked to a vast imperial defense scheme and to the export of bullion that was the envy of the poorer, less-developed colonies of the North.[2]

Under such circumstances the defense of the island came to be a metropolitan function; one carried out with relatively little assistance from local colonial forces. Colonial troops were not numerous or very important until after the uprisings against Spain in the first quarter of the nineteenth century. Those movements for independence were eventually successful everywhere on the continental landmass. However, no island colony saw a serious effort at emancipation in those years after the Haitian Revolution (1791). Word of the Haitian experience, where numerous whites were slaughtered in the slave rebellions of the late eighteenth and early nineteenth centuries, raised fears among the ruling groups on the islands. They worried about rebellions by their numerous black slaves, and the presence of Spanish garrisons helped ensure continued loyalty to Spain, not only in Cuba but also in Puerto Rico and Santo Domingo.

Despite occasional troubles, it was only in 1868, almost half a century after the revolutions on terra firma (continental soil), that a major revolution broke out in the form of the Ten Years' War of 1868–78. In response to the hostilities, local forces began to be organized in a serious fashion, including rebel units and colonial militias loyal to Spain.[3] The war was followed by an uneasy, seventeen-year peace with all manner of compromise solutions proposed and eventually proven unworkable. The role of Spanish intransigence in this negative context, after the independence movements in South and Central America, seems to reveal Spain's desperation to hold on to its last colonies.

In 1895, war broke out again with the *mambises* pitted against the Spanish regular forces and the *voluntarios* or guerrillas of the loyalist cause.[4] During three years of warfare, the rebels became a formidable force. The debate still continues as to whether U.S. intervention was necessary to bring about the collapse of the Spanish war effort. Instead of remaining in the eastern provinces, as had happened in the Ten Years' War, the insurgents invaded most of the island and at one time were close to the capital itself. The Spanish responded with massive force and repression, including internments in concentration camps. After declaring war on Spain in 1898, the United States sent an expeditionary force that collaborated little with the Cuban forces but managed to dislodge the Spanish army from key positions, including the city of Santiago de Cuba. The modern U.S. fleet in Cuban waters also defeated the Spanish squadron in the area.[5]

Cuba was thus delivered from Spain by a quick and decisive campaign. The United States occupied the island from 1898 until 1902 and, when withdrawing, made sure that it could return to protect its interests or to keep order at its discretion. The United States also retained the naval base at Guantánamo Bay east of Santiago and has done so to this day.

The United States did not attempt to create armed forces on the pattern of the *mambises* who had confronted Spain in the struggle for independence. Washington feared that the rebel forces would develop an anti-U.S. stance similar to that seen in the occupied Philippines.[6] Thus, the services developed by the U.S. troops on the island were to be little more than constabularies of a kind to become famous as the century moved on in other republics of the Caribbean where the U.S. Marines held sway. Arms purchases, doctrine, training, uniforms, drill, and other elements of military life were based on the U.S. model. And the force was kept small so as to provide no threat if and when Washington decided to intervene again.[7]

The rather traditional role of the armed forces of Latin America, that of interpreter of what was good for the country, emerged in Cuba as well. In the years between 1902 and 1958, the military, or elements thereof, intervened to unseat leaders, to reestablish order, or to place one of their own in key posts of government.

Attempts were made to make the forces less dependent on the United States, but these were few and far between. When Cuba and other Caribbean countries declared war on the Central Powers in World War I, and even more so when all of Latin America eventually joined forces against the Central Powers during World War II, the Cuban armed forces became extremely closely connected to their U.S. mentors and suppliers. U.S. military missions became permanent on the island and remained until well after Castro's revolutionary government was installed.

The army raised by the republic was not impressive. During the Batista regime (1952–58), itself brought to power by the army in a coup, the practices of corruption became even more marked.[8] Despite the weakness of the Castro forces in the field, they proved more than a match for a vastly larger, better equipped, but morally bankrupt Batista army.[9]

Castro's army, the basis for today's FAR, was a small field force never greater than a couple of thousand fighters, and generally poorly trained at that.[10] It was, however, allied to an urban guerrilla arm of the movement whose actions in the major cities sapped the energy and self-confidence of the dictatorship's security forces. The *barbudos,* or rebels, operating initially from the Sierra Maestra mountains, followed a westward series of military actions leading to the occupation of Havana toward the end.

The Early Years of the FAR

In 1959 the army of the dictatorship was quickly disbanded, its personnel dispersed, and some of its commanders shot. The insurgents became the armed forces of the republic. In addition to internal security and external defense roles, they were also active in national development tasks, no small responsibility for a revolutionary force newly out of the Sierra Maestra. Most of the new leaders of the country were also serving as members of the armed forces; their determination and connections ensured them a formidable position in the formative years of the government.[11] In many ways it was difficult to see any obvious division between the rebel army (*Ejército Rebelde*) and the government of the country.

The armed forces had enormous advantages that they could use to solidify their strong position in the state. They had the moral ascendancy that victory over Batista's army brought them. They were an army of the poor that had overcome great odds. As opposed to the urban fighters, the rural rebels were mostly from the peasantry and labor elements, although this composition is easy to exaggerate. They were unassailable in their proven loyalty to the regime and to the key figure in it—Fidel Castro himself. Frequently put into key positions in education, the judicial system, land reform institutes, and the police, rebel officers and even senior noncommissioned officers soon brought the forces to even greater prominence.

Converting the army of the mountains into a professional force took time. A ministry of defense was established in October 1959, and soon Communists in the movement were given important positions in it. The army was soon deeply divided on the subject of the proper role for the Communists, and only a serious purge was able to preserve order as the sharp move to the left began in earnest. Popular militias appeared to be the answer, and these were soon established as a means to ensure that there was no possibility of successful counterrevolutionary activity. The existence of these two elements offered great flexibility to the government at various times in recent decades since it became possible to shift emphasis from the regular army to the militia or vice versa as different political contexts came to the fore.

Other revolutionary groupings of the Batista era were brought under the umbrella of the armed forces, politicized, and given further training, as were many other Cubans. The foreign threat appeared in the form of the Bay of Pigs invasion of mid-April 1961.[12] The prestige of the armed forces and even of the militia was already high, but great successes in repelling the attack rapidly and immeasurably reinforced the public's trust of the armed forces and the leadership. Also, the elimination of opposition groups in the Escambray Mountains demonstrated the capabilities of the revolution's key guardians, and especially the regulars. The importance of the militia declined slowly, a trend reinforced by the decision to implement compulsory military service in 1963 as well as the success of purges of the army's anti-Communist elements.

Settling In

The years after 1963 showed the armed forces increasingly at home with wide responsibilities and a special position within the state. With the government far from certain about which way to turn in terms of its organizational basis, the armed forces ensured security against foreign and domestic opponents. The army expanded its role in society, moving on from agrarian reform to agricultural production and a host of other fields. While the threats to the regime appeared to be diminishing over the years, the budget and roles of the FAR seemed to be on the increase.

Raúl Castro inspired steady progress in creating an institutional linkage between the armed forces and the other central pillar of the state, the Cuban Communist Party (PCC).[13] Key individuals came to hold both party and military positions of importance. The FAR seemed to have much the better of it. The PCC was being subordinated to the military and not the reverse. There was to be only one chain of command, and this was to be dominated by the defense ministry, MINFAR, and not by the party.

From 1962 to 1968, Cuban foreign and defense policy was dominated by the "export of revolution," which suggested that the answer to U.S. attempts to isolate the regime was to try to overthrow neighboring governments that collaborated in the anti-Castro campaign. Ernesto (Che) Guevara was a key figure in this period, and only his death in 1967 allowed new trends to become dominant. The end of the export-of-revolution phase signaled an improvement of relations with the Soviet Union, and this advanced the armed forces' standing immensely and quickly. Raúl Castro was instrumental in obtaining more, and better, weapons and equipment from Moscow, and this also did much to solidify his own position as leader of MINFAR.

The subsequent years, moving into the late 1970s, were dominated by a drive to professionalize the armed forces. This meant that Castro would have a powerful foreign policy tool, one he was to use in dramatic fashion. Already by 1975, significant Cuban troop levels were being maintained in Angola. Later in the decade, entanglements in Ethiopia likewise called for the deployment of up to seventeen thousand men in that even farther-away country.[14]

An era of internationalism was upon Cuba with a vengeance. Havana proved to be prepared to pay a high price for supporting like-minded "reformist" regimes, especially in Africa, although on occasion Soviet gratitude for Cuba's actions seemed to make up for the losses. Some asserted that Castro was proving to Washington that it could ignore the little country only at its cost and that Havana's "nuisance value" was considerable. The FAR, for the first time, had sustained battle experience abroad, on occasion against quite sophisticated armies such as that of South Africa. And it had proven itself a force to be reckoned with in military terms.

With time, however, the political and economic costs of this policy of support for revolutionary causes around the world proved simply too great for Cuba to sustain.[15] The isolation of the regime in the Americas, demonstrated when the usually understanding Canadian government cut off assistance in 1976 as a result of Havana's involvement in Angola, was particularly hurtful. And with the mid-1980s evolution of Soviet policy on these matters, Cuba got little out of such efforts as the years went by. Moscow was not interested in destabilizing its bilateral relationship with Washington by adventures of that sort, and thus pressures to desist were growing as were Cuba's own frustrations with foreign, especially some African, partners. Probably more than two hundred thousand Cubans had at one time served in Angola, the Congo, Ethiopia, and Mozambique, and some two thousand had died in the effort. Little could be shown for all this loss.[16]

Domestic issues increased the relative importance of the reserve forces, already "the backbone of the national defense."[17] Social mobilization regained prominence, and the dominant strategic concept became what was termed "War of All the People." From its beginnings in 1980, this new defense stance has been more effective than other attempts to tie together regulars and reserves in national defense schemes. This time MINFAR gave the idea its full support, including assigning good officers and resources to making it work. A sense of urgency was stimulated by the invasion of Grenada in the autumn of 1983 and by the U.S. role in the Central American civil wars then raging. The need to deter invasion was central to a key policy speech by Raúl Castro after the return of the bodies of thirteen Cubans killed in Grenada. The minister of defense referred to the necessity of being able to wage war against an invader as the means to deter him from attempting an attack.[18]

Party and armed forces worked closely together to ensure that needed reforms were implemented and were effective. The system survived relatively unchanged until the end of the decade.

FAR and the Special Period

Few countries were to be as hard hit as Cuba by the events unleashed in 1989 in much of Eastern Europe. Cuba's overseas trade and capital relationships had been shattered in the early 1960s by the U.S. response to its reform program. Three decades later, Havana had to face an even more severe jolt when its assistance arrangements with Moscow and other Communist capitals were rapidly dismantled.

A critic of Gorbachev's perestroika and glasnost, Castro railed against the changes in the Communist camp and criticized the Soviet leadership as early as 1988. Responding to the criticism, Moscow moved to a cash basis in the bulk of its dealings with Havana, a change that spelled massive dislocation for the beleaguered Cuban economy and government.

In July 1990, Fidel declared the beginning of a "special period," one in which drastic measures would be necessary and a tightening of belts not seen in many years. The economy shrank between 35 and 50 percent from 1989 to 1993. Exports were hard hit, but this also meant Cuba's ability to import was dealt a massive blow. Before the collapse, the Soviets took 63 percent of Cuba's sugar, 73 percent of its nickel, 95 percent of its citrus, and 100 percent of its electrical components. The Soviets exported 63 percent of what Cubans imported to eat, 98 percent of what they used for fuel, 80 percent of their intake of machines and equipment, and 74 percent of other manufactured goods. In only four years, the island lost 80 percent of its purchasing power abroad.[19] The importance of other markets and sources could not have been more stark. Before the special period, Europe was the source of only 6.7 percent of Cuban trade and the Americas a mere 5.7 percent. This would have to change if the revolution was to survive.

The special period saw all manner of economic reform but limited political reform to answer the challenges posed by the new context.[20] The United States moved quickly to reinforce its embargo through the 1992 Torricelli Act (and later the 1996 Helms-Burton Act) and thus put even more pressure on the government. Rumors of impending doom abounded.

The armed forces seemed particularly hard hit by the Soviet collapse and the end of the Warsaw Pact. Acquisition of equipment and weapons quickly became part of the new cash-only policy being applied by the Russians. This simply meant that no equipment or weapons could be acquired. While the threat from Washington seemed to be growing, the ability to counter it was waning. The siege mentality prevalent on the island redoubled, and the long decline of Cuban military capabilities began.

The problem of no new acquisitions was serious enough. But worse was the lack of access to spare parts, those so essential elements of military operations and even training. Very soon into the special period it became obvious to observers that the cannibalization of aircraft and vehicles had begun in earnest and that many of them were being taken out of service to ensure that others remained operational.

Training was also curtailed. The shattering loss of fuel supplies led to cuts in training, deployments, service flying, and general operations. Useful live-fire exercises, dependent on ammunition replacement, became much less frequent. Related to these trends was an even more dramatic drop in the rate of call-ups of conscripts. Many of those called up were increasingly put to work not in training for field operations but rather in sugar and other essential crop production. Still others, especially those with language or related skills, were sent to jobs in the tourist industry. There had always been a program whereby some young men did their military service in non-military tasks such as education and medicine, but now this became a major portion of the annual call-up of personnel. The length of service was likewise reduced.

In line with the above, the military was asked to contribute to getting through the special period by taking on new jobs and responsibilities in the tourism industry. Soon the armed forces were running hotels and taxis, doing language training, and spiriting tourists around the island on tours, and they were involved in any number of other activities, all paid for in hard currency. Aircraft normally used for parachute and other training were converted to tourist-carrying planes that could reach remote areas of the island. The forces were also asked to feed themselves and not be a burden on the national agricultural production system.

Finally the armed forces were charged collectively or individually with the reorganization of what were called *industrias militares*. These "military industries" were, however, neither the defense industries one normally thinks of (industries producing for defense needs), nor the companies owned by the military in some other parts of Central and South America whose profits go directly into defense ministry (or military officials') pockets.[21] In Cuba, such industries can be any state or even mixed enterprise that, in the view of the government, requires the benefits of military discipline, hierarchy, structures, and the like in order to function efficiently. Since the state considers the running of such industries to be vital to the country's well-being, military officers are put in charge, and military operational regimes are put in place to ensure that they run well. In addition, those industries often benefit from other advantages that militarization brings them, such as easier access to transport, fuel, personnel, and so on.[22]

All of this is impressive in the context of a national effort to beat the effects of the embargo and the special period. But the military reality is that those activities detract from training and other essential military tasks. There is simply no doubt that the overall effect has been a reduction in the efficiency of the armed forces in terms of their main military role of national defense in case of invasion, and deterrence short of that. The priority is given to those combat units that are most likely to be needed in order to defeat an invasion, and it does seem those units are much better off than most. However, it is also true that the cannibalization of vehicles and the rest of the conditions facing other units in order to provide the necessary assistance to maintain high readiness units as such are damaging to morale and efficiency in the forces as a whole.

Almost as drastic has been the cutting of military linkages with the outside world. The Cuban armed forces, and especially their security and intelligence services, had an unrivaled international network on which to draw for what was, after all, still a developing country. Before the end of the cold war, Cuban forces were of course actually deployed in many overseas countries. Equally important were the activities of military attachés in embassies in much of the world. The military had access to much of the Warsaw Pact's intelligence network, and indeed the island, especially through the Lourdes intelligence establishment run by the Soviets, also contributed to that wider network through its proximity to the United States.[23]

Little of all this remains. Military cooperation with Cuba was one of the first casualties of Gorbachev's determination to improve relations with the United States at virtually any cost. The Lourdes facility quickly became a shadow of its former self (it was later closed down). Soviet, East German, and other Warsaw Pact training of Cuban intelligence personnel ceased.

Sharing of information seems to have virtually ended as well, although the long-term connections of individual Russian and Cuban intelligence officers might ensure some continuing linkages. Very few Cuban embassies still have military attachés, and if they do, they are unlikely to have them in such numbers or with such personnel and financial support as to make them fully effective. Thus the Cuban armed forces, after being so connected for so long, are now virtually blind where analyses of the outside world are concerned. This has required them to concentrate on the central issue: where the United States is going on security and wider issues related to the island. In this, MINFAR intelligence still appears to be doing very well. And it must be said that strategic analysis and planning in this vital area, especially the work of the exceptional CEDSI think tank, is impressive indeed.[24]

A Word about MININT

Reference has been made in this chapter to the security forces deployed by the Ministry of the Interior (MININT), set up in 1961, and it is important to understand who they are. MININT provides the "elite rapid-reaction force" for the country. They are well trained and fit, and appear to be both devoted to the regime and well motivated when going about their duties. This force is much more visible in many areas than are the armed forces, especially where there is a major tourist presence. However, even they are not as present in small towns and rural areas as the national security forces present elsewhere in Latin America.

The numerical strength of this force is much debated. Their total force is estimated at something on the order of fifteen hundred personnel. But it is likely that this is merely the rapid-reaction component, for that figure is belied by the wide presence of the force in some key areas of exposure to tourism and other foreign elements.

What is clear is that MININT forces enjoy better equipment than any of the other security forces and in some ways better than the FAR itself. General Abelardo Colomé, minister of the interior, is an FAR officer of considerable prestige. He is also known to be close to Raúl Castro and is clearly a member of the central elite of decision makers in the country. This alone ensures a linkage between the two institutions, which is of great importance today and perhaps of even greater importance tomorrow.

The whole subject of the connection between the FAR and MININT and its sizable and semimilitary personnel is, however, difficult in the extreme to understand. This relates to the special period and its demands on Cubans in general and the security forces in particular.[25] The island's siege mentality is especially difficult to handle in a special period where even loyalists are being forced to compromise their loyalty in order to eke out a living. The frustrating cry *"En el periodo especial todos somos ilegales"* (During the special period we all are illegals) expresses so much hard truth that it needs no further explanation to Cubans.[26] The 1994 Havana riot left the security forces under no illusions about how these troubled times could lead to serious public disturbances that could threaten the regime. Although quelled by both loyalist trade union members and security elements, not to mention through the personal intervention of Castro himself, the riot left deep marks on the security system as a whole.

Thus MINFAR has begun to close ranks with MININT to an even greater extent. Several senior officers and even generals have been posted from the FAR to the interior ministry forces. There is speculation about whether this means that the armed forces will be more tailored to internal security in the future or whether they are determined to avoid any such role and are thus helping out with individual personnel rather than taking on this role in any direct way themselves.

The FAR rejects the idea of taking on internal security duties. It is quick to point out that in revolutionary Cuba, *"el ejército no tira contra el pueblo,"* that is, the army here, as opposed to elsewhere in Latin America, "does not fire on the people." In this sense, it can be imagined that MINFAR is attempting to support MININT in these difficult days but without tarnishing the popular credentials of the military institution.

Thus the special period has hit hard at the military, which has carried much of the weight of the changes brought on by the economic crisis. MINFAR has responded with many original ideas and employed its manpower, organizational capabilities, and skills to face the extraordinary challenges posed to it and to the nation at this time. Its influence as a result has no doubt grown, reinforced by the absolute requirement of the government to have at its disposal a loyal and effective defense establishment.

A Snapshot of the Armed Forces Today

The FAR's context within society as a whole is easier to assess than is its link with MININT. A vast percentage of Cuba's male population, and a fair section of the female, is serving, has served, or will soon be serving in the regular armed forces of the state. In addition, an even larger portion of the population as a whole has been or is currently part of the massive reserve system.

The presence of the FAR and the reserves and the strength and deployment of the Ministry of the Interior forces attest to what has been termed a "militarized" society. However, one should not exaggerate. In a social context where everywhere one sees calls to defend the country, the revolution, and Socialism, the day-to-day presence of the armed forces is not great, especially if compared with only a few years ago. And while MININT personnel seem ubiquitous in the capital, this is not true of the armed forces, except of course near their bases, nor is it true of MININT outside the major cities.

A word is necessary here on the police force and its relations with the FAR. The Policía Nacional Revolucionaria (National Revolutionary Police, PNR) is the major element of the security system visible to all and growing in strength at the present time. The growth of the crime rate, prostitution, and other antisocial behavior has meant that in many ways the expansion of the police has been looked upon with favor by much of the population. Most Cubans appear to agree that something had to be done about crime, especially petty crime, in the streets. Cubans were, and still are, spoiled when it comes to the standards of safety in their neighborhoods. Levels of crime that are the long-term objectives of most cities in the Americas are considered unacceptable by the Cuban population.

Thus the expansion of the police has not raised as much disapproval as might be imagined outside of Cuba. The often high-handed actions of the police have, however, been the cause of great dissatisfaction among many sectors of the population, especially the young. While this phenomenon is most noticeable in Havana and other tourist centers, the fact is that the PNR is more present and more active than ever before. Its expansion has included many people unfamiliar with the cities in which they serve and who appear to have been only half trained during whatever rush program they undertook.

The police force has begun to gain a reputation for minor corruption, something not seen since the Batista era, although so far at levels that compare very favorably with either that of the Batista period or current Latin American practice in general. Fining of offenders for all manner of small misdeeds causes bafflement among Cubans who often do not feel they are doing anything at all wrong. Given the need to be involved in what might be vaguely illegal in order to survive, many citizens feel the police are being unreasonable and hypocritical in arresting or fining people for such deeds. Almost all policemen are ex-military servicemen of one kind or another. Thus there is an indirect effect on the prestige of the armed forces here as well. Other linkages between the FAR and the PNR are less well known and less often analyzed.

Despite these linkages, the armed forces are well received by the population at large, which knows them well and generally seems to have considerable respect for them. This contrasts with the experience of some Latin American populations. Service in the armed forces, while not popular among the young men who have to undertake it, does appear to be accepted to a degree unknown elsewhere in the Spanish-speaking countries of the Caribbean Basin and Central America.[27]

Young people often carry away a sense of achievement from their military service. And in what is still a *machista* society, service in the armed forces is seen as a coming of age for a young man. Not being selected has, at least in rural areas, been seen as a failure, causing suspicions as to one's mental state, physical fitness, or other characteristics. Cubans know they will serve at one time or another in the forces or in national service of some kind, and in general they do not appear to be troubled excessively by this fact.

Service in the reserve components is widespread, but they are not particularly professional, at least in a strictly military sense. In the context of the War of All the People and its objective of deterring invasion, the role of these forces is a real one. Over a million personnel in the Territorial Troop Militia (TTM) and the Youth Labor Army create a huge force.[28] The TTM, successor force to the revolutionary militias of the early revolutionary years, has about one thousand battalions, but they are hardly combat ready except perhaps in the strictest sense of territorial defense. The Youth Labor Army is really a civic action force with only rudimentary military training and can in no sense be considered a real army.[29]

Organizations like the TTM and the Youth Labor Army insert the idea of national defense deeply into the body politic and keep the military structures of the country present at the local level. While poorly equipped and not very well trained, they also provide a nationwide base upon which to conduct a prolonged defense of the country in case of invasion by a vastly superior force. And they retain a potential for internal security tasks as well.

Thus between regular and reserve cadres, the armed forces are both reasonably popular and widely dispersed within the Cuban population. They are rarely seen as a force of repression at the service of a hostile state, even by opponents of the regime. When compared with MININT, the Policia Nacional Revolucionaria, the border guard force, or particularly with the Comités de Defensa de la Revolución (Committees for the Defense of the

Revolution, CDR), the FAR forces appear well received and respected. They are seen as a major defense of the government in case of trouble. Some analysts believe they are a guarantee of security and stability for what might come in Cuba's future.

The FAR in a Transition

One day there will be a successor to Fidel Castro. The regime may change rapidly or slowly and may be headed by Fidel's chosen successor Raúl. Time does not stand still. Fidel was seventy-seven years old in 2003 and has referred to his eventual retirement from politics and even to his death.

There clearly will be a transition at some time even if the outcome and the circumstances remain unknown. The armed forces will certainly play a role. This section begins with a discussion of what the armed forces have to offer Cuba in the inevitable transition. (See table 13.1 and appendices B and C.)

The FAR, as we have seen, is an extraordinary mix of influences—historical, ideological, economic, external, and internal. Its members have stood the test of time, including considerable combat experience in many spheres. And they have proven their loyalty to Cuba and to Castro time and again. But for a transition period, and in order to have a major role at such a time, what are their special attributes?

The first of these is that they enjoy widespread respect among the population, even among the young who do not wish to serve in their ranks. This is rare in Latin America, and could easily be seen as still more unusual in a country where disaffection with the Communist system, while hardly universal, is still common, especially among the young. Cubans are often truly proud of their armed forces, their role in deterrence, their past internationalist posture, the way they have proved themselves in combat, and the like.

A second element giving the armed forces a likely special context in a situation of transition is their presence throughout the country, especially if one considers all the reserve branches. When combined with the first attribute, this can be telling indeed.

The armed forces are, of course, hierarchically organized. They are accustomed to a chain of command that allows for the rapid transmission of orders, a clear system of subordination to higher authority, a tradition of service, and a sense of their place in the system as a whole. While there is much in Cuba that is organized in a hierarchical fashion, the military hierarchy is, as elsewhere in the world, special in the sense that it is considered

Table 13.1. Evolution of the Cuban armed forces, from 1981–82 to 1997–99

	1981–82	1997–99
Total armed forces	227,000	50,000
Total reserves	130,000	39,000
Military expenditures (in millions of $)*	1,135	350
MBT (IS-2, T-34, T-54/55, T-62)	710	1,500
AIFV (BMP-1, BRDM-1)	NA	400
APC (BTR-40/-50/-60/-152)	400	700
ARTY (including towed arty, SP arty, MRL, mortars, static defense arty)	NA	2,040
Army personnel	200,000	38,000
Fighters (MIG-17/-21/-23/29 versions)	371 (175 combat aircraft)	156 (130+ combat aircraft)
Helicopters (Mi-1, Mi-4, Mi-8/-17, Mi-25/-35 incl. Attack and ASW and transport)	59	90
Air force personnel	16,000	10,000
Submarines (Foxtrot and Whiskey classes)	3	2
Frigates (Soviet Koni class)	None	2
Patrol and coastal combatants (incl. Ex-Sov SO-1, Kronstadt, Osa-I, Osa-II, Komar, fast attack craft Turya, P-6, P-4, Zhuk, Pauk II)	81	5
Minesweepers (incl. Sonya, Yevgenya)	9	10
Navy personnel	11,000	5,000
State security, border guards, PNR, special troops, civil defense force, Youth Labour Army and Territorial Militia)**	118,000	1,146,600

Sources: International Institute for Strategic Studies, *The Military Balance, 1981–82, and 1997–98* (London: IISS, 1998), 214–15; ACDA, *World Military Expenditures and Arms Transfers 1996, 1999–2000* (Washington, D.C.: U.S. Department of State, Bureau of Verification and Compliance, 1996, 2002).
*Figures for 1985 and 1995.
**In 1981–82 the Territorial Militia was still being formed.

sacred for the conduct of the armed forces' role, which is itself seen as sacred for the nation.

The FAR members are also disciplined. They obey the orders they receive. Many observers have remarked upon the lack of that scourge of Latin American militaries, the tradition of *acato pero no cumplo,* in the Revolutionary Armed Forces. This is the long-established reaction of local commanders in Latin America, from well back in colonial times, of receiving and accepting orders from above but not obeying them.[30] That tradition simply does not exist in the Cuban armed forces, or so most observers believe.

In addition, the FAR is mobile. While not as well equipped as they were some years ago, the armed forces still maintain a capability to get around the island, deploy troops and weaponry, and make their presence felt, which is the envy of other state agencies. Indeed, linkages with tourism and other dollar-earning activities, while not without disadvantages for the military and its professionalism and honesty, do ensure it has access to fuel, and this is of course vital for the mobility that forces need.

The question of their own in-house access to dollars and other hard currencies is a major one. The reality of the possible corruption of armed forces officers, often with relatively easy access to dollars, fuel, food, and vehicles, is now obvious. And while it is easy to exaggerate the pervasiveness of this corruption, especially by Latin American standards, corruption there is.[31] Despite these disadvantages, access to dollars through their own activities in tourism, agriculture, and other spheres of the economy gives the forces great weight at every level of Cuban society. Here again, it is an advantage shared by few other organized elements of the state and society.

Related to this last factor, the FAR is also relatively self-sufficient in many key matters of concern to most in Cuba. In addition to the mobility provided by access to transport and to fuel, the FAR's agricultural interests, combined with in-house manpower resources, ensure that its forces are virtually self-sufficient in food. And this could act as a source of loyalty to an institution on an island where food scarcity was not uncommon in the early 1990s. The same can be said of lodging; accommodation for the members of the armed forces is relatively abundant and often of reasonably good quality.

The standard of fitness in the Cuban armed forces is also striking. Even the officer corps, rather in contrast with most Latin American militaries, is generally fit and soldierly looking. Priority is given to readiness in the FAR and a lack of fitness, especially among officers, would quickly give the lie to that readiness. Hence that priority is maintained.

Related to this last factor is another: the armed forces personnel of Cuba are inured to hardship. Wags in Cuba would say, "And in Cuba, who isn't?" But the reality is that armed forces exercises, especially before the special period, tended to be realistic and long lasting, especially by Central American and Caribbean standards. Many officers and senior noncommissioned officers are veterans of rough campaigns in Africa. Life is not easy for them even if they have been one of the relatively cushioned elements of Cuba's society.

In addition to these factors, it must also be said in the context of any transition that the Cuban armed forces are generally respected by another institution that could conceivably matter greatly in some scenarios for change. I refer to the U.S. armed forces. As has been seen repeatedly in recent years, the U.S. military tend to have at least a grudging respect for the Cuban forces. Even where they find nothing good to say about the Castro government, American senior officers have often said and written things in praise of Cuban military seriousness, combat effectiveness, deterrence capabilities, even reliability in matters such as the drug war, handling of issues around Guantánamo, illegal immigration, overflights for humanitarian reasons, and confidence-building measures. It is not inconceivable that this respect, which is often mutual where Cuban officers are concerned, could provide a bridge in case of difficulties with the transition.[32]

Most important, however, of the factors that would suggest a major role for the military in a transition is the simple one that the Cuban armed forces are just that—armed. In times of trouble and uncertainty, the wielders of weaponry become by that fact alone vital for the future of the state. This is a major part of the reasoning behind the fact that Fidel has wanted Raúl at the head of MINFAR for so many decades, has named him his successor, and has ensured the loyalty of the military command structure for so long.

It is then important to ask which other sectors of the Cuban polity will have an important role in any transition. The second pillar of the Cuban system is the Communist Party. Here again, we have an institution with a number of advantages that it has offered Castro since early in the revolutionary process. The PCC ensured that Castro had a guiding ideology and a structure for the amorphous political and military system, based essentially on his personality and leadership, which he had established in the years after 1959. Also, it has been able to produce a real organizing element for the regime. The party trained and the party administered. The party inspired and the party produced new cadres at all levels of the state.[33] But the PCC does not command the level of popular respect that the FAR does. The Communist Party also sees that its popularity could be on the wane.

It is difficult to imagine the party being an acceptable interlocutor about the country's future for anyone outside of Cuba. Certainly the U.S. armed forces would include few senior officers willing to show interest in the PCC as an interlocutor. Such is the peculiar nature of politics and discussion of power transition in Cuba.[34]

FAR's Role in a Power Transition

As for the armed forces in such a transition, it is clear that Raúl, while hardly as revered as his brother is by the military, has their basic loyalty, and they could live with his leadership. The armed forces, while hardly mono-lithic or unthinkingly standing aside while political events transpire, still have all the institutional advantages discussed earlier. The armed forces would doubtless prefer to stay well clear of direct rule in any transition. However, they are the last defense of the state, and serious disorder would almost certainly quickly put paid to such sentiments.

The armed forces are imbued with the traditions of a heroic past and the achievements of the revolution. They will not be keen to see those achieve-ments dismantled, but they are likely to be willing to see more changes than many observers credit them with accepting. But they will want change to be controlled and orderly. They will not tolerate widespread disorder or vio-lence. They will be watchful of the privileges of the armed forces and their role in Cuban society. And they will be concerned about foreign influences in the designing of the island's future.

Conclusions

The Fuerzas Armadas Revolucionarias have a major role in Cuban society and government today. They are one of two key pillars of the state and government of the island. The unique series of benefits they bring to the Castro government ensures that they have a role to play in the running of the state and a significant word to say on major issues of policy, especially those touching the security field.

This role has evolved in recent years in a number of key ways. Before the special period, the War of All the People strategy had already placed defense in a long-term central position in government decision making. But the special period has meant that, despite massive problems of cuts, lack of funds, lack of training, and operations difficulties of every imaginable kind, and even problems of corruption and loss of morale, the armed forces have increased their importance. However counterintuitive this might appear, it is natural that a government in trouble has to look to its main pillars, espe-cially its armed one, for reassurance.

Thus the role of the armed forces during and after a national crisis would be a central one. The strength, weaponry, and the host of other advantages of the armed forces would ensure it has a say in policy, if not the direction thereof. After that crisis, essentially no matter what the outcome (short of military defeat and occupation of the country by an outside power), that role would still be vital. And even in a peaceful transition, they may be expected to provide the guiding hand, the reassurance to all parties that disorder and violence are not an option, and the means to ensure that things do not come unstuck. This would hardly be the first time an armed force played such a role in Latin America, or indeed anywhere else. Cuba is a very special place, but it is not unique in every sense. Many circles in Cuba want change. But few of them want it to come with disorder and violence. While that remains the case, the armed forces will be central to any Cuban political process and any prospects for change.

In this, relations between the Ministry of the Interior and the FAR may well be important. While those links have become stronger of late with crosspostings and even transfers apparently more common, it is extremely difficult to know what is actually going on. There may be a militarization of the MININT. There is certainly concern to ensure that the military, if called upon, would be able and willing to support the internal security responsibilities of MININT. But how this is being played out is shrouded in secrecy. MINFAR will want little direct role in such activities, unless real disorder spreads. However, if such were to come to pass, it is difficult to escape the conclusion that the military would then not only wish to have control; they would insist on it. And MININT would simply have to come under the military's wing as its equivalents have had to do in so many places in Latin America and around the world when the going got really tough and prospects were dim.

With all this discussion of negative factors and change, it is tempting to leave this subject thinking that real change is actually almost upon us. Close observation of the Cuban scene, however, does not necessarily afford such a perspective. The government in fact seems more firmly in the saddle at this moment than for some time past. There is a strong sense among the Cuban leadership that the worst is now behind this beleaguered little country and its government. Some of the recent tightening of control on the island and the rollback of certain reforms suggest that this development has had major policy implications. And there is little doubt that the armed forces, while troubled and hurt, are not out of the game. Fidel is doubtless wise to try to keep them happy. It may well be they who to a considerable extent decide the nature of the future game and who the players in it are to be.

Notes

1. The author has benefited from the assistance of the Department of Foreign Affairs and International Trade of Canada, which has been extremely generous in helping him continue his studies in the area of Cuban defense policy.

2. Eric Williams, *From Columbus to Castro: The History of the Caribbean 1492–1969* (London: André Deutsch, 1970), 52.

3. Very little is written on this war in English. In Spanish, the best, if not most

unbiased, account is by Ramiro Guerra, *La guerra de los diez años* (Havana: Editorial Ciencias Sociales, 1972).

4. It is somewhat odd to see the use of the term "guerrilla" in the context of loyalist forces fighting an insurgency, but the nature of their employment, in relatively small groups harassing the rebels, made the term appear appropriate to a Spanish army raised on the epic defense of Spain against Napoleon at the beginning of the century. See Francisco Peréz-Guzmán, *La guerra en La Habana* (Havana: Editorial Ciencias Sociales, 1976).

5. Jack Cameron Dierks, *A Leap to Arms: The Cuban Campaign of 1898* (Philadelphia: Lippincott, 1970).

6. See the summer 1998 special issue of *Temas,* the main Cuban journal of intellectual exchange, dealing with this and related historical matters.

7. Such interventions were permitted, under the infamous Platt Amendment, from 1902 to 1934, when, as part of the Good Neighbor Policy of the Franklin Roosevelt government, they were officially discontinued. See Hugh Thomas, *Cuba: The Pursuit of Freedom* (London: Eyre and Spottiswoode, 1971), 452–57.

8. See, for example, John J. Johnson, *The Military and Society in Latin America* (Stanford, Calif.: Stanford University Press, 1964), 110–12.

9. Interesting new elements of this story are brought to light in a new biography of Ernesto Guevara. See Jorge Castañeda, *La vida en rojo* (Mexico: Editorial Alfaguara, 1997), 137–55.

10. There was considerable debate about the strength of Castro's forces before the capture of Havana. See Neill MacAulay, "The Cuban Rebel Army: A Numerical Survey," *Hispanic American Historical Review* (May 1978): 284–95.

11. This is discussed in greater detail in Damián Fernández, "Historical Background: Achievements, Failures and Prospects," in *The Cuban Military under Castro,* ed. Jaime Suchlicki (Miami: University of Miami, North-South Center, 1989), 1–26.

12. Michael Mazarr, "The Cuban Security Apparatus," in *Cuba: The International Dimensions,* ed. Georges Fauriol and Eva Loser (New Brunswick, N.J.: Transaction Press, 1990), 257–92.

13. Ibid., 266.

14. Fernández, "Historical Background," 15.

15. Jorge Domínguez, "Cuban Military and National Security Policies," in *Revolutionary Cuba in the World Arena,* ed. Martin Weinstein (Philadelphia: Institute for the Study of Human Issues, 1979), 77–97, esp. 82.

16. These figures may be too low. See Raúl Marín, *¿La hora de Cuba?* (Madrid: Editorial Revolución, 1992), 99–101.

17. Domínguez, "Cuban Military," 84.

18. Leon Gouré, "Cuba: Military Doctrine and Organization," in Suchlicki, *The Cuban Military,* 61–97, esp. 69–75.

19. These figures come from what is perhaps the best single work on the special period: Homero Campo and Orlando Pérez, *Cuba: Los años duros* (Mexico City: Plaza y Janés, 1997), 14–15.

20. Carmelo Mesa-Lago, *Are Economic Reforms Propelling Cuba to the Market?* (Miami: University of Miami Press, 1994), 23–56.

21. See Arnoldo Brenes and Kevin Casas, *Soldiers as Businessmen: The Eco-*

nomic Activities of Central America's Militaries (San José, Costa Rica: Arias Foundation, 1998).

22. Such advantages, of course, make it extremely difficult to decide whether improved efficiency is actually a result of military methods or merely of better conditions from which to compete.

23. For the early years of the setting up of the Cuban military intelligence system, see Domingo Amuchástegui, "Cuban Intelligence and the October Crisis," in *Intelligence and National Security* 13, no. 3 (autumn 1998): 88–119.

24. CEDSI is the Spanish acronym for the Centro de Estudios de Defensa y Seguridad Internacional (Center for the Study of Defense and International Security).

25. There has for years been a considerable degree of distrust between the two ministries. See Mazarr, "The Cuban Security," 284.

26. "In the special period we are all illegal," that is, involved in some sort of illegal activity.

27. For comparative purposes, however, it is worth noting that the Cuban forces, and service in those forces, is not seen as favorably as in Chile or Ecuador.

28. Mazarr, "The Cuban Security," 283.

29. These elements of the armed forces are discussed in the Cuban national chapter of Adrian English, *The Armed Forces of Latin America* (London: Jane's, 1984).

30. See Hal Klepak, "Cross-Cultural Dimensions of Non-proliferation and Arms Control Dialogue in Latin America," in *Culture and Society: Multilateralism, Arms Control and Security Building*, ed. Keith Krause (London: Frank Cass, 1999), 159–88, esp. 173.

31. In recent years there have been several cases of corruption among both junior and senior military officers. And while some have been related to drugs, these are the minority. Most have been connected with the dollar-earning activities to which the forces are closer than ever before. Punishment, especially by Latin American standards, has been swift and harsh.

32. Interviews with Cuban senior military officers, Havana, May, 1998.

33. Juan M. del Aguila, "The Changing Character of Cuba's Armed Forces," in Suchlicki, *The Cuban Military*, 27–59, esp. 37–40.

34. Marín, *¿La hora de Cuba?* 162.

VII

Migration to the United States

Migrating to the United States

Evolution, Change, and Continuity

Félix Masud-Piloto

Evolution of Cuban Migration

For more than four decades, the United States and Cuba have been engaged in a political war marked by crises, hostilities, and confrontations. These tensions have deeply affected the flow and process of Cuban migration to the United States. Since the 1960s, Cubans arriving in the United States, by whatever means—including hijacking of U.S. commercial airplanes—or under any circumstances, have expected and usually received political asylum simply by claiming persecution by, fear of, or disaffection with the Cuban Revolution and Castro's government. The U.S. government's Cuban migration strategy has always had clear ideological and political objectives: every Cuban who came to the United States would serve, willingly or not, the cause of discrediting and undermining the Cuban Revolution. To accomplish that goal, U.S. laws would have to treat Cubans as a privileged immigrant group, at least until the Castro government was overthrown.

As the migration increased and the revolution became consolidated, ten successive U.S. presidents have coped with the Cuban migration within the parameters of the cold war and on a crisis-to-crisis basis. The Kennedy administration created the emergency Cuban refugee program, the Johnson administration organized and financed the Cuban airlift program (the so-called freedom flights), the Carter administration did the best it could to manage the Mariel boatlift, and the Clinton administration confronted the rafters' crisis in the summer of 1994. That last crisis, however, resulted in one of the most significant changes in U.S. immigration policy toward Cuba in nearly forty years.

Hoping to stop illegal and uncontrolled immigration from Cuba, on May 2, 1995, the Clinton administration decided to stop granting political asylum to those Cuban migrants who did not arrive with U.S. visas or were not able to prove a well-founded fear of persecution by the Cuban government. The decision marked the end of an era of virtually unrestricted admission and preferential treatment of Cubans based strictly on political considerations. From that point on, the thirty-six-year-old unwritten policy of welcoming almost every politically disaffected Cuban to the United States was effectively revoked. Overnight and without warning, most Cubans arriving in the United States without the proper documentation were no longer welcomed nor considered special.

The Cuban community in the United States reacted vociferously and with great indignation to the policy and status change, accusing the Clinton administration of treason; they staged demonstrations and acts of civil disobedience in Miami, Union City, and Washington, D.C. The Cuban government, on the other hand, praised Clinton for trying to normalize the migration flow between the two countries. In reality, the administration's policy shift had more to do with international political changes and U.S. domestic policies than with the long-standing political animosities between the United States and Cuba.

With the end of the cold war in 1989 and the disintegration of the Soviet Union in 1991, Cuba's importance on the U.S. foreign policy agenda declined considerably. The USSR's demise brought severe economic dislocations and hardships to Cuba, thus limiting the Cuban government's capacity to challenge U.S. hegemony in Latin America.[1] In that context, the Clinton administration was willing to keep up the anti-Castro rhetoric of the cold war, while at the same time exploring diplomatic channels that would lead to a normal and controlled migratory process from Cuba. In order to achieve that objective, however, the Cuban migrants' privileged status would have to be changed or at least adjusted to be more compatible with the changing U.S. foreign policy.

Evolution of the Cuba Issue in American Politics

After several years of low visibility, the Cuba issue returned to the center stage of U.S. political debate in 1992. The return was propelled mainly by the disintegration of the Soviet Union, the fall of Communism in Eastern Europe, and the "official" end of the cold war. The United States no longer had to worry about the "Soviet threat," so it again turned its attention to the "Cuban threat." The United States accused Cuba and Castro of going against the tide of democracy engulfing Latin America, instigating and supporting political subversion in the region, drug trafficking, and violating the human rights of Cubans. And in a highly ironic and contradictory tone, the United States, which for more than thirty years had justified its attacks against Cuba by citing Cuba's close alliance with the Soviet Union, now urged the Cuban government to emulate the Soviet model for change.

That same year, 1992, was also a presidential election year in the United States, and as in past presidential elections, the Cuba issue figured prominently in the campaign. Just a few months before the elections, U.S. representative Robert Torricelli (D-NJ), chairman of the House Western Hemisphere Subcommittee, proposed a bill designed to tighten the U.S. economic embargo against Cuba and to strengthen the prospects for democracy in the island. The Cuban Democracy Act (CDA), also known as the Torricelli bill, aimed to hasten Castro's fall from power, and like other strategies with that objective, generated a spirited debate among the presidential candidates. Although the CDA proposed a hard-line policy toward Castro, its potentially negative repercussions for U.S. foreign relations troubled many who, at least in principle, supported the proposal. The bill, among other things, would prohibit trade with Cuba by U.S. subsidiaries established in third countries, and block access to U.S. ports for ships that had recently visited Cuban ports. Even President Bush was concerned; he refused to support the CDA on the grounds that the subsidiary provision would damage U.S. relations with important allies.[2]

The Democratic candidate, William (Bill) J. Clinton, also refused to support the bill. However, as the campaign intensified during the summer months, Clinton surprised the political world when he declared himself in favor of the Torricelli bill. At a fund-raiser in Miami, organized by the predominantly Republican and conservative Cuban American National Foundation (CANF), Clinton justified his new position by explaining: "I think that this administration [Bush-Quayle] has missed a big opportunity to put the hammer down on Fidel Castro and Cuba."[3] Not to be outdone by his challenger, several days later President Bush also reversed himself and endorsed the CDA.

The Cuba issue served Bill Clinton well during the campaign, and although he failed to carry Florida, he managed to defeat George Bush in the November elections. Despite Clinton's position on the CDA, the Democrats' electoral victory raised the Cuban government's hopes and expectations for better relations with the United States. Cuban officials were hopeful that Bill Clinton's hard-line position on the CDA was only campaign rhetoric. They expected a liberal Democrat to be an improvement over the previous twelve years of conservative Republicanism under Reagan and Bush.

As part of its overall strategy to survive after the disintegration of the Soviet Union and the signing of the Cuban Democracy Act into law in October 1992, the Cuban government aggressively pursued foreign investments and trade relations with Europe, Latin America, and Asia. At the same time, Cuba sought to establish a new dialogue with its émigré community. In April 1994, at a conference organized and hosted by then foreign minister Roberto Robaina, the government invited 220 Cubans living in twenty-five countries for three days of talks in Havana. Although modest in scope, the talks were perceived as serious by most participants, and they concluded with the government's commitment to improve communications between itself and the émigrés, to relax most travel restrictions to the island, and, most important, to hold more meetings with a wider agenda.[4]

Changes in Cuban Migration in the 1980s

Despite the crisis the Mariel boatlift created for the Carter administration and the state of Florida, Washington continued to treat Cuban immigration on a crisis-to-crisis basis—as part of a political strategy designed to overthrow the revolution—instead of instituting a rational and humane immigration policy. Havana was also guilty of playing politics with the migratory process and of treating emigration—especially the Mariel boatlift—as a domestic political issue with the objectives of eliminating political opposition and consolidating the revolution. As a result, as soon as the immediate crisis was over in the fall of 1980, both governments returned to their familiar cold war positions and resumed their war of words.

The creation of Radio Martí in 1985 and the CANF's lobbying efforts against the Cuban government justified Cuba's reluctance to negotiate an immigration agreement with the United States. By the same token, the Reagan administration, responding to the Republican Party's most conservative constituents, was equally reluctant to negotiate with Cuba. After all, during the 1980 presidential campaign, Reagan and the Republicans had harshly criticized Carter's "soft stance on Cuba" and the way he had "mishandled" the Mariel boatlift. Under those circumstances, a comprehensive agreement on immigration would have to wait until the political climate between the two nations changed or another crisis forced the parties to negotiate.

Ironically, despite the Reagan administration's hard line against the Cuban government, in 1984 the two governments agreed to settle the status of some twenty-eight hundred Cuban "excludables" who had been detained in U.S. prisons since 1980. This was a good move on both sides because it showed a willingness to settle controversial and sensitive immigration issues. The agreement was short-lived, however, as Cuba suspended it to protest the administration's creation of Radio Martí in May 1985.

In the absence of a working immigration agreement between the United States and Cuba, a rare government–private sector collaboration emerged. The CANF created and the State Department approved the "Exodus" program, to arrange the immigration to the United States of Cubans who had managed to arrive at third countries. Using a combination of public and private funds and working with the potential immigrants' relatives in the United States, the foundation sponsored more than ninety-five hundred Cubans between 1988 and 1993, providing medical insurance and employment opportunities for them for one year. It is estimated that the CANF's Exodus Relief Fund received about $2 million in federal assistance during those years.

The program was quite successful, but it was not nearly enough to satisfy the Cubans' growing demands to emigrate. In addition, the program also raised some questions about its legality and politics. Wayne Smith, the State Department's senior representative in Havana during the Carter and Reagan administrations, told the *New York Times*: "I do not know of any other political organization in the United States that has ever received this kind of privilege. . . . It is one [privilege] they have clearly used to their advantage, saying to people, we can get your uncle in Madrid to the U.S. and, oh, by the way, you do support the Foundation, don't you?"[5]

An issue that the United States was willing and hoping to negotiate with the Cuban government was the return of more than twenty-five hundred Mariel excludables who remained in U.S. prisons, most since 1980. The "Marielito" stigma seemed to be getting worse, as the U.S. mass media continued making the "criminality" of the Marielitos the focus of numerous news stories.[6] Thus, responding to a combination of pressures ranging from those who wanted the "criminals returned to Castro" to human rights groups who underlined the illegality of detaining individuals indefinitely without a trial, in 1987 the United States entered into negotiations with Cuba to try to settle the excludables issue and to reactivate the 1984 accords. Although the Cuban government saw the return of the Mariel excludables as a political defeat, it was under great pressure to reopen a legal and direct migratory channel to the United States.

The renewed agreement was welcomed by both governments but received a violent response from those who would be most adversely affected

Table 14.1. Number of rafters by years, 1985–1994

Year	Immigrant visas issued by the United States	Illegal rafters to the United States	Rafters detained by Cuba
1985	1,227	—	—
1986*	—	—	—
1987*	—	—	—
1988	3,472	—	—
1989	1,631	—	—
1990	1,098	467	1,593
1991	1,376	1,997	6,596
1993	964	4,208	11,564
1994	544	4,092	10,975
Total	11,222	13,275	7,801

Source: Fidel Castro, *La razón es nuestra* (Havana: Editorial Política, 1994), 54.
*Cuba suspended the 1984 agreement, in protest of the Reagan administration's creation of Radio Martí.

by it, the excludables who would be deported to Cuba. Ignored by the U.S. justice system as they served their seemingly endless sentences, the Cuban inmates at the federal penitentiaries of Oakdale, Louisiana, and Atlanta, Georgia, rioted and demanded individual asylum hearings. The riots left more than two hundred inmates and prison officials injured and more than $100 million in damages.[7]

The 1987 agreement merely reactivated the 1984 accords, which were expected to normalize the migratory process between the two countries. Most important among the measures were the continued deportation of the Mariel inmates and the renewed promise of the United States to issue up to twenty thousand visas a year to qualified Cubans. The agreement, however, was never executed as intended. The U.S. Interests Section in Havana, blaming the overwhelming number of visa requests, never came close to issuing the twenty thousand visas a year permitted by the accord, a point that did not escape Castro's political analysis of the situation. In a 1994 speech, the Cuban president accused the United States of dragging its feet and violating the spirit and letter of the agreement. With the aid of figures provided by Cuban (and U.S.) official sources (see table 14.1), but using much lower 1994 rafter data than that of the U.S. Coast Guard (see table 14.2), he explained that from 1985 to 1994, the United States had issued 11,222 visas, only 7.1 percent of the 160,000 the two governments had agreed to under the accord. Castro also explained that during the same period, the United States had admitted 13,275 Cubans who arrived in Florida illegally.[8]

It is important to note, however, that during the speech Castro referred to the twenty thousand visas as if that number was guaranteed or absolute. In reality, the accords stated that the United States would issue up to twenty thousand visas a year.

Castro's arguments and reasoning were not very different from a report prepared by the U.S. Interests Section in January 1994. In a top-secret memorandum to the State Department, the CIA (Central Intelligence Agency), and the INS (Immigration and Naturalization Service), visa officers in the U.S. Interests Section discussed the difficulties they were having identifying visa applicants with legitimate human rights cases. As reported in Havana's daily *Juventud Rebelde,* the visa officers observed:

> The processing of refugee applicants continues to show weak cases. Most people apply more because of the deteriorating economic situation than a real fear of persecution . . . . Although we have tried hard to work with those human rights organizations on which we exert greater control to identify activists truly persecuted by the government, human rights cases represent the weakest category of the refugee program.[9]

By 1990 it was clear that the 1984/1987 immigration accords were not working to anyone's satisfaction. At the same time, the collapse of the Soviet Union and most Communist governments in Europe eliminated most of Cuba's trading partners. That, in addition to low productivity and mismanagement, sent the Cuban economy into a tailspin. The economic crisis, coupled with increased pressure and opposition from human rights groups, presented the Cuban government with one of the most potentially explosive social situations since 1959. As a result, the number of people leaving the country illegally by sea increased dramatically, from 467 in 1990 to 3,656 in 1993. In 1994 the numbers increased steadily from 716 in April to 21,300 in August.[10] The steady rise in arrivals worried many Florida officials who feared another Mariel-style boatlift from Cuba.[11]

The fast and steady increase in Cuban rafters gave rise to the Hermanos al Rescate (Brothers to the Rescue, BTTR) organization. The BTTR, founded in May 1991 by José Basulto and twenty-five volunteer pilots, scoured the sea between Florida and Cuba, looking for rafters. The organization then informed the U.S. Coast Guard of the rafters' location, contributing to their rescue, and continuing the flow of Cuban migration to the United States.

Basulto is a Bay of Pigs veteran[12] who claimed to be above politics and insisted that BTTR is an organization guided by humanitarian motives:

"We [were] trying to break through the partisanship that exists in Miami by communicating a message of love, understanding, and hope."[13] But his motives have been questioned. The existence of a private rescue operation, operating with the approval of the U.S. government, raised important legal and political questions.

Chief among concerns are the contradictions in and unfairness of U.S. immigration policy. In 1991 and 1992, the United States reinforced its Haitian interdiction program by deporting thousands back to Haiti and detaining more than thirty thousand Haitians in Guantánamo Bay to await deportation.[14] The double standards in U.S. immigration policy, as applied to Cubans and Haitians, were illustrated by Washington's actions, which were denounced by policy critics. How could the United States justify encouraging and allowing the rescue of Cubans while denying Haitians the opportunity to plead their cases for asylum? The policy's unfairness became an issue during the 1992 U.S. presidential election: During the campaign, Clinton bitterly assailed George Bush's cruel Haitian policies, particularly his harsh treatment of refugees. Shortly after Clinton's election, however, he moved quickly to make these policies harsher still by extending the (flatly illegal) blockade on Haiti to prevent refugees from escaping the mounting terror—allegedly done "for humanitarian reasons, [as] the goal was to save lives." Among those who fled Haiti, some remained in the United States as "economic refugees." Clinton's increased brutality proved to be a grand success. Refugee flow, which had reached over thirty thousand in 1992, sharply declined under Clinton's ministrations to about the level of 1989, before the decline under President Jean-Bertrand Aristide.[15]

A New Migration Crisis: The Summer of 1994

In scenes reminiscent of the events and incidents leading to the Mariel boatlift of 1980, a series of embassy invasions and boat hijackings by Cubans seeking asylum disturbed the usually peaceful city of Havana during the months from May to August 1994. On May 28, more than one hundred people forcefully entered the Belgian ambassador's residence. On July 13, twenty-one people entered the German embassy. Two days later, nine people entered the Chilean consulate. The embassy crises were resolved without violence or fatalities. Most boat hijackings, however, had violent outcomes. On July 13, at least thirty-two people drowned when a hijacked tugboat was rammed by two Cuban Coast Guard tugboats in the port of Havana. On July 26 and August 3 and 4, the boat that had transported passengers from Havana to the city of Regla for nearly one hundred years was hijacked to Miami. Violence was used in all these hijackings, and one resulted in the death of a Cuban police officer on August 4.[16]

As these incidents became more frequent and more violent, on August 5 President Castro held a televised news conference to explain the Cuban government's position. Castro was visibly angry, not with his national television audience, but with the U.S. government. Earlier that day, Cuban police had put down a small riot in the city of Havana. The riot, Castro claimed, was caused by rumors of a "United States-sponsored boatlift to Miami." He went on to say that if the United States continued encouraging illegal migration, the government of Cuba would discontinue its policy of stopping people trying to emigrate illegally. "Either they [the United States] take serious measures to guard their coasts, or we will stop putting obstacles in the way of people who want to leave the country, and we will stop putting obstacles in the way of people [in the United States] who want to come and look for their relatives here."[17]

Castro's words were not unfamiliar to his audience. He had used similar language in 1965 when he announced the boatlift from the port of Camarioca, and again in 1980 to announce the Mariel boatlift. Even more portentous, however, was the fact that, as during the previous boatlifts, Cuba was experiencing a period of economic hardship and crisis. The big difference was that, unlike the situations in 1965 and 1980, the 1994 economic crisis was the worst in the revolution's history. The economy seemed to have hit bottom, and as consumer goods, food, and petroleum supplies became more scarce, the people became increasingly tense, hungry, and restless.

News of the August 5 riot in Havana appeared in most major newspapers in the United States, but the news was bigger and more ominous in Miami, where many analysts saw the incident as the beginning of the end for Castro. Many Cuban American political activists were convinced that Castro would not be able to survive the usually fatal combination of economic crisis and popular discontent.[18]

The riot clearly added to the Cuban government's problems, and as the severe economic crisis continued in 1994, the number of Cubans arriving on the coasts of Florida in homemade and extremely unsafe *balsas* (rafts) reached alarming proportions. Thousands of Cubans reached the conclusion that the economy would not improve any time soon and decided to emigrate by whatever means possible. Ernesto Rodríguez Chávez, a Cuban analyst who has studied the factors influencing Cuban emigration, argues that in addition to Cuba's economic crisis, rafters were also driven by the historical guarantee that they would be welcomed by the U.S. government, "[a] welcome that had been specially warm for those arriving in July and

August 1994, after stealing boats, using violence, endangering the lives of people who did not wish to emigrate, and even committing murder." Rafters were further assured and encouraged by the U.S. government's pledge to "not change its immigration policy toward Cubans under any circumstances."[19]

The United States responded to Cuba's economic and political crises with clear signs of encouragement for those who tried to escape from the island. Indeed, so many tried that August 1994 soon became a record-setting month in the history of the Cuban migration to the United States, a fact that captured the attention of the U.S. mass media. The *New York Times, Miami Herald, El Nuevo Herald, Time,* and *Newsweek* were among the many newspapers and magazines that tried to keep up with the record-setting numbers by publishing daily or weekly tables and graphs.[20] It was estimated that at least twenty-five thousand *"balseros"* (rafters), traveling on anything that floated, had headed north from the Cuban port town of Cojímar, during the month of August 1994 (see table 14.2). The migration from Cuba was back on the front pages, and the headlines were as dramatic as ever: "U.S. Coast Guard to Guard Florida Straits";[21] "Vessels Prepared to Head Off Any Exodus from Cuba";[22] "We won't allow another Mariel,"[23] and "U.S. hints at blockade."[24] As in the past, the United States seemed to have been caught by surprise and was again reacting to a Cuban immigration crisis, with little control over the events.

The U.S. government's lack of control over the migration and the high number of daily arrivals prompted some analysts to compare the August exodus with the Mariel boatlift of 1980. The comparison was not without merit. For example, it was clear that Castro could control the migration at will. In three televised addresses to the Cuban people—one carried live by CNN in the United States—Castro repeatedly explained that due to the long history of encouragement from the United States for Cubans to leave the country illegally, and in light of the recent series of hijackings of state-owned vessels, his government would stop putting obstacles in the way of people wishing to leave the country.[25]

At least three factors, however, made the new crisis different from the Mariel boatlift: First, the numbers had the potential of being higher in 1994 than in 1980. On August 23, the U.S. Coast Guard rescued a single-day record of 2,886 Cubans in the Florida Straits. And in the twelve-day period of August 13 to 25, the Coast Guard rescued 13,084 rafters, a much larger number than the 9,340 who arrived during the first twelve days of Mariel. The total number of rescues for the month of August was 21,300.[26] Second, unlike Jimmy Carter's inability to stop the Mariel boatlift during its early days, Bill Clinton announced on August 19 that Cubans would not be al-

Table 14.2. U.S. Coast Guard Cuban rescue statistics, 1981–94

Year	Number of people rescued	Increase over previous year (%)
1981	NA	—
1982	NA	—
1983	47	—
1984	19	-60
1985	43	+56
1986	27	-37
1987	44	+63
1988	59	+34
1989	391	+563
1990	467	+19
1991	2,203	+372
1992	2,557	+16
1993	3,656	+43
1994	37,139	+916

Source: U.S. Coast Guard Public Affairs Office, Miami, as cited in Max J. Castro, "Cuba: The Continuing Crisis," *The North South Agenda,* 13 (April 1995): 4.

lowed to enter U.S. territory. Instead, they would be rescued at sea and detained indefinitely by U.S. naval authorities.[27] Third, also unlike Jimmy Carter's reluctance and failure to negotiate with Castro, the Clinton administration was able to negotiate an agreement with the Cuban government to stop the exodus.

President Clinton was determined to prevent another Mariel. So when the governor of Florida declared a state emergency, Clinton, after consulting with the governor, Jorge Más Canosa of the CANF, and other Florida political and civic leaders on August 19, announced that Cuban rafters would no longer be transported to the United States. They would instead be detained indefinitely in the U.S. Naval Base at Guantánamo. The next day (August 20) the president announced that in addition to detaining rafters, the U.S. government would take the following measures: (1) limit visits to Cuba by Cuban Americans, except in extreme humanitarian cases, (2) no longer allow Cuban Americans to send money remittances to their relatives in Cuba, and (3) require a special U.S. Treasury Department license for journalists and academics wishing to travel to Cuba.[28]

The president's orders to stop the Cuban rafters represented a complete reversal of a thirty-five-year-old immigration policy designed to welcome, as political refugees, almost any Cuban claiming to be escaping Fidel Castro's repression. Cubans, who had had the doors to the United States opened since 1959, were suddenly not only denied entry but were being intercepted at sea and taken to what they came to call concentration camps at the U.S. military base at Guantánamo Bay, Cuba. Once on the base, they were technically in safe haven, out of danger, and without the right to claim political asylum in the United States. U.S. attorney general Janet Reno emphatically announced that the more than twenty thousand Cuban rafters at Guantánamo would be held there indefinitely and "not be processed for admission to the United States."[29]

The change in policy came as a shock to Cubans, who had come to believe that immigrating to the United States was a natural right. Still, the announcement did not deter the flow of rafters right away. On the contrary, the days following Clinton's orders set new one-day records. On August 22, the U.S. Coast Guard picked up 2,338 rafters, and 2,886 on August 23.[30]

To show its resolve, the administration, in an unprecedented move, asked the Cuban government to dissuade rafters from leaving Cuba. Cuba's agreement to use only "peaceful persuasion," coupled with Washington's threat of "indefinite detention," dashed the hopes of the would-be refugees. For the first time in thirty-five years, the United States was refusing to allow immigration from Cuba. It was also the first time in thirty-five years that the U.S. and Cuban governments had joined forces to stop refugees fleeing from a country categorized as a serious human rights violator by the U.S. Department of State. The U.S.-Cuba collaboration gradually ended the exodus, and on September 1, 1994, the United States and Cuba initiated a round of conversations on immigration issues affecting both countries. Cuba proposed a wider agenda to discuss all issues preventing the two countries from having normal diplomatic relations—particularly the U.S. economic embargo, maintained against Cuba for more than three decades. The Clinton administration insisted on discussing immigration issues only and prevailed.

The first round of talks was held in New York City and concluded on September 10 with the Cuban government's promise to continue its policy of peacefully dissuading potential migrants from taking to sea in unsafe vessels. The Cuban government also agreed to allow any detained rafters wishing to return to Cuba to do so without fear of reprisals. In return, the U.S. government agreed to accept at least twenty thousand Cuban immigrants each year and to persuade all detained rafters to return to Cuba to apply for visas to the United States.

The twenty-eight thousand rafters in U.S. custody reacted with anger and violence to the U.S.-Cuba negotiations. Some twenty-five hundred Guantánamo detainees rioted, injuring more than two hundred U.S. soldiers, and more than one hundred detainees escaped from the detention camps in Panama, where they were interned on a temporary basis at Washington's request. They felt betrayed and confused by the new U.S. position.

Nevertheless, despite the Clinton administration's hard-line rhetoric of "indefinite detention," most rafters and their relatives in Miami were optimistic and convinced that sooner or later they would be allowed to immigrate to the United States.

May 2, 1995: End of the Open Door Policy?

The Clinton administration's policy of indefinite detention received harsh criticism from the powerful Cuban American community in Miami, human rights organizations, some Latin American governments, and the rafters. Reacting in part to the pressures, in October 1994 the administration announced that while most rafters were destined to remain indefinitely at Guantánamo, those seventy years of age or older, the critically or chronically ill, pregnant women, and minors with their parents would be allowed to immigrate to the United States. This change, along with the nearly one thousand rafters who had voluntarily returned to Cuba, gradually reduced the detainee population by almost 20 percent, but the United States would still have to find a way of settling another twenty-one thousand Cubans.

The policy revision was the first indication of the administration's attempts to find a way out of a policy that in addition to being unpopular and controversial was extremely expensive. Start-up costs for the Guantánamo tent city were estimated at $100 million. Another $35 million was invested in improvements to the base infrastructure in order to accommodate the long-term population. Finally, the daily operations cost $1 million. Based on operating costs alone—at least $365 million a year—it was highly unlikely that the administration could keep the Guantánamo operation going for a long time.

In addition to the high costs of the Guantánamo operation, there was also the fear of more rioting and violence due to the deplorable living conditions in the camps. In April 1995, the Pentagon issued a report that reflected those fears, and recommended closing the camps as soon as possible. Despite a significant increase in military personnel at the base, the summer months were still expected to bring unrest and possibly more violence among the rafters.

On May 2, 1995, the Clinton administration relieved the military's preoccupation with the explosive situation in the camps when it announced that after secret negotiations with the Cuban government, the two nations had reached a mutually beneficial immigration agreement. The new agreement eliminated the indefinite-detention provision in effect since August 1994, news that brought cheers from the detained rafters and their relatives in Miami. All detainees were gradually admitted to the United States until

Guantánamo was emptied of rafters in March 1996. The agreement, however, also called for the direct deportation of any rafter attempting to enter the United States illegally.

As could be expected, reaction to the Cuba-U.S. agreement on deportation was mixed and emotional. The U.S. government believed it was the best solution for a bad situation. It could not continue holding people indefinitely, nor afford to continue taking in unlimited numbers of refugees. The agreement set a generous immigration quota for Cubans—a minimum of twenty thousand per year—and established an orderly immigration procedure in Cuba that guaranteed the safety of deportees and of new applicants. The Cuban government hailed the agreement as sound. In particular, Ricardo Alarcón, the chief Cuban negotiator, was pleased because the accords eliminated the Cubans' "exclusivity," a weapon the United States had used against Cuba since 1959: "[F]rom this moment on, Cubans will be treated the same way as people of other nationalities." The Cuban American community in the United States saw the new agreement, though, as U.S. treason against Cuba's liberation.

On May 9, 1995, exactly a week after the agreement, an unprecedented, and until the previous week unthinkable, event took place in the small Cuban port town of Cabañas. A U.S. Coast Guard cutter docked at the port and surrendered thirteen Cuban rafters to Cuban immigration officers. On the dock, representatives of the U.S. Interests Section in Havana greeted the deportees and offered them guidance on how to apply for U.S. visas.

The arrival in Cuba of the first deported rafters proved that the new immigration accords could work and that the United States and Cuba were capable of reaching agreements and working together when the interests of both countries were at stake. Yet, despite that rare show of cooperation, neither government could stop illegal immigration from Cuba. In 1999, as the Cuban economy continued to falter, 2,254 rafters arrived in Florida. This was the highest number of arrivals since the drastic decline—only 209 arrivals—following the signing of the 1995 agreement.[31] Discouraged by migration policy changes, the ensuing number of illegal migrants interdicted at sea by the U.S. Coast Guard decreased, especially from the peak year of 1994. The number of interdictions started to increase again in 1998–2000 but decreased slightly in 2001; the data for 2002 is incomplete. (See table 14.3.)

Cuban Migration after Elián

As the twentieth century drew to a close, U.S.-Cuban migratory relations had compiled an extensive but mixed record of accomplishments and short-

Table 14.3. U.S. Coast Guard's Cuban interdictions at sea, 1991–2002

1991	1992	1993	1994	1995	1996	1997	1998	1999	2000	2001	2002*
1,722	2,066	2,882	38,560	525	411	421	903	1,619	1,000	777	366

Source: U.S. Coast Guard, *Migrant Interdictions at Sea, 1991–2002* (Washington, D.C.: U.S. Department of Transportation, Public Affairs Office, 2002)
*As of July 26, 2002.

comings. Within the context of the hostile and confrontational political relations between the two nations during the previous four decades, the fact that several major migratory agreements and collaborations had been possible can be considered a major achievement. In addition, since the signing of the 1995 agreement, the United States and Cuba have been holding several meetings a year to monitor and adjust the accord if necessary.

Unfortunately, the two countries' ability to work together on immigration issues has not reduced the hostility between them. In February 1996, the U.S. Congress approved the Cuban Liberty and Democratic Solidarity Act (also known as the Helms-Burton bill). In addition to further tightening the U.S. economic embargo against Cuba, it threatened to retaliate against foreign businesses investing in Cuba, and gave Cuban nationals residing in the United States the right to sue the Cuban government in U.S. courts to recover lost property in Cuba. President Clinton, who had strong reservations about the act's extraterritorial implications, signed it into law after the Cuban air force shot down two Brothers to the Rescue planes claiming that they had violated Cuban airspace.

The Helms-Burton law increased the hostile environment between Cuba and the United States. It was yet another reminder, perhaps the strongest, that the cold war between the two nations was far from over, and that as long as that environment existed, it would be extremely difficult, if not impossible, to have a normal migratory flow between Havana and Miami. In fact, even before the enactment of the Helms-Burton law, an unwritten immigration policy affecting only Cubans had been in effect: the wet feet versus dry feet policy. That is, any Cuban migrant who was rescued or stopped by the U.S. Coast Guard before reaching U.S. soil—wet feet—would be immediately deported back to Cuba. On the other hand, any Cuban migrant arriving in the United States undetected by U.S. immigration authorities—dry feet—would gain the right to have a hearing for political asylum.

The wet/dry feet policy has developed into an extremely dangerous and often fatal cat-and-mouse game in the Florida Straits between the U.S. Coast Guard and private *lancheros* (high-speed boats). According to Coast Guard estimates, from October 1998 to April 1999 more than one thousand *lancheros* made it to Florida. Each of the surviving passengers, and those who did not survive the voyage, paid at least two thousand dollars and up to ten thousand dollars to improve their chances of arriving in the United States with dry feet. In accordance with U.S. immigration regulations and the U.S. Refugee Act of 1980, all survivors are granted a political asylum hearing as long as they prove a "well-founded fear" of political persecution at home. In addition, thanks to the Cuban Adjustment Act of 1966, after only one year of residence in the United States, Cubans are entitled to apply for permanent residency.

The Cuban Adjustment Act and the wet/dry feet policy continue to keep the Cuban migration to the United States in a peculiar yet privileged situation vis-à-vis migrants from the rest of the world. The latest and perhaps most extreme case was that of Elián González, the six-year-old Cuban boy found floating off the coast of Ft. Lauderdale, Florida, on November 25, 1999, after his mother, stepfather, and eight others had drowned attempting to make it to the United States with dry feet. Little Elián met all the requirements to be sent back to Cuba to his natural father. Instead, the boy was turned into a political symbol of the exile community's political war against the Cuban government. Not to be outdone, the Cuban government also turned Elián into a political symbol of its war against U.S. imperialism.[32]

Elián González's case was disputed in U.S. courts for nearly seven months, despite the fact that his father, the only person who could properly speak on his behalf, asked for the boy's immediate return to Cuba. Most importantly, although the INS initially ruled in the father's favor, Elián remained for five months in the custody of distant relatives in Miami who willingly and consciously politicized the case to the extreme. Most analysts and jurists, and the majority of the American public, agreed that had Elián been from any other country in the world except Cuba, he would have been returned to his father just a few days after his rescue.[33] Instead, due to the irrational emotions that dominate relations between the United States and Cuba and the peculiar immigration regulations applied to Cubans, the boy, like the U.S.-Cuba policy, became a hostage of politics.

Notes

1. The collapse of the Soviet Union and the end of Communism led many—especially in the Cuban American community—to believe that Castro's days were numbered. The expectations were so high that in 1990, the *Miami Herald* held a contest for readers to predict Castro's final days. The winning contestant would be awarded an all-expenses-paid vacation in Cuba's famous resort at Varadero Beach. The contest was suspended two years later without a winner. An equally speculative

and presumptuous book was Andrés Oppenheimer's *Castro's Final Hour* (New York: Simon and Schuster, 1992). For serious academic analysis on U.S.-Cuba relations after the cold war, see Guillian Gunn, *Cuba in Transition: Options for U.S. Policy* (New York: Twentieth Century Fund, 1993); Enrique Baloyra and James Morris, eds., *Conflict and Change in Cuba* (Albuquerque: University of New Mexico Press, 1993); Carollee Bengelsdorf, *The Problem of Democracy in Cuba* (New York: Oxford University, 1994); and Sandor Halebsky and John Kirk, eds., *Cuba in Transition: Crisis and Transformation* (Boulder, Colo.: Westview, 1992).

2. Gunn, *Cuba in Transition*, 20–26.

3. Ibid., 21.

4. The three days of talks between the Cuban government and Cuban exiles caused quite a stir in Miami, where participants were accused of treason in the local press and some were threatened with physical violence. For more on the Cuban American community's reaction to the conference, see the *Miami Herald* and *El Nuevo Herald*, April 20–30, 1994; *Contrapunto*, May 1994 and June 1994; Human Rights Watch, "Dangerous Dialogue Revisited: Threats to Freedom of Expression Continue in Miami's Cuban Exile Community," report (November, 1994). The conference's proceedings were published as *La nación y la emigración* (Havana: Editora Política, 1994). A second conference took place in Havana November 3–6, 1995.

5. *New York Times*, May 8, 1995.

6. For more on the mass media's increased interest in the criminality of the Marielitos, see Félix Masud-Piloto, "Changing Public Opinion toward Mariel Entrants: The Evolution of the 'Marielito' Stigma" (paper presented at the Twenty-eighth Congress of the Latin American Studies Association, March 1994).

7. *Miami Herald*, December 3, 1987.

8. Fidel Castro, *La razón es nuestra* (Havana: Editora Política, 1994).

9. *Juventud Rebelde*, March 6, 1994.

10. *Miami Herald*, August 26, 1994, January 9, 1995.

11. Executive Office of the Governor, "The Unfair Burden: Immigration's Impact on Florida" (March, 1994). The federal government also developed a confidential emergency plan called "Operation Distant Shore" in anticipation of a Mariel-style exodus. *Miami Herald*, August 18, 1994.

12. The Bay of Pigs is the failed 1961 invasion of Cuba by Cuban exiles who were organized and financed by Washington. Basulto participated in the invasion and has a long association with the U.S. Central Intelligence Agency. (Editor's note.)

13. *Miami Herald*, July 5, 1992.

14. For a good discussion on the Haitian interdiction program and the living conditions for Haitians at Guantánamo, see Paul Farmer, *The Uses of Haiti* (Monroe, Me.: Common Courage Press, 1994): 225–96.

15. Noam Chomsky, introduction to Farmer's *The Uses of Haiti*, 37–38.

16. Ernesto Rodríguez Chávez, *La crisis migratoria* (Havana: Casa de las Américas, n.d.), 14. For more details about the hijackings and their impact on Cuba and the United States, see *El Nuevo Herald*, July 14–August 10, 1994.

17. *Miami Herald*, August 6, 1994.

18. *El Nuevo Herald,* August 6, 1994.

19. Rodríguez Chávez, *La crisis migratoria,* 15.

20. In addition to the extensive coverage on the rafters and the record numbers, the popular press produced some interesting pieces. One of the most interesting was on changes in the language used by the press. For example, *Time* had a cover article titled, "Cubans go home," words never before used in reference to the Cuban migration. *Time,* September 5, 1994. For daily statistics on the rafters, see the *Miami Herald* and *El Nuevo Herald,* July 1–September 30, 1994.

21. *Miami Herald,* August 11, 1994.

22. Ibid.

23. *Miami Herald,* August 19, 1994.

24. *Miami Herald,* August 22, 1994.

25. Castro, *La razón,* 33.

26. *New York Times,* September 9, 1994.

27. *Miami Herald,* August 20, 1994.

28. *Miami Herald,* August 21, 1994.

29. Ibid.

30. *Miami Herald,* August 24, 1994.

31. Karen de Young, "U.S., Cuba Discuss Immigration Pact," *Washington Post,* December 13, 1999; "Castro Vows to Halt New Exodus by Sea," *Financial Times of London,* August 5, 1999.

32. The Elián González case attracted more media attention than any other recent event or crisis in the long Cuba-U.S. conflict. During the seven months that it took to finally settle the case, thousands of articles, editorials, opinions, and photographs were published in newspapers and magazines throughout the United States. For details about the case and the political confrontation between Cuba and the United States, see, among others, *Miami Herald, El Nuevo Herald, New York Times, Washington Post, Chicago Tribune, Time,* and *Newsweek,* from November 25, 1999, to July 30, 2000.

33. Elián González finally returned with his father to Cuba on June 28, 2000. According to witness reports, he is living a normal life after having adjusted well to his family and to being back in his hometown, Cárdenas, Matanzas province. In November 2001, Manny Diaz, the attorney representing Elián's Miami relatives and a central figure in the legal custody battle, was elected mayor of Miami, thanks to his "lock on the decisive Cuban-American vote for the run-off election." The losing candidate, former Miami mayor Maurice Ferre, who is Puerto Rican, "accused his opponent of spreading a rumor in the Little Havana section that he supported Janet Reno, the Democratic candidate for governor who has been vilified among many Cuban-Americans for ordering the raid that returned Elián to his Cuban father while she was attorney general in the Clinton administration." "Lawyer for Cuban boy's relatives is elected Miami mayor; Cuban-Americans' vote proves decisive." *New York Times,* November 14, 2001. (Editor's note.)

VIII

International Relations

15

Policy Changes and New Objectives in World Relations

H. Michael Erisman

The interplay between continuity and change has long fascinated those who chronicle the human condition. Often the latter consideration receives primary attention, if for no other reason than that the challenges implicit in confronting the unknown tend to be seen as much more dramatic and hence much more interesting than business as usual. It should, therefore, hardly be surprising that the landscape surveyed by political analysts is littered with references to new deals, new frontiers, and new international orders. Recently this tendency has been especially evident among Cuba specialists, for the winds of change have been swirling around the island with near-hurricane force over the past decade.

Although all facets of the revolution have been affected by this maelstrom, the impact has probably been greatest with respect to its external affairs, where the disintegration of the Socialist bloc destroyed the central pillar of the country's foreign policy and thereby presented Havana with the daunting task of radically reconfiguring its network of international relations (particularly with respect to trade and related economic concerns).

Yet no matter how spectacular any changes may be, the basic rule of thumb is that elements of continuity will remain part of the scene and cannot be overlooked if one wishes to have a truly accurate picture of the overall situation. Or, to put it in historians' terms, the present is always to some degree a product of the past. This cautionary note holds true with respect to contemporary Cuban foreign relations, for juxtaposed against the restructuring that has taken place are certain important elements of the policy equation that have persisted over time. Specifically, revolutionary Havana has *always* defined its role on the world stage in terms of promoting and protecting three national attributes: effective sovereignty, economic security, and international stature.

Effective Sovereignty

Many observers, particularly those who are influenced by the Realist school of thought, are not very optimistic about the prospects for small countries to be able to control their own destinies. Instead, the tendency is to see such states as victims of global power differentials whose weaknesses often result in their incorporation into some other country or region's sphere of influence.

William Demas, president of the Caribbean Development Bank, eloquently summarized such sentiments when he noted:

> Many people in the [Caribbean] region . . . hold pessimistic and deterministic positions regarding our prospects for any degree of *effective* independence vis-à-vis the outside world. They believe that we are doomed to abject subordination because of our small and in some cases minuscule size, and because of our long colonial history as mere political, economic, military, and cultural appendages of the metropolitan countries. They consider that we . . . [are] impotent, unable to control our destiny, . . . and inevitably subject to the decisions, and indeed the whims, of outside countries.[1]

Demas is suggesting the very important need to distinguish clearly between *formal* sovereignty and *effective* sovereignty. The former is in many respects symbolic, involving such things as admission to the United Nations and other similar badges of acceptance into the international community. Effective sovereignty, on the other hand, refers to circumstances wherein a country and its people truly control their own destinies; they are, in other words, exercising their right of national self-determination to the greatest extent possible.

The architects of the Cuban Revolution, acutely aware of the island's tragic history of encounters with imperial Spain and a hegemonically inclined United States, have enthusiastically embraced the proposition that their highest priority must be to maximize their country's effective sovereignty. Indeed this pursuit represents the leitmotif underlying much of Havana's foreign policy; it long has been and remains probably the single most important consideration influencing the dynamics of the revolution's international relations.

Economic Security

Economic security, like many other general concepts, has been defined in various ways. One common approach is to conceive it in terms of the progress that occurs within a society toward higher levels of industrialization and modernization.

But for smaller, lesser-developed countries, defending against potential external economic threats is often the most important dimension of the economic-security issue. Applied to Cuba's foreign policies, such concerns have translated into efforts to configure the island's relations in such a manner as to minimize its vulnerability to hostile economic penetration or economic sanctions. In particular, Havana has sought to use its international ties as a buffer against the economic warfare that Washington, using such tools as the trade embargo and the Helms-Burton law, has long waged against the Fidelistas.

International Stature

Most revolutionary experiments are messianic to some degree, if for no other reason than their supporters often tend to see their actions as having a relevance or a mission that goes beyond the borders of the societies from which they emerged.

In this respect, the Fidelistas have not been markedly different from other rebels who have managed to triumph against tremendous odds, for they also have aspired to carve out a special niche on the world stage for their movement. Many critics have, of course, expressed serious reservations about such ambitions, considering that Cuba, a small country with a population of only eleven-plus million people and very limited natural resources, simply cannot realistically hope to exert any significant influence in international affairs. A contrary view was, however, expressed at one point by Jorge Domínguez, a specialist on the revolution, who was widely quoted when he observed that "Cuba is a small country, but it has a big country's foreign policy. It has tried to carry out such a policy since the beginning of the revolution, but only in the second half of the 1970s did it have conditions . . . to become a visible and important actor actually shaping the course of events."[2]

Even if one does not agree with Domínguez's conclusions, the record demonstrates that he is correct in suggesting that revolutionary Cuba, in stark contrast to many small countries that (reluctantly) accept their fate as pawns in world affairs, has long harbored aspirations to play a significant, proactive role in the great game of nations.

From a broad conceptual perspective, then, Cuba's foreign relations can be understood in terms of the various strategies that Havana has employed in its efforts to guarantee the integrity of these three key national attributes.

In other words, the pursuit of these goals, which in practice are often mutually reinforcing, represents a constant within the revolution's foreign policy equation, while the methods used to try to secure them have often had to be adjusted to developments in the larger global environment. Accordingly, while admittedly simplifying the situation somewhat, the changing nature of this ends/means interplay will be characterized here in terms of two broad configurations—classical Fidelismo and neo-Fidelismo—associated with the two international systemic structures—cold war bipolarism and the post-Soviet transition—within which the revolution has operated. In the following discussion of each paradigm, primary attention will be devoted to neo-Fidelismo since it represents the international dimension of the contemporary survival and renewal process being examined in this book.

The Cold War and Classical Fidelismo

Ironically, by the early 1970s the cold war tensions that had spawned serious threats to the Fidelistas' security had likewise engendered an international environment within which Havana was able to implement a sophisticated grand strategy that capitalized on its special ties with the USSR and the Eastern European Socialist nations in order to promote its three core foreign policy goals.[3] The key contributions that this highly lucrative Soviet bloc connection made to Havana's international agenda can be summarized as follows:

> The Soviet connection provided the revolution with a sense of military security that had been sorely lacking in the more turbulent 1960s. Although Cuba never became a formal member of the Warsaw Pact (the Soviet mutual defense alliance that functioned as the Kremlin's response to the West's NATO treaty), the island nevertheless was widely considered to be covered by the pact's deterrent umbrella. Moreover, the massive amounts of military aid from the Socialist bloc transformed the Cuban armed forces into a highly formidable organization that even the Pentagon was not anxious to confront.[4] As such, Havana was able to jettison its prior obsession with the possibility of a U.S. attack and turn its foreign policy attention to other concerns.
>
> The Soviet connection gave Cuba assured access to a broad menu of socioeconomic aid programs that allowed it to achieve levels of development comparable in some respects to those of the most modernized nations. The main vehicle for such assistance was the Council of Mutual Economic Assistance (CMEA), which Havana joined in 1972

and which functioned as the Soviet bloc's rough equivalent of the European Economic Community.

A crucial security aspect of these ties was that they significantly reduced Cuba's exposure to the economic warfare that the United States was trying to wage against the revolution, thereby allowing Havana to concentrate on developing its own distinctive role on the global stage rather than (as had previously been the case) being obsessed with responding to Washington's hostility; it enhanced the resources, both human and material, upon which rested the Fidelistas' capability to pursue an extremely audacious global agenda, particularly in the realm of third-world affairs. In other words, Havana could be more ambitious in terms of its international activities because it now had the power necessary to operate on a much broader scale.

In effect, then, Cuba was tapping Eastern European resources to bolster its security, stabilize its economy, and modernize its armed forces, and thereby put itself in a position where it could begin to explore foreign policy options that heretofore had not been high on its priority list.

The most sensational of these initiatives saw Havana seeking to interject a much more vigorous South-South dimension into the overall fabric of its international relations by widening and strengthening its ties with other developing countries. For example, a major Cuban effort to reconnect with its Latin American and Caribbean neighbors ultimately generated sentiment to lift the sanctions imposed on Castro's government by the Organization of American States (OAS) in 1964. It was, however, in sub-Saharan Africa where Cuba registered its most spectacular gains by instituting numerous developmental as well as security assistance programs and by deploying thousands of combat troops that were decisive in winning two wars (in Angola, 1975–76, and, cooperating closely with the USSR, in Ethiopia, 1977–78). Havana also assumed a dramatically higher profile in the Nonaligned Movement, the pinnacle of its rise coming in 1979 when Fidel Castro succeeded Sri Lanka's president as the sixth head of state to lead the organization.

During the 1970s and much of the 1980s, the combination of these two elements—establishing a highly lucrative economic coalition with Eastern Europe that also included large infusions of military aid and expanding significantly its relations with developing nations throughout the Southern Hemisphere in an effort to bolster its third-world leadership aspirations—was the defining hallmark of Cuba's foreign policy. To some extent these two areas of activity were geared to servicing distinct interests. The Soviet bloc connection, for instance, addressed such basic concerns as political security and economic viability, while the South-South campaign was geared toward enhancing the revolution's international stature. It was, however, the mutually supportive fusion of these various threads into an impressive strategic package that was the key to the success of classical Fidelismo's approach to international affairs. For almost two decades the Cubans performed brilliantly in managing the dynamics of their Soviet connection in a manner that furthered the revolution's vital foreign policy interests. Cuba established a special and highly beneficial relationship with the Kremlin that enhanced the nation's effective sovereignty by generating an extremely high degree of security (both economic and political) and creating conditions whereby the island's international stature would rise to unprecedented heights. Ultimately, however, this edifice came crashing down when the USSR and the Soviet bloc disintegrated in the early 1990s. In its place emerged Havana's response to the exigencies of the new world order—neo-Fidelismo.

The Post-Soviet World and Neo-Fidelismo

In contrast to the more unitary nature of classical Fidelismo, wherein practically all threads in Cuba's cold war web of international relations were anchored in Havana's Soviet bloc connection, neo-Fidelismo represents a more segmented approach that relies upon two distinct (or disaggregated) strategies as the vehicles to pursue Cuba's core foreign policy goals. The first strategy, trade restructuring, promotes economic security, while the second strategy, neo-Bolívarianism (which admittedly entails some developmental-cooperation dimensions), centers on enhancing the revolution's international stature and influence. To the extent that there is success in these two endeavors, the island's effective sovereignty should be enhanced.

Circumstance rather than choice forced radical reconfiguration of Cuba's economic relations, particularly its trade networks, to the top of Havana's international agenda in the early 1990s. The catalyst for this process was, of course, the turmoil that was engulfing the USSR and Eastern Europe. One major casualty of the chaos was CMEA, which was disbanded in June 1991, and with it went the privileged trade regime and developmental-aid packages that had long provided Cuba with a high degree of economic security.

Such a disruption in the increasingly interdependent modern world would be a matter of serious concern for practically any government, but it represented a disaster of epic proportions for Cuba, an island country

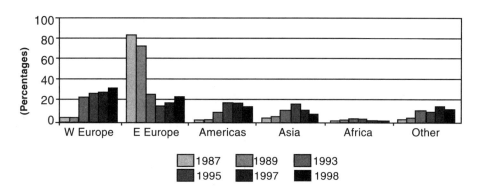

Fig. 15.1. Cuban export profile. Data from selected editions of U.S. Central Intelligence Agency, *Cuba: Handbook of Trade Statistics* (Springfield, Va.: National Technical Information Service).

whose economic health tends to be heavily reliant on foreign trade. Making the situation even more precarious, of course, was Washington's eagerness to intensify the crisis in yet another effort to drive a dagger through the Fidelistas' political heart. This gloomy scenario led many observers to conclude that the revolution was finished—it would follow its Eastern European compatriots into oblivion. Such dire predictions proved, of course, to be false, one major contributing factor being Havana's ability to radically restructure its shattered web of international economic relations. Supporting the campaign to expand its trade and related ties were such major initiatives as a drive to develop new export product lines (for example in the biotechnology field) and efforts to attract foreign investors by further liberalizing the laws governing joint ventures on the island.

A global overview of Cuba's export/import activity covering both the late cold war and the post-Soviet periods is presented in figures 15.1 and 15.2, which indicate the percentage of the island's total exports going to various regions and the percentage of total imports coming from those same areas (a number that is sometimes referred to here as market share). Admittedly the data is often less complete than one might prefer.[5] Nevertheless, the general trends that emerge provide a good outline of Havana's evolving trade partner priorities as it has attempted to respond to the exigencies of a new international economic order.

Looking first at transformations that have occurred in the island's export profile, figure 15.1 shows that by 1995 Western Europe had rather handily surpassed Eastern Europe as the world's main destination for Cuban goods

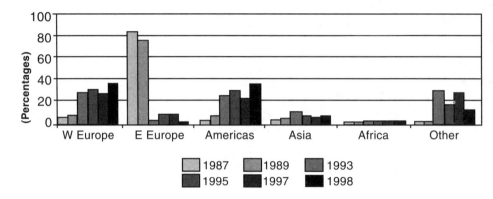

Fig. 15.2. Cuban import profile. Data from selected editions of U.S. Central Intelligence Agency, *Cuba: Handbook of Trade Statistics* (Springfield, Va.: National Technical Information Service).

and services (29 percent versus 17 percent) and would maintain that position for the rest of the decade.[6] The status of the Americas (which includes Canada) has vacillated somewhat in recent years, moving into the number two slot in 1995 and then subsequently losing ground to a resurgent Eastern Europe.[7] A somewhat different picture emerges, however, if one takes a longer-term perspective. For example, a comparison of 1987 and 1998 market shares reveals that the Americas had expanded their position by 475 percent in the post-Soviet period while trade with Eastern Europe had shrunk by 65 percent.

The broad contours of the island's evolving import situation parallel in many respects its general export patterns, the major exception in terms of regional categories being Eastern Europe's much weaker position relative to Western Europe and the Americas (see figure 15.2). Indeed, if the time frame is again extended back to 1987, the status of CMEA and Eastern Europe as a source of Cuban imports plummets from an 85.8 percent market share in 1989 to a 3.5 percent share in 1998 (a 95.9 percent decline). In short, the numbers confirm what even the most casual observer could have predicted—that as a result of CMEA's demise and with it the trade preferences that Havana enjoyed (discount prices, lucrative barter deals, and so on), Eastern Europe would pale into relative obscurity on the revolution's import profile.

Overall, then, the post-Soviet data clearly demonstrate that Havana has been quite successful in its efforts not only to restructure its trade and related ties but also to interject into Cuba's basic fabric an important element

Table 15.1. Destination of Cuban exports, 1992–98 (in millions of U.S. dollars)

	1992	1993	1994	1995	1996	1997	1998
Europe							
France	44	39	44	57	50	48	53
Germany	21	14	25	31	22	26	25
Italy	51	33	50	54	38	19	13
Netherlands	131	89	101	172	230	264	253
Spain	85	65	78	96	132	123	134
United Kingdom	23	13	16	13	30	25	26
Americas							
Canada	212	133	143	234	294	255	220
Argentina	2	2	48	7	8	4	7
Brazil	16	10	57	40	32	22	7
Colombia	3	3	14	23	21	28	19
Mexico	7	4	12	6	23	36	28
Venezuela	20	3	5	2	2	5	2

Sources: Compiled from U.S. Central Intelligence Agency, *Cuba: Handbook of Trade Statistics* (Springfield, Va.: National Technical Information Service, 1998 and 1999).

of diversification. Gone is the near-monopolistic position, rooted in the revolution's membership in CMEA, that Eastern Europe once occupied. In its stead has emerged a much more complex web of economic relations, with the most important and multifaceted new threads radiating out to Western Europe and the Americas where in both cases Havana has developed a fairly varied menu of trading partners (see tables 15.1 and 15.2 for a listing of some of the main countries involved in each region). However, while such achievements can generally be seen as having a positive impact on the island's quest for greater economic security, they contribute little, at least in a direct fashion, to the revolution's international stature and influence. Instead, this latter dimension of post-Soviet foreign policy has played itself out primarily in terms of Havana's efforts to encourage its hemispheric neighbors to embrace an alternative to Washington's proposed conceptualization of the nature and dynamics of the economic-integration process in Latin America. Stripped to its bare essentials, the Cuba-U.S. rivalry here centers upon the competing paradigms of neo-Pan-Americanism and neo-Bolívarianism.

Neo-Pan-Americanism, which Washington champions, revolves around the notion of implementing an economic manifestation of the classical Pan-American ideal of hemispheric cooperation with respect to political and security questions. The OAS was created in 1948 to facilitate and orches-

Table 15.2. Sources of Cuban imports, 1992–98 (in millions of U.S. dollars)

	1992	1993	1994	1995	1996	1997	1998
Europe							
France	90	127	133	148	193	216	259
Germany	59	40	41	70	70	57	76
Italy	104	64	63	81	114	122	192
Netherlands	42	55	50	71	54	50	33
Spain	199	191	289	396	465	474	549
United Kingdom	50	21	40	30	38	32	56
Americas							
Canada	98	108	84	200	197	260	308
Argentina	63	72	48	65	125	114	70
Brazil	17	19	25	42	43	50	60
Chile	4	5	15	18	18	17	17
Colombia	14	20	35	18	22	19	22
Mexico	117	188	269	394	369	327	250
Trinidad/Tobago	12	9	7	20	26	23	14
Venezuela	79	120	90	112	119	21	433*

Sources: Compiled from U.S. Central Intelligence Agency, *Cuba: Handbook of Trade Statistics* (Springfield, Va.: National Technical Information Service, 1998 and 1999).
*This dramatic spike in Cuban imports was probably related to the emergence of Hugo Chávez as the new power in Venezuelan politics (he easily won the presidential elections in 1998 and 2000) and his interest in extending trade preferences to Havana.

trate this more traditional view of collaboration. Like its predecessor, neo-Pan-Americanism implies participation by and, at least from Washington's perspective, a leadership role for the United States.

Inextricably linked to this vision is Washington's desire to convert the entire hemisphere to a neoliberal economic system. The five main points of the "neoliberal consensus," according to Elizabeth Martinez and Arnoldo Garcia, are (1) the rule of the market, which calls for liberating private enterprise from any bonds imposed by the government and for total freedom of movement for capital, goods, and services; (2) cuts in public expenditures for social services; (3) deregulation; (4) privatization of (i.e., selling off) state-owned enterprises and services such as banks, airlines, and power plants to private investors (local or foreign); and (5) elimination of the concept of "the public good" or "community," replacing it with a regimen of "individual responsibility."[8] Many Latin Americans are skeptical about this scenario, doubting that their individual countries will be able to fare very well in what appears to be a no-holds-barred competition with one of the world's greatest centers of economic power. The most vociferous critics, with the Cubans at the forefront, see this blueprint as little more than a formula for the United States to reestablish tight economic hegemony over the region and thereby drive the hemispheric nations back into counter-developmental dependency relationships with Washington.

In the context of the early twenty-first century, the Free Trade Area of the Americas (FTAA) project embraced by both Bush administrations as well as by President Clinton has been widely seen throughout the hemisphere as the organizational framework within which the United States hopes to put into place its reformulated neoliberal version of Pan-Americanism.

Neo-Bolívarianism, on the other hand, represents the Hispanic (and Anglophone Caribbean) alternative to a landscape dominated by the United States. The key idea here is that any contemporary developmental-cooperation schemes launched by hemispheric states should be modeled along the lines of Simón Bolívar's vision of a politically unified Latin America that would be clearly separate from and independent of the colossus to its north. As such, this approach rejects, at least for the time being, any significant involvement in the process by Washington. Instead, it sees the whole enterprise unfolding under Latin American (rather than U.S.) leadership, the ultimate goal being to achieve a level of integration that would put the hemispheric community (defined as South America and the Caribbean Basin countries) in a position where its pooled economic power would be sufficient to counterbalance that of the United States.

Cuba's position with regard to these two models has been and remains unequivocal—it seeks to function as a catalyst for the development of neo-Bolívarianism and as a facilitator of progress toward achieving its integrative agenda. Havana's commitment to this path stems not only from its affinity with the concept of a viable, independent Latin American community on the larger international stage within which the revolution would be a major participant; it is also grounded in the fact that neo-Bolívarianism is highly compatible with the Fidelistas' policy of strengthening both their political and their economic ties with a wide range of Latin American and Caribbean countries.

Although Havana launched some neo-Bolívarian initiatives during the cold war's heyday, such endeavors have accelerated and especially have become more ambitious in the post-Soviet era. In November 1998, for example, the island was admitted to ALADI (the Latin American Integration Association), which aspires to become a free-trade federation at some time in the future.[9] Currently, however, the organization is concentrating on the more modest goal of encouraging limited commercial and related agreements among its members with the hope that this foundation will serve as the basis for a comprehensive free trade accord at some undefined future point.

Recently Cuba has also intensified the efforts that it had been making throughout the 1990s to improve its relations with CARICOM (the Caribbean Community and Common Market), a fifteen-member regional-integration group serving primarily (but not solely) the English-speaking islands of the West Indies. The high point of this campaign came in August 1998 when the CARICOM countries included Havana in the vehicle that they were using (called CariForum) to represent their interests in negotiations to update their collective trade and aid agreement with the European Union. But despite such collaboration and an impressive expansion of economic relations, Cuba has yet to take the ultimate step to full CARICOM membership.

The newest organization to attract Havana's attention has been the Association of Caribbean States (ACS), which was inaugurated in Cartagena, Colombia, on July 24, 1994, with Cuba as a charter participant. ACS has twenty-five members that (by the late 1990s/early 2000s) have an overall population of 210 million people, a combined gross domestic product of approximately $500 billion, and a total annual trade volume of roughly $140 billion.[10] The basic objectives of the ACS, which have a distinct neo-Bolívarian quality to them, have been summarized by the writer Andrés Serbin as follows:

> To maximize regional trade and to promote the economies of scale needed to achieve insertion into the international economic system through trade liberalization; to optimize bargaining power with third parties (given the area's post–cold war decline in strategic importance) through the forging of tightly focused regional alliances based on identification of common (primarily geoeconomic) interests; and to move toward various forms of cooperation (and eventual integration) by forging consensus on matters of mutual interest and consolidating a regional identity, based on shared cultural and social traits, that will overcome existing divisions and heterogeneity and benefit the population of the entire region.[11]

Among the various neo-Bolívarian initiatives that it could pursue within this ACS framework, Havana seems to have become increasingly attracted to the idea of serving as a broker for greater cooperation between the ACS and the better-established MERCOSUR (Southern Cone Common Market) group. Considered by many to have the potential to be a regional integrative powerhouse due to the already considerable economic strength of some of the countries involved, MERCOSUR was founded in 1991 with Argentina, Brazil, Paraguay, and Uruguay as its full-fledged participants. Bolivia and

Table 15.3. Evolution of intra-MERCOSUR trade (in billions of U.S. dollars)

Years	1985	1990	1991	1992	1993	1994	1995	1996	1997	1998
Commerce	1,953	4,127	5,103	7,215	10,028	12,049	14,452	17,043	20,478	20,373

Source: ALADI Secretariat.

Chile hold associate membership. Certainly progress of any kind toward increased ACS/MERCOSUR collaboration would be extremely gratifying for the Cubans.[12] But the ultimate prize—midwifing a merger of the two organizations—would represent a triumph of unprecedented proportions for Havana's post-Soviet Latin American policy.

The hurdles confronting such a brokerage effort seem, however, to be quite daunting. For example, MERCOSUR has been not only very determined but also very successful in its endeavors to entice its participants to give top priority to intraorganizational trade (see table 15.3, which indicates that commerce among MERCOSUR members has increased almost 300 percent since the group was established).

Investigating the implications, both national and international, of such practices for the World Bank, Alexander Yeats concluded:

> The findings of this study appear to constitute convincing evidence that regional preferences can affect trading patterns strongly and detrimentally for . . . nonmember countries. . . . Domestic producers reoriented exports to local markets, presumably in order to charge the higher prices associated with the most restrictive trade barriers. This reduced the potential exports of third countries to Mercosur.[13]

Certainly these exclusionary propensities seem to be evident in Cuba's trade with MERCOSUR. Havana has normally run a trade deficit with the countries involved, but in recent years its exports to them have been dropping precipitously, down 86.5 percent from 1994 to 1998, and down 71.2 percent from 1995 to 1998 (see table 15.4). This decline becomes even more dramatic when considered in terms of MERCOSUR's status within the overall Latin American and Caribbean community as a consumer of the island's goods and services (see figure 15.3, which illustrates the declining percentage of Cuba's Latin American and Caribbean exports going to MERCOSUR). What these data seem to indicate, then, is that the MERCOSUR countries have been (increasingly) restricting Havana's access to their domestic markets while simultaneously being quite willing to take advantage of the island's post-Soviet reconfiguration of its trade patterns—see figure 15.4, which shows that MERCOSUR has been capturing a

Table 15.4. Cuban trade with MERCOSUR (in millions of U.S. dollars)

Year	1985	1991	1992	1993	1994	1995	1996	1997	1998
Exports to MERCOSUR	4	29	20	12	111	52	41	26	15
Imports from MERCOSUR	211	176	81	92	73	107	168	165	134
Trade balance									
Deficit	210.6	147	61	80		55	127	139	119
Surplus					38				

Source: Compiled from U.S. Central Intelligence Agency, *Cuba: Handbook of Trade Statistics* (Springfield, Va.: National Technical Information Service, 1998 and 1999).

steadily larger share of the island's growing imports from Latin America. In short, Cuba has apparently suffered from the broader protectionist tendencies that Yeats uncovered in his MERCOSUR study, tendencies that do not bode well for greater cooperation and integration between MERCOSUR and other hemispheric groups.

But perhaps the greatest obstacle threatening Havana's desire to nurture closer ACS/MERCOSUR ties lies in the fact that the ACS did not seem to be demonstrating any significant viability as the new millennium dawned. Many observers were not particularly surprised by this turn of events, noting that the two main regional groups within the ACS—the West Indian islands and the mainland Hispanic states—have never displayed much capacity for sustained cooperation. Such institutional lethargy was put vividly on display in September 2000 at a major ACS meeting convened in Port-of-Spain, Trinidad, to assess its performance, to make any necessary revisions in its long-term strategic vision, and to set some concrete cooperative goals that could be met in the near future. Participation was lackluster; only fourteen of the twenty-five members attended, with host Trinidad being the only CARICOM country present. Whether this development was just an anomaly or an indication that West Indian countries have essentially given up on the ACS remains to be seen.

In any case, Cuba remains strongly committed to the neo-Bolívarian ideal. Hence Havana can be expected to accord high priority on its future hemispheric agenda to initiatives seeking to transform the concept into political and economic reality. Such ambitions will, of course, encounter strong opposition from the United States, but the potential for confrontation with Washington has never deterred the Fidelistas in the past and is unlikely to do so in this instance.

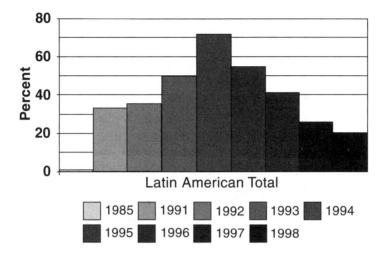

Fig. 15.3. Cuban exports to MERCOSUR. Data from selected editions of U.S. Central Intelligence Agency, *Cuba: Handbook Of Trade Statistics* (Springfield, Va.: National Technical Information Service).

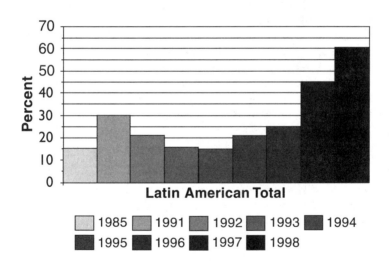

Fig. 15.4. Cuban imports from MERCOSUR. Data from selected editions of U.S. Central Intelligence Agency, *Cuba: Handbook Of Trade Statistics* (Springfield, Va.: National Technical Information Service).

Notes

1. William Demas, *Consolidating Our Independence: The Major Challenge for the West Indies* (Distinguished Lecture Series, Institute of International Relations, University of the West Indies, St. Augustine, Republic of Trinidad and Tobago, 1986), 12.

2. Jorge Domínguez, "Cuban Foreign Policy," *Foreign Affairs*, no. 57 (fall 1978): 83.

3. This section draws heavily upon material that is developed more fully in H. Michael Erisman, *Cuba's Foreign Relations in a Post-Soviet World* (Gainesville: University Press of Florida, 2000), chapter 4, and sometimes incorporates text verbatim from that source.

4. Cuba enjoyed special status with regard to Soviet security aid when compared to Moscow's allies who were members of the Warsaw Pact. Normally the Eastern European states were expected to at least partially reimburse the Kremlin for the equipment and other types of military assistance that they received. Cuba, on the other hand, paid nothing; the arms, the logistical supplies, the training, the advisory services, and so on were all provided free of charge by the USSR.

5. Such problems are exemplified by what appears to be the sometimes excessive appearance of numbers consigned to the "Other" category in the charts provided here. The basic rule of thumb seems to be that it takes some time to process Cuban trade data to determine exactly where particular pieces of information (temporarily warehoused in the "Other" category) belong in the overall classification scheme. Thus, over time the "Other" category shrinks to more reasonable proportions. For example, in comparable statistics from the 1980s, "Other" normally represents only about 1 percent of the total and never exceeds 6 percent (as opposed to the 15–20 percent—and even higher—numbers that often appear in the 1990s tables). While it may be necessary to use this designation as a temporary classification for some incomplete findings due to problems in the reporting process, the practice may very well distort the total picture for a while until the ambiguities are resolved and the information is then moved to its proper station.

6. Actually Western Europe moved to the forefront in 1994 by the fairly slim margin of 27.5 percent, compared to 23.4 percent for Eastern Europe. But in 1995 its lead increased to double digits and has generally remained close to that range for the rest of the 1990s (the specific percentages for 1997 were 30.1 percent for Western Europe and 20.2 percent for Eastern Europe, and in 1998, 33.0 percent for Western Europe and 25.8 percent for Eastern Europe).

7. The specific percentages were:

	1995	1997	1998
Eastern Europe	16.8	20.2	25.8
The Americas	20.6	19.5	17.0

8. See Elizabeth Martinez and Arnoldo Garcia, "What Is 'Neo-Liberalism?: A Definition for Activists," at www.igc.org/neolib.htm (on line). For another good summary of neoliberalism, see David N. Balaam and Michael Veseth, *Introduction*

to International Political Economy, 2nd ed. (Upper Saddle River, N.J.: Prentice-Hall, 2001), 333.

9. For details about Cuba's entry to ALADI, see the Inter Press Service's story from Havana, "Trade—Cuba: Admission to ALADI boosts ties with region," CNN (on line), November 9, 1998. See also "Cuba New Member of Latin Trading Bloc," *CUBAInfo* 10, no. 15 (November 16, 1998): 5. Havana's entry as ALADI's twelfth full member was officially validated in mid-August 1999 after a study concluded that the island's economy was sufficiently open to allow it to be incorporated into a free-market system such as ALADI—see *CUBAInfo* 11, no. 10 (August 4, 1999): 7.

10. The twenty-five full members of the ACS are Colombia, Costa Rica, Cuba, the Dominican Republic, El Salvador, Guatemala, Honduras, Nicaragua, Panama, Mexico, and Venezuela, plus fourteen of the fifteen CARICOM countries (Montserrat, a member of CARICOM, is not included because it is not independent). The associate members are Aruba, the Netherlands Antilles, and France (on behalf of French Guiana, Guadeloupe, and Martinique).

11. This list comes from Andrés Serbín, "Towards An Association of Caribbean States: Raising Some Awkward Questions," *Journal Of Interamerican Studies and World Affairs* 36, no. 4 (winter 1994): 64.

12. In early November 1999 the author participated in an international academic conference held at the Universidade Estadual Paulista in Araraquara, Brazil (November 3–5, 1999), dealing with the topic "Inter-American Relations: Continuities and Change on the Verge of a New Millennium." Various members of the Cuban delegation indicated, both privately and within the public context of the conference, that Havana supported the neo-Bolívarian concept in general, and specifically they were hoping that a much higher level of ACS/MERCOSUR collaboration would be forthcoming in the near future.

13. Alexander J. Yeats, "Does Mercosur's Trade Performance Raise Concerns about the Effects of Regional Trade Arrangements?" *World Bank Economic Review* 12, no. 1 (January 1998): 25.

16

The Cuba-U.S. Conflict in a New Century

Esteban Morales Domínguez

This chapter discusses some of the theoretical and methodological approaches used to study Cuba-U.S. relations. Using familiar macro- and microvariables, the focal points of three interrelated scenarios are examined: internal Cuban reality, internal U.S. reality, and international reality. The study's analytical value increases as we move from macroanalyses to microanalyses, examining the possible scenarios as well as the processes involved in the bilateral discord that has endured for more than forty years.

Scenarios and Variables

Cuban studies dealing with the Cuba-U.S. conflict emphasize almost exclusively U.S. policy toward Cuba and how that policy is formulated, executed, or adjusted. Scholars seem to overlook the fact that troubled Havana-Washington relations involve two active parties. Hence, I examine here the role Cuba plays, without overlooking the United States within the conflictive relationship. I move this way into a level of analysis in which Cuba, in spite of being treated as a political object, plays an active role.

Methodologically, I interrelate a foreign policy analysis in which Cuba is a constant in a bilateral relation, and an analysis of the points at which the two countries interact. Such treatment is largely justified by the changes in Cuba-U.S. relations since the second half of the 1980s. Although these revisions do not entail a significant change in the Cuban policy of the United States, they have caused important variations within the boundaries of that policy.

For over forty years U.S. policy toward Cuba has essentially remained unchanged—it was and continues to be based on aggression. The world stage (as well as the hemispheric and regional arenas) where the bilateral conflict is acted out has changed, leading to new situations that create new scenarios. The majority of political observers, both in Cuba and abroad, concentrate on moments of crisis, losing sight of trends that allow a better understanding of the subtle, underlying issues.

Thus, rather than prioritizing the critical features that typify the Cuba-U.S. conflict, I present an analytical model for a conflict that has really lasted about two hundred years, while giving Cuba its corresponding place as an active object.

The United States, since the end of the 1980s, has maintained economic growth (which slowed noticeably starting in 2001), and has extended its world hegemony as probably never before—as demonstrated in the 2003 Iraq war.[1] For its part, Cuba has experienced the most difficult economic crisis of its revolutionary period, a situation that has improved slowly without yet reaching a necessary stability.[2] Still, growth rates in the gross national product (GNP), such as the high 6 percent attained during the first half of 1999, attest to an ongoing process of economic recovery.

Both situations are the result of the asymmetric impact that the collapse of the Socialist camp and the Soviet Union had on Cuba and the United States. The events that flowed from that collapse continue to influence both countries, although they have affected Cuba's internal and international contexts more intensely. Havana lost not only its main economic allies but also the political and ideological pillars for its Socialist building process. The legitimacy and fortitude of the Cuban Revolution have been amply demonstrated during these years of resistance and difficult economic recovery. Conditions have tended to improve since Cuba began to overcome the crisis of 1989–94, but the economy was seriously harmed by the 1996 Helms-Burton law, which intensified the international economic pressures of the U.S. economic blockade. And yet, this law has failed to paralyze economic growth and the island's process of international trade reintegration.

The Bilateral Conflict's Variables

There are six long-term, fundamental macrovariables of the model in the context of the conflict beginning with the events of the 1986–96 period, and beyond:

- the internal Cuban situation,
- congressional power relations and the U.S. Cuba policy,
- internationalization of the economic blockade,
- international resistance to the internationalization of the blockade,

- failure of the search for international political consensus to subvert Cuba,
- the attitude of the U.S. executive branch toward the Cuba policy of the United States (a conjunctural variable).

There is also a seventh variable represented by certain U.S. sectors and their heterogeneous economic interests in Cuba. This group has become in practice an antiblockade lobby, since the blockade is the main obstacle to normalizing economic and trade relations with Havana.

Now let us examine these macrolevel variables by looking into the specific arenas where the conflict has been and is still enacted at the micro- and midlevels of political and social interactions.

The Internal Cuban Situation

Once the most pressing difficulties of the Cuban economy during the period 1989–94 started to subside with minor GNP growth in 1995, the economic impact of the Soviet collapse could be broken down into a small set of intimately related elements: the dynamics of economic recuperation, the development of economic reforms, and the social and political impact of the new economic policies.

The stratification implicit in the initial macrovariables is valid, for there is a close relationship among the necessity to maintain economic recuperation, the measures needed for economic reform, the impact of these measures, and the evolving social and political (ideological) situation in Cuba. The regime sought to avoid any more shock therapy than that which the population had experienced in the initial years of deprivation caused by the collapse of the Soviet economy. The government drastically reduced its own size, taking such steps as reducing the number of civilian functionaries and armed forces and decreasing purchases of gasoline and consumer items used by workplaces.

The government strategy was successful to the extent that, in spite of the critical situation, the revolution survived, and the political leadership managed to safeguard its political project while maintaining its capacity to lead. Nevertheless, the government was not able to avoid certain social inequalities and social problems such as prostitution and corruption at various levels. In addition, a negative correlation among labor capacity, employment, and income affected the ability to manage the economy. This led to intense efforts to maintain the workforce, particularly the most qualified workers, in the positions most needed by the country: industry, agriculture, basic services, education, and public health. Although tourism, foreign investment, and the legalization of transactions in foreign currency impacted dynamically on the economic crisis, at the same time these activities competed with the rest of the economy, especially those parts that did not operate within the new schemes. Thus, it was imperative to take the necessary measures to undo the negative conditions present in the internal economy.

The economic challenge seriously threatened the distribution, stability, and renovation of the country's qualified labor force. It also encouraged families to search for added income, and it promoted emigration. Dual forms of income and growing inequalities decreased the incentive to work and even promoted criminal behavior. Such situations brought into play social, political, and ideological contradictions that undermined the Socialist project. These were the kinds of situations the Cuba policy of the United States sought to encourage for their potential for inciting an overthrow of the political leadership and the Socialist system.

Congress, Other Political Actors, and U.S. Cuba Policy

The United States Congress has been the center of debate of U.S. Cuba policy since Helms-Burton became law, precisely because under this law only Congress can make any significant policy change (as the Republican-dominated House tried to do in 2002, but without follow-through from the Senate). The power of Congress to affect U.S. policy toward Cuba derives less from its constitutional power than from the prerogatives that President Clinton granted to the legislative branch when, in the midst of the 1996 electoral campaign, he signed the Helms-Burton law.

In addition to Congress, there are other actors within the U.S. government and within the political system in general that aim to secure their participation in the debate. Additionally, the influence of nongovernmental organizations should not be underestimated.

On the governmental front, the Drug Enforcement Administration, the United States Information Agency, and the Defense Department are among the best known actors representing perspectives that separate them from the aggressive stand of extreme conservatives.

On the nongovernmental front are found extreme conservative and right-of-center organizations within the Cuban community. Foremost among these is the conservative Cuban American National Foundation (CANF). Many other nongovernmental organizations maintain an interest in Cuban affairs:

- Academic and cultural organizations interested in U.S. policy toward Cuba;

- Organizations such as the Chamber of Commerce and other business groups (especially farm interests);
- The media, including newspapers like the *New York Times* and the *Washington Post*, which publish points of view sometimes critical of U.S. Cuba policy;
- Religious organizations of various denominations;
- Solidarity groups and organizations such as Pastors for Peace;
- Left-leaning organizations, including Cuban American groups;
- An important part of the African American, Hispanic, and labor community.

Whatever the consequences, there is a wide array of political actors within U.S. society concerned with Cuban policy, spanning the whole internal political spectrum. Their number has grown as the conflict has dragged on in the face of ineffective policies. There has been a qualitative change regarding Cuban policy. Today, it is not possible to count those interested in Cuban policy, while ten years ago such a count was easy to accomplish. Also, solidarity with Cuba and opposition to the blockade are no longer ignored, as in the past. Moreover, the extreme right has lost control of a great deal of what is said about Cuban policy. In the United States Congress, positions against the blockade are not limited to the small group of liberal legislators who for years have called attention to the contradictions of Washington's Cuba policy.

Today, the antiblockade stance is the relevant alternative. Within Congress, the number of legislators supportive of at least a partial lifting of the blockade has grown. This development was prompted by the bilateral conflict itself and brought along an increasing number of political actors involved in Cuban policy. In the end the debate sprang from the very survival of the Cuban Revolution—without a Socialist Cuba such political dynamics would not have evolved. The contexts for analysis are the domestic Cuban situation and the so-called national interests of the United States vis-à-vis the island. The two positions may be summarized as follow:

One sector believes there ought to be a change in policy because the island continues to progress in its social project and U.S. policy is clearly ineffective. Thus, a new mode of relations with Havana must be found. Most of all, this position is upheld by the business and farming community, which understands keenly that it is missing profitable trade opportunities.

A second sector maintains that, while Cuba has begun to overcome its economic crisis, it still faces difficult challenges, and current U.S. policy is effective and must be strengthened. This sector included the Clinton administration but is more stridently represented by President George W. Bush's administration, the Cuban American political right (as exemplified by the CANF and the changing political tactics it has followed since the death of its founder, Jorge Más Canosa), and counterrevolutionary and terrorist groups. In coalition with them are four members of Congress: Lincoln Díaz-Balart (R-FL), Ileana Ros-Lehtinen (R-FL), Mario Díaz-Balart (R-FL), and Bob Menéndez (D-NJ).

Legislative efforts to roll back the economic embargo have not made headway because of the dominance exercised by conservative groups operating in the inner circles where U.S. Cuba policy is made. The ever-increasing number of individuals and groups who advocate a real policy change have been deterred by the prevailing political context. The political reality is that a long road has yet to be traveled before Washington's Cuba policy is transformed into the kind of change that the Cuban side of the conflict would welcome. The domestic Cuban reality should support the kind of political dynamics needed for a policy change within the United States. While it is in the United States where the policy must change, Cuba's role in promoting it is by no means insignificant.

The Blockade's Transnationalization

The Torricelli law, as well as the Helms-Burton law enacted four years later, expressed the will in American politics to continue using the blockade as the cornerstone of U.S. policy toward Cuba.[3] These laws provoked conflicts in the international arena with traditional U.S. allies. Still, the United States and its allies have made every effort to avoid turning Cuba into an "apple of discord" among them. Arguably, when the United States stands as the only world hegemonic power, it is inclined to impose its will on its own allies. In this sense, Cuba has become a test case by which the United States has probed how far it can go in forcing its policies on the international community. By defining the blockade as a transnational political action, the United States has turned it from a bilateral to a multilateral action.

With passage of the Helms-Burton law, the contradiction between the United States' Cuba policy and the sovereign rights of nations became clearly visible. This triangular conflict became manifest during the process of Cuba's international economic reintegration in the 1990s. While many nations sought to establish economic links with the island, the United States aimed at creating all kinds of obstacles. The situation underlined the international dimension of the conflict, although it has been mostly decided and perpetuated by American domestic politics. Since the United States has had a long-standing desire to make Cuba an extension of its territory (or to keep Cuba within its sphere of influence, as a feasible alternative), it chose to legislate transnationally to accomplish its objectives with Cuba. Hence, this political factor has been formed by three basic components: U.S. blockade policy, Cuba's national and economic sovereignty, and the sovereign rights of nations that would like to start or continue trading with Cuba.

These three categories are expressed in the conflict of interests that resides at the international level, including the many fronts of resistance to U.S. policy. The confrontation is then acted out at three parallel levels, between the U.S. blockade and (1) other states, (2) U.S. business circles, and (3) solidarity groups with Cuba.

The United States could not reach any accommodation with the solidarity groups but tried to pressure them to stop providing aid to Cuba or tried to infiltrate them in an attempt to subvert Cuban civil society. The situation has been more complex, however, with the first two sets of conflicting interests. There have been many instances involving U.S. allies that have required an avoidance of direct confrontation. Negotiations have been necessary whenever sensitive issues arose as the European Union and Canadian interests confronted U.S. economic pressure. But from the perspective of the economic reintegration of Cuba, the confrontation at the international level takes a triangular shape on the following stages:

- Cuba—Latin America—United States
- Cuba—Caribbean—United States
- Cuba—European Union—United States
- Cuba—Asia—United States

Within Europe, more specifically the European Union, it is important to highlight Russia and the former Socialist countries of Eastern Europe. Russia was a primary U.S. concern due to its continuing relationship with Cuba, to the point that it received special attention in the Helms-Burton law. The Eastern European nations were also of particular interest to Washington, which made significant efforts to prevent their establishing economic rapprochement with Cuba. As far as the Asian triangle is concerned, China, Vietnam, and Korea require special consideration for their position vis-à-vis Cuba since they did not heed U.S. pressure aimed at isolating them from Havana. China, above all, is a special case because of its complex relations with the United States.

It is within this context of contrasting and conflicting views that negotiations became unavoidable. The White House sought to abate the problems

Helms-Burton created with U.S. allies. In practice, however, negotiating Helms-Burton's international acceptance was Washington's tool to forge a worldwide consensus aimed at subverting Cuba's national interests.

Several stages of confrontation and negotiations ensued in the late 1990s, with the potential of repeating themselves under President Bush. At first the Helms-Burton bill was not viewed as a proper U.S. policy, but once Clinton found himself "forced" to sign it, he used the new law as an instrument to pressure American allies and other international actors. The president's special envoy, Stuart Eizenstat, played an essential role in explaining Helms-Burton to skeptical allies in an attempt to make U.S. Cuba policy acceptable at the international level. It must be pointed out that U.S. allies do not grant Cuba any priority in their foreign policy, except basically for their desire to prevent Washington from using Cuba to demonstrate its ability to impose its own interests (as was manifest in the Iraq war). The bottom line here is whether sovereign nations can exercise and defend their own rights, and whether their business communities can develop economic relations with Cuba—or with anyone else, for that matter. In addition, the stage where these negotiations have been carried out has been dominated by the interests of the United States and its allies. The dispute is taking place within a complex political space that includes the following components:

- The interest of the United States in pressuring Cuba into accepting a "democratic-liberal market" modality, which dominant economic powers are trying to impose on the world by means of a process of globalization that they aim to control;
- The interest of U.S. allies in maintaining a strategic agreement with the United States, although they oppose an ineffective political method that hurts them as competitors at the international level.

It is within this framework, riddled with contradictions between the United States and its allies, that Cuba finds an opportunity to move forward with its international economic integration. Still, while these pressures to impose a particular policy approach against Cuba have not been fruitful on the economic front, the United States and its allies still maintain strategies that do not differ markedly on the political front. The allies share with the United States the strategic objective of returning Cuba to capitalism. The difference lies in the strategy, whether to demand it overtly, negotiate it discreetly, or seek it merely as a desirable goal. Hence, the contradictions lie mainly in the methods, not the desired ends.

The methods used to further the goal of returning Cuba to capitalism differ in the various arenas: the United States, Latin America and the Caribbean, the European Union, and Asia.[4]

The U.S. Cuba policy has been conceived as an amalgam of blockade pressures, the absence of economic relations (notwithstanding the paid-in-cash American food trade initiated in late 2001, and continued since), and setting political obstacles to the acceptance of Cuban Socialism and characterizing it as incompatible with peaceful hemispheric and international coexistence. U.S. pressure to move Cuba toward "liberal democracy" really seeks to forge the internal conditions that would destroy Cuba's political system. This includes creating the domestic circumstances that could precipitate and justify U.S. military intervention. The conditions have been pragmatically stated (and repeated by President Bush): Havana must carry out free elections, certified by an international team of observers, as a demonstration of its willingness to promote a transition to democracy and capitalism. Cuba's current political leadership is to be excluded from such transition, as defined in Helms-Burton and the "common position" that was agreed upon with the European Union in 1996. But the U.S.-EU negotiating process on Cuba has remained mostly stagnant: after several sessions, only two meetings led to concrete agreements.

The fundamental difference between the European Union's position and that of the United States is that the former maintains economic relations with Cuba and has not accepted the dictates of Title III of the Helms-Burton law because of its extraterritorial reach and its insensitivity toward other nations' sovereignty. The dispute even led to the selection of a panel of judges to review charges brought by the European Union against the United States at the World Trade Organization (WTO). After much negotiation, a standoff has remained. Even though all have been willing to use Cuba as a negotiating piece, the unmistakable transnational scope of Helms-Burton gets in the way of any settlement.[5]

One issue that should not be overlooked has been Cuba's participation as an observer in the African, Caribbean, and Pacific (ACP) group of states during the Lomé Convention negotiations, which had the potential of opening the door for alternative relations with the European Union. (Lomé was replaced later by the Cotonou Agreement.) The White House was standing with the extreme Right demanding a stronger hard line against Cuba on one side while the U.S. allies were on the other. However, it was a weak performance indeed, since the United States remained in favor of maintaining the blockade and pressure against Cuba—a position supported by President Bush.

In the Latin American and Caribbean area, what stands out is Cuba's progress in its economic relations with the region, the gradual reestablishment of diplomatic relations, and the cooperation the island has promoted with Central America, especially in its provision of medical aid and its willingness to train specialists from and for the region. Also, Cuba has become a participant in such organizations as the Association of Caribbean States (ACS), ALADI (Latin American Integration Association), SELA (Latin American Economic System), CARIFORUM (Caribbean Forum), and others. This has taken place in spite of Washington's attempt to exclude Cuba from hemispheric economic dynamics. The linkage against the obstacles caused by the blockade could open so-called windows of vulnerability. A most interesting case is Canada, a Western country that has maintained a permanent political dialogue with Cuba while also expanding economic relations with it.[6]

Such Cuban foreign policy initiatives as its membership in ALADI, its observer status in the negotiating group for Lomé, its numerous United Nations resolutions against the U.S. blockade, its role hosting the Iberian-American Summit in November 1999, its medical aid to Central America, its presentations at the Group of 77 meetings, as well as the speeches by Cuba's foreign minister at the United Nations on numerous occasions provide factual indication that the island has recovered the international activism for which it was noted prior to 1989.

This recovery process is not only economic but also political and includes Cuba's new image in the hemisphere. The positive emerging image has diluted any lingering animosity from previous times. Thus, such issues as Havana's participation in the Organization of American States (OAS) and its transition to liberal democracy have lost their urgency under the political reality of a new century (demonstrated by the newly elected leftist and center left presidents in Latin America). Cuba is repeatedly maintaining its personality as a nation in the hemisphere and on the world stage. In turn the United States has been continuously condemned by the General Assembly of the United Nations for its blockade against Cuba.[7] Although Washington keeps its pressure over the hemisphere and internationally to enforce discriminatory practices against Cuba, the policy has lost support and suffered numerous defeats.

In Asia, China, Vietnam, and Korea ignore U.S. pressure against Cuba. Japan responds to American pressure by maintaining a degree of independence in its relations with Cuba and has looked for ways of widening its economic links with the island.[8]

Havana has been steadily recovering its international links. "Today the country has more than 360 joint ventures with foreign capital, 170 of which were created after the signing of the Helms-Burton law. Marketing and investment agreements have been signed with forty countries. It has been elected or appointed to twenty governing bodies of the United Nations, and currently has 118 diplomatic, consular, or interests offices abroad—ninety-eight of them are embassies, the highest number in the history of Cuba."[9] Furthermore, Cuba has commercial relations with seventeen hundred companies from 150 nations, hosts seventy-nine embassies representing countries from all continents, and has accredited 138 foreign correspondents from 104 media organizations and thirty-one countries, compared with 93 correspondents from 62 media organizations a decade ago.

Faced with this reality, is it proper to speak of Cuba's isolation, or is it more accurate to speak of the growing international opposition to U.S. policy, particularly the blockade against Cuba?

Clinton's and Bush's Approach to Cuba

The Clinton Years

William Clinton began his first term as president in 1993 with no real commitment to support the United States' long-held aggressive policy against Cuba. In contrast to George W. Bush in 2000, Clinton did not have a strong Miami connection "deciding" his Cuba policy. However, during the 1992 presidential campaign, Clinton supported the Torricelli bill, in his search for South Florida Cuban American votes. He even forced President Bush (the father) to sign the Torricelli bill into law to avoid having Cuban Americans switch to Clinton. In the end, Bush (father) won Florida but lost the reelection, while Clinton lost the Cuban American vote but won the White House. Still, an electoral seed was planted for a future political campaign strategy vying for Cuban American votes—George W. Bush's troubled victory depended largely (to some analysts, entirely) on Florida's electoral mishaps, including the Cuban American vote and political activism.[10]

The Clinton administration kept its Cuba policy on hold until the August 1994 *balseros* (rafters) crisis. Until then, two contradictory incidents were salient. On the one hand, wanting to keep some distance from the head of the conservative CANF, the White House did not invite Jorge Más Canosa to the May 20 (a Cuban national holiday) celebration. On the other hand, the appointment of a political moderate, Carlos Baeza, as undersecretary of state for Latin America was cancelled after a lobbying campaign by Más Canosa's CANF. Clinton decided in favor of extant Cuba policy and used the Cuban Democracy Act (Torricelli bill) as his political mantra.

For reasons escaping objectivity, the extreme right suspected that Clinton was going to make changes in U.S. Cuban policy at the beginning of his administration. The signing of the immigration accord in September 1994, aimed at ending the rafters' crisis, and the Dennis Hayes–Ricardo Alarcón exchange during the signing of the second immigration accord in May 1995 reinforced the conservative belief that Havana and Washington were negotiating in secrecy.

Throughout the 1996 election year Clinton confronted the contradictory dilemma of having signed Helms-Burton into law in spite of his initial intention of having Cuba policy be decided more rationally. Before signing the Helms-Burton bill, Clinton knew that it could cause serious problems for his reelection if Congress decided to approve it without his support. His search for a formula that would make Helms-Burton politically profitable paid off when two planes flown by Brothers to the Rescue (BTTR), an anti-Castro Miami organization, were shot down on February 24, 1996, by the Cuban air force. Richard Nuccio (Clinton's Cuban policy advisor) would state later that he had warned about the possibility of such an incident and the dangers it would bring.[11]

The most intimate and real causes of the incident could be found in the numerous provocative threats to Cuban national security by Brothers to the Rescue and the repeated warnings and complaints Cuba had filed with American authorities. Washington turned a blind eye to these warnings and complaints. It seems certain that Havana's downing of the Brothers to the Rescue planes allowed Clinton to overcome some of the political difficulties encountered during his first term. However, under Helms-Burton the White House could only decide its Cuban policy within the narrow limits established by this law. Hence, Clinton continued supporting the blockade and used Helms-Burton adroitly, seeking a consensus for the political subversion of the Cuban Revolution. Clinton's final Cuba policy was mostly a mix of antagonistic rhetoric and actions hardened by the blockade (although he decided to ease it partly by the end of his administration), and of pressures on U.S. allies to make them accept Torricelli's Track II and some of the Helms-Burton measures.[12] The Clinton paradox is evident: the president who appeared as least committed to extreme-right-wing aggressiveness contributed to some of the most contentious means to put an end to the Cuban Revolution.

Cuba Policy under George W. Bush

In 2000 a Council of Foreign Relations task force, chaired by Julia Sweig, Bernard Aronson, and Walter Mead, issued a report, "US-Cuban Relations in the 21st Century," that provided positive guidelines for the United States' Cuba policy. Since the first months of President George W. Bush's administration, an array of hostile initiatives toward Cuba have been approved; however, Title III of the Helms-Burton Act continued to be suspended in 2001, 2002, and 2003, as was done by the Clinton administration. The financing of the internal opposition to the Cuban government in the amount of $100 million was one of the early Bush initiatives. Paradoxically, with such an action Washington was confirming Havana's long-standing charge that regime opponents were being paid by the U.S. government.

Despite the Senate's opposition but with the CANF's blessing, and taking advantage of a congressional recess in December 2001, President Bush appointed Otto Reich, a conservative Cuban American, as undersecretary of state for Latin America, an appointment that lasted until the end of 2002, when Reich was moved to the National Security Council. Another hard-line Cuban American, Col. Emilio González, was assigned to the Western Hemisphere post at the National Security Council.

The situation that ensued after the attack on the Twin Towers and the Pentagon on September 11, 2001, turned tense due to Cuba's opposition to the way the war against terrorism was being pursued. In his address to the United States Congress, President Bush had dichotomized the world into countries "supporting the United States or supporting terrorism," which posed a hegemonic challenge to the international community. Cuba reacted, making public its opposition to the war in Afghanistan. Havana had offered earlier its sincere condolences and deepest sympathy for the horrific attack against the American people and had expressed its willingness to share intelligence and to permit its airports and airspace to be used as needed to fight terrorism. Finding it of little value, Washington dismissed Havana's good-faith offer.

Pleasing the hard-line Cuban Americans that made up the audience, Bush used a Miami political rally celebrating a Cuban holiday on May 20, 2002, to announce his Cuba policy. Repeating issues raised earlier, he demanded that Havana allow internationally supervised free and democratic elections, freedom of expression, and freedom for all political prisoners, before an end to such punitive measures as trade and travel restrictions could be considered. By then the White House had welcomed the 2001 UN Human Rights Commission's condemnation of Cuba by a majority of one vote. (The close decision was made possible by the relentless campaign of the United States seeking support for the anti-Cuba resolution, including arm twisting of reluctant delegations whenever necessary.)

The diplomatic situation was appraised by the head of the Cuban Interests Section in Washington, Dagoberto Rodríguez: "What we hear from the American public is that there is a great desire to have normal and civilized relations . . . . [But] what we hear from government officials is that there are no great possibilities that it could ever happen." And yet, "we are always ready to sit down to discuss in a civilized fashion any bilateral issue, but never our internal affairs," added Rodríguez.[13]

Nonetheless, some events contrary to Bush's Cuba policy were already taking place during the administration's first years. Notably, acting against Washington's long-held restrictions, Americans continued visiting the island. By the end of 2001, approximately one hundred eighty thousand U.S. tourists had traveled to Cuba, demonstrating a growing interest in their neighboring island. In spite of the severe penalties increasingly imposed on travelers without the required Washington-issued license, the flow of visitors continued in 2003. However, after the administration stopped issuing licenses for the people-to-people educational program, the number of American visitors was expected to decrease—the Washington-granted licenses were not renewed after their expiration date.

Representing a cross-section of American society, visitors seemed bound by their common concern for finding proper ways to relate to Cuba. Americans from many walks of life—political leaders, students, teachers, personalities, industrialists, businessmen, farmers, and many others—were included among the visitors. Several hundred students participating in the University of Pittsburgh's Semester at Sea program, members of Congress, city mayors, Illinois governor George Ryan (for the second time), former president Jimmy Carter (who was later honored with the Nobel Peace Prize), the 2000 presidential candidate Ralph Nader, and others were welcomed personally by President Castro.

The general secretary of INTERPOL, Ronald Noble, during a visit to the island in early 2002, supported Cuban efforts against drug trafficking and the illicit use of credit cards. Noble stated that "Cuba has sustained an outstanding campaign combating drug trafficking as well as the illicit transit of people and the use of counterfeited credit cards." Noble also endorsed Cuba's condemnation of terrorism and of the terrorist attack suffered by the United States on September 11, 2001, characterizing it as "sincere and honest." He added that both "Cuba and the INTERPOL agree that a 'refuge/paradise' [in any country] for criminals and especially for terrorists could not be tolerated."[14] While attending a regional conference studying ways to stop drug trafficking, Congressman William Delahunt (D-MA) proposed a cooperative approach by Washington and Havana to combat the problem. Ricardo Alarcón, head of the Cuban National Assembly, responded, saying,

"I see no reason that could prevent the United States and Cuba from having an antidrug agreement."[15]

In the year 2000 President Clinton approved the sale of food and medicines to Cuba under restrictive conditions: no private or public credit or financing were allowed; all sales had to be paid in cash. But until Hurricane Michelle caused major havoc to the island in the fall of 2001, Clinton's partial softening of the long-held embargo had no real impact. With winds of 250 kilometers per hour, affecting 53 percent of the population and 45 percent of the national territory, Michelle caused material losses estimated in the millions of dollars, which harmed severely the nation's gross domestic product (GDP) for that year. In the face of such disaster, Washington offered humanitarian aid to relieve the hardship. After respectfully declining the Bush administration's offer, Havana reversed its earlier refusal to proceed with needed purchases under such onerous conditions and announced its willingness to pay cash for U.S. food products. The administration refused at first but then accepted Cuba's offer—an initial dispute concerning how to transport the cargo ended when it was agreed to use third countries' merchant ships. Soon thereafter, the first shipments of food from U.S. ports in over four decades were sailing for Havana.

Characterizing it as a "Castro political maneuver," southern Florida Cuban Americans voiced their disapproval of the ensuing, mutually profitable commercial exchange. Showing her frustration, Rep. Ros-Lehtinen stated that "it is up to American farmers if they want to run the risk of not being paid by Castro for their products." Contrary to such gloomy predictions, however, the shipments arrived on time throughout 2002 and since and have been properly paid for in cash by Cuba.

The political fallout generated by American farmers' sales to Cuba gained a life of its own. Under pressure, Congress became sympathetic to ending restrictions, in order to facilitate further trade (although allowing Cuban products to enter the United States was not part of the legislation under consideration). The Republican-dominated House approved in 2002 the commercial financing of sales to the island, as well as putting an end to travel restrictions and lifting the limits imposed on money remittances by Cuban Americans to their relatives. (The Senate failed to vote on the proposed changes before it adjourned for the 2002 December recess.)

Rather than political abstractions and partisanship, the social and economic needs of American farmers and businessmen were the force behind the growing movement seeking to end the politics of sanctions and embargo against Cuba. However, militant conservative forces in Congress and in the

Republican Party, acting with the administration's support, were adamant in their opposition to even a partial softening of Bush's Cuban policy.

Final Considerations

Substantial changes have appeared on the stage occupied by the Cuba-U.S. conflict. No model could be used as an analytical tool without a recognition of the role of such changes.

Meanwhile, Cuba continues to emerge from its 1989–94 crisis—slowly consolidating its economic recovery and completing its international political and economic reintegration. At the same time, the difficult social conditions that followed the economic downfall are lessening as Havana widens its political and diplomatic links in the hemisphere and beyond. Recent years, 1994–2003, indicate that Havana has secured its rightful place in hemispheric and international undertakings and organizations. Cuba's reintegration process enhances its international activism and prestige and legitimizes its domestic policy, while the United States' blockade and other punitive policies become increasingly isolated internationally.

By discussing some of the intervening macro- and microvariables, one can see how Washington has maintained its position within the conflict, even though that position has become increasingly untenable internationally and even domestically. Meanwhile, Cuba has steadily continued its social project, even under tremendous difficulties. Seemingly, the bilateral conflict has moved to a stage of development where the international context, long-term factors, and the newly developed American commercial and political dynamics may predominate. The United States will remain isolated on its Cuban policy if it continues clinging to outdated modalities. This is exemplified by the U.S. delegate's speech at the United Nations on September 24, 1999, deriding Cuba. But Washington lacks today the diplomatic impunity it had in the late 1980s and early 1990s. In contrast, Cuba is now over its worst moments and is moving forward socioeconomically while securing its political objectives.

While the island's internal consensus remains and the political leadership manages to safeguard the national project, the U.S. policy consensus is increasingly lost—only politically extreme groups and individuals continue supporting the old methods used to try to destroy the Cuban Revolution.[16] Slowly the newly emerging forces (especially economic ones) have served to ward off further punitive action in favor of at least a partial lifting of the blockade. The American economic sectors' interests in Cuba, although not large enough yet to turn the tide nationwide, have led to active questioning of the long-held Cuba policy. It will not be politically advantageous to the present Republican administration to ignore the emerging informal business and farming coalition.

Not even in its own "historical backyard" has the United States been able to isolate Havana—especially with the public support Cuba receives from Venezuela, Brazil, Ecuador, Argentina, and others. It is one thing for the United States and its European allies to agree on the desirability of a transition to "Western" democracy in Cuba, and another to agree on isolating the island. U.S. allies, while remaining contentious on the ideological and political level, have traditionally chosen the road to rapprochement. This is evidenced by the actions taken by some regional powers, as well as, more cautiously, by Japan.

As a sovereign nation, Cuba is reaping the fruits of its long struggle, which permits it to play an independent role on the international stage. But Havana also needs to widen its political impact both in the United States and internationally. This objective, however, is only feasible if Cuba continues its economic recovery, preserves its social projects, and guarantees the stability of its political system. It is not possible to know for sure when the present U.S. policy toward Cuba will change. But what appears certain is that if the island cannot continue resisting U.S. pressure, difficult economic conditions and their internal social consequences, and the other problems facing it and moving forward on all fronts, no change in U.S. policy agreeable to Cuba can ever take place.

Notes

This chapter was translated by Professor Enrique Sacerio-Gari, Bryn Mawr College, Pennsylvania.

1. See *Survey of Current Business* (March 2002): D-38; and *Business Week,* August 12, 2003, 29.

2. Figures and analysis may be found in *Revista de Economía y Desarrollo,* no. 3–4 (1996): 91–110.

3. A "dog" and a "throwback to the 1960s" was the language used by congressional aides to characterize the Torricelli law (Cuban Democracy Act, CDA) when it was initially introduced in the House. Still, "then-Congressman Robert Torricelli (D-N.J.), chairman of the House Subcommittee on Western Hemisphere Affairs, . . . and the Cuban American National Foundation [CANF] leader at the time, Más Canosa—the real force behind the bill—were committed to having it become law. [Congressman, later Senator] Torricelli, [Senator Jesse Helms, R-N.C.], . . . and other elected officials benefited from the support by the . . . [CANF] and its leaders (soft money) for politicians and political parties who would play an anti-Castro

role." The Torricelli bill was finally signed into law by President George Bush just before the 1992 presidential elections.

"The Helms-Burton Act [signed into law by President Clinton in 1996] is organized in four separate titles or sections. Title I solidifies a . . . network of sanctions against Cuba [i.e., seeking an international embargo, opposing Cuba's business with international lending organizations, sanctioning former socialist countries aiding Cuba, supporting independent organizations and individuals on the island, and codifying the embargo]. . . . Title II covers U.S. aid to a free and democratic Cuba. . . . Title III protects American citizens who lost property [nationalized by the Cuban government]. [Included in this category are Cuban Americans who are American citizens today but were not at the time. However, the legislation authorizes the U.S. president to cancel its application for security reasons for a six-month period, which Presidents Clinton and Bush have done with no exception.] . . . Title IV empowers the secretary of state and the attorney general to suspend visas of officials from corporations trafficking in American property and those officials' spouses and children" (Max Azicri, *Cuba Today and Tomorrow: Reinventing Socialism* [Gainesville: University Press of Florida, 2000], 181–83, 208–9).

4. See Esteban Morales Domínguez, Carlos Batista, and Kanaki Yamaoka, *The United States and Cuba's International Economy Reinsertion,* Joint Research Program Series no. 126 (Tokyo: Institute of Developing Economies, 1999).

5. See, for example, "José Maria Aznar's, Spain President," statement in *Granma,* September 11, 1999.

6. Morales Domínguez, Batista, and Yamaoka, *Reinsertion,* 139–44.

7. "For the 10th year in a row [twelfth year in 2003], the General Assembly voted overwhelmingly . . . for an end to the United States trade embargo against Cuba. The vote was 167 to 3, identical to [the year before]. Those opposing the resolution, in addition to the United States, were Israel and the Marshall Islands, which also supported Washington in 2000. Latvia, Micronesia and Nicaragua abstained, as they did last year. Despite United Nations support for American positions since the Sept. 11 attacks against the United States, sympathy for Cuba's financial plight and condemnation of the blockade remained unchanged." "U.N. again chastises U.S. on Cuba trade," *New York Times,* November 28, 2001.

8. Morales Domínguez, Batista, and Yamaoka, *Reinsertion,* 152–77.

9. "Informe del Ministro de Relaciones Exteriores," *Granma,* September 15, 1999.

10. For a discussion of the different political forces that brought President Bush to the White House, see Michael Lind, *Made in Texas: George W. Bush and the Southern Takeover of American Politics* (New York: Basic Books, 2003).

11. *El Nuevo Herald* (on line), February 21, 1999.

12. The Torricelli law (Cuban Democracy Act, CDA) and its two-track policy have been implemented by the administrations of President George Bush, President Bill Clinton, and President George W. Bush (who in 2003 suspended its person-to-person exchange provision to curb further the inflow of U.S. dollars to Cuba). Under this legislation, "while the embargo [has been] tightened (track one, the stick), at the other end (track two, the carrot) a window [has been] opened facilitating exchange

of information and travel by certain individuals. To Havana and some political analysts, under the guise of increased person-to-person relations, Washington's real objective with track-two [has been] to undermine the revolution from within" (Azicri, *Cuba Today and Tomorrow,* 189).

13. *El Nuevo Herald* (on line), January 24, 2002.

14. *Granma,* January 17, 2002.

15. *El Nuevo Herald* (on line), November 11, 2001.

16. For a discussion of Cuba's April 2003 crackdown and its impact on relations with Washington and the European Union, see chapter 1. (Editor's note.)

Appendix A

Cuba
Selected Economic Indicators

Gross National Product (GNP)

Year 2000 GNP: $27.6 billion
Productivity
  1999: 5.4%
  2000: 4.6%
Annual growth rate
  1989–2000: 3.2%
  1995–2000: 5.0%
  2000: 5.6% (85% of the 1989 level)

International Trade

Year 2000
Exports: $4.5 billion
Imports: $4.9 billion
Trade deficit: $0.4 billion
Trade by region
  Europe: 45%
  Latin America: 37.4%
  Asia: 16%

External Debt

Year 2000: $11 billion (negotiated or in the process of renegotiation with Japan, Italy, England, and Belgium)

National Budget

From GNP revenues: 48%
Expenditures: 50% (62% on education, health, pensions, social welfare)
Deficit: 2.7%

Social subsidies: 75% reduction since 1995
Taxation: 11 types of taxes, three different rates, one income tax
Taxable transactions/activities: self-employment, artwork, sugarcane, production of different goods, private transportation, leasing of private land, farmers' markets, middleman activities, etc.

Foreign Investment

Objectives: To generate U.S. dollars for the local economy and to promote import substitution policy
Year 2000 results: 392 joint ventures with 46 countries in 32 economic sectors
Investors by region/country
   European Union members: 52%
   Canada: 19%
   Latin America: 18%

Foreign Investment Performance

Announced investment: $1.5 billion
Committed investment: $4 billion in tourism, nickel, telecommunications, oil
Finalized investment: $550 million
Investor protection agreements: 51 agreements signed with 45 countries
Free trade areas: 3, including 294 international enterprises
Risk investment rate: D, 62 points

Domestic Indicators

Unemployment
   1999:   6.0%
   2000:   5.5%
Inflation
   2000: 3% reduction due to lower prices in agricultural products and in the black market
Supply sources for consumers
   State markets: 76%
   Farmers' markets: 8.0%
   Self-employed outlets: 8.5%
   Black market and other sources: 7.5%
Central bank reserves: US$731 million

Economic/social dollarization
   Access to U.S. dollars: 62% of the population
   Tourist industry inputs: 64% from national producers
   Sales in dollar stores: 48% of sales are national products paid in hard
currency
Workers' dollar incentives: $52 million reaching 1.7 million workers
Economically active population: approximately 4 million
Dollar remittances: $864 million (approximately a third of national revenues)

Tourism

International tourists in 2000: 1.8 million (13.2% over 1999)
Hotels: 150 hotels (66% dedicated to international tourism)
Average visiting days per visitor: 11 days
Average daily expenditure per visitor: US$185
Nationality of tourists
   Canadians: 271,000
   Germans: 186,000
   Cuban Americans: 180,000
   Other: 80,000

Enterprise Reform (*Perfeccionamiento* administrative improvement)

Objectives: To achieve management autonomy, financial self-sufficiency,
decentralized profit management, enterprise reinvestment, salary reform,
and a new management system
Program requirements: Enterprise to be approved by the supervising central
commission and to demonstrate sound accounting practices
Enterprises involved: 130 enterprises (including 1,024 economic entities, of
which only 3.4% are releasing employees)
Sales growth: 18%
Profit growth: 120%

Compiled by Esteban Morales Domínguez, University of Havana, 2003. Sources:
CEPAL, *Cuba: Evolución económica, 1999* (United Nations, 2000); The Economist
Intelligence Unit, *Cuba Country Risk Service, 2000*; *Granma* (several issues);
Centro de Estudios de la Economía Cubana, *Workshop 2000*. Also see Centro de
Estudios de la Economía Cubana, *La economía Cubana en el 2000—desempeño
macroeconómico y transformación empresarial* (Havana: Fundación Friedrich
Ebert, 2001).

Appendix B

A Comprehensive Review of the Cuban Military, 1989–99

Year	ME ($ million)		AF (1,000)	GNP ($ million)		CGE ($ million) Constant 1999	People (million)	ME/AF Constant 1999	ME/GNP %	ME/CGE %	ME per capita Constant 1999	AF soldiers per 1,000 people	GNP per capita Constant 1999
	Current	Constant 1999		Current	Constant 1999								
	E	E		E	E			E	E		E		E
1989	1,380	1,730	297	35,500	44,600	NA	10.4	5,820	3.9	NA	166	28.5	4,270
1990	1,380	1,670	297	33,700	40,700	NA	10.5	5,630	4.1	NA	158	28.1	3,860
1991	1,160	1,350	297	27,000	31,400	NA	10.6	4,560	4.3	NA	127	27.9	2,950
1992	NA	NA	175	23,900	27,200	NA	10.7	NA	NA	NA	NA	16.3	2,530
1993	600E	667E	175	25,000	27,800	NA	10.8	3,810E	2.4	NA	62E	16.2	2,580
1994	600E	654E	140	25,700	28,000	NA	10.8	4,670E	2.3	NA	60E	12.9	2,580
1995	600E	640E	70	26,900	28,700	NA	10.9	9,140E	2.2	NA	59E	6.4	2,630
1996	700E	732E	70	29,600	30,900	NA	11.0	10,500E	2.4	NA	67E	6.4	2,820
1997	720E	739E	55	30,800	31,600	NA	11.0	13,400E	2.3	NA	67E	5.0	2,870
1998	700E	710E	55	31,500	32,000	NA	11.1	12,900E	2.2	NA	64E	5.0	2,890
1999	630E	630E	50	34,000	34,000	NA	11.1	12,600E	1.9	NA	57E	4.5	3,060

Source: *World Military Expenditures and Arms Transfers, 1999–2000* (Washington, D.C.: U.S. Department of State, Bureau of Verification and Compliance, 2002), 69.

Notes:(1) Abbreviations used in the appendix:

AF   Armed forces
CGE   Central government expenditures
E   Estimate
GNP   Gross national product
ME   Military expenditures
NA   Not available

(2) Some statistical observations:

Military expenditures were 63.5 percent lower in 1999 than in 1989, at constant 1999 dollars.

The armed forces decreased 83.16 percent from 1989 to 1999.

The military expenses/armed forces ratio was 53.8 percent higher in 1999 than in 1989.

Military expenses per capita were 65.66 percent lower in 1999 than in 1989, at constant 1999 dollars.

The population was 6.3 percent greater in 1999 than in 1989.

The number of soldiers per 1,000 people was 85.9 percent lower in 1999 than in 1989.

Military expenses as a percentage of GNP were 51.2 percent lower in 1999 than in 1989.

The GNP was 28.33 percent lower in 1999 than in 1989.

Appendix C

Central America and Caribbean Military Expenses by Region and Selected Countries, 1989–99

	U.S. Dollars (billions) 1999	Growth Rate (%) 1989–99	1995–99
Central America/Caribbean	1.0	-6.3	-12.9
Cuba	.6	-9.3	-0.6
Panama	.1	2.1	5.4
Dominican Republic	.1	6.4	-6.3
Guatemala	.1	-4.6	-6.9
El Salvador	.1	-11.7	-6.9

Source: *World Military Expenditures and Arms Transfers, 1999–2000* (Washington, D.C.: U.S. Department of State, Bureau of Verification and Compliance, 2002), 4, 179.

The Central American and Caribbean region military spending decreased 6.3 percent from 1989 to 1999, and 12.9 percent from 1995 to 1999. Cuba's spending reduction from 1989 to 1999 (-9.3 percent) was second to El Salvador's, but Cuba remained the region's highest spender in 1999. Weapon deliveries to Cuba from the Soviet Union ended in 1991. Small deliveries were made in 1992–93 by Russia under prior-year agreement, but there is no record of more weapon deliveries since then.

Contributors

Arnold August is the president and director of education tours and academic programs at EduTours to Cuba, Voyage Culture Cuba, Quebec, Canada, and is author of *Democracy in Cuba and the 1997–98 Elections* (1999). He has visited Cuba over thirty times, conducting field research. He resides in Montreal, Canada.

Max Azicri is political science professor at Edinboro University of Pennsylvania and author of *Cuba: Politics, Economics, and Society* (1988), *Cuba Today and Tomorrow: Reinventing Socialism* (2000), and numerous studies on contemporary Cuban politics and society.

Sonia L. Catasús Cervera is a professor at the Demographic Studies Center of the University of Havana and author of scholarly studies on Cuba's population growth and demographic policy.

Margaret E. Crahan is Latin American Studies professor at Hunter College, University of New York and was a visiting scholar at the Woodrow Wilson Center, Washington, D.C. She has authored numerous studies on religious life in contemporary Cuba.

Elsie Deal is professor emerita of English at Edinboro University of Pennsylvania and is a long-time editor of scholarly studies on Cuba and Latin America, bioethics, and fiction.

H. Michael Erisman is professor of political science at Indiana State University, Terre Haute. He has written extensively on Cuba's and the Caribbean's international relations, including *Pursuing Postdependency Politics: South-South Relations in the Caribbean* (1992) and *Cuba's Foreign Relations in a Post-Soviet World* (2000).

Amanda Frantz-Mamani is professor of Spanish and head of the Latin American Studies Program Academic Committee at Edinboro University of Pennsylvania.

Judith D. Gramley is professor of Spanish at Edinboro University of Pennsylvania and head of the foreign languages department.

Hal Klepak is professor of Latin American diplomatic and military history at the Royal Military College of Canada, Kingston, Ontario, and author of numerous studies on the Cuban armed forces. He is currently conducting field research in Cuba for a book-length project on the military.

William M. LeoGrande is dean of the School of Public Affairs and government professor at American University in Washington, D.C. He has written extensively on Cuban and Central American politics and American foreign policy in the region, including *Our Own Backyard: The United States in Central America, 1977–1992* (1998) and *Cuba's Policy in Africa* (1980).

Carlos Mamani is professor of foreign languages and culture at Gannon University, Erie, Pennsylvania.

Félix Masud-Piloto is history professor and editor of the Center for Latino Research's *Diálogo,* at De Paul University, Chicago, Illinois. He has authored numerous studies on Cuban migration, including *With Open Arms: Cuban Migration to the United States* (1988), and is currently working on a new book.

Esteban Morales Domínguez is former director of the Center for the Study of the United States (CESEU) and is currently professor of economics at the University of Havana. In recognition of his scholarly research and national and international publications, he has received some of the most prestigious Cuban academic awards.

José A. Moreno is former sociology professor at the University of Pittsburgh and author of numerous studies on Cuban society and culture; he regularly conducts field research in Cuba. He is an adjunct faculty of the University of Pittsburgh's Semester at Sea program, Institute for Shipboard Education, traveling with students to Cuba and Brazil.

José Luis Rodríguez García is minister of the economy and planning of the Cuban government, and economics professor at the University of Havana. He has authored numerous books and studies on the Cuban economy and Socialist economic and political issues.

Peter Roman is professor of political science in the Behavioral/Social Sciences Department at Hostos Community College, New York, and member of the doctoral faculty in the political science program at the CUNY Graduate Center. He is the author of *People's Power: Cuba's Experience with Representative Government* (1999) and is at work on a new book on Cuba's National Assembly.

Enrique Sacerio-Gari is Dorothy Nepper Marshall Professor of Hispanic and Hispanic American Studies at Bryn Mawr College, Bryn Mawr, Pennsylvania, and author of books on poetry and studies on Cuban literature and culture.

Nelson P. Valdes is currently visiting professor at Duke University and sociology professor and director of the on-line news and information service *Cuba-L* at the University of New Mexico. He is the author of numerous books and studies on Cuba.

Norma Vasallo Barrueta is head of the women's studies program and professor of psychology at the University of Havana. She is the author of numerous studies on contemporary Cuban women.

Jean Weisman is the administrative coordinator of the City College Center for Worker Education in New York City University, New York. She is codirector of the documentary film *From Maids to Compañeras* and has served as executive member of the Latin American Studies Association (LASA) task force on scholarly relations with Cuba.

Andrew Zimbalist is the Robert A. Woods Professor of Economics at Smith College. He has published numerous studies and several books on the Cuban economy and is coauthor of *The Cuban Economy: Measurement and Analysis of Socialist Performance* (1989). He is also a consultant in the sports industry, and his latest book, *May the Best Team Win: Baseball Economics and Public Policy,* was published in 2003.

Index

Note: Tables, notes, and figures are shown by italic notations *t*, *n*. and *f* after the respective numbers.

Abreus municipality (Cienfuegos), 231, 234

Accor Group, 25

accountability of elected officials, 234–35, 241*n*.8

Acosta de Armas, Carmen María, 77

ACP. *See* African, Caribbean, and Pacific (ACP) group

ACS. *See* Association of Caribbean States

ADM. *See* Archer Daniels Midland

administrative units, 101

Afghanistan, bombing of, 11, 332

Afghan prisoners, 11–12

Africa, 264; international profile, 307

African, Caribbean, and Pacific (ACP) group, 328

ages, of population, 105

aggression, 35, 320

aging population: fertility rates, 105; forecasts, 115–16; mortality rates, 107; savings rate, 168

agricultural fairs, 9

agriculture: cooperatives, 156, 157; decentralization, 59; growth rates, 158; military activities, 274; prices, 156–57; privatization and national security, 249

ALADI (Latin American Integration Association), 313, 329

Alarcón, Ricardo, 20, 210–11, 234

Aldana, Carlos, 185, 190, 192; dismissal, 192–93, 252; Union of Young Communists (UJC), 191

Alfonso, Ada, 78

Alvarez, Pedro, 10

American people: Castro speech, 20, 38*n*.34; July 4 honor, 21; normalized relations, 333; visits to Cuba, 333

Americas, trade, 309*f*, 310*f*, 310, 311

Amnesty International, 23

ANAP, 208, 210; legislation on cooperatives, 216–17

"A New Heaven and a New Earth" (pastoral, 2000), 138–39

Angola, 264, 307

Annan, Kofi, 14

anomie, 53

Archer Daniels Midland (ADM), 8, 9

archipelago, 101

armed forces: equipment, 273*t*; future concerns, 276; personnel, 273*t*; respect for, 271, 272, 274–75; role, 261; state enterprises, 158

Asia, 329

Asian triangle, 326

Association of Caribbean States (ACS), 314, 315, 316, 319*n*.10

axis of evil, 36*n*.36

Axis of good, 5

Aznar, José Maria, 24

Baeza, Carlos, 330

Balaguer, José Ramón, 6, 191, 193

balseros. *See* rafters crisis of 1994

banking system, 157

barter economy, 154

Basic Units of Cooperative Production (UBPCs): economic reforms, 188; incentives, 156; private sales, 156–57; state farms, 157; subsidiaries, 156

Basulto, José, 289–90, 299*n*.12

Batista regime, corruption, 262

Bay of Pigs, 128, 263, 299*n*.12

Beijing women's conference, 76, 78–79

Berlusconi, Silvio, 24

bilateral conflict, 35

biological warfare, charges, 16

biotechnology, 166

black Cubans, 176*n*.4

black market, 165, 169; *cuenta propista*, 60

Blair, Tony, 12

Blanco-Alonso, María Manuela, 74

blockade. *See* embargo

Bolívar, Simón, 313

Bolton, John, 16

Brazil, street merchants, 60–61

broadcasts to Cuba from U.S., 43*n*.81. *See also* Radio Martí

Brothers to the Rescue planes, 194, 289–90, 331

budget deficits, 156, 158–59, 164, 167; financing options, 177*n*.7

Bush, George H. W.: Haitian policies, 290; Torricelli Act, 285

Bush, George W., 19–21; embargo, 42*n*.75; new Cuba policy, 19, 325, 331–35

Bush, Jeb, embargo, 42–43*nn*.75, 81

CADECA. *See* exchange houses

Cairo population conference, 100, 101

campaign practices, 32, 228–29

Camps Cruell, Carlos, 135–36

Canada: Angola policy, 264; exceptional relationship, 329; OAS as forum, 24; U.S. economic pressure, 326

candidacy commissions, 208, 209, 211–12

CANF. *See* Cuban American National Foundation

capital consumption allowances, 168

Cargill, 8, 9

Caribbean: foreign policy, 307; military spending, 344*t*; trade, 314–16

CARICOM (Caribbean Community and Common Market), 314

CariForum, 314

CARITAS, 132

Carmona, Pedro, 15

Carter, Jimmy, 16–17, 41*n*.70, 218, 333

casas de cambio, 53

Casas Regueiro, Julio, 249

Cason, James, 21–26

Casteñada Gutman, Jorge, 13, 14, 15

Castro Porta, Carmen, 67

Castro Ruz, Fidel: age, 254*n*.2; Aida Pelayo, 68; armed forces' loyalty, 262; authority, 196; diplomatic campaign, 7; lobbying, 196; National Assembly, 217–18; on power, 160*n*.4; proximity to, 196; rafters crisis, 291, 292; on religion, 133–34; on retirement, 254*n*.1; Rosita Mier, 68; special period reforms, 189

Castro Ruz, Raúl, 195, 196; age, 254*n*.2; armed forces link, 263; constitutional succession, 246, 247, 248; Council of Ministers, 247; economic reforms, 31, 193; Political Bureau, 247–48; Soviet

arms, 264; style, 242; succession, 32, 204*n*.63, 243, 245, 252, 275–76

Catholic Center for Civic and Religious Formation, 140

Catholic Church: baptisms, 132; before 1959, 28, 127; church and state roles, 136; conflicts with Revolution, 127–28; criticized, 194–95; dimensions in mid-1990s, 132; divisions, 142; Eastern Europe compared, 123; economic situation, 138; growth factors, 131–32; historical role, 125; rapprochement, 129; revitalization of hope, 136–37; rivalry with government, 29; *Vitral* viewed, 141–42

CDR. *See* Committees for the Defense of the Revolution

CEA. *See* Center for the Study of the Americas

CEC. *See* Cuban Council of Churches

CEDSI think tank, 268, 279*n*.24

Center for Genetic Engineering and Technology, 16

Center for International Policy, 23

Center for Psychological and Sociological Studies (CIPS), 133

Center for the Study of the Americas (CEA), 193, 194

Central America: military spending, 344*t*; wars of 1980s, 265

Central Committee, generational succession, 197–98

Central Intelligence Agency (CIA), terrorism in Cuba, 11

Central Planning Board (JUCEPLAN), 186

Chafee, Lincoln D., 12

chain of command, 263, 272

Chávez Frias, Hugo: coup attempt, 15–16, 40–41*nn*.56, 59, 61; Cuban imports, 312*n*; election, 5

Cheney, Dick, 12

Christian Center for Reflection and Dialogue, 139–40

churches, civil society, 124

church publications, 125

church-state relations: Camps on, 136; democratic transition, 126; increased communication, 129

CIEC. *See* Cuban Council of Evangelical Churches

CIPS. *See* Center for Psychological and Sociological Studies
civil liberties: Ralph Nader, 17–18; U.S. and Cuba compared, 12–13, 18
civil society, 55; churches, 124; church view, 136–37; Poland compared, 126; religions, 123–24
classical Fidelismo, 308
class system: early reforms, 51; values, 53–54
Clinton, William (Bill) J., 285
Clinton administration: approach to Cuba, 330–31; asylum halted, 284; food and medicine, 334; Haitian refugees, 290; Helms-Burton law, 297, 327; new migration policy, 284; paradox, 331; rafters, 293
CMEA. *See* Council of Mutual Economic Assistance
Coast Guard: Cuban interdictions at sea, 297t; Cuban rescue statistics, 293t
cocaine trafficking, 187
Cold War: classical Fidelismo, 306–8; migration, 283. *See also* end of the Cold War
cold war bipolarism, 305
Colomé Ibarra, Abelardo, 249, 268
Committees for the Defense of the Revolution (CDR), 190; nominations, 226; people's councils, 208
communication professionals, 75–79
Communism, international, end of Cold War, 4
conciencia (consciousness), 61
Concilio Cubano, 194
conflict with U.S.: change in policy advocates, 324–25; final considerations, 335–36; macrovariables summarized, 321–22; scenarios and variables, 320–21; three variables, 34–35
conglomerates, 249–50
conscription, 271
consejos populares (popular councils), 234, 240
consensual unions, 112
Constitution: amending, 18–19, 42n.72; equality of sexes, 86; population policy, 114; presidential succession, 245–47
Constitution of 1976, 129
Constitution of 1992, Council of State powers, 246
consumer goods, 59

consumer price index, exchange rates, 159
consumption, economic crisis, 151
cooking fuel, 93
cooperatives, 188; legislation, 216–17
corruption: Batista regime, 262; causes, 58; *cuenta propistas*, 61; emerging sectors, 239; frequent types, 58–59; military, 274, 279n.31; police force, 270; state enterprises, 239; trials, 187
Cotonou Agreement, 25
Council of Ministers, 246–47
Council of Mutual Economic Assistance (CMEA), 306–7, 308
Council of State, 245–46
criminal underground, 241n.11
CTC. *See* Cuban Confederation of Workers
Cuba Adjustment Act (1966), 33
Cubalse, 250
Cubana Airlines bombing, 11
Cubanacán, 250
Cubana de Aviación, 175
Cuban Adjustment Act (1966), 33
Cuban American lobby, 164
Cuban American National Foundation (CANF): embargo, 9; Exodus program, 287; lobbying, 286; as political actor, 323; Torricelli bill, 285
Cuban Americans: blockade, 52; Bush links, 21; Bush speech, 19, 332; Elián fallout, 300n.33; frustration with Bush, 43n.81; immigration accord, 296; pandering to, 20; policy to Cuba, 324–25; post-Fidel Cuba, 251, 253
Cuban Communist Party (PCC): adaptive change, 195–96; armed forces-party link, 263; believers admitted, 131; Castro's role, 196; Central Committee, 184–85, 186, 189, 195–96, 247; debate, 30–31; divisions within, 191–95; downsizing of bureaucracy, 189; economic reform, 31; first secretary, 247; founding congress, 185; generational leadership succession, 31; grassroots membership, 198; individual beliefs, 130; legislation, 209–10; limited-reform strategy, 195–96; as Martí's heir, 195; membership, 247; membership growth, 198; mobilizational capacity, 199; municipal nominations, 226, 227; National Assembly, 209–11; new members, 191; nominations to

Cuban Communist Party—*continued*
National Assembly, 220; origins, 183–87;
population policy, 114; presidential succession, 247–48; reformers vs. hard-liners, 191–95; religious affairs, 140; role
and significance, 30; role as institution,
252; size, 184–85; Special Period, 187–
91; transition role, 275
Cuban Confederation of Workers (CTC):
dominance, 126; legislation, 217; municipal nominations, 226; people's councils,
207–8
Cuban Council of Churches (CEC), 134
Cuban Council of Evangelical Churches
(CIEC), 129
Cuban "exceptionalism," 33
Cuban Revolution, non-communist origins,
183–84
Cuban Revolution "institutionalization,"
184, 185
Cuba Policy Foundation, 23
Cuba-U.S. conflict. *See* conflict with U.S.
cuenta propistas: described, 60; licensing,
60; regulations and controls, 61. *See also*
self-employment
cultural demands, 90
cultural diversity, 78
currency devaluation, 156
customs agents, 59

Dacosta Pérez, Caridad, 70
daughters' generation, 90–91, 96
day care centers, 72, 87
de Armas, Modesta, 73–74
debt crisis, 187
decentralization: economic, 59–61; resource
management, 157; state enterprises, 157
de la Torriente Brau, Pablo, 25
delegates, Provincial Assembly, 211
Del Valle, Sergio, 186
democracy, concept of, 125
democratic transition, 126; churches, 134;
Eastern Europe, 127
democratization, religion linked, 126, 143
demographic policy, development strategy,
28
demonstration transition, churches, 134
dependent capitalism, 53, 54, 56
deportation policy, 296
depreciation, 168, 178*n*.24

deputies, National Assembly, 211
deregulation, 312
developed countries: Cuba compared, 105–
6; demographic indicators compared,
107*t*
developing countries: demographic indicators compared, 107*t*; workforce, 94
Díaz-Balart, Lincoln, 325
Díaz Vallina, Elvira, 69–70
diplomatic interests sections, 17
direct vote, 31–32
disaster relief, 8–9
discrimination, mothers' generation, 89–90
dissent: tolerance for, 193; within elite, 251
dissidents: Bush's speech, 20; Carter, 16–17;
Catholic Church, 137–38; crackdowns,
44*n*.86; groups, 194; international solidarity, 45*n*.89; movement, 193; spoiled
and blank ballots, 232–33
dollarization: agriculture, 165; class system, 58; depenalization, 177*n*.13; described, 154–55; distribution, 159; dollars-only shops, 7; exchange houses,
177*n*.14; functioning, 53; impact, 57;
negative social effects, 156; perceptions
of, 98; social divide, 7
dollar-peso double economy, 57
dollars, peasants, 59
dollar shops/stores. *See* hard currency stores
domestic skills, 91
domestic workers: before 1959, 65, 85;
post-1959, 66; poverty, 74; schools for,
72–75; special period, 94; transformations, 80
Domínguez, Luis, 187
Dominican Republic, 344*t*
double morality, 245
drug interdiction, 12, 333–34
dual economy, 174
dual monetary system, 154

Eastern Europe: churches, 126–27; church
role compared, 123; continuing relationship, 326; domino effect, 4; economy
compared, 163; lack of regulation, 62;
party legitimacy, 198; resources to Cuba,
306–8; successor strategies, 197; trade,
309*f*, 310*f*, 310, 311, 318*nn*.6, 7
economic crises of 1990s, private initiatives,
60

economic crisis: alternatives for women, 94–95; analyzed, 322–23; boatlifts, 291; changes in relations, 335; daughters' educations, 96; decisive factors, 151; economic recovery, 149; family, 135; feminine subjectivity, 94–97; foreign debt, 151, 161*n*.9; Fourth PCC Congress, 160*n*.3; internal policy, 154; measures, 97–98, 150; migration increasing, 289; perceptions, 97–98; population growth, 115; prostitution (*jineterismo*), 96–97; rafters, 291–92; self-esteem, 98; social security, 96; statistics, 150; women affected, 92–94; workers' parliaments, 236–37; workforce participation, 95
economic development: population policy, 28, 100–101, 113; revolutionary model, 150
economic growth, 158, 339; historical, 150; U.S., 321
economic indicators, 29; post-Cold War, 6; recent years, 158–59
Economic Planning and Management System (SDPE), 186, 202*n*.24
economic policy: budgets and plans, 215; PCC debates, 191–95; rectification campaign, 186; significant changes, 154; special period, 188–89
economic problems, in 1990s, 7
economic recovery: assessed, 35, 321, 322–23; balance, 158–59, 1995–99; oil, 98; preamble, 149–51; reasons for, 165–66; road to, 151–58; statistics debated, 176*n*.2; tourism sector, 173
economic reforms: analyzed, 322–23; armed forces, 249; deceleration, 151; domestic, 156; external economic policy, 152; first experiments, 249; impact, 199; PCC, 31; state enterprises, 193, 341
economic sanctions, EU, 25
economic security, 304–5, 308
economy: debate summarized, 29–30; decentralization, 59–61; early 1990s, 52; female participation, 87; Latin America compared, 163; population as variable, 116; present economic reality, 164–66; presidential succession, 253; problems of 1990s, 7; three distinct economies, 166; tourism, 56
ecumenical groups, 139

ecumenism, 134, 142
education, 197; attainment levels, 159; women, 86
effective sovereignty, 304
egalitarianism: early changes, 26; erosion, 7; measures of 1960s, 51, 54; special period, 27
Eizenstat, Stuart, 327
elderly population. *See* aging population
elected officials: nonelected officials, 241*n*.8; three levels, 224
elections: of 1902–1958 period, 224; accountability of officials, 234–35; campaigning and requirements, 228–29; fairness, 236–37; municipal, 223; national deputies, 229–34; noncompetitive, 212, 236; revocation process, 235–36; spoiled and blank ballots, 232*t*, 232–33, 233*t*; U.S. sympathizers in Cuba, 232–33; *voto unido* system, 212
Electoral Law (1992), 213–14, 219, 228, 236
electoral system, 31–32; past experience, 223–24; weaknesses, 238–40
electric energy, 153
electric power rationing, 93
Elián González case: church support, 142; Cuban American right wing, 224; Cuban people, 62; elected officials, 237; immigration regulations, 298; Internet use, 48*n*.110; Miami politics, 300*n*.33; nationalism, 197; solidarity, 62, 63; summarized, 33–34; values expressed, 62
elite decision making, 196
elite rapid-reaction force, 268–69
El Salvador, 344*t*
embargo: antiblockade stance, 324; anti-Castro exiles, 52; anti-embargo business forces, 9–10; Carter, 16; churches on, 133; costs of, 161*n*.10, 164; Cuba Policy Foundation, 23; economic crisis, 152; economic impact, 30; immigration talks, 294; population growth, 115; post-Cold War, 266; price levels, 57–58; recent U.S. votes, 175; social welfare impact, 8; transnationalization, 325–30; Washington support for, 10; White House support, 42–43*n*.75 and 81; women on, 75; women's role, 81. *See also* Helms-Burton law

emerging entrepreneurial class, 199
emerging modern economy, 253
emerging sectors: corruption, 239; elected officials and, 238, 239–40; employment for women, 95; organization, 245; traditional compared, 97–98
émigré community, 133
émigré conference in Havana, 286, 299n.4
employment: developing countries, 94; population growth, 103
empresas mixtas. See joint ventures
end of the Cold War, 165; Cuban exiles, 298n.1; Cuban threat, 284–85; debates, 187; domino effect, 4; economic crisis, 149, 321; economic record since, 163; foreign policy, 306; impact on Cuba, 4, 265; impact on women, 66; international relations, 303; international stature, 308; Marxism, 3, 4–5; neo-Fidelismo, 308–16; population growth, 115; presidential succession, 123; reinvention, 52; Socialist survivors, 3; stages since, 3; tourism, 55; trade before, 265; U.S. foreign policy to Cuba, 284. See also Cold War
ENEC. See National Cuban Church Encounter
energy, 158
enterprise improvement movement, 157–58
Enterprise-Perfecting Plan, 193
equipment, military, 266, 273t
equity and equality, norms of, challenged, 164
Esperón, Hidelisa, 68–69
Espín, Vilma, 69, 71
Ethiopia, 307
EU. See European Union
European trade, 309f, 309–10, 310f, 311, 318nn.6, 7
European Union (EU): Castro critique, 25, 47n.99; Helms-Burton law, 326, 328; support for US policy, 24–25; U.S. policy, 24, 47–48n.105, 326, 328
exceptionalism, 33
exchange houses, 177
exchange rates, 155–56, 167; dual economy, 174; historically, 177n.14; official, 178; role in economy, 57
excludables in U.S. prisons, 287
Exodus program, 287
export enclave, 166, 177n.11

export of revolution phase, 263–64
exports: by country, 311t; earnings, 153; MERCOSUR, 315–16, 316t; to MERCOSUR, 317f; by region, 309f, 309–10; restructuring, 309

family, 27; daughters' generation, 90–91; economic crisis, 135; grandmothers' generation, 88–89; mothers' generation, 89–90; reorganization, 95–96
Family Code, 74, 86
family planning, 86
FAR. See Revolutionary Armed Forces
farmers' markets, 59, 166, 186, 188; dollars, 57; reinstated, 99n.8; shortages, 193
Father Ramón Clapers Center for Religious Formation, 139
FCMM. See Women's Civic Front José Martí
Federation of Cuban Women (FMC), 66, 71–72; bureaucratism, 190; municipal nominations, 226; people's councils, 208; role, 80–81; status, 27
Federation of Cuban Workers, (CTC), 208
Federico García Lorca Cultural Center, 24–25
feminine subjectivity, 94–97
feminism: acceptance, 81; before and after 1959, 80; revolutionary social project, 85; Socialism, 81; struggle of 1950s, 70–71; success of revolution, 80
ferry hijackers, 22, 45n.87, 46n.92
fertility rates, 28, 109–12; after 1970, 104; early, 102; global (GFR) and gross reproduction (GRR), 111t; historical, 109–10; Latin America compared, 106; regional homogeneity, 110; second stage, 103; urban and rural, 110
fitness standards, 274
FMC. See Federation of Cuban Women
Fonte, Lugo, 217
food imports, shortages, 93–94
food sales: early, 8–10; leverage, 35; net sales, 37nn.24, 27; political fallout, 334; private agriculture, 156–57; transport costs, 92; U.S. terms, 92
food supplies, armed forces, 274
foreign affairs, 185
foreign currency collection stores (TRDs), 154. See also hard currency stores

foreign debt, 165; liquidity, 153, 161, 162n.14
foreign direct investment (FDI), 170
foreign investment: acceleration, 152; amounts, 170; attracting, 171; as catalyst, 170; challenges, 29; concessions, 56; contracts, 170; economic crisis, 165; extant origins, 170; FDI flows, 170; joint ventures, 309; lack of investment, 168–70; obstacles, 171; rectification period, 201n.16; tourism, 52, 56
foreign policy, 34–35; big country's, 305; cold war, 34; Cuba side, 320; new Fidelismo, 34
foreign relations: continuity, 303; three attributes, 303
foreign trade, restructuring, 152
formal sovereignty, 304
Fox, Vicente, 13–15
Free Trade Area of the Americas (FTAA), 313
free-trade federations, 313–16
Friends of Venezuela group, 16
FTAA. See Free Trade Area of the Americas
Fuerzas Armadas Revolucionarias (FAR). See Revolutionary Armed Forces

García, Guillermo, 186
García Franco, Raimundo, 128, 139
gasoline scarcity, 58
Gaviota corporation, 249, 250
GDP: growth, 158; special period, 188
gender: life expectancy, 108–9; mass media, 77, 78; meanings explored, 77
gender equality, FMC, 71–72
gender issues, 27, 71; revolutionary values, 65
gender ratio, 102
generational leadership succession, 197–98
Geneva Convention, 12
Gil, Elena, 72
glasnost, criticized, 265
glass ceiling. See women: senior posts
global economy: challenges, 52; competitiveness, 52; new practices, 52
global fertility rates (GRF), 111t
Global Pastoral Plan 1997–2000, 137
González, Elián. See Elián González case
González, Emilio, 332
Gorbachev, Mikhail, 4, 185

governmental decrees, 237
Grand Hall, 18
grandmothers' generation, 88–89
Great Depression, 102
Green Party, 17–18
Grenada invasion, 265
gross mortality rate, 106–7, 108t
gross reproduction rate (GRR), 111t, 117n.16
Group of 77 meetings, 329
GRR. See gross reproduction rate
Guantánamo base: Afghan prisoners, 11–12; costs of detaining rafters, 295; Haitians detained, 290; rafters, 293–94
Guatemala, 344t
guerrilla, use of term, 278n.4
Guevara, Ernesto Che, 54, 186, 263–64, 161n.8
Gutiérrez, Lucio, election, 5

Haitian interdiction program, 290
Haitian Revolution, 260
handicraft market, 156
hard currency, 154; bonuses for workers, 166; military access, 274; as work incentive, 156
hard currency stores (tiendas de recuperación de divisas, TRD), 166, 172; Cuban products, 153, 161n.13
hard-line policies, 18; Miami support, 19–20; motivation, 21
Havana, administrative role, 101
Havana riot (1994), 269
health care, 197
health system. See public health
Helms-Burton law: Clinton reelection, 331; described, 297; economic impact, 321; FDI flows, 170; immigration policy, 297; as macho law, 80; reinforcing embargo, 266, 325; Title III, 332; triangular conflict, 325–26; U.S. allies, 326–27
Hernández, María Teresa, 73
Hernández, Melba, 69
higher education, 86, 87, 95
hijackings: ferry, 22, 45n.87, 45n.92; wave in 2003, 22
historical events: demographic growth, 101; summarized, 102
hope, 135, 136
hotels, white personnel, 7

house churches, 132
human rights: Afghan prisoners, 12; Bush on, 332; Carter, 41n.70; Fox on, 13; refugee flow stemmed, 294; social justice, 195; visa requests, 289
Hurricane Michelle, 163; economic impact, 30, 334; U.S. relief offer, 8, 334
Hyde, Henry J., 36n.6

Ibáñez, Elda, 72–73
ideological hegemony, 189; religion, 130; Vitral challenges, 141
Iglesias, Maruja, 68
illegal immigration, 296
images of women, 77
immigrants to Cuba, 102
immigration policy, U.S., 286, 290, 293–94, 297–98
immigration quotas, 296
imports: by country, 312t; economic recovery, 153; from MERCOSUR, 317f; by region, 310f; substituting, 153
import substitution, tourism, 171–72
income distribution, 164; growth rates, 30
income redistribution, 103
indefinite detention policy, 294–95
independence, wars of, 102, 260–61
independent foreign visitors, 23
individualism, 53, 54
industrialization, 104
industrial markets, 165
industrial sector, 156; growth rates, 158
infant mortality, 159; decrease, 106; developed countries compared, 105–6; program, 107; rural and urban, 110–11
inflation, hard currency, 154
informal economy, 154; role, 157; women, 94
informal sector, 166; cuenta propista, 60; investment, 168–69
institutional religion, status, 127–35
Integrated Revolutionary Organizations (ORI), 184
intelligence personnel, 267–68
interest sections, 19
interlocking power network, 250–51; Castro brothers, 243; separation of roles and powers, 251
internal security, 268–69, 270, 277

International Meeting on Population and Development (Cairo), 100, 101
international relations, 34–35; end of the Cold War, 303
international stature, 305, 308
International Women's Conference (Beijing), 76, 78–79
INTERPOL, 333
invasion by U.S. See overthrowing the Cuban government
investment: Cuba's share, 161n.12; economic crisis, 151; EU, 25; ratio, 168
Iraq war: Cuba on, 11; Italy, 24; Spain, 24
islands of autonomy, 200
Italy, adversarial EU position, 24

Jewish community, 133, 143n.1
jineterismo. See prostitution
John Paul II: anticipated fall of Cuba, 123; impact of visit, 138; Iraq War, 38n.34; visit analyzed, 133–34
joint ventures, 152; military industries, 267; military retirees, 249; numbers, 329–30; tourism, 56; worker benefits, 56–57
JUCEPLAN. See Central Planning Board

Kirchner, Néstor, 5–6

labor program, 128
labor unions: Solidarity labor union, 126; women, 74. See also Cuban Confederation of Workers
Lage, Carlos, 6, 171, 191, 192, 196; amending constitution, 18; Council of Ministers, 247
Lasaga, José Ignacio, 128
Latin America: ACS/MERCOSUR links, 315; demographic indicators compared, 107t; economies compared, 163; fertility rates compared, 106; foreign policy, 307; historical, 109, 110; infant mortality compared, 107t; leftist politics, 5; opposition to coup attempt, 15; population growth, 103; population growth compared, 106; teen mothers, 112
Latin American Left: origins and status, 5; revival, 6
Law Decree No. 140 (1993), 154
Lazo, Esteban, 194

leadership style, 32
leftist politics, history, 5
legislation, 209–10; how bills become law, 214–18
legislative practices, 31
legislatures, 233
Leninism, reforms, 188
liberation theology, 129, 131
life expectancy, 108t, 108–9; developed countries compared, 105
liquidity, 153, 164–65, 167, 177n.8
literacy campaign, 86
Local Organs of People's Power (OLPP), 207
Lomé Convention, 328, 329
López Miera, Alvaro, 248
Lorca Cultural Center, 24–25
Lourdes intelligence establishment, 267
"Love Hopes All Things," (pastoral, 1993), 136
Lula da Silva, Luis Inácio, election, 5

Machado, Antonio, 25
Machado Ventura, José Ramón, 191, 192
MAGÍN, 27, 75–79; creation, 66, 76; disbanded, 79; future, 81; Helms-Burton impact, 66; U.S. policy, 79, 80; workshops, 76
Mariana Grajales women's platoon, 70
Mariel excludables, 287–88
Mariel exodus: Castro on, 291; crisis for U.S., 286; political legitimacy, 187; rafters crisis compared, 292–93; stigma, 287
market sector, 166
market system: Castro on, 160; economic pressures on Cuba, 327–28; impact, 29; neoliberal consensus, 312; PCC reformers, 192; political erosion, 200; role, 150–51, 160n.4
marriage: daughters' generation, 90–91; grandmothers' generation, 88–89
Martínez, Osvaldo, 211–12
Martínez Puentes, Rubén, 249
Martin Luther King Jr. Center, 139–40
Marxism, end of Cold War, 3, 4–5
Marxism-Leninism, 130
Más Canosa, Jorge, 293, 330
mass media, 194; gender, 77, 78; religions' access, 130; U.S., 324

materialism: ideological hegemony, 130
media. See mass media
median population age, 105
medical care, 159; Batista era, 70, 71; compromised, 164
medical schools, women, 86
medicine shortages, 94
Meliá, 25
Menéndez, Bob, 325
MERCOSUR (Southern Cone Common Market), 314–16; intra-MERCOSUR trade, 315t; trade with Cuba, 315–16, 316t
Methodist Church, 130
Mexican Embassy (Havana) incident, 13–14
Mexico: Catholic donations, 139; cool relations, 39n.52; Pascoe censure, 39n.51. See also Fox, Vicente
Miami Spanish-language radio, 13–14, 43n.81
Mier, Rosita, 68
migration: as act of war, 45n.88; after Elián, 296–98; Catholic parishes, 128; Cuban "exceptionalism," 33; evolution, 283–84; hijackings, 22; historically, 283–84; Mariel, 104; nationalization, 103–4; new policy, 33; overview, 33–34; population growth, 103, 104; Protestants, 128; U.S. refusal, 294
Migratory Accords (1994), 22
military, 32–33
military attachés, 267, 268
military hierarchy, 272–73
military industries, 267
military intelligence, 267–68
military missions, 261
military service, 271
Military Units to Aid Production (UMAP), 128
MINFAR. See Ministry of Revolutionary Armed Forces
MININT. See Ministry of the Interior
Ministry of Revolutionary Armed Forces (MINFAR): heads, 248–49; as institution, 252; War of All the People, 265
Ministry of the Interior (MININT), 268–69; FAR link, 268–69, 277; ubiquitous in cities, 270
mixed enterprises. See joint ventures

Miyares, José Manuel, 129
modernity, 78
Moncada barracks, attack, 68
money supply, 164–65
Monterrey UN conference, 14
moral incentives, 186, 187
Moro, Sonia, 76
mortality rates: cause of death, 109; children, 109; developed countries compared, 105; early decline, 102; gross mortality rate, 106–7, 108t; historical patterns, 106–7; stages, 103
motherhood, grandmothers' generation, 88–89
mothers' generation, 89–90
municipal assemblies, 207, 229, 238, 240
municipal elections, 223, 224–28, 236
municipality, concept of, 224–25

Nader, Ralph, 17–18, 33
National Action Plan, 79
National Assembly: bill's passage into law, 214–18; Castro Ruz, Fidel, 217–18; Communist party, 209–11; contacting the population, 212–14; Council of State related, 245–46; deputies, 211; electing deputies, 229–34; elections, 211–12; fieldwork (research), 206–7; nominations, 220; Permanent Commission on Childhood, Youth, and Equal Rights for Women, 86–87; structure and functions, 208–9; terms of office, 213–14; unanimous voting, 218–19
National Assembly of People's Power, 190–91
National Candidacy Commission, 230, 233–34
National Catholic Congress, 127–28
national crisis, armed forces, 276–77
National Cuban Church Encounter (ENEC), 14, 131, 140
national deputies, 229–34
national dialogue, 135, 138
National Foreign Policy Council, 23
national identity, 126
nationalism: challenges to system, 124; political legitimacy, 197; regime change, 124
nationalization: migration from Cuba, 103–4; small business, 52–53

national liberation movements, 130
National Revolutionary Police (PNR), 270–71
National Security Council, 21
National Union of Writers and Artists (UNEAC), 192
neo-Bolivarianism, 308, 313–16; neo-Pan-Americanism vs., 311
neo-Fidelismo, 308–16
neoliberal consensus, 312
neoliberal economic model: readjustment rejected, 151–52; religious publications, 141; Socialist model vs., 149
neoliberalism: impact, 29; political reaction to, 5
neo-Pan-Americanism, 311–12
New, Arnold, 23
New, Zachary, 44
Newberg papers, 66
"new man": Committees for the Defense of the Revolution (CDRs), 54; compromises, 27; Cuban Communist Party, 54; day care centers, 54; Federation of Cuban Women, 54; ideals, 54; institutions, 54; internalized, 62; militias, 54; trade unions, 54; Union of Young Communists, 54
NGOs. See nongovernmental organizations
Noble, Ronald, 333
nominations, electoral, 212, 220; municipal, 225–26; national deputies, 229
Non-Aligned Movement, 307
nongovernmental organizations (NGOs): democratic paradigms, 124; FMC, 79; government organized, 124; MAGÍN, 79; U.S., 323–24
Nuccio, Richard, 331

OAS. See Organization of American States
Oblate nuns, 139
occupation, U.S., 261
Ochoa, Arnaldo, 187
Ochoa-La Guardia affair, 244
Office of Attention to the Population, 214
oil: alternative fuels, 92; Castro on, 40n.58; economic recovery, 98; impact on women, 92–93; reduction impact, 92–93; Venezuela, 15
OLPP. See Local Organs of People's Power

one-party system, 195
open discussion, grassroots, 189–90
open mass assemblies, 224
OPP. *See* Organs of People's Power
opposition: analyzed, 245; Bay of Pigs, 263; Bush-Cason scheme, 21–26; Cason strategy, 22–23; lack of support, 245; in National Assembly, 220; running candidates, 233
Organization of American States (OAS): Cuban expulsion, 47*n*.97; Cuba participation, 329; opposition to coup attempt, 15; Pan Americanism, 311–12; Powell initiative, 23–24; sanctions lifted, 307
Organs of People's Power (OPP), 190, 191, 207
Ortega y Alamino, Jaime, 136
outreach, 139
overthrowing the Cuban government, 23, 253, 265; justifying (Bush), 328; preparedness, 267, 271

paladares: corruption, 58; dollar economy, 57; regulation, 168–69
Panama: military spending, 344*t*; rafters detained, 294
parallel market rate, 178
Paris Club, 162*n*.14
parliamentary system: representation, 31; weakest link, 31
participation, civic society, 54
Passionist novices, 139
patron-client network, 71
Payá Sardiñas, Osvaldo, 17, 46–47*n*.94
PCC. *See* Cuban Communist Party, 30
peace processes, church roles, 135
peasants, women, 95
Pelayo, Aida, 67, 68, 70–71
Pentecostals, 133
people-per-doctor rate, 159
people's councils, legislation for, 215–16
"people to people" educational exchange: diplomats expelled, 22; visas, granting, 22
perestroika, 185, 186, 252, 253; criticized, 265
Pérez, Humberto, 186
Pérez, Irma, 6–70
Pérez Betancourt, Miguel, 249

Pérez Roque, Felipe, 196, 198; amending constitution, 18
petition, right of, 218
petty crime, 270
pharmaceuticals, 9
Pinar del Rio, Church, 132
Pinero Corporation, 25
Plan for the Advancement of Women, 72
Platt Amendment, 278*n*.7
Plaza de la Revolución: accountability of officials, 235; *consejos populares*, 234; electoral candidates, 230, 231*t*, 231–32
PNR. *See* National Revolutionary Police
Poland, 28–29, 123, 125, 126, 143
police force, 270–71
Political Bureau: generational leadership succession, 197–98; national and party leadership, 210–11; presidential succession, 247–48, 248–49; purge, 194
political consciousness, 150
political culture: compromises, 27; early period, 26; special period, 27
political institutions: early reforms, 188; special period reforms, 189
political legitimacy: debates, 199–200; diminished, 197; elections as plebiscite, 232–33; PCC, 252; post-Castro, 197
political reforms: hopes for, 252–53; state bureaucracy, 157
political representation, U.S. as model, 207
politics, 30
popular militias, 262–63
Popular Socialist Party (PSP), 184
population, 101–6
population conferences, 100–101, 113
population growth, 28; current characteristics, 116; economic development, 100–101, 113; future, 114–16; historical, 102; Latin America, 103; Latin America compared, 106; main indicators, 1988–2000, 105*t*; migration, 103, 104; phases, 103; salient characteristics, 102–6
population policy, 112–14; economic development, 28; objectives, 116; quality of life, 116; socioeconomic development, 101
poverty, domestic workers, 74
Powell, Colin: biological warfare, 16; OAS initiative, 23–24
Preamble, 149–51

presidential succession: anticipation, 123; armed forces role, 272; constitutional provisions, 245–47; economy, 249–50; elite agreement, 196–97; historical context, 242–43; military, 248–49; PCC, 247–48; political openings, 242; ruling elite, 250; significance, 243; succession context, 243–45; summarized, 32; unrealistic exile views, 63; U.S. media on, 254n.4

price levels, embargo, 57–58

Prieto, Abel, 192

prime minister position, 192

prisoners of war: Afghan, 11–13; Geneva Convention, 12

private productive work, 53

private schools, 128

private sector, 156; economic decentralization, 60; reforms avoided, 189; rural sector, 59

privatization, 312

productivity, 158

professional status, mothers' generation, 89–90

prostitution (jineterismo): black women, 72–73; controversies, 7; economic crisis, 96–97; new forms, 55–56; part-time, 56; self-esteem, 97; tourism related, 55

Protestantism: pope's visit, 134; recent activities, 139–40; resurgence, 132–33

Protestants: rapprochement, 129; revolutionary government, 128

provincial assemblies, 207

Provincial Assembly, delegates, 211

pseudorepublic, 102, 103

PSP. See Popular Socialist Party

public education, 130

public good, 312

public health: death, cause of, 109; expenditures, 159; mortality patterns, 109; system in 1990s, 8; universal coverage, 107–8; women's lives, 86

public opinion surveys, 214

public sector, 166

public spending, 312

Quintana, Nora, 78, 80

racism, 73–74; women on, 75

radio, Miami Spanish-language, 13–14, 43n.81

Radio Martí, 13, 19, 45–46n.90, 43n.81; U.S. policy, 286, 287

rafters: end of open door policy, 295–96; numbers of, 288t, 288

rafters crisis of 1994, 188, 193, 290–95; Clinton policy, 330–31; Mariel boatlift compared, 292–93

rationing books, 57

rationing system, 159

Raulistas, 32, 242, 251, 252, 253

Reagan administration, 286–87

Realist school, 304

Rebel Army, 183, 262

rectification of errors and negative tendencies, 4; economic policy, 150; focus, 186–87

reforms: Cuban, 4; Gorbachev, 4; impact on former USSR, 4

regime change: Cuba, 126; issues raised, 124; Poland, 126

Reich, Otto: appointment questioned, 43–44n.82; biological warfare, 16; Bush appointee, 21, 332; coup attempt in Venezuela, 15; Mexico-Cuba relations, 13

religion, 28–29; consensual agenda lacking, 142; status of institutional, 127–35; in U.S., 324

religious activism, 28

religious belief, 130

religious believers, party membership, 190, 191

religious education, 125

religious formation, 139

religious freedom, 129, 130

religious publications, 132, 140

religious vocations, 139

remittances: amount, 177n.15; authorized, 154; before 1993, 53; hard currency reforms, 53, 154; political impact, 162n.17; significance debated, 162n.18

rendering-accounts sessions, 234–35, 238

Reno, Janet, 294

rent-seeking behavior, 167; concept of, 178nn.21, 22

research centers, 194

reserve forces, 264, 269, 271

revocation process, 235–36

Revolutionary Armed Forces (FAR), 32, 183; chain of command, 263; discipline, 273; early advantages, 262; early history, 260–62; early years, 262–63; expenditures (1989–99), 342*t*, 343; expenditures compared, 344*t*; high command, 248–49; MININT link, 268–69, 276; mobility, 274; professionalization, 262, 264; role in power transition, 275–76; role in society, 263; snapshot today, 269–72; source of stability, 259; special attributes, 272–75; Special Period, 265–68; transition role, 272–75; U.S. generals on, 48*n*.109

Revolutionary Directorate, 184

revolutionary political culture: ambivalence in feminine subjectivity, 91; feminism, 85; social project, 85; summarized, 51

Revolutionary Tribunals, 193

revolutionary values, changes discussed, 61–62

revolutionary vanguard, 202

Rio Group conference, 5

Robaina, Roberto, 191, 192, 195–96, 286

Roca, Blas, 186

Roca, Vladimiro, Bush's speech, 20

Rodríguez, Dagoberto, 23

Rodríguez, Esther María, 72

Rodríguez Caldéron, Mirta, 70

Roman, Olga, 67

Romay, Olga Dotre, 70

Ros-Lehtinen, Ileana, 1, 13, 325, 334

Ruiz Narváez, Irene Esther, 77

ruling elite: changes of 1990s, 55; factions lacking, 244; interlocking power network, 250–51; presidential succession, 32, 243, 244; resources, 244; support for Raúl, 250–51

Rumsfeld, Donald, 12

rural areas, fertility rates, 110

Ryan, George, 9, 333

salary levels, 159

Sánchez, Celia, 69

Sánchez, Elizardo, 233

Santamaria, Haydee, 69

santería, 133, 143*n*.1

Sao Paulo forum, tenth, in Cuba, 6

satellite accounts, 174

Scott, Anne, 8

Scott, James, 7

Scott, Walter, 6

SDPE. *See* Economic Planning and Management System

secret ballot election, 189

secularization, 123–24

self-employment, 188; controversies, 7; cooperatives, 165; economic recovery, 156; numbers, 156, 169; social costs, 7; taxes, 169; women, 95. *See also cuenta propistas*

self-esteem, 97, 98

September 11, 2001 attacks: Cuba response, 37*n*.30, 332; Cuba stand, 10–11; economic impact, 30; tourism, 98

service occupations, trend to, 57, 58

sexist images, 75–76

sexual abuse, 74

sexual harassment, 73

sexual work, 55

siege mentality, 266, 268–69

slavery, 260

social costs, 7, 149

social demands, 90

social indicators, recent trends, 159

Socialism: concept of, 124–25; Cuban case, 125; end of the Cold War, 3; feminism, 81; historical overview, 3; law of value, 161*n*.8; materialism, 129; nationalism related, 197; persistence of monetary-mercantile relationship, 160, 161*n*.5; reforms, 188; survivors, 3; women's liberation, 79

Socialist Council of Mutual Economic Assistance (CAME), 54

socialist value culture, 198–99

social mobilization, 264

social reality, 87

social safety net, 164; presidential succession, 197; spending levels, *n*3, 176

social security system, women and families, 96

social services, 163

social welfare: churches, 134–35; church role, 131; as claim to legitimacy, 134–35

societal change, churches, 135–43

Society, 26

solidarity groups with Cuba, 324, 326

Solidarity labor union, 126

South-South campaign, 307, 308

sovereignty: challenges to system, 124; Elián González case, 142; formal vs. effective, 304; Helms-Burton law, 325–27; political and economic independence, 34; U.S. allies, 327

Soviet arms, 306, 307, 318n.4; end of the Cold War, 266; Raúl Castro, 264

Spain, adversarial EU position, 24

Spanish American War, 260–61

Spanish Empire, 260

Special Period in Peacetime: armed forces, 265–68, 276; Catholic Church's standing, 29; changes assessed, 35; Communist party, 187–91; declared, 265; domestic work, 94; economic impact, 265; egalitarianism, 27; external factors, 149; impact on women, 66; initiatives, 52–53; objectives and limits, 150, 160n.4; origins, 4; positive impact, 94; quality of life, 105; women's lot, 75, 84

Specter, Arlen, 12

speculation, goods obtained through, 156

spiritism, 127, 143n.1

spiritualism, 133

state enterprises: corruption, 239; deficits, 177n.12; excess workers, 169; military industries, 267; military retirees, 249; reform objectives, 162n.20; reforms, 193, 341; subsidies, 157, 162n.19, 165

state investment, FDI flows, 170–71

state sector, 166, 167; described, 178, 179n.26

stereotypes, 76, 77

street merchants, 60–61

Stuttgart, 8, 9

Suárez, Raúl, 139

subjective level, 87–91, 94–97

sugar industry, 7, 110, 188

teen pregnancies, 112

Ten Years' War of 1868–78, 260

Territorial Troop Militia (TTM), 271

terrorism: Cuba on, 10–13; Cuba on State Dept. list, 44n.84; five Cubans in Miami, 39n.43; September 11 response, 37n.30; U.S. State Dept. list, 21, 38n.38

Toledo, José L., 218

Torricelli, Robert, 285

Torricelli Act (1992), 266, 285, 325, 330, 336n.3, 337n.12

tourism, 55–57, 171–74; armed forces, 266; basic indicators, 173t; demand, 174, 175; economic gains, 152–53; EU, 25; focus, reasons for, 171; foreign investment, 171; gross investment, 172; growth, 172; holding companies, 172–73; investment, 168; lack of free time, 98; limitations, 174–76; local value-added, 174; military service, 266; multiplier effect, 152–53; overview, 52, 55; perceptions of, 97–98; significance, 7–8; size, 8; as strategy, 55

tour operators, 174–75

trade: before end of the Cold War, 265; "Other" category, 318n.5; post-cold war, 7; summarized, 329–30

trade restructuring, 308

training, military, 266

travel restrictions: ban amendment, 8; Carter era, 17

TRD. See hard currency stores

triangular conflict, Helms-Burton law, 325–26

TTM. See Territorial Troop Militia

Twenty-sixth of July Movement, 65, 184

UBPCs. See Basic Units of Cooperative Production

UMAP. See Military Units to Aid Production

unemployment, 159; measures, 52–53; sugar industry, 7

Union of Young Communists (UJC), 191, 252

United Nations: anti-embargo vote, 337n.7; Cuba on terrorism, 10–11; Cuba speeches, 329

United Nations Development Financing Conference (Monterrey), 14

United Nations Human Rights Commission, 14

United Party of the Socialist Revolution (PURS), 184

United States: Congressional role, 323; consensus slipping, 335–36; Cuba policy summarized, 328; economic warfare, 305, 307; evolution of Cuba issue, 284–86; funding opposition groups, 332; hegemony, 321; migration policy, 283, 286; military missions, 261; neo-Pan-Americanism, 311–12; political actors, 323–25; rafter crisis, 292; respect for military, 275; war on Spain, 261. See also conflict with U.S.

universities, women in, 86

upward mobility, 87

Uruguay, 14

U.S. Interests Section: Cason strategy, 22; opposition groups, 218; visa requests, 288–89

U.S. National Endowment for Democracy, 15, 40n.56

U.S. Refugee Act of 1980, 298

USSR, former: advantages of connection, 306–7, 308; aid, 164; collapse, 4; dependency, 6; internationalism, 264; military aid, 264, 266, 306, 307, 318n.4; reforms, 4, 185–86, 187; subsidies, 164; trade, 265

U.S. State Department, terrorism, 21

Valdés, Ramiro, 186

value change, 54

Varela Project, 17–18, 46–47n.94, 199; cost to dissidents, 23; legality, 218; right of petition, 218

Vatican II, 127, 131, 140

Venezuela, 15

Vera, Maité, 77–78

violent deaths, 109

La Virgen de la Caridad del Cobre, 139

visas, granting, 22, 288–89

Vitral, 132, 140–41

Vivarium, 132

voluntary labor, 186

voter cards, 71

voter registration, 225

voting, 228–29; spoiled and blank ballots, 232t, 232–33, 233t

voting rates, 229

voto unido system, 212

wage inequalities, 186

war against terrorism: Castro on, 12; Cuban view, 10–13; Guantánamo base, 11–12; Latin American complaints, 24

War of All the People, 264–65, 271, 276

Warsaw Pact, 306, 318n.4

Western Europe, 309f, 309–10, 310f, 311, 318nn.6, 7

West Indian countries, 316

wet/dry feet policy, 297–98

women: benefits, 66; combatants, 70; consensual unions, 112; demographic structure, 111–12; domestic responsibilities, 88, 90, 91, 92–93, 96; femaleness, 85; future scenarios, 81; history, 27; invisibility in history, 76; multiple circumstances, 84–85; national vs. local elections, 237; policies affecting, 27–28; population growth, 104; role, 27–28; senior posts, 27, 80; social subjects and objects, 85, 88; special period, 28

women communicators, 75–79

Women's Civic Front José Martí (FCMM), 67–69

women's liberation, 74, 79

workers' parliaments, 217, 236–37

workforce: developing countries, 94; domestic workers, 85; economic crisis, 96, 323; female, 85; women and economic crisis, 94–95; women's majority, 95

Working Group on Cuba, 10, 23

workplace, criticism, 97

World Trade Organization (WTO), 328

World Wars I and II, 261

Youth Labor Army, 271